The Schneider Trophy

A history of the contests for

LA COUPE D'AVIATION MARITIME

JACQUES SCHNEIDER

David Mondey

Robert Hale · London

First published in Great Britain 1975

ISBN 0 7091 5011 3

Robert Hale & Company
63 Old Brompton Road
London SW7

Filmset and printed in Great Britain by
BAS Printers Limited, Wallop, Hampshire

Contents

Illustrations

PLATES

SIAI-Marchetti, No. 12, 44; Aeronautica Macchi, No. 13, 15, 16, 24, 28, 37; United States Air Force, No. 25, 26; Curtiss-Wright, No. 27; *The Aeroplane*, No. 29; Short Brothers & Harland, No. 35; Società per Azioni Fiat, No. 41; Industrie Aeronautiche e Meccaniche Rinaldo Piaggio, No. 42, 43; Air Vice Marshal F. W. Long, No. 51, 52, 53, 54; Mr R. Morris, No. 55.

The remaining pictures are from the collection of John W. R. Taylor.

THREE-VIEW DRAWINGS

SCHNEIDER TROPHY CONTEST COURSE MAPS

Acknowledgements

My list of persons to whom I owe so much for invaluable information could add a number of pages to this book if I expressed in detail my appreciation to each of them. Consequently my reference has to be curtailed, but at the head of the list must go Air Vice Marshal F. W. Long, who was the first most willing 'victim' of my enquiries. He is followed by Air Commodore D. D'Arcy A. Greig and my friends and colleagues John W. R. Taylor and Kenneth Munson.

Companies have been most generous with help, information and drawings, and I must thank most sincerely Jim Oughton of British Aircraft Corporation, Jim White of Short Brothers and Harland, A. M. Humphries and C. W. Morton of Rolls-Royce, Vico Rosaspina in Italy and the Fiat and Macchi companies. Speeds were difficult to establish with accuracy, and I am most grateful for the assistance received from the Fédération Aéronautique Internationale and the affiliated Aero Clubs in the countries which participated in the contests.

Librarians and their staffs have been both patient and kind, and in particular I would mention Arnold Naylor of the Royal Aeronautical Society and Mrs Jean King of the Trenchard Hall Library at the Royal Air Force College, Cranwell. The librarian and staff of the Surbiton public library deserve more than passing mention for never failing to track down and produce obscure books from far flung libraries.

In answer to requests for information that were published by the courtesy of the editors of *Flight International* and the services magazine *Airmail*, I received dozens and dozens of letters from service, ex-service and civilian enthusiasts who wrote to express their interest, give personal reminiscence and supply photographs. I cannot possibly mention them all, but must single out as their representative Mr G. W. Horne of Auckland, New Zealand, who not only sent me a summary of detailed references which he had compiled on the subject of the Schneider Trophy Contests, but who also called to see me and discuss progress during a visit to Britain.

It is imperative also that I should mention those who have contributed to the production of the book itself: Michael Badrocke for his immaculate three-view drawings and Tony Theobald for the design of the dust jacket. Perhaps it may be considered unusual to include the publisher in an acknowledgement, but I cannot omit reference to Gordon Chesterfield and record my appreciation of his patience and encouragement.

To all of these people – and any others that I may have failed to mention by name – I offer a most sincere thank-you. I trust that they, and you the reader, consider my summary of their efforts worthwhile.

Surbiton
March 1974

D.M.

For my patient, long-suffering and beloved wife Joyce—far better known as 'Lucy' to a host of friends in the world of aviation.

I

Cart before the horse

Fickle memory retains an impression that day after day, in the fall of that historic year, the sun blazed down from a cloudless sky, making nonsense of a calendar which had already slipped quietly into Autumn.

A casual onlooker might have been excused the belief that his gaze embraced a land of bountiful peace, for so far as the eye could see the countryside of Kent and Sussex, folded into the gentle contours of the South Downs, basked quietly in sunlight that dappled its fields in russet and gold. Roads and lanes carried little traffic: an occasional farm vehicle was to be seen, taking advantage of the fine weather to carry the harvest home.

But here and there, the landscape was scarred by patches of torn and burned earth. Clearly these were too savage in origin to be a normal part of the scene and immediately posed a question. Yet it was one to which any workers in the fields could have provided a clue without uttering a word, by simply pointing upward to where invisible pens were tracing white lines across the late Summer sky.

This, to so many persons, whether servicemen or civilians, was their prime impression of the Battle of Britain, a machine-age joust fought high in the blue; remote, exciting and very nearly beautiful.

It was only when combat was sufficiently low for the staccato bark of machine-guns to be heard; or when a mortally-wounded machine came plummeting to earth, its often brief life ending in an eruption of disintegrating metal, a blossom of crimson flame and funereal pall of oily black smoke, that one began to understand the scarred fields. Then it became alien, more personal, and perhaps a little frightening.

For Britain's twentieth-century knights—the Churchillian 'few'—little remained of the niceties of mediaeval combat. No question of yielding to superior numerical force: their homeland had its back to the wall and it had become a simple case of kill or be killed. Only their mounts retained a vestige of the glamour that graced the chargers of heraldic days, for they bore the proud names Hurricane and Spitfire.

Oddly enough, the courageous hearts of these metallic beasts, that enabled their knights to scale effortlessly the invisible pathways of the heavens, had the name Merlin—one that seemed to derive directly from

King Arthur's court. It was almost as if wizardry had provided this superlative engine at precisely the right moment of time—for Britain. Yet, it had no ancient history.

Indeed, the spell which began its creation had been cast a scant twenty-eight years earlier when a Frenchman, Jacques Schneider, first offered a trophy for annual competition by water-borne aircraft. In even his wildest dreams he could never have imagined that this simple action of a racing enthusiast could speed the evolution of aircraft that would one day change the face of history.

Yet, towards the end of July 1940, some 600 to 700 single-engined fighter aircraft of the British Royal Air Force were assembled to oppose the might of Germany's seemingly invincible *Luftwaffe*. This opposition was mounted with such courage and determination that, after a bitter and protracted struggle, they succeeded in denying to the Germans the freedom of the daylight skies above Britain.

This was a turning point in the war. A supreme moment of actual and psychological triumph, that was to warm the hearts of British men and women during the see-saw fortunes of battle that filled the years until our victory was certain. From that moment defeat was unthinkable.

It needed the mind of Winston Churchill to distil the immortal words with which he gave a nation's thanks to those gallant men of the Royal Air Force's fighter squadrons: 'Never in the field of human conflict was so much owed by so many to so few.'

Before we begin to follow the history of the Schneider Trophy Contests, we must first learn something of the state of aviation progress in those years immediately preceding the first World War. This information is necessary if we are to understand why Jacques Schneider was prompted to encourage the development of water-borne aircraft. And it is as well, too, that we know the origin of this Frenchman who died almost penniless in 1928, at the early age of 49. Ironically, his death came at a time when competition for his trophy was reaching a climax, and rival nations were spending thousands of pounds to develop aircraft that would secure for one or the other a prize that, over the years, had acquired great international prestige.

Jacques Schneider, son of an armaments manufacturer, was born near Paris on 25 January 1879. Thus, he was twenty-four years of age when the Flyer, built by the Wright brothers in America, made the first-ever powered, sustained and almost-controlled flight in history. Nearly three years after the Wright's success, on 23 October 1906, he might well have been one of the close on a thousand excited and half-frozen spectators who stood for almost eight hours to see the tribulations of the diminutive and Chaplinesque Alberto Santos-Dumont turn to triumph. In the fading light of that October afternoon, the ungainly No 14*bis*, powered by a 50 hp Antoinette engine, left the uneven surface of the Bagatelle field in the Bois de Boulogne, Paris. It was a flight of seconds only, covering almost 200 feet, but was witnessed by so many people, photographed at take-off and in the air—just—that the newspapers of the world heralded this event as the world's first powered flight in a heavier-than-air machine. And because the flight was officially observed and timed, Santos-Dumont became the holder of the first official world air speed record, at 25·657 mph (41·291 km/h)!

How was it possible that the first realisation of powered flight, which had taken place almost three years earlier, was not common knowledge throughout the world? It can be explained only by facts such as the reaction of news editors to the garbled report of a free-lance reporter; that the Wright brothers failed to appreciate the importance of publicity; and that when they finally gave a demonstration for the press, in May 1904, they were unable to provide anything more exciting than a 60 ft (18 m) glide. Little wonder that the American press found nothing worth reporting and that, consequently, the news failed to make its impact in any other country.

Particularly ironic is the fact that just over a year before the first flight made by Santos-Dumont, on 5 October 1905, the Wrights' No 3 Flyer had made a non-stop flight of just over 24 miles (39 km).

During the fifteen months that followed the flight of Santos-Dumont's 14*bis*, little real progress was made in French aviation. By the end of 1907, for example, only the Voisin-Farman 1 was capable of remaining airborne for about a minute.

The real change began in August 1908, when Wilbur Wright arrived in France with a new Model A which he assembled at Léon Bollée's factory near Le Mans. On the 8th of the month, at Hunaudières racecourse, near Le Mans, a critical audience of French pilots, proud and confident of their own superiority, assembled to see if this American would be able to get his machine into the air.

Wilbur's first demonstration flight, which lasted for just under two minutes, was sufficient to convince the most sceptical among the Frenchmen that they were only the veriest of beginners. His graceful banks and circles, the smooth, controlled landing, emphasised how crude were their own achievements. At first there was only shocked silence, but this gave way to a roar of acclamation and, to give those men their due, they were at a loss to find adjectives able to express adequately their admiration of the Wrights and their, by comparison, superb machine.

Presumably, Jacques Schneider would have been numbered among the spectators of at least some of the more than 100 flights made by Wilbur during the remainder of that year. That made on 31 December lasted for 2 hours 20 minutes, during which time the Model A covered a distance of 77 miles (124 km).

France was alight with enthusiasm for 'les aviateurs', and this country soon led the world in this new field of sport. For sport it was then, still unblemished by military applications. Indeed, so great was the interest in these new heavier-than-air craft that, at any rate temporarily, they attracted the crowds that formerly had flocked to watch the other rich man's sport of motor racing. One of the participating devotees of this latter sport was Jacques Schneider and it is hardly surprising that he, with plenty of money behind him, should become keenly interested in aviation, albeit in lighter than-air craft. His first balloon flight was made in 1909 and two years later he gained his pilot's brevet, qualifying soon afterwards as a pilot of free balloons. In 1913, in his balloon *Icare*, he gained an altitude record of 33,074 ft (10,081 m) for his country, and also made a cross-country flight from France to the Black Sea.

Unfortunately, in 1910 he had been involved in an accident that caused multiple fractures of both arms, and this limited his activities which, otherwise, might well have extended to flight in heavier-than-air craft. It did not, however, prevent him from taking a leading part in the organisation of aviation events and competitions, and he was one of the judges at the first hydro-aeroplane meeting held at Monaco in 1912.

That such a meeting was possible at all is surprising when one considers that a little less than four years had elapsed since Wilbur Wright's first European demonstration flights. The pioneer designer/pilots were then having quite enough difficulty in coaxing their fragile machines from the bosom of mother earth, without adding the complexities of operations on water.

Nevertheless, the first heavier-than-air craft to take off from water had been demonstrated in France as early as 1905. This was a glider mounted on floats, the co-operative design of Gabriel Voisin and Ernest Archdeacon. On 8 June 1905, towed by a motor boat, it broke loose from the surface of the Seine with Voisin at the controls, completing an initial flight of some 490 ft (150 m) before landing again on the river.

But it was not until five years later, in March 1910, that another Frenchman, Henri Fabre, made the world's first successful take-off from water in a powered heavier-than-air craft. His aircraft is of particular interest, not only because it was the first, but due to its curious blend of nautical and aviation design.

Perhaps this factor should not be surprising, for Fabre was the son of a family of ship-owners. At the time of the Wrights' first powered flight he was twenty-one years old, and thus of an age to become keenly interested in the activities of the French aviation pioneers. To him it seemed quite natural that, with a maritime background, he should devote his energies to the development of an aircraft that would operate from water.

Initial experiments began in 1907, and his first machine was completed in 1909. He soon discovered this to be a failure, primarily because it wouldn't fly, so was wise enough to waste no further time on it. It had provided a

The Voisin/Archdeacon floatplane glider on the Seine on 8 June 1905

Henri Fabre's hydro-aeroplane, the world's first successful powered seaplane

great deal of information that was to be of value in the design and construction of his second aircraft.

This was a strange-looking machine, its 'fuselage' comprising two beams that supported biplane surfaces at their forward end and an immense vertical fin and monoplane wing aft. Each of the lifting surfaces had unique lattice-girder spars, strong as a box spar but lighter, which allowed air to pass between the upper and lower flanges. Mounted at the rear end of the upper beam was a 50 hp Gnome engine, driving a two-blade wooden pusher propeller.

But the most important feature was the three floats that supported the craft on the water, one at the forward end and two aft, beneath the wings. Designed by Fabre, they were flat-bottomed and had a curved upper surface. A contemporary description told how they were '. . . so designed that when the machine is moving either through the air or on the surface of the water, or with the floats completely submerged, there is always a vertical lift on them due to the speed.' Hence, it is clear that they were so mounted and wire-braced to have positive incidence.

Seated somewhat precariously at a mid-position on the upper beam, Fabre succeeded in getting this aircraft into the air at Martigues, near Marseilles, on 28 March 1910, covering a distance of some 1,500 ft (457 m) at a height of about 6 ft (1·8 m). It was a remarkable feat, particularly as it was Fabre's first flight for, unlike many of the pioneers, he had no previous glider experience upon which to draw. Fabre had something to celebrate that evening: the world's first take-off from water by a powered heavier-than-air craft. That it was a machine of his own design and construction, and also his first flight, must surely have added the topping to the cake.

When fully loaded Fabre's hydro-aeroplane weighed 1,047 lb (475 kg), and it seemed surprising to many observers that the three comparatively small floats were capable of supporting the craft on the water. In fact, it was for this design feature that Fabre was to become best known, and floats of his construction equipped many early water-borne aircraft.

Contemporary with Fabre was the American, Glenn Curtiss, who began to experiment with hydro-aeroplanes towards the end of 1908. It was not until just over two years later, on 26 January 1911, that he succeeded in making a first take-off from water, at San Diego, California, flying in a floatplane version of his famous *June Bug*. By comparison with Fabre's aircraft it was a far more practical aeroplane of biplane configuration—even if still wedded to a forward elevator operating in conjunction with a similar rear-mounted control surface—and is regarded generally as the first practical floatplane in history.

It was powered by a Curtiss water-cooled engine, mounted between the wings, this driving a two-blade wooden pusher propeller. With a wing span of 26 ft (7·92 m), it was capable of sustained flight at speeds between 50 and 55 mph (80–88 km/h).

Commander Oliver Schwann with the Avro Type D at Barrow-in-Furness after its conversion to floatplane configuration in August 1911

The Voisin canard hydro-aeroplane in flight

Britain was not far behind the Americans in recording a first take-off from water, the machine being an Avro Type D converted by Commander Oliver Schwann. A. V. Roe's Type D was an honest-looking biplane, almost conventional by later standards except that lateral control was by wing warping. The prototype, powered by a 35 hp Green four-cylinder in-line liquid-cooled engine, had been flown by Howard Pixton at Brooklands for the first time in March 1911. Three months later it was bought by Commander Schwann and railed to Barrow-in-Furness, where the wheels were removed and a series of different floats, designed by Schwann and his colleagues and built by Navy personnel, were attached to the skids that were then a common feature of landplanes. Extending forward of the wheels, the skids were intended to prevent the aircraft from nosing-over when landing on dubious surfaces.

If Schwann had expected his task to be simple, he was doomed to disappointment. Seven different sets of floats were designed, built and fitted, and an extra 10 hp coaxed from the engine before, on 18 November 1911, he was able to get the Type D into the air for a brief flight. Like Fabre he had no previous experience as a pilot, but was not so fortunate as the Frenchman: the little machine had barely become airborne before it proved too much of a handful for Schwann and both received a ducking. This machine had a wing span of 31 ft (9·45 m), take-off weight of 1,000 lb (454 kg) and a maximum speed of 40 mph (64 km/h).

It is interesting to record that some four months later, when it had been salvaged and repaired, the Type D was flown successfully by Sydney V. Sippe on a number of occasions. Endurance was limited to twenty minutes; not by reason of inadequate fuel capacity, but because this was generally the length of time that elapsed before the cooling water had reached boiling point!

That it flew at all as a floatplane is amazing, for the all up weight of the Type D prototype in its original landplane configuration was 500 lb (227 kg), just half that of Schwann's floatplane conversion. He was certainly expecting a great deal from the engine's modest 35 hp, and one can see why it was necessary for Green's engineers to persuade it into providing an extra 10 hp—no mean achievement.

In France, during 1911–12, the development of hydro-aeroplanes was following a similar pattern. Successful landplanes (and remember that the word successful is something of an exaggeration) were being given, in the main, poorly-designed floats to enable them to operate from water. With increased all up weight and only marginal engine power it was inevitable that performance was 'only just'.

In fact, in calm water conditions, it was quite impossible for many floatplanes to get airborne. This was a bitter pill: roughish water was necessary to break the adhesion of float to surface, but this was really more than their frail structures could withstand. The turbulent water in the wake of their floats was a clear indication of the tremendous drag they induced. 'If only the engine would develop more power' was the cry, the theoretical demand always being much in excess of practical reality.

It pinpoints the problem that beset all aircraft designers in the early days: there was never enough power. This meant that engines were always overloaded and soon began to perspire. But engines that overheat are under stress and, in consequence, unreliable. This wasn't really terribly important at a time when aviation was for fun, and it was common practice to strip down an engine after each flight: but it was more than a little frustrating for ambitious designers with mental images of huge aeroplanes flying effortlessly over continents and oceans.

Small engines, say up to 50hp, had become fairly reliable, beyond that sort of power output the problems grew rapidly. France, however, gained an early lead in engine design as a result of the advances which came from experience in long-distance motor car racing, which was then the rage of Europe. This was true particularly in respect of in-line liquid-cooled engines developed for the motor car. But they were big and heavy, quite unsuited for the frail aircraft of the day, and the weight of the essential cooling system only added to the difficulties.

One of the most inspired engine designers in France was Laurent Seguin who, together with his brother, began in 1907 to give serious thought to aircraft power plants. Both realised that a good power to weight ratio was essential, that air cooling was desirable to keep the weight as low as possible, and that there would be a big market for a successful engine. The small frontal area of the in-line engine offered great advantages, but this was offset by the weight of the complete power plant: the radial engine which was of such a shape that air could flow over all of its cylinders was low on power. Low power meant slow forward speeds, poor airflow and, consequently, overheating.

Seguin's solution was the rotary engine, one in which propeller, cylinders and crankcase rotated as one, the crankshaft being stationary and fixed, indirectly, to the airframe. The rotating mass of this engine gave excellent flywheel inertia, providing smooth running at low throttle openings, and solved the problem of cooling the cylinder. When their first five-cylinder engine ran in 1908, it produced about 34hp and weighed approximately 112lb (51kg), 3·3lb (1·5kg)/hp. Their seven-cylinder model of 1909 produced 50hp at a similar power/weight ratio, at a time when contemporary engines averaged about 6lb (2·7kg)/hp.

By the end of 1912, the year of the first hydro-aeroplane meeting at Monaco, there was a series of six Gnome engines. These ranged from 50 to 160hp, the latter producing one horsepower for each 1·95lb (0·88kg) of weight. The clear lead held by the Gnome engines is apparent if one glances at a comparison of four well-known engines produced at that time in other countries:

Manufacturer	Country of origin	Cyls	HP	Weight lb (kg)	Pounds (kg) weight per hp developed
A.B.C.	Britain	8	115	380 (172)	3·32 (1·51)
Anzani	France	3	44	154 (70)	3·50 (1·59)
Curtiss	America	6	60	315 (143)	5·26 (2·39)
Daimler-Mercedes	Germany	6	100	510 (231)	5·10 (2·31)

Within less than half a decade Seguin had produced a power plant that, on average, produced double the power for an equivalent weight. On the debit side the Gnome used vast quantities of castor oil, which soon provided a liberal waterproof coating for the aircraft's wings and fuselage; it was noisy, and it certainly looked a bit off-putting. Nonetheless, it represented the biggest single advance in powered flight to that time, and there is little wonder that the aviation brotherhood soon realised *en masse* that this odd-looking piece of machinery was, in fact, *the* power plant they had all been waiting for.

It was all jolly fine for the airframe designer to blame the engine builder for the marginal performance of the aircraft as a whole. When engines of increased power first began to appear airframe designers were soon to discover that their repeated incantation 'give us more power', and now realised, was no magic password to the perfection of flight. It they had hoped for a touchstone to transmute their leaden aircraft into golden eagles they were doomed to disappointment.

Instead of being satisfied merely with the realisation of flight, the time had now come for them to improve the airframe. There was a reasonable margin for improvement. Today we tend to label aircraft of that era as 'stick-and-string', implying rather inaccurately and unkindly that their technology of aircraft construction was something more than primitive. In fact, study of an aircraft of that age is very revealing, belying the layman's mental image created by the 'stick-and-string' label. Varnished wooden framework shows the craftsmanship of the cabinet maker; no less lovingly fashioned are the metal fittings and beautiful hand-carved propellers. Our eyes are held by the multiplicity of king-posts and wires that brace the frail structure. Indeed there were usually so many wires that innumerable and inevitable humorists suggested a bird could be kept safely within their confines: if it escaped it was reasonably certain that a wire was missing.

There was one advantage to this frangible structure: it disintegrated quite gently on impact, and many of the pioneers owed their lives to this factor. Somewhat shaken, they would disentangle themselves from the wreckage and stagger back to the drawing-board. There were, of course, those for whom a drawing board was too splendid and sophisticated. They arrived at a configuration that experience, personal or observed, suggested might fly. If it did, surprisingly, a constant trial and error sequence dictated its further development or dissolution.

Bamboo, a strong, lightweight and flexible tube had been a favoured constructional material for early aircraft. It was replaced gradually by light, strong and flexible woods, such as spruce and ash, and as designers began to realise that their innumerable struts and wires created resistance to movement through the air (drag), they began to use streamline sections and clean up the airframe generally. Thus, by the end of 1911, it was possible to see aircraft that looked as if they could fly and which, with the availability of more reliable engines, proved that they were able to stay in the air for quite extended periods. France led the field, for during that year Edouard Nieuport had set a world speed record of 82·73 mph (133·14 km/h) in a monoplane of his own design; another Nieuport monoplane, flown by A. Gobé, had covered a distance of 449·2 miles (722·92 km) in a closed circuit; and Raymond Garros had coaxed a Blériot XI monoplane to a height of 12,828 ft (3,910 m).

This was significant progress, and the same year recorded also some notable 'firsts', including a 90-mile (145-km) over-water flight, landing on and take-off from a ship, a non-stop London–Paris flight, the flight of an amphibian and the beginning of airmail experiments. This year introduced also one sad but inevitable event: a Blériot monoplane was the first heavier-than-air craft to be used in warfare, the Italians making use of it for reconnaissance in their conflict with Turkey.

The foregoing gives an appreciation of the state of the art which, in 1912, set Jacques Schneider thinking how he could best help his country to maintain their lead in aviation. It was clearly a form of transport that would grow in scope and which, with steady improvement in airframe and power plant design, would allow international, and perhaps intercontinental, passenger and cargo services to be established. Since seven-tenths of the earth's surface is covered by water, it was reasonable then to assume that aircraft able to operate on and from the surface of oceans, lakes and rivers, would represent the ultimate form of transport. Perhaps he shared also a then fairly common belief that, in the event of a crash landing, the yielding surface of the sea would prove far more hospitable than that of solid land.

Thoughts along these lines must have been very much in his mind when the world's first hydro-aeroplane meeting was held at Monaco at the end of March 1912. Organised by the International Sporting Club, it had attracted a total of ten entrants, seven of which finally presented themselves and their aircraft to take part in the various tests. These, to use the phraseology of a contemporary report, included 'starting from a calm sea, resting on calm water, resting on broken water and rising from broken water'. In addition, for those amphibious machines with both wheels and floats, a landing on the sea offshore between Monte Carlo and Mentone; the aircraft was then required to taxi ashore so that pilot and passenger could alight without getting their feet wet. Subsequently, the machine had to be taxied back into the water, taking off again to land at Monaco.

Those actually taking part in the contest were as follows:

Pilot	Aircraft	Engine	Final position in contest
M. Benoit	Sanchez Besa biplane	Salmson Unne	6th
R. Caudron	Caudron biplane	Anzani	5th
M. Fischer	Henri Farman biplane	Gnome	1st
L. Paulhan	Curtiss biplane	Curtiss	3rd
A. Renaux	Maurice Farman biplane	Renault	2nd
H. Robinson	Curtiss biplane	Curtiss	4th
M. Rugère	Voisin biplane	—	7th

Clearly, the biplanes built by the Farman brothers led the field, Henri Farman's being the first of his design to dispense with a forward elevator, while the Maurice Farman, powered by a 70 hp Renault engine, was a typical 'longhorn' biplane. The latter had floats attached between each pair of bicycle-type wheels and at the tail, whereas Henri Farman's machine had a clean-looking purpose-built float installation.

Appearing completely outdated was the Voisin biplane of canard configuration. Its outward appearance seemed to suggest at all times imminent disaster. This became fact when a heavy landing wrecked the four 'Fabre' floats, lower flying surfaces and propeller. Its pilot, with M. Colliex as passenger, escaped with sodden clothing and injured dignity. Benoit also received a ducking when the Sanchez Besa 'caught a crab' while taking off, but was fortunate to escape without injury.

Perhaps most significant was that points awarded for the take-off tests varied according to the number of passengers carried. Highest went to the Maurice Farman, flown by Renaux, who managed to get airborne with a total of five passengers clinging to any reasonably fixed object. This factor was not overlooked by the eagle-eyed Captain Godfrey Paine, RN, who was present as a representative of the British government. He lost little time in instructing George Holt Thomas, who held sales rights within the British Empire for the products of the Farman brothers, to arrange for Lieutenant Arthur Longmore, RN, to carry out flight testing of the Farman machines. These factors help explain selection of the Farman 'longhorn' for the R.F.C., for whom it gave excellent service as a primary trainer.

But despite the outstanding performance of the Farman biplanes, it was quite apparent to Jacques Schneider that, in the main, performance and reliability were both very marginal. A great deal of progress was needed before there was any chance of hydro-aeroplanes fulfilling the task that his mind had conjured up for them.

How could he help accelerate this development. It seems inevitable that his thoughts must have returned to the sphere of motor racing where, he was well aware, the evolution of fast and reliable vehicles had forged ahead under the spur of competition. Slowly emerged the idea of an international contest to encourage designers to concentrate on the development of fast and reliable aircraft that could operate on and from water. His emphasis was on speed, because he believed that the search for speed produced also reliability. Carefully he marshalled his facts and proposals, soon needing only an appropriate moment to announce his ideas.

He chose the Gordon-Bennett banquet of the Aero Club of France as his venue, this being held on 5 December 1912. *Flight* duly recorded: '. . . the announcement was made of a splendid offer by M. J. Schneider of a prize for hydro-aeroplanes. Briefly, M. Schneider has offered for international competition a trophy of the value of £1,000, to go to the club which the pilot represents; and in connection with this he also offers to give £1,000 annually for three consecutive years.'

The full title of the competition was *La Coupe d'Aviation Maritime Jacques Schneider*, soon abbreviated internationally as the Schneider Cup. The main rules stipulated:

(i) The contest must take place over open sea
(ii) It must be a race of at least 150 nautical miles
(iii) Competing aircraft must be seaworthy. (Initially, the seaworthiness tests were somewhat complicated, but were modified gradually over the years)
(iv) Each country competing in a race would be limited to a maximum of three entries
(v) Each entry must be sponsored by the body governing sport aviation of that country
(vi) The trophy was for annual competition
(vii) A country gaining three wins in five years would become final holder of of the trophy

Thus, Schneider envisaged this as an international inter-club contest, and the rules allowed for any club affiliated to the Fédération Aéronautique Internationale (FAI) to challenge the club holding the Trophy. The holder was to have the responsibility of organising the next contest.

In this way the scene was set for the first trial of strength, scheduled as a comparatively small item in the very full programme of the Monaco Hydro-Aeroplane Meeting of April 1913. In fact, it created initially very little stir in the world of aviation: it was just another of the many and growing number of meetings where the devotees of the sport would forgather. It is extremely unlikely that anyone could have foreseen the excitement that would eventually be generated by these races, or that within their eighteen-year span speeds would climb from a mere 60 mph (96·5 km/h) to over 340 mph (547 km/h).

In the eighteen years ahead there were to be moments of triumph and disaster: men would sacrifice their lives in the attempt to win the 'Cup'. Even Jacques Schneider would not survive long enough to see a nation become the proud holder of the Trophy for all time. But all that is far in the future. On Wednesday 16 April 1913, golden sun, blue sky and calm water dominated the scene at Monaco: the day of the very first Schneider Trophy race had dawned.

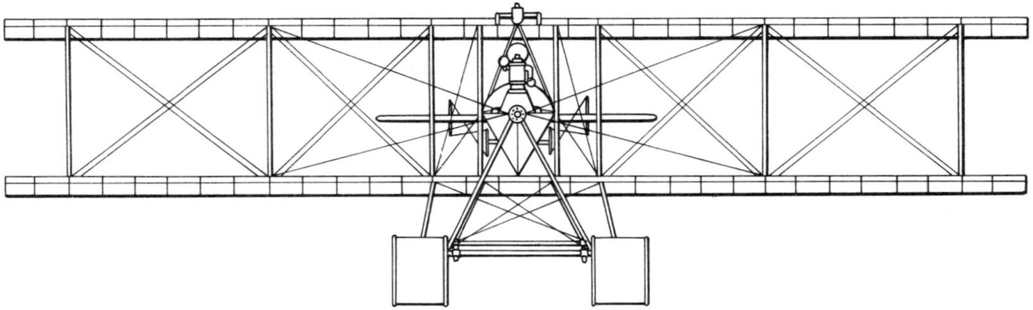

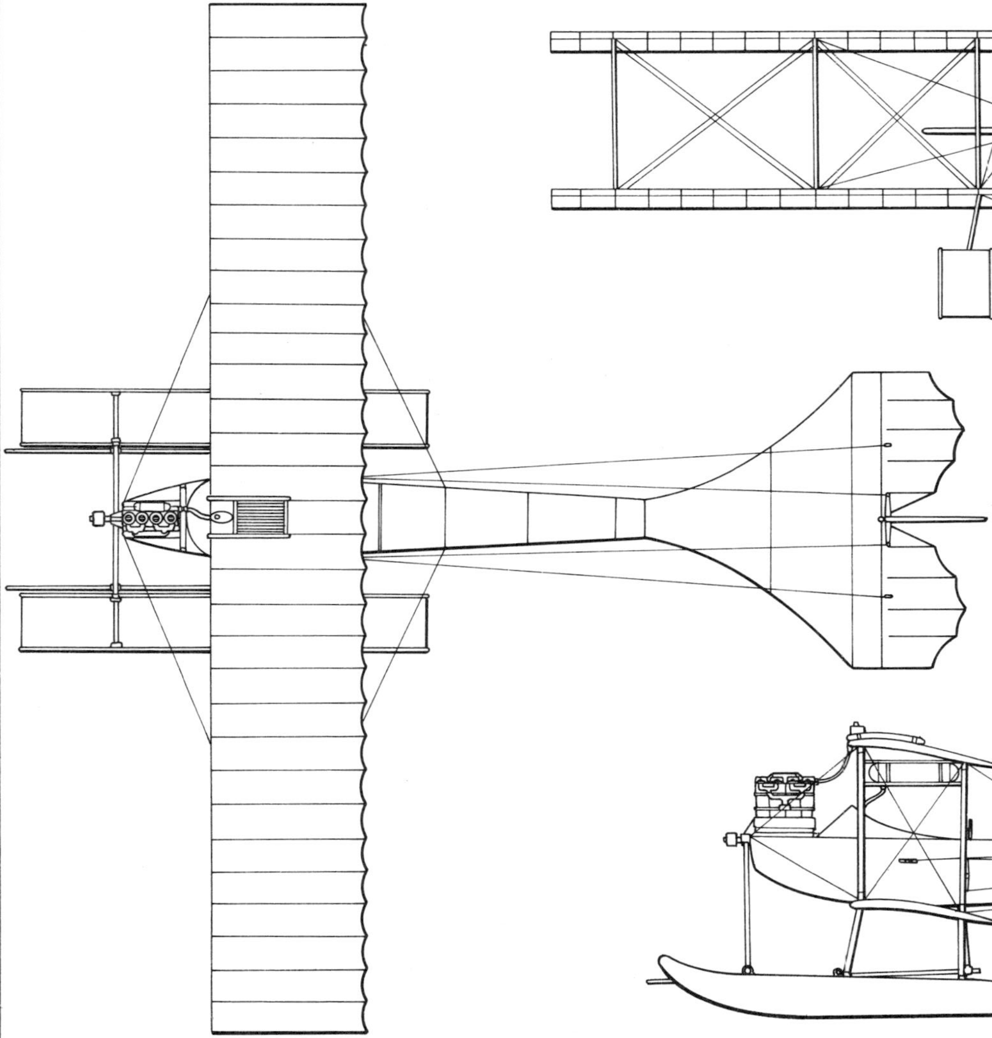

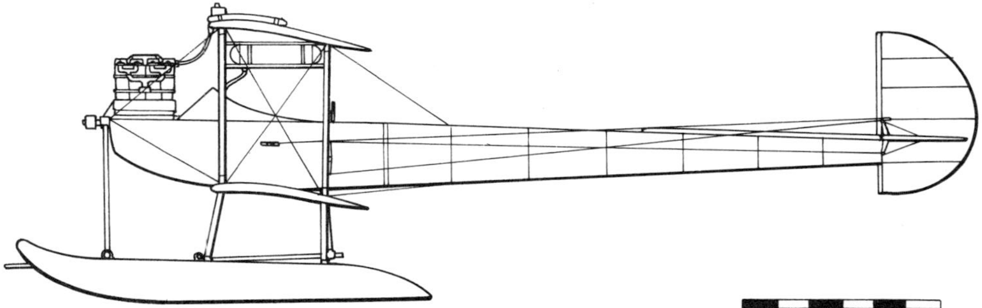

Avro Type D (1911)

Wing Span: 31 ft (9·45 m)
Length Overall: 26 ft (7·92 m)
Wing Area: 310 sq. ft (28·80 m²)
T-O Weight: 1,000 lb (454 kg)
Max Wing Loading: 3·23 lb/sq. ft (15·77 kg/m²)
Horsepower of Power Plant: 35 hp

2

First Contest at Monaco
1913

If the aircraft, which their proud owners had brought to take part in the second Hydro-aeroplane Meeting at Monaco, were not particularly beautiful, there could not have been a more pleasant venue for the meeting, which was to include also the first Schneider Trophy contest. The little principality, situated on the Mediterranean coast of France, enjoyed normally more than a fair share of delightful weather, and the beautifully-sited yacht harbour provided a wonderful setting for what promised to be an exciting fortnight, beginning on 3 April 1913.

Not surprisingly, the meeting attracted a great deal of attention, and visitors from as far afield as America had travelled to Monaco to enjoy the spectacle of sea, sunshine and hydro-aeroplanes. That it was of interest also to 'les aviateurs' was demonstrated clearly by the fact that the number of entries had almost trebled, by comparison with 1912, to provide a total of twenty-six would-be competitors for the events.

Once again the aircraft of the two Farman brothers were represented, but there were also many new types appearing for the first time, attracted by the worthwhile prizes. It must be remembered that at a time when there was a very limited sale for aircraft, they being the toys of the wealthy, success in competition not only provided valuable income to help pay for new ideas and their development, but was also the best possible means of advertising the superiority of the winning design. Unfortunately, in the same process, it scorched in the fullest blaze of publicity the performance of the not-so-successful contenders.

Let us take a look at some of the aircraft entered for the Grand Prix de Monaco, scheduled for Saturday 12 April, after early eliminations and withdrawals had produced a hard core of sixteen contenders. This is not superfluous to our history, for it is desirable to retain as wide a view as possible of the development in seaborne aircraft throughout the periods of the Schneider contests.

To take them alphabetically, first came the Artois biplane (entry No. 7), powered by an 80 hp Gnome seven-cylinder air-cooled rotary engine, driving via a chain a four-blade propeller. To be piloted by Louis Gaudart, this was of particular interest to those assembled, builders, pilots and knowledgeable onlookers, for it was one of two embryo flying-boats competing. Both were on the lines of the Donnet-Lévêque flying-boat of 1912, and which has since become regarded as the first European 'classic' flying-boat.

Next came the Astra biplanes, built by Cie. Générale Transaerienne, robust-looking aircraft with their two large floats mounted on circular-section tubular-steel struts, and which were supplemented by a third under-tail float. Those entered for the Grand Prix, Nos. 24 and 25, were to be flown by M. Labouret and M. Barra respectively. Both had 110hp Salmson (Canton-Unne) engines driving tractor propellers, and this particular type of power plant was somewhat unusual, since it was a water-cooled radial engine.

A Borel biplane (No. 9), was the second machine to have a true flying-boat hull in lieu of floats. This was to be flown by M. Daucourt, and was powered by a 100hp Gnome fourteen-cylinder air-cooled rotary engine driving a tractor propeller. The second Borel (No. 10) was of monoplane configuration, and had a fairly conventional float installation. To be flown by M. Chemet, it had begun life with an 80hp engine and a different set of wings, but a change to a 100hp Gnome and new wings was expected to enhance performance, giving it a good chance in the Grand Prix. Unfortunately, no one appears to have given any thought to the fact that the more powerful Gnome engine was also somewhat heavier: with no change in the float position to offset the additional weight forward, it presented a depressing, hopeless nose-down attitude on the water, requiring a rapid reversion to the original power plant and wings.

Two Breguet biplanes (Nos. 14 and 15) differed considerably in their float installations, demonstrating clearly that Louis Breguet was a man of ideas and was not afraid to experiment. No. 14, to be flown by M. Bregi, had a fairly conventional twin-float installation and was powered by a 110hp Salmson (Canton-Unne) nine-cylinder radial engine. That to be flown by M. Moineau, No. 15, had a single large central float mounted on four struts, the rear pair having oleo-pneumatic suspension supplemented by external helical springs. A balancing float was attached to the under-surface of each lower wing, approximately at mid-span, and a fourth float beneath the tail completed the installation. This arrangement was to prove highly successful in rough water conditions. Power plant was a 200hp Salmson (Canton-Unne) fourteen-cylinder radial engine. Of this particular machine, Fred T. Jane, who founded *Jane's All the World's Aircraft* in 1909, was to comment that it was the first aircraft to deserve the name of seaplane.

Of special interest, and a strong favourite, was the monoplane designed by Louis Béchereau for the Armand Deperdussin company. To be flown by Maurice Prévost (entry No. 19), it was a clean-looking machine, the only ugly features being the two angled cabane struts serving as king-posts to support with wire bracing the monoplane wing. Béchereau was a young man, something of an engineering genius, who had taken a keen, appraising look at the Blériot and Nieuport designs of the period and had decided that he could go one better. In this he succeeded, creating a circular-section monocoque fuselage of wood, the larger diameter of the forward fuselage being adequate to allow provision of a cowling that streamlined neatly the 160 hp Gnome fourteen-cylinder air-cooled rotary engine, driving a two-blade tractor propeller. A large spinner completed the neat lines of engine and propeller installation and this power plant created considerable interest as it was the first appearance of this twin-row rotary. Even the float installation was more tidy than most, each float being carried on an N-type strut, wire-braced to each other and the wings, and a third small float was mounted beneath the tail unit. Fin and rudder extended above and below the tapered rear fuselage, while the fixed tailplane and elevators were mounted in alignment with the fuselage upper surface. Roll control was by wing warping.

The Deperdussin started favourite, as two landplane versions of the same machine had taken first and second places in the all-French Gordon-Bennett contest held at Clearing, near Chicago, Illinois, on 9 September 1912, the winner with an average speed of 105·5 mph (169·8 km/h). Though floats would reduce performance the prospects for a win seemed very good.

The success of the Farman brothers' machines at the 1912 Monaco meeting meant that they, too, had a strong following for the 1913 Grand Prix, but few of their supporters had considered the extent to which aircraft like the Deperdussin represented a completely new generation, with far cleaner lines and the benefit of tractor propulsion. This year's Farmans differed little from the 1912 entries except for increase in engine power; the Henri Farman No. 2, piloted by M. Fischer, had another of the new 160 hp Gnome rotaries, driving a two-blade pusher propeller of 12 ft 3 in (3·73 m) diameter. With a wing area of 660 sq. ft (6·13 m²) and maximum take-off weight of 2,850 lb (1,293 kg), wing loading was only 4·32 lb/sq. ft (21·0 kg/m²), which helped considerably to overcome the disadvantage of inefficient floats. Power plant of the Maurice Farman, No. 4 piloted by M. Gaubert, was a 110 hp Salmson (Canton-Unne) nine-cylinder radial. Wing area of this machine was slightly greater at 700 sq. ft (65·03 m²), also giving a very low wing loading, and span of the upper wing was 70 ft (21·34 m).

Considerable interest was aroused by the de Marcay monoplane, No. 18, which was to be flown by M. Bielovucic. Feature of this design was wings which could be folded when the aircraft was at anchor, but even more startling was the fact that the wings were held forward in their rigged position by steel cables, they serving also as the roll control system. In lieu of wing warping, one wing or the other was given slight sweep by slacking off the control/rigging cable. Power plant of the de Marcay was a 100 hp Anzani ten-cylinder air-cooled radial engine, driving a two-blade tractor propeller.

The Morane-Saulnier biplane No. 13, to be flown by M. Gilbert, was supported on the water by two large main floats on rigid tubular section mountings, together with a small under-tail float. This aircraft, as well as the two Farmans, were the only contenders with an uncovered fuselage structure, and still showed the strong influence of the Wright biplane. Power plant was an 80 hp Le Rhone nine-cylinder air-cooled rotary engine driving a pusher propeller. Also taking part in the events of the week, but not entered for the Grand Prix, was a far more business-like Morane-Saulnier monoplane, flown by Roland Garros, and this skilled pilot gave several demonstrations of the potential of this comparatively new machine.

This left only the Nieuport machines, but those who knew the 'form' realised that these, Nos. 5 and 6, to be flown by Charles Weymann and M. Espanet respectively, and the Deperdussin, were the most likely aeroplane/pilot combinations to take the Grand Prix. Charles Weymann had won the 1911 Gordon-Bennett Cup at Eastchurch with the landplane version of the Nieuport monoplane, at a speed of 78 mph (125·5 km/h) and followed this by taking the Grand Prix at St Malo in the hydro-aeroplane version. To emphasise its reliability, he had topped off the St Malo win by recording what was then the longest over-water flight in a machine of this type. A clean-looking monoplane, with its 100 hp Gnome rotary engine neatly cowled, it had single-step floats which promised quick take off. It had one major unconventionality, the wing-warping being effected by foot-operated pedals, while the conventional control column took care of rudder and elevators. It must have represented a nightmare for a pilot converting

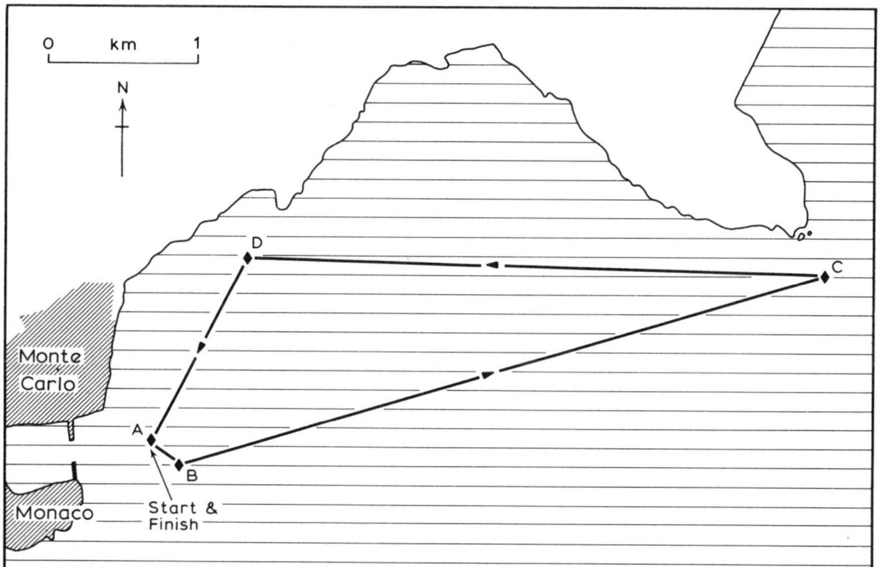

1. Schneider Trophy Contest Course: Monaco 1913 and 1914

from the more usual arrangement of pedal-operated rudder. Wing span of these machines was 39 ft 7 in (12·07 m), length overall 28 ft (8·53 m) and wing area 230 sq. ft (21·37 m^2).

Amongst other aircraft which had arrived for the meeting were several Deperdussins, and a Breguet of canard configuration.

The affair opened in grand style on Thursday 3 April, sixteen of the total entry being anchored for exhibition in the yacht harbour, and thus qualifying for participation in the ensuing tests. There were six in all, five of which had to be carried out in the open sea. The sixth (handling) took place in the harbour, the competitor having to negotiate his craft so that it was beneath one of the harbour cranes. This was to enable it to be hoisted from and lowered again on to the water, but its purpose was a little obscure as no attempt was made to weigh the aircraft. It was also a time-consuming business, competitors seeking to ensure the safety of their machines with, sometimes, amateurish knots. There were, of course, no lifting eyes or really suitable attachment points for slings.

The open water trials were quite demanding, and it is well worth recording the details here:

(1) *Getting under weigh.* The hydro-aeroplane brought to a standstill on the water, the motor stopped, the pilot must be able, with the resources he can command on board, and with solely the assistance of the passenger, if he carries one, restart the motor without retouching the propeller, and cover a distance of 100 metres between two lines of buoys.
(2) *Altitude.* Mount from water, at least 500 metres high, and return to water in less than 30 minutes.
(3) *Volplaning.* Rise from water to at least 100 metres altitude, descend *vol plané*, without the aid of the motor.
(4) *Towing.* The machine must be taken in tow by any one craft, either rowing or motor boat, and be trailed over the course for test No. 1.
(5) *Navigability.* Travel without leaving the water by aid of the motor over a course of six kilometres and a quarter.

The first item, on the face of it, was quite a problem. However, the rule had been known well in advance with the result that there were some ingenious devices for engine starting, including lever mechanisms, geared hand-turning devices and more sophisticated compressed-air starters. The fourth item appeared so harmless that few had given it any serious consideration, and a lack of suitable attachment point(s) for the tow caused far more problems than anyone had forseen.

The weather at Monaco is notoriously kind, but on this occasion decided to enter into the competitive spirit in the air by providing some opposition.

During the afternoon of 3 April a gale blew up and, with the exception of the de Marcay monoplane and Prévost's Deperdussin which rode out the storm, the other aircraft were removed to the security of dry land.

The storm continued to rage throughout Friday and most of Saturday, and it was not until Sunday that the first tentative trials were attempted. But things began in earnest on Monday and it was not long before tests not included in the official schedule—namely airworthiness and sea-worthiness—began to take their toll. Among the four victims of the first full day were three Deperdussins, one of them flown by Prévost, all of which made landings that were too heavy for their float-supporting structure. One Astra ducked a wing tip with disastrous results but there were, fortunately, no casualties.

Tuesday and Wednesday passed without serious incident, during which period Prévost's machine was repaired and completed the tests. Then, on Thursday evening, Chemet set off to flight test the Borel No. 10. Eye-witnesses said that he pulled it off the water too soon and that it stalled in on one wing, causing considerable damage to the machine.

Friday was devoted to the eliminating trials for the Schneider Trophy, for which there were only four entrants. Three were French: Prévost, Garros and Espanet, and Charles Weymann represented America flying a French Nieuport machine. All four qualified for the race to be run during the following week.

Once again the weather decided to participate and on Saturday, the day set for the Grand Prix, there was a gale blowing and a heavy swell on the sea. Despite the conditions it was decided to make a start at 10 a.m.: after all, the basic idea of meetings like this was to speed the development of aircraft that could operate in weathers other than a complete calm.

Fischer was first away in the Henri Farman, followed by Gaubert in the Maurice Farman after the scheduled interval of five minutes, to try their skill over the course of about 90 km. Neither had any difficulty in getting off the rough water, but the navigability test at Beaulieu was a very different matter. Fischer landed and completed his 500 metres stretch on the surface of the sea, but as he attempted to take off his machine was caught by a sudden gust of wind and capsized immediately. Gaubert was more fortunate, but his floats had been damaged during the landing and he had to put into Beaulieu harbour.

The Farman biplanes were followed by two Breguet machines and by Weymann in the Nieuport monoplane, the stepped floats of the latter proving to be of great assistance and enabling him to attain full flying speed before lifting off the water. However, it was a different story as he came in to make his landing at Beaulieu: caught in a violent squall the Nieuport was literally blown off the water on to its tail unit, the shock shattering the fuselage and allowing it to fold backwards over the tail. Weymann, fortunately, escaped with a ducking.

Meanwhile, Espanet in the second Nieuport was sent off at Monaco, but as he left the shelter of the yacht harbour he found the open sea so rough that he decided to give it best and turned back. He was followed by Prévost

Gabriel Espanet's Nieuport, seen at Monaco, provides an excellent view of the Fabre-type floats in the Deperdussin, determined to press on, but he had barely started his take-off run before a propeller tip was damaged by a wave and he was eliminated.

At Beaulieu both the Breguets had got down safely and Bregi, in the No. 14 with conventional float installation, decided that enough was enough and retired to the safety of the harbour. Moineau, finding that his machine handled reasonably well on the new Breguet float installation, decided that he might be able to finish the course. His take off and subsequent landing at San Remo, the next compulsory stopping point, presented no difficulties, but while attempting the second navigability trial, off San Remo, his engine was doused by an extra large wave. Not only did it cease to function after such unreasonable treatment, but stubbornly refused all attempts at a re-start. The only remaining course was a tow back to harbour, during which a high degree of co-operation between a wave and a cunningly directed blast of wind was sufficient to put the Breguet on its back.

It was the last straw: the organisers had by then decided that everyone had suffered quite enough and declared the elements triumphant, stopping the race and declaring it void. For his gallant attempt in reaching San Remo, Moineau was awarded 13,000 of the 50,000 francs prize money, and those who reached Beaulieu were each awarded 3,000 francs. This left a balance of 25,000 francs, which was proffered as prize for a hastily-introduced new event to take place on Tuesday 15 April, the eve of the first Schneider Trophy Race—weather permitting!

The stormy weather continued to dominate the scene on Sunday and Monday, but had eased sufficiently on Tuesday to allow an attempt at the new event which had been substituted for the abandoned Grand Prix. The race was one of 50 10-km laps, but even this proved too much for the four entrants, Bregi, Espanet, Gaubert and Prévost, for not one of them completed the course. Best effort was that of Gaubert, with a total of 270 km, followed by Bregi with a distance of 260 km.

It was something of an anti-climax: none had exceeded the 280 km distance of the Schneider course and it began to look as if it, too, might end in failure. To add to the general air of depression, the day was marred by a fatal accident when Louis Gaudart set out to test the Artois biplane. He appeared to be making a perfectly normal take-off, when the machine left the water in a very steep climb and almost immediately nosed over to dive into the sea, carrying the pilot to his death. It would have needed only the slightest degree of non-co-operation from the weather at that point for the Schneider Contest to be anulled.

Fortunately, Wednesday 16 April dawned fine and clear, complete with the brilliant blue sea and sky that is a normal accompaniment to the Monaco scene. The sea had, apparently, succumbed to the same mood and there was scarcely a ripple on the water as the contestants readied themselves for the race. There were, in fact, only four of them: Espanet, Garros and

Prévost for France; Weymann represented the United States—flying a French machine!

The course for the race was one of 280 km, comprising 28 laps of 10 km, with the starting and finishing point off the mouth of the yacht harbour at Monaco. First came a short south-east leg of 0·24 km, with an easy turn there to the next point 4·49 km distant at Cape Martin on an approximate east north-east course. There a hairpin bend set them flying almost due west for the 3·87 km to the last turn at Point de la Vielle, giving a final short leg of 1·4 km on a south south-east heading back to the starting point.

As the moment for the start of the race approached, Prévost must have been the most apprehensive, for his favourite Deperdussin—that with the clean-strutted float installation—had to be withdrawn due to engine trouble. Instead he had to fly the earlier version, which had been used by the French team to familiarise themselves with the course and which was given a hastily painted race number 19. As he gazed at the veritable birdcage of wires that braced floats and wings, Prévost must have felt that his chances had been reduced to nil.

The race plan called for the competitors to be started at intervals, their take-off order decided by lottery. Thus, it was a race against the clock rather than each other, so avoiding the potential dangers of crowding at the turns and, furthermore, allowing the pilots to concentrate on the task of keeping their capricious aircraft in the air.

First away was Maurice Prévost in No. 19, at about 8.08 a.m., taxying smoothly to the starting line, from where the first 5 km had to be covered on the surface of the water to demonstrate the seaworthiness of the machine. All went well, the sea penitent and co-operative, and as Prévost opened the throttle fully at the mid-point of the first lap the Deperdussin responded nobly, climbing up on her floats to scud smoothly over the water before lifting off without any apparent effort.

Before Prévost gained the end of his first lap, Roland Garros was sent to the starting line in the Morane-Saulnier No. 2. This aircraft, it will be remembered, was similar to those built by the Farman brothers and, like them, demonstrated its best take-off performance on choppy water. Today it was an oily calm and No. 2, having completed the taxying trial, was reluctant to become airborne. Its progress developed into a series of up and down hops as Garros tried to wrestle it into the air, but one of the downs supplied a drenching of sea water for the engine which promptly decided that it had had enough. Garros signalled frantically for assistance, and a motor boat was soon on the scene to tow the dejected pilot and his machine back to the yacht harbour. There it was surrounded quickly by a mass of supporters, with a wealth of suggestions and little practical help, but all determined to get him back into the race again as quickly as possible.

Meanwhile, at 08.50 a.m., Gabriel Espanet in Nieuport No. 6 had got away and although slightly slower than Prévost in completing the compulsory seaborne trial, was able to get into the air without difficulty. Last away was Charles Weymann in Nieuport No. 5, but extreme caution in negotiating the seaworthiness trial cost him valuable time. By the time that he had joined the others in the circuit, Prévost had a lead over him of more than seven minutes.

Prévost was forging ahead as fast as he could go, well aware that the Nieuports held an advantage over him in respect of speed, and determined to use all his skill as a pilot to hang on to his lead. But it was soon apparent, for those keeping a close watch on lap times, that while this was enabling him to gain on Espanet, Weymann was steadily clipping seconds off the Frenchman's lead.

It promised to be an exciting event: to a back-cloth of blue sky and sun-kissed sea, the three machines raised their voices to a crescendo as, at full throttle, they raced round the course. Unfortunately, the pace soon proved too much for Espanet's Nieuport as, with engine misfiring, he headed back reluctantly to Monaco's harbour. A quick check showed that a fuel line had fractured and that it was beyond speedy repair. Then there were two!

Almost certainly this must have been the first moment when officials and spectators felt the thrill of excitement that was to characterise these contests in later years. Two aircraft, representing America and France, were battling for supremacy. That both were of French design and construction was purely academic: in the end result the Trophy would go to the nation represented by the pilot, and the first hint of international prestige could be felt. There was another question: would engines and airframes withstand the pounding of the remaining 75 per cent of the 280 km course.

As lap after lap was marked off, the tension increased, for it was clear that despite Prévost's skilful handling of his machine the superior speed of the Nieuport was beginning to tell. With just over half of the race completed they were literally neck-and-neck.

The result appeared to be a foregone conclusion when, with 75 per cent of the race completed, Weymann was ahead on time. Shortly after the result seemed certain: Prévost having completed his 28th lap alighted on the sea 0·5 km short of the finishing line. Some conviction was in his mind that he must land and cross the finishing line on the surface of the sea.

His belief was entirely wrong: the rules required that the finishing line should be crossed in the air. One can imagine the voluble and excited French voices raised in protest and counter-argument, added to those who were trying to urge Prévost to take off again to complete another lap. They were all wasting their time: Prévost was certain that Weymann was so far ahead in time that even if he took off and completed another lap the situation would remain unaltered, particularly as there was now the time spent on the ground to be added. His opponent had merely to complete the remaining laps at a less demanding speed to win comfortably.

In mounting tension the spectators watched Weymann continue to pile on the laps . . . 21, 22, 23, 24. Only four more to go. It was now fate's turn to take a hand in a slight readjustment of the sequence of events: suddenly, and completely unexpectedly, the Nieuport was seen to alight on the sea. A motor boat was alongside in minutes, and no time was lost in towing the machine and its disappointed pilot back to harbour. There it was discovered that a burst oil pipe was responsible for the forced landing. It was fairly easy to replace and men and tools almost fought to get at the machine; could he get back into the race in time? It might have been possible had not a prudent check showed traces of metal in the filter: the engine had been damaged by lack of oil and Weymann was right out.

A near state of panic took over the French camp, for it was essential that they should do something quickly to establish themselves as the winners. The Morane-Saulnier of Roland Garros had been rendered serviceable by this time, and he was bustled off to the starting line to begin once again the seaworthiness trial. This time he was able to coax his machine from its affinity for the water, and was soon bustling round the course, making impeccable turns. Those who watched his performance found emphasis, if it had been needed, of this pilot's ability to handle aircraft in a skilful and technically sympathetic manner. Excitement rose to new heights as Prévost was seen to be taxying the Deperdussin out again: he became airborne without difficulty and had quickly completed the extra essential lap, this time *flying* triumphantly over the finishing line. Thus, the first Schneider Trophy contest was awarded to Maurice Prévost and France: his official speed, after inclusion of the period spent on the ground after the invalid 28th lap, was 45·75 mph (73·63 km/h). Second place went to Roland Garros, who went on to complete the 28-lap course in fine style.

There was general agreement that the Schneider Trophy contest had been the most successful event of the Monaco meeting, creating great excitement and interest, which augured well for the future. Furthermore, Monaco would be the venue for next year's event and the French, being on home ground, must start as keen favourites.

On the other hand, the Grand Prix had been far from successful, demonstrating effectively that there was still very considerable scope for improvement in the structural integrity of the hydro-aeroplane. Stanley Spooner, then the Editor of *Flight*, summed it up in an editorial, commenting:

'. . . There are phases of hydro-aeroplaning that can only be appreciated on the spot. A swell on the sea and a lee shore close at hand are not in the least comparable with any sort of aerodrome, prepared or natural.

'It is not only the wind, but the sea with which one must contend, for the sea, unlike the land, may upon occasion rise to strike the machine a disabling blow.'

How right he was, and the sea was to raise a watery hand to strike many blows during the series of Schneider Trophy contests.

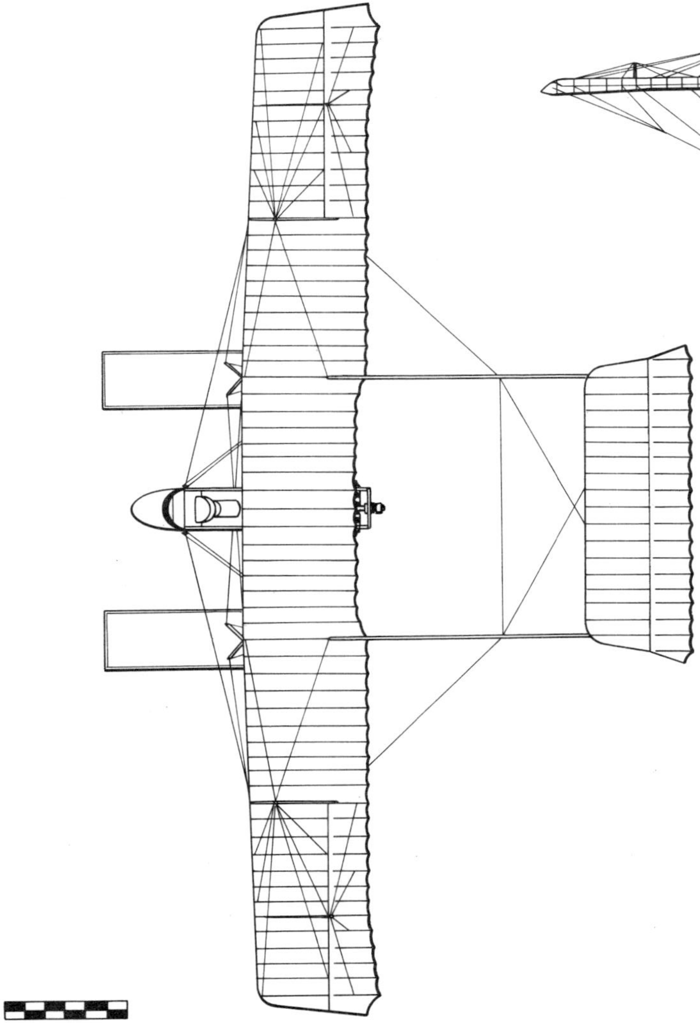

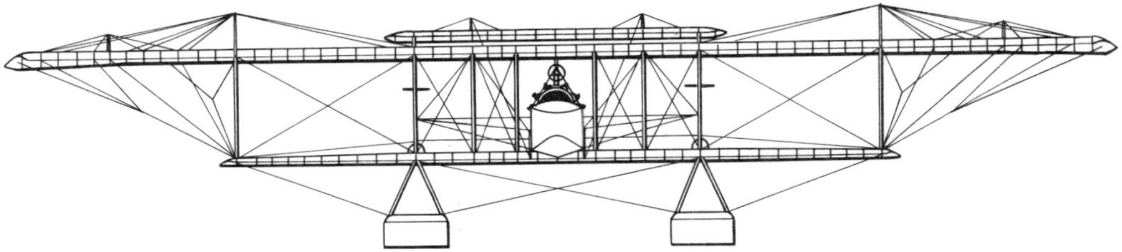

Henri Farman (1913)

Wing Area: 660 sq. ft (61·32 m²)
T-O Weight: 2,850 lb (1,293 kg)
Max Wing Loading: 4·32 lb/sq. ft (21·09 kg/m²)
Horsepower of Power Plant: 160 hp

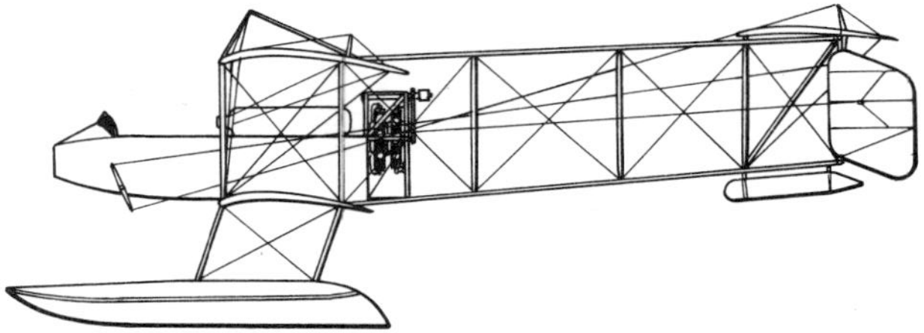

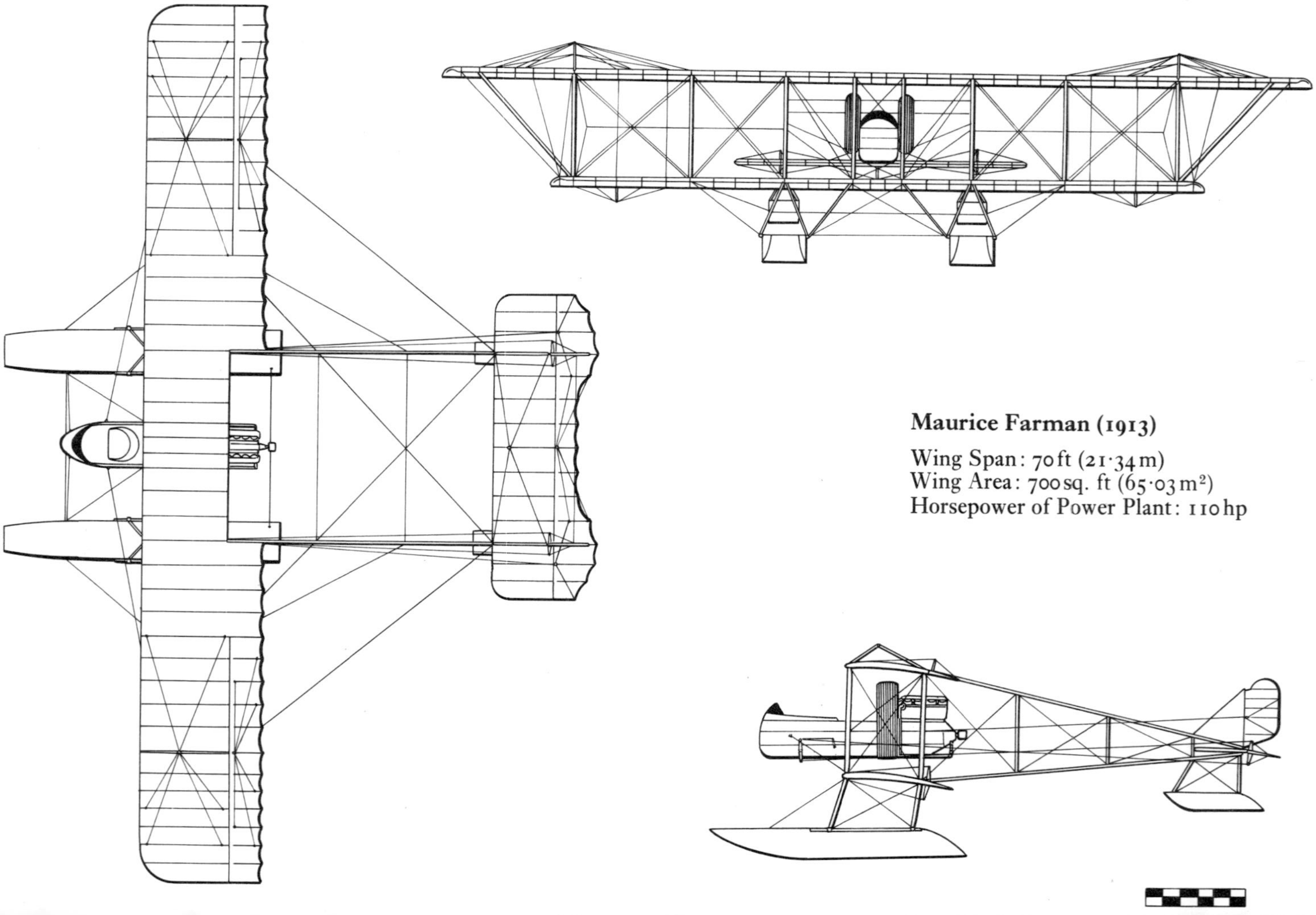

Maurice Farman (1913)

Wing Span: 70 ft (21·34 m)
Wing Area: 700 sq. ft (65·03 m²)
Horsepower of Power Plant: 110 hp

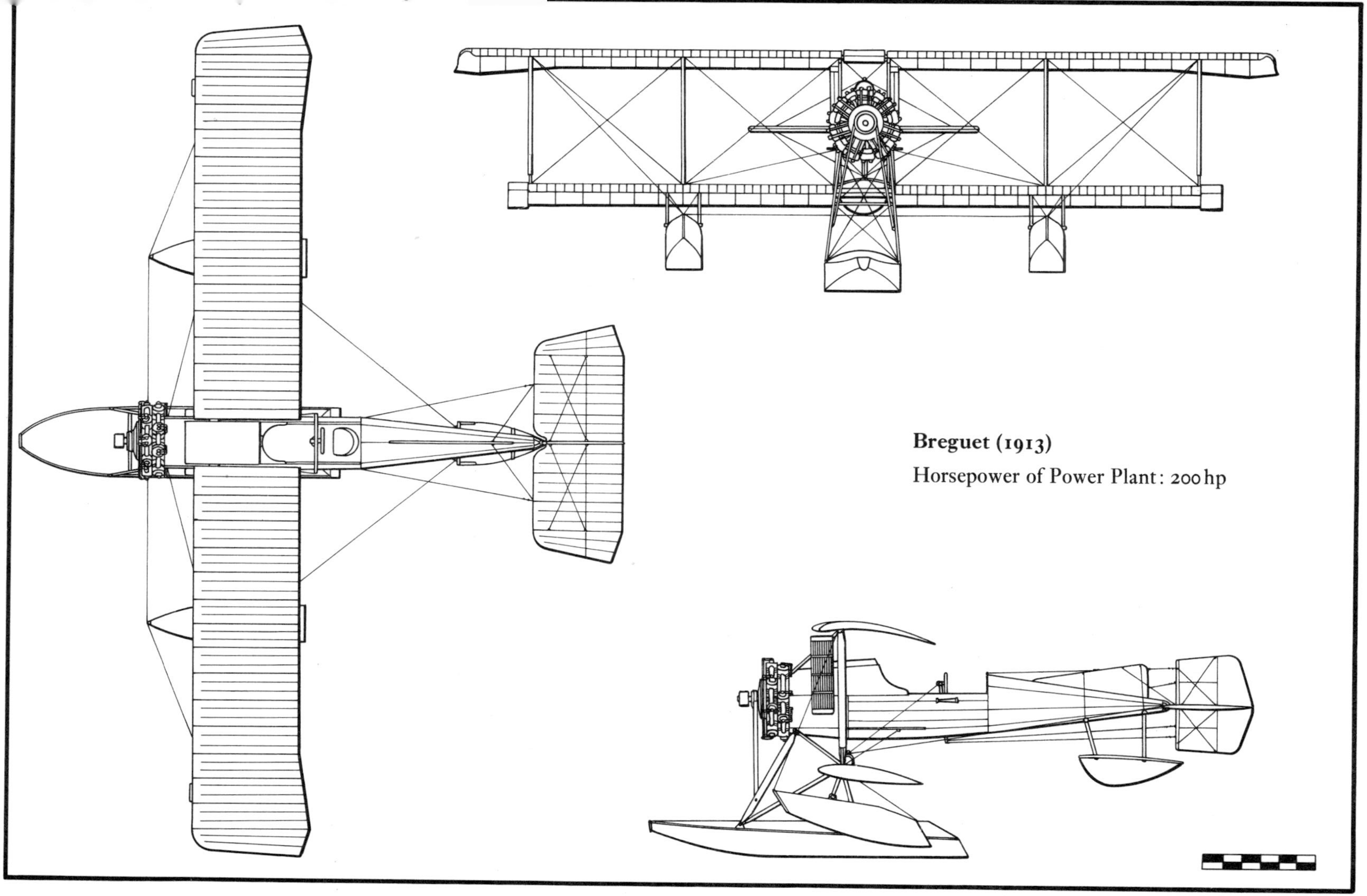

Breguet (1913)

Horsepower of Power Plant: 200 hp

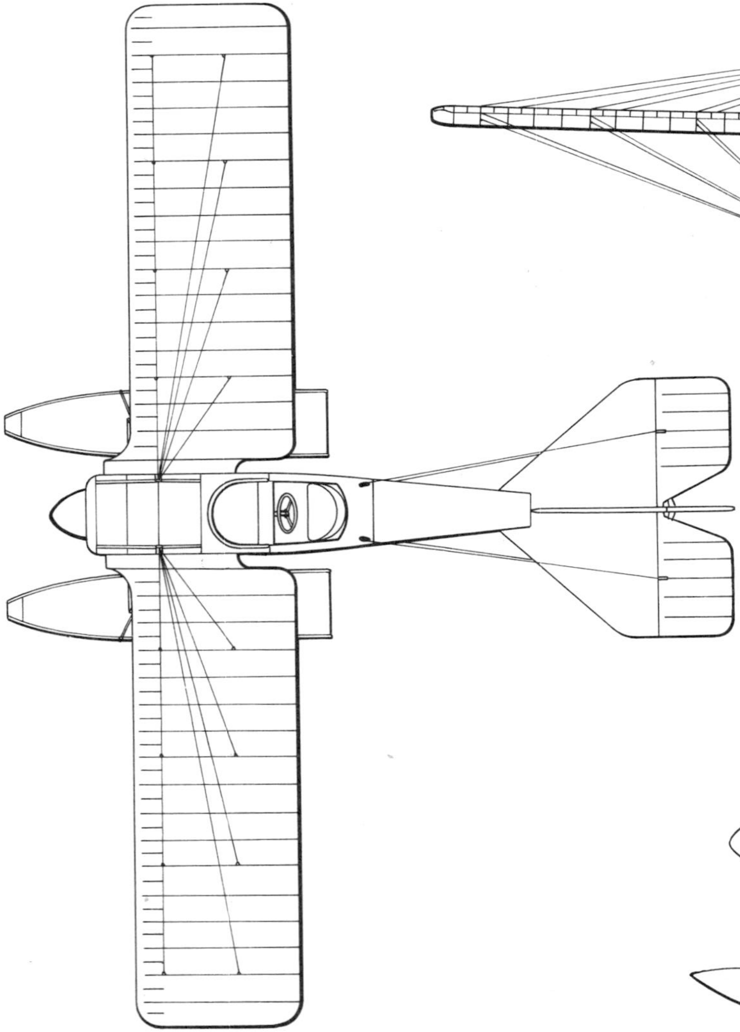

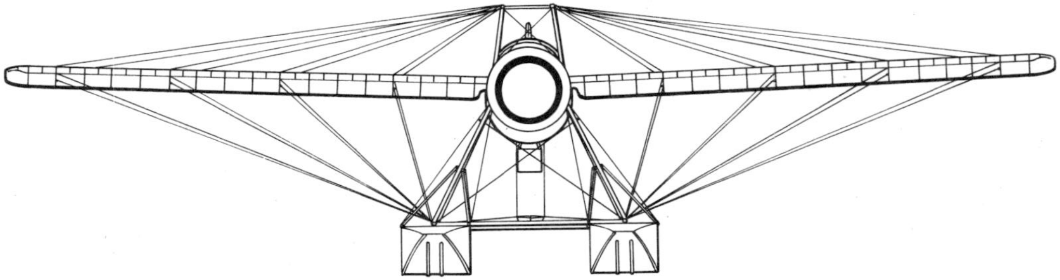

Deperdussin (1913)

Wing Span: 44 ft 3 in (13·49 m)
Length Overall: 29 ft 6 in (8·99 m)
Wing Area: 301 sq. ft (27·96 m²)
Weight Empty: 2,095 lb (950 kg)
T-O Weight: 2,645 lb (1,200 kg)
Max Wing Loading: 8·79 lb/sq. ft (42·92 kg/m²)
Horsepower of Power Plant: 160 hp

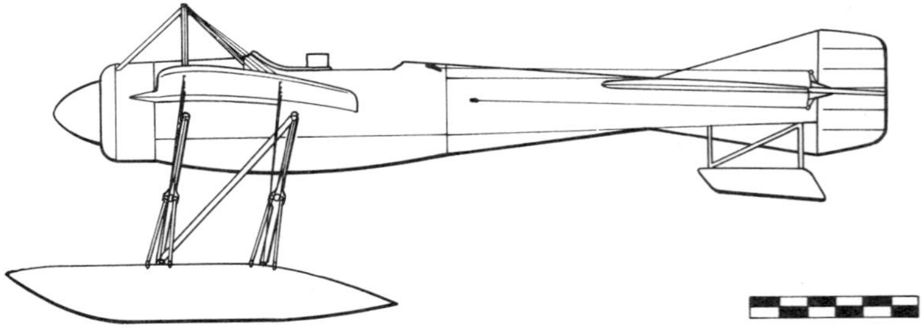

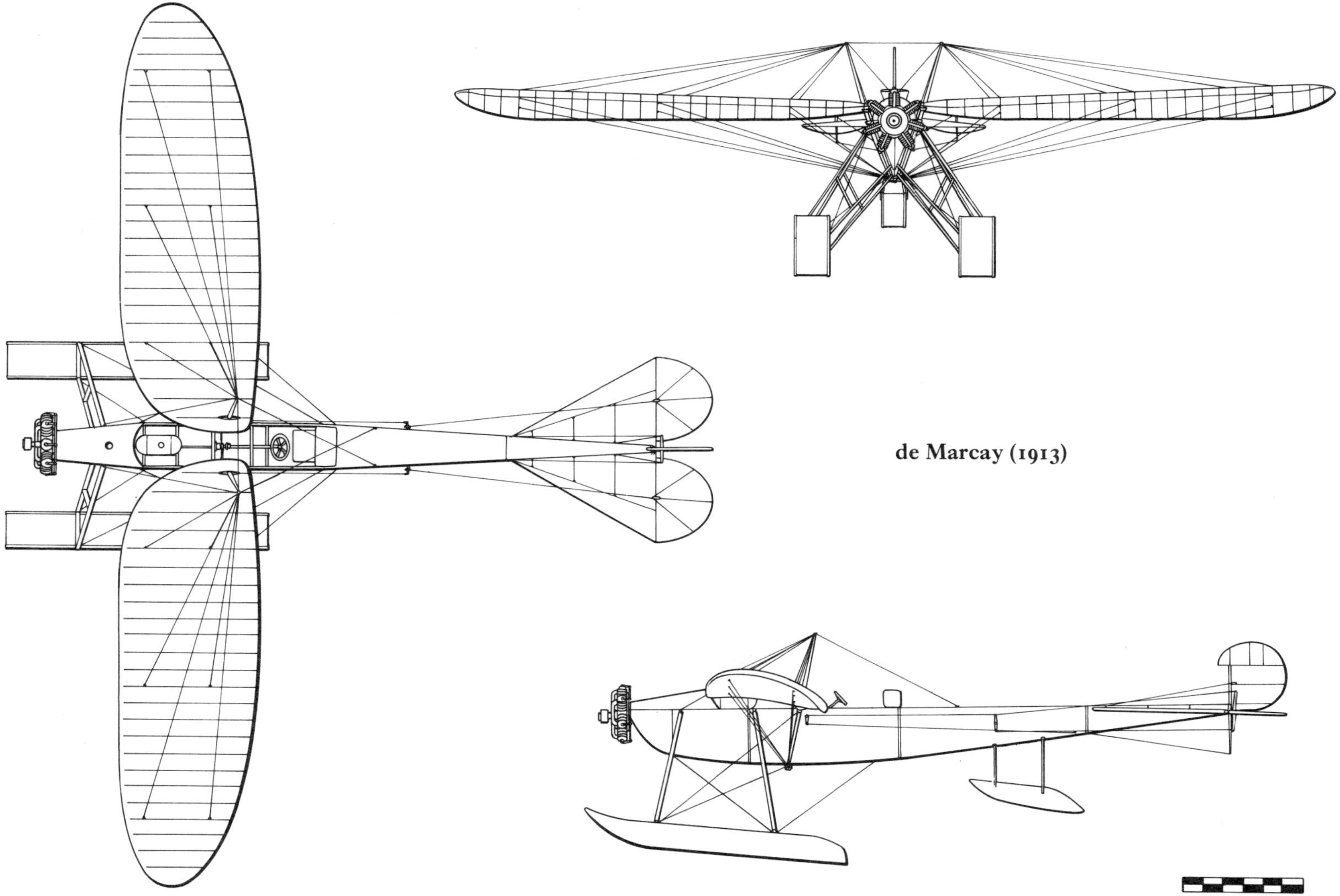

de Marcay (1913)

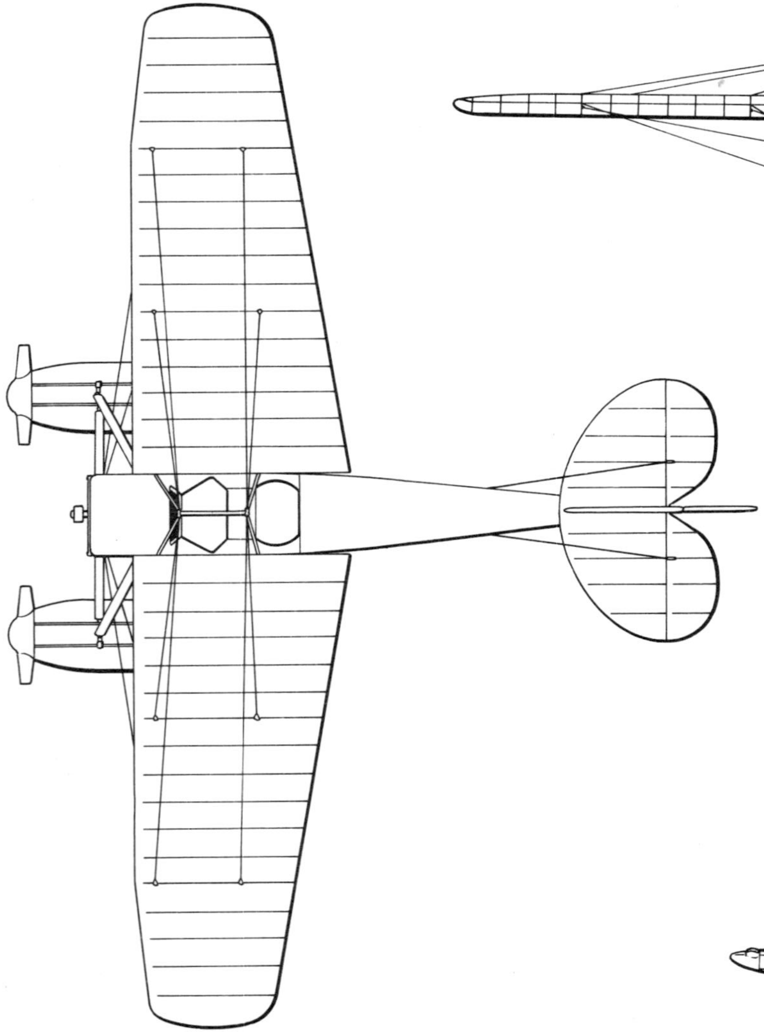

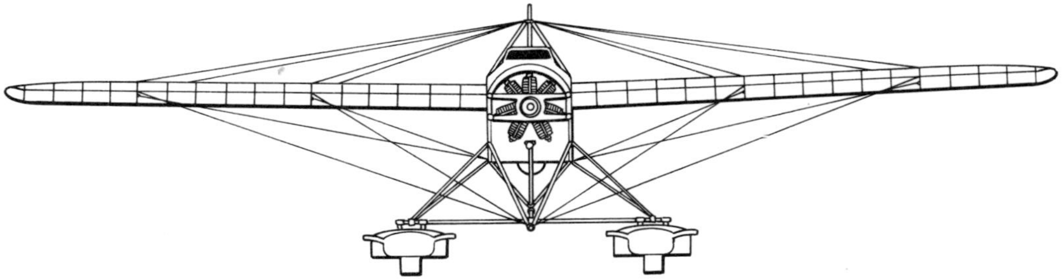

Nieuport (1913)

Wing Span: 39 ft 7 in (12·07 m)
Length Overall: 28 ft (8·53 m)
Wing Area: 230 sq. ft (21·37 m²)
Weight Empty: 1,320 lb (599 kg)
T-O Weight: 1,875 lb (851 kg)
Max Wing Loading: 8·15 lb/sq.ft (39·79 kg/m²)
Horsepower of Power Plant: 100 hp

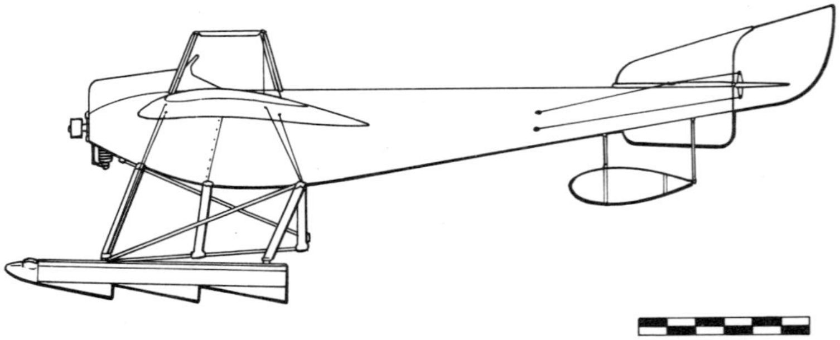

3

Again at Monaco

1914

Organisers of aviation events in the days prior to the first World War were either extremely naive or supreme optimists. Possibly without either or both of these characteristics they would never have become involved in such a dicey business. Those responsible for arranging the 1914 Hydro-Aeroplane Meeting at Monaco must, in addition, have been stricken with short memories. Ignoring the near-fiasco of the previous year, which had shown that the elements then held clear domination over man's frail flying machines, they produced far more ambitious plans for the next event.

Instead of hydro-aeroplanes racing around a number of laps to complete a 500km course (achieved by none of the 1913 competitors), an Aerial Rally was substituted with seven optional starting points. These included Paris, London, Brussels, Gotha, Madrid, Milan and Vienna; the first five routes terminated at Marseilles, the last two at Genoa. At these coastal terminals of the seven routes, each of which were 1,083km (673 miles) in length, there remained an overwater crossing of 210km (130 miles) to be completed. And since Marseilles and Genoa were not equidistant from the finishing point, the discrepancy was to be adjusted by additional laps of the 10km Schneider Trophy Course at Monaco. Thus, when those pilots who were fortunate enough to complete the rally course came in to their water landing outside the yacht harbour, each should have completed a distance of 1,293km (803 miles). Competitors could attempt their chosen route at any period between 1 and 15 April 1914: it was also allowed that after completion of one route they could, if they wished, attempt another route in the hope of bettering their time.

One complicating factor, if any was necessary, arose at the end of the land routes. Here the competitors had the choice of converting their landplane for water-borne operation, for which a period of forty-eight hours was allowed to complete the installation of floats and launch their aircraft. Alternatively, a second hydro-aeroplane could be used for the overwater stage, but this had to be of the same make and type as the landplane which had carried the pilot to Marseilles or Genoa.

Although the number of entries was the same as for 1913, there were contestants from countries which had not entered previously, as well as from manufacturers which had not been represented before. Of the tried and true, there were three Deperdussins, four Farmans, six Morane-Saulniers and three Nieuports. The remaining entries comprised two Albatross, two Aviatiks, two Breguets, one R.E.P., one Schemmel and two Taube-Gothas. And in a somewhat tentative attempt to avoid attention from the eye of the 'evil one', no machine had been allocated the entry number 13.

The first five competitors set out on 3 April, and Garros in a Morane-Saulnier had to force-land at Orange when his machine caught fire. Moineau, flying a Breguet, hit some overhead electric cables when attempting a forced landing at Cantinolles, near Bordeaux, seriously damaging his aircraft. Most successful of the first five starters was Brindejonc des Moulinais, who set out from Madrid in a Morane-Saulnier. He was the first to arrive at Monaco, on 4 April, having set a time of 16 hrs 2 mins $31\frac{3}{5}$ secs, but damaged his aircraft slightly while landing in rough water conditions. After hasty repairs, he set out again to better his time, this time selecting the Italian route, but only to wreck his machine at Antibes.

Moineau, Verrier and Legagneux all had their aircraft damaged in landing accidents, and most competitors had adventurous journeys. By no means all of them completed the course chosen, suffering a variety of mechanical failures or dominated by unco-operative weather.

Garros proved to be the hero of the meet, however, for after effecting repairs to his machine at Orange, he went on to reach Monaco in a total flying time of 12 hrs 11 mins $34\frac{1}{5}$ secs, which put him well in the lead. Not satisfied with that he made a second attempt to better his time, choosing the Brussels–Monaco route, to record 12 hrs 27 mins 13 secs, thus gaining first and second places. He was, in fact, the only competitor to better the time set up by des Moulinais, who gained third place.

On 8 April the French held eliminating trials at Monaco to finalise their team for the Schneider Trophy Contest. Each was required to fly four laps of the 10 km course, and those taking part were Brindejonc des Moulinais, Gabriel Espanet, Roland Garros, M. Janoir, Pierre Levasseur and Maurice Prévost. It proved to be a depressing business, for only Espanet flying a Nieuport was able to complete four laps. Levasseur in another Nieuport managed two; Garros on his Morane-Saulnier completed only a single lap, and so these three comprised the French team. Prévost and Janoir in Deperdussins and des Moulinais in a Morane-Saulnier failed to complete a lap and were nominated as reserves.

Despite this poor showing in the eliminating trials, the French felt pretty confident of gaining the Trophy for the second time. That Prévost and Janoir had failed to make the team must have come as a pretty severe shock, for the Deperdussins had been developed into the most streamlined aircraft of that era and their top speed was in excess of 120 mph (193 km/h). In the

1913 Gordon-Bennett Cup race held at Rheims in September, the Prévost/Deperdussin combination had taken first place at 124·5 mph (200·36 km/h). Emile Vedrines in a Ponnier racing monoplane had come second at 123 mph (197·94 km/h), and Gilbert flying another Deperdussin had completed the French triumph with a third place at 119·5 mph (192·3 km/h). With two Gordon-Bennett Cups and the first Schneider Trophy contest tucked beneath their belts, the French had every reason to feel confident. The big question mark emanating from the eliminating trials was whether the Nieuports would have sufficient speed to meet any foreign challenge. They were slow by comparison with the Deperdussins, but there was no alternative other than to abide by the result of the trials.

The excitement generated by the first Schneider Trophy Contest had suggested that the number of entries would be greater for the 1914 event. This proved to be fact, for America, Britain, France, Germany and Switzerland were all fielding competitors. Speculation amongst the more knowledgeable posed the question as to whether France was correct in her assumption of an easy win. Although France had held the lead in European aviation for some time, there was no doubt that both Britain and Germany had been concentrating on the development of improved aircraft.

America was again represented by Charles Weymann, his mount being a Nieuport as in the previous year, but this time powered by a 160 hp Le Rhone rotary engine. The second American was a little-known pilot, named William Thaw. His machine was a somewhat tired-looking Curtiss biplane flying-boat of pusher configuration, which so clearly had no chance of surviving the full course that he jumped at a generous offer of the loan of a French Deperdussin.

German interest centred on the Aviatik Arrow to be flown by Ernst Stoeffler. This was a clean-looking biplane with a large central float, under-wing balancer floats at the wing tips and a small under-tail float. Power plant was a 150 hp Benz in-line water-cooled engine, driving a two-blade tractor propeller. With a wing area of 484 sq. ft (45 m^2) and take-off weight of 1,984 lb (900 kg), the resulting low wing loading of 4·4 lb/sq. ft (21·4 km/m^2) suggested that it might perform well on the water. Unfortunately, its maximum speed was only about 75 mph (121 km/h), so that its only real hope was to keep going if all the others failed.

The Swiss entry, an F.B.A. flying-boat was of interest also, being constructed by the Franco-British Aviation Company, which had been founded in 1913 by Beaumont and Schreck to build a production version of the Donnet-Lévêque biplane flying-boat. Emanating from the French designer Denhaut, this machine had a stepped nacelle-type hull and small balancer floats at the wing tips. Power plant was a 100 hp Gnome Monosoupape rotary engine, driving a two-blade pusher propeller. With a wing area of 279·8 sq. ft (26 m^2) and maximum take-off weight of only 1,036 lb (470 kg), the resulting 3·7 lb/sq. ft (18 kg/m^2) wing loading promised spectacular take-off performance. It did; providing amusement for spectators but something of a nightmare for the pilot, Ernest Burri, for it twisted and wallowed over the water like a baby porpoise at play. However, with a maximum speed of about 68 mph (110 km/h) it was reasonably clear that this machine presented no challenge whatsoever to the French.

Its most interesting feature was the new Gnome Monosoupape (mono—single; soupape—valve) engine, and this is perhaps an appropriate moment to look at the rotary engine which, at this period of time, was by far the most effective power plant available to the aviation industry or pioneer constructor.

As has been mentioned earlier, Laurent Seguin had been concerned primarily in dealing with the problem of overheating which had plagued earlier aircraft engines. The solution of a fixed crankshaft, requiring the cylinders, crankcase and attached propeller to revolve was instrumental in providing better cooling, while the flywheel-inertia of the engine's mass gave a far smoother running engine than any other then available.

Fuel and oil were fed into the crankcase via the hollow crankshaft, and so that the lubricating medium was not diluted to impotency by the fuel, a vegetable oil not miscible with petrol was essential. This accounted for the selection of castor oil, the smell of which pervaded aircraft, flying clothing and pilot to provide that magic aroma of nostalgic memory.

Lubrication began at an oil tank which fed a gear-driven pump that, in turn, supplied oil under pressure to the main crankshaft ball races, big-ends, little-ends via connecting-rod ducts and valve gear. Practically all of this lubricant ultimately reached the cylinders by centrifugal action and was either consumed by combustion or duly ejected through the exhaust valves. The oil intake of early Gnome engines could vary from 25 to 50 per cent of fuel consumption, according to engine condition, and was clearly a wasteful and filthy business.

Seguin sought to overcome some of these shortcomings by introduction of the Monosoupape version. Dispensing with inlet valves offered a weight saving; and improved design allowed higher rpm and power output. This, in turn, allowed reversion to a single bank of nine cylinders for a 100 hp engine, resolving the overheating problem. Provision of obturator (oil control) piston rings helped reduce oil consumption, but at best it remained between 20 and 25 per cent of the fuel consumed.

The working cycle of the Monosoupape was interesting, for the elimination of mechanical inlet valves led to their replacement by an elementary sleeve-valve idea, the skirt of the piston doubling as sleeve. Petrol was introduced into the crankcase from a pressurised tank, spraying out of a crankshaft jet. This was partially vapourised by incoming air supplied through a forward-facing funnel-shaped scoop, and the fuel droplets were further broken up by the churning action of the crankshaft and connecting rods.

Starting point of the four-stroke cycle was with piston at top dead-centre (TDC) and exhaust valve open. As the piston descended in the cylinder, as a result of its rotation, air was drawn in through the exhaust valve until at 60° before bottom dead-centre (BDC) the exhaust valve was closed. Further downward movement of the piston created a partial vacuum in the cylinder so that when at 20° before BDC the ports in the cylinder wall were uncovered, petrol mixture flowed from crankcase to cylinder. This was compressed on the up-stroke of the piston, fired just before TDC, and after 90° of the power stroke the exhaust valve re-opened. When the piston reached TDC the cycle re-commenced.

The primary drawback of the rotary engine was, of course, the power wasted in turning the mass of the engine through the slipstream. In fact, for a nine-cylinder engine, this method of achieving cooling cost almost 30 per cent of the power output. So while the rotary was to dominate the aviation scene for some time, by far the most efficient engine available in those years just before and during the war, it was really but an interim design until more effectively air-cooled radial and lightweight liquid-cooled engines were developed.

But to revert to the 1914 Schneider Trophy Contest: we have seen that the French feared little from German and Swiss opposition, while the American challenge was almost disregarded. There remained Britain, but it seemed likely that this would be of little concern. Two entries had been received: that of Lord John Carbery flying a Morane-Saulnier and the French knew that, barring accidents, they more than had the measure of that aircraft. The second entry was that of an unheard of Sopwith machine, to be flown by a Mr C. Howard Pixton, also unknown. That a new and untried machine should have any chance against the proven Deperdussins and Nieuports was not worthy of consideration.

Unfortunately for the French, the Sopwith machine was something of a dark horse, produced under conditions of considerable secrecy by T. O. M. (later Sir Thomas) Sopwith. Basically an engineer, Tommy Sopwith was an early victim of the ballooning bug, the somewhat virulent disease spreading rapidly throughout his system, taking the extreme form of the complaint which manifested itself in an irresistible urge to become involved in powered flight.

The son of a wealthy civil engineer, young Sopwith had few problems in acquiring a Howard Wright monoplane in which at Brooklands, on 22 October 1910, he had essayed his first flight. Overconfidence was his undoing, and within no time at all the little monoplane had a broken propeller, landing gear and a crumpled wing.

It was not until 4 November that the machine had been repaired and was once again ready for flight. This time, adopting a more cautious approach to acquire a feel of the controls, he succeeded in making his first self-taught solo flight. The monoplane was quickly substituted for the latest Howard

Wright biplane with which, on 21 November, Sopwith acquired his pilot's certificate (No. 31).

A month later, on 18 December, he competed for a prize of £4,000 offered by the Baron de Forest for the longest flight from England to the Continent, completing a distance of 177 miles (285 km) in 3 hrs 40 mins, before his 60 hp E.N.V.-powered biplane was buffeted by winds which forced him to land. This achievement was unbeaten by anyone else before the closing date of the contest, 31 December, and Sopwith took the £4,000 prize.

He followed this by an American tour, taking with him a new Gnome-engined Blériot monoplane. Unfortunately, this was soon wrecked, and a new model was ordered from France to supplement his Howard Wright biplane which had then arrived. It proved to be an adventurous tour, and was sufficiently successful to earn him a considerable sum in prize money.

On his return to England he set up a flying school at Brooklands, counting among his pupils Major Hugh Trenchard and Harry G. Hawker, and immediately he considered the school well established he turned from pilot to constructor. Acquiring a newly-closed skating rink in Canbury Park Road at Kingston upon Thames, Surrey, he established there in 1913 The Sopwith Aviation Company. Involved with him in the new company was Harry Hawker, with prime responsibility as pilot and management of the works staff, and Fred Sigrist, an engineer employed by Sopwith originally to look after his yacht *Neva*. It was planned that while Hawker concentrated on building aircraft and flying them, Sopwith and Sigrist would busy themselves with the design of new machines.

One of the earliest products of the new organisation was the Tabloid, a two-seat biplane intended for demonstration and racing. The choice of a biplane configuration, with its multiplicity of drag-inducing struts and bracing wires, may have seemed a little odd for an intended racing aircraft, especially having regard to the speeds demonstrated by the clean-looking monoplane of the French Deperdussin company. There was good reason for the choice, however, for as a result of accidents involving monoplane aircraft, coupled with a report by Louis Blériot that the monoplane configuration had inherent structural weaknesses, both the British and French governments had been induced to place a temporary ban on the construction of monoplane aircraft for military use.

Consequently, if a manufacturer entertained any hope of acquiring military contracts, all-important to the early constructors, a biplane structure was essential. Tommy Sopwith was unconvinced that a biplane must necessarily be inferior to a monoplane. On the contrary, he argued that the biplane structure lent itself to a compact, robust and lightweight aircraft which, with reasonable attention to streamlining, should produce a machine equal to, if not better than, contemporary monoplanes.

The prototype Tabloid was what we would regard as a modern-looking

Posing for the photographer, Howard Pixton leans nonchalantly on the lower wing of the Sopwith Tabloid

The Sopwith Schneider during construction at Kingston upon Thames

biplane, with side-by-side seating for pilot and passenger in a single open cockpit. The single-bay wings of equal span had only one pair of interplane struts on each side, and landing and flying wires were reduced to a minimum. Roll control was still by wing warping, although later production versions were to acquire ailerons. The tail unit consisted of a fixed tailplane, two elevators and a balanced rudder: there was no fixed fin. However, following the modified tail unit developed for the Sopwith Schneider, the fin and rudder combination became standard.

Power plant was an 80 hp Gnome rotary, and perhaps the strangest feature of the Tabloid was that this engine, designed to rotate in the air to keep it cool, was completely enclosed in a rather ugly cowling. Cooling air was admitted through two slots.

Initial flight tests were carried out at Brooklands, but when Harry Hawker flew it for an official demonstration at Farnborough, a speed of 92 mph (148 km/h) was recorded, as well as an initial rate of climb of 1,200 ft (366 m)/min with pilot and passenger. Clearly it was quite some aircraft, and while the factory got on with production, Hawker shipped out to Australia, taking with him the prototype for demonstration flights in the hope of gaining some sales in that country.

Somewhat out of context, it is interesting to record a few statistics of the production Tabloids which had a wing span of only 25 ft 6 in (7·77 m), length of 20 ft 4 in (6·20 m) and height of 8 ft 5 in (2·57 m). Wing area totalled 241·3 sq. ft (22·42 m²), which with a maximum take-off weight of 1,120 lb (508 kg), gave a wing loading of only 4·6 lb/sq. ft (22·4 kg/m²), helping to account for their excellent performance.

Best known of the some forty Tabloids that were built were Serial Nos. 167 and 168, operated by the Royal Naval Air Service (RNAS) at the beginning of the first World War. In these two machines Squadron-Commander Spenser Grey and Flight-Lieutenant R. L. G. Marix set out on 8 October 1914 to bomb the German Zeppelin sheds at Cologne and Düsseldorf. Spenser Grey was unable to locate his target in conditions of bad visibility, but Reggie Marix succeeded in planting his bombs neatly on the Zeppelin hangar at Düsseldorf, being rewarded by an enormous explosion which destroyed the hangar and its contents, the new Zeppelin Z.IX.

Well aware that success in an international contest could provide the best possible publicity for his new company, Tommy Sopwith decided that a floatplane version of the Tabloid might have a good chance of success in the 1914 Schneider Trophy Contest. Accordingly, he set out with characteristic enthusiasm to prepare a special version, dubbed the Sopwith Schneider, to compete at Monaco.

There were two main requirements: a more powerful engine and a suitable float installation. The former need was that most easily resolved, for Sopwith had heard of the new 100 hp Gnome Monosoupape and lost no time in a visit to the Gnome works and was soon back in Kingston complete with an example of the engine.

The floats were a somewhat bigger problem, and considerable effort went into devising what was thought would provide the most stable arrangement. This consisted of a long single central float with wing tip balancer floats. The other variation from the prototype consisted of modification to the tail unit, by the addition of a triangular fixed fin and a plain rudder.

In this form the Schneider was broken down for transit to Southampton, where it was to be tested on the River Hamble. By 31 March, just eighteen days before the scheduled date for the contest, it had been re-assembled, rigged and was ready for test. Unfortunately, its chosen pilot was confined to bed with a severe chill, so that it was not until the next day when, looking rather the worse for wear, he stood and shivered in his flying clothing as the team from Kingston waited for the tide to raise the water level in the river sufficiently for them to launch the little biplane.

This pilot was C. Howard Pixton, taken on as a test pilot by Sopwith to keep things moving during Harry Hawker's absence in Australia. He was not, as many French reporters were to comment later, a young and inexperienced pilot. Young, yes; but he held British pilot's certificate No. 50 and had gained considerable success in competitions at Brooklands. Additionally, he had served with the Bristol Aeroplane Company for a spell before joining the new Kingston firm.

Gradually the tide rose and, at last, came the moment when the pilot was able to climb aboard and start the engine. He opened the throttle slightly and began to taxi away, but a pronounced nose-down attitude on the water suggested that the main float was too far aft. This was confirmed seconds later as Pixton pushed the throttle a little further open and the Schneider cartwheeled and sank. Despite being hampered by his heavy clothing, Pixton managed to wriggle out of the cockpit and gain the security of dry land, while the rest of the party looked dejectedly at the Schneider which, now controlled by the tide, had drifted towards midstream. The immediate problem was to ensure that it remained within reach when the tide ebbed, and it was not long before ropes were attached to the aircraft, securing it to the jetty. At low tide it presented a sorry sight to those first on the scene, balanced precariously on its nose, tail high in the air.

It was a critical situation, now with only sixteen days to go. A lesser man would have decided there and then that enough was enough. Not so Tommy Sopwith. No time was lost in getting the machine back to Kingston, where willing hands set to work to repair the damage.

The biggest problem was, of course, the float installation; and the design and construction of an alternative arrangement within the time available. Practical rather than theoretical remedy had to be adopted, and the large single float was sliced longitudinally, the resulting uncovered sides being boxed in to make two single floats. Each was then mounted on two struts, in the then orthodox floatplane layout, with strut and wire bracing. The wingtip balancing floats were removed and a small under-tail float fitted. This latter float had a small square water rudder attached to its trailing-edge.

By 6 April all was ready once again, but with the race only twelve days ahead there was no time to go back to the Hamble River. Instead, Old Father Thames would have to suffice, and in the absence of permission to launch a floatplane on the surface of the Thames Conservancy's sacred water, a little touch of the clandestine was essential.

Accordingly, at 5.00 a.m. on the morning of 7 April the Schneider was taken down to the river just below Kingston bridge, but delays in making final adjustments took so long that it was 9.30 a.m. before all was ready. By that time relentless officialdom, unconcerned of national prestige, had arrived on the scene and Sopwith and his men had to be satisfied with flotation tests only. At least the Schneider sat more happily on the water than at Hamble.

But more than mere flotation tests were needed to give some assurance of satisfactory take-off performance before becoming involved in the costly business of getting the aircraft to Monaco. It was decided to try their luck again on a stretch of water coming under the jurisdiction of the Port of London Authority, for Sopwith's chief mechanic—Victor Mahl—was aware that the Thames Conservancy's authority ended at Teddington lock.

So, in the early hours of the following morning, Mahl and his men surreptitiously got the Schneider on to the water, not too far distant from the present Hawker factory at Kingston. Launched opposite to Glovers Island, near Ham, Howard Pixton lost little time in 'having a go' before officialdom could intervene. The new float installation seemed to be entirely satisfactory, lifting quickly to plane the calm surface of the Thames, despite a roughly-running engine. There was little room for manoeuvre, but confirmation that the floats were capable of shouldering their task was all that was needed. There was no doubt of the potential of the aircraft, which was hustled back to the factory and crated for the journey to Monaco and the Schneider Trophy, now only ten days away.

Tommy Sopwith was confident that his machine with Pixton at the controls stood a very good chance barring accidents: the most worrying factor was the time that would be involved in getting the Schneider from Kingston to Monaco. In fact, it was not until two days before the race that Sopwith and his team got possession of the crated aircraft.

Willing hands speeded the uncrating and assembly, but when the French saw the diminutive biplane that had been erected, powered by an engine of only 100 hp, their delight had no bounds. It was clear that even one of the most experienced pilots, Prévost for example, would have no chance at all in such a machine, never mind an unknown pilot with no record of experience in international competition. The Trophy was theirs for the taking.

The most pathetic-looking feature of the Sopwith machine was its engine, which had gained no benefit from its immersion in the Hamble River. Not only did it look like a rusty relic from some scrapyard, it was not too keen to enter into the spirit of the occasion, running so erratically that Mahl and his men worked on it almost incessantly until late on the night of 17 April. The race was due to commence the following morning.

Fortunately, the weather intervened once again, so that on Saturday morning the organisers decided to postpone the contest for twenty-four hours. This gave Sopwith and his men an additional day in which to ensure the Schneider was as fit as possible for the gruelling task ahead. Their main concern, and particularly that of Howard Pixton, was that there had been no opportunity to fly the aircraft to discover whether any adjustments were needed to rigging or control settings. The only flight experience at that point had been limited to a brief hop from the Thames.

Sunday morning 19 April dawned clear with moderate sea, and Sopwith quickly had the team astir. At the near-nocturnal hour of 5.00 a.m. the Schneider was fuelled, a somewhat heavy-eyed Pixton bundled into the cockpit, and the little machine launched on to the waters of the yacht harbour. It did not sit too happily on the water, decidedly tail-down, but at least the little water rudder aft of the tail float simplified Pixton's task of taxying out to the open sea.

The great moment had arrived, and as Pixton pushed the throttle forward to give the Monosoupape full power, he must have wondered whether he was about to repeat his ducking in the Hamble. Instead, she lifted gallantly on to the floats and, benefiting from the light wing loading, was off the water almost before the few spectators of the event were aware that it had happened. Only a few minutes in the air were needed to satisfy Pixton that the machine handled well, and coupled with its excellent take-off performance he had every reason to feel pleased with his mount. One problem had revealed itself: the engine was tending to exceed its recommended maximum rpm, and for a race which could last for anything over two hours there was a sure danger of overheating, leading to engine failure.

Soon after his landing the breeze freshened, and as the sea began to weave itself into unpleasant-looking shapes, the organisers decided once again to postpone the race for another twenty-four hours. This proved the undoing of John Carbery and Ernst Stoeffler who, taking advantage of this extra day, decided to put in some practice. Both succeeded in damaging their aircraft, putting them out of the race. For Stoeffler it was the end, but Carbery managed, by exercising his very considerable charm, to borrow a Deperdussin from Janoir, one of the French reserves.

For the Sopwith team, on the other hand, this extra twenty-four hours proved invaluable, for it gave time for discussion with the Gnome representatives. Their recommendation was installation of a reduced-diameter coarser-pitch propeller to limit the maximum rpm of the Monosoupape. One other area of uncertainty remained, for there had been no opportunity to check fuel consumption of the float-equipped version of the Tabloid. Clearly this would be increased by the float installation, and to make sure that lack of fuel should not endanger its chances in the contest, the standard 24 Imp gallon (109 litre) fuel tank was supplemented by a 6 gallon (27.3 litre) tank installed alongside Pixton's seat, and which was piped into the standard fuel system. To complete the preparations, more robust bracing wires were attached to the floats. It was now a question of waiting for the weather.

The course was precisely the same as that of the 1913 event, but a change in the rules eliminated the early taxying test of the previous year, substituting two touch-downs and take-offs within a specified distance during the first lap. This was to serve as the seaworthiness test.

Monday 20 April dawned clear with only a slight wind, and it was announced that the race was on: competitors could start at any time between 8.00 a.m. and sunset. Long before the starting hour John Carbery and Howard Pixton went out to familiarise themselves with the course, and Ernest Burri and Charles Weymann also made short trial flights.

Excitement mounted as the starting hour approached, with the sea in co-operative mood. Promptly at 8.00 a.m. the starting maroon shattered the peace, setting all the gulls screaming their derision. The predominantly French crowd shouted their enthusiasm as they saw that the first two machines to taxi out were those of the nationally-entered favourites, the Nieuports piloted by Gabriel Espanet and Pierre Levasseur.

The latter was first off the water, and at Cap Martin executed his two landings and take-offs skilfully within the allotted distance. Espanet was not so fortunate, his second touch-down being beyond the confines of the test area, requiring a second attempt which added to the time of his first lap. Meanwhile, Burri had delighted and excited the spectators at Monaco with a no-he-won't-yes-he-will take-off run that, somewhat surprisingly, ended with him being airborne. His compulsory seaworthiness tests at Cap Martin were virtually a couple of spray-flinging bounces, but complied with the regulations and enabled him to record a first lap time almost three minutes better than the two Nieuports. French consternation. Still, not to worry. The superior speed of the Nieuports would tell in the end.

Howard Pixton was fourth away, at 8.16 a.m., making easy work of the take-off and was obviously travelling quite fast as he headed for Cap Martin and the seaworthiness test. This he accomplished superbly, his floats merely skimming the surface of the water twice, with hardly any reduction of his flying speed. It was a neat piece of flying and as he completed the first lap in a steep bank at each of the two close turns facing the yacht harbour, it caused British elation and French concern to discover that his lap time was only 4 mins 27 secs. If he could complete the course at anything like that lap speed it was clear that the Sopwith machine would run away with the race.

In fact, Pixton's lap times proved the undoing of the Nieuports as, for ten laps, he maintained a speed of almost 90 mph (145 km/h), nearly 15 mph (24 km/h) faster than the French machines. Espanet and Levasseur flew superbly, using their undoubted skill to clip every possible second off each lap. But in the attempt to hold off this very serious British threat, both engines were running at full throttle, which proved too much for the twin-row rotary Gnomes that powered the Nieuports. Soon the rear banks of cylinders were overheating, and lap times grew longer as their power output fell.

In the meantime, John Carbery had got off in his borrowed mount, but came to grief during the seaworthiness test when his 160 hp Le Rhone rotary took exception to the salt spray. Towed in to Beaulieu, and with the engine dried out, he managed to get going again, only to complete one more lap before being forced to retire due to engine failure during his third lap.

Four machines continued to lap the circuit with growing precision, but all the time Pixton's lead was increasing and it seemed inevitable that he would be first home. The moment had arrived for the fates to intervene. During his 16th lap, Espanet had to make a forced landing: the pace had proved too much for his Gnome engine which had seized pistons in the rear bank. This was enough to bring excited comment and speculation from the voluble French. Could Levasseur hold out? Levasseur couldn't. On his 17th lap he met the same fate as Espanet, engine failure ending his chance.

This left the despised British and Swiss machines roaring round the circuit, for although the French could still field a reserve it seemed a little pointless in view of the speed being set by the Sopwith aircraft.

If Jacques Schneider had wanted to create a cliff-hanger situation, he could not have expected the ingredients to spill together at precisely the right moment. On his 15th lap, Pixton's Monosoupape began to misfire, one of its nine cylinders deciding that it had already done more than could reasonably be expected of it.

But despite falling lap times the Sopwith machine stayed in the air. There followed six laps of sheer drama, each a little slower, when it seemed that at any moment the British machine would be out of the race. French hopes began to revive, but there was still Burri to consider. Lapping steadily with the F.B.A., its engine sounded far too healthy, as hearty and full of life as when it first took to the air.

For Pixton each lap must have seemed an eternity, expecting that at any moment his engine might fail. But gradually it dawned on him that the Monosoupape, though lacking the power of one cylinder, had no intention of letting him down. With this realisation came a new feeling of possible success, and forgetting the engine Pixton concentrated on impeccable turns and accurate flying to gain desperately important seconds. It paid off; lap times reduced and almost before he knew it the last lap became reality. It was accomplished to a roar of congratulation from the large crowd of spectators, but if they expected him to come in to a triumphant landing they were disappointed. Instead, by prior arrangement with Sopwith, Pixton kept going for two more laps in a successful attempt to set a new floatplane record for a 300 km closed circuit.

But even with Pixton's victory the drama had not ended. During his 23rd lap Burri's Monosoupape, which had been running so sweetly, banged and clattered to a stop. With considerable skill Burri brought the little flying-boat down on to a rising sea. This brought a new stir of excitement, for Maurice Prévost was seen to be taxying out in his Deperdussin. If Burri's engine failure was serious, France could still capture second place. Fate had other ideas, for the F.B.A. had merely run out of petrol, and the engine of Prévost's Deperdussin decided to give up as soon as the floatplane reached the open water.

Burri's F.B.A. was soon refuelled, and he took off again to complete his 28 laps. In a last despairing effort to retain some French prestige, Pierre Levasseur borrowed Weymann's Nieuport in a second attempt to complete the course and record this place for France. This, too, was doomed for failure; after completing nine laps he was brought down when yet another engine decided that it was time to call it a day.

This meant that the representatives of Britain and Switzerland were the only two to complete the course, and it is significant that both machines were powered by 100 hp Gnome Monosoupape engines. If confirmation was needed for Seguin's grasp of the problems relative to improved power plants, the 1914 Schneider Trophy Contest had given emphasis to his brilliant leadership. In each case the twin-row rotary engines had failed from overheating: the Monosoupape which he had designed to overcome just this problem had lasted the course. Even Pixton's engine might have completed its thirty laps without faltering if it had not suffered previously from immersion in the water of the Hamble River.

The Sopwith Schneider had recorded a speed of 86·78 mph (139·66 km/h) for the Contest, and of 86·6 mph (139·37 km/h) for the 300 km closed circuit. The Swiss F.B.A. had achieved only 51 mph (82·08 km/h), but the reliability of the engines of these two aircraft had proved too much for the French competitors. If French prestige had been damaged, there was at least some consolation that the power plant of the two successful aircraft were of national design and construction.

At an informal luncheon given by the Royal Aero Club, on Tuesday 12 May 1914, to honour the achievement of Tommy Sopwith and Howard

Pixton in winning for Britain the 1914 Schneider Contest the Chairman, the Marquess of Tullibardine, was not slow to emphasise this point:

'. . . in the Sopwith machine', he said, 'the motor was French, but we must not grudge this share of the victory to our good friends across the Channel, and it is only fair to recollect how much the Gnome motor has assisted all constructors and pilots in advancing the science and practice of aviation for the past four years . . .'

To the disgust of Britain's then limited aviation press, national newspapers failed to enthuse over the achievement at Monaco. The French press, however, was vociferous in their praise of the British achievement and, quite naturally, were elated at the success of the new Gnome engine.

Most significant, however, was the following extract from the report in *Le Temps*, hinting that the British and German aviation industries were beginning to make serious efforts to catch up on the lead held by French aviation:

'In the interests of our industry we must consider the importance of this victory, which will arouse great enthusiasm on the other side of the Channel. In a country where the Navy is held in great honour, the triumph of an English hydro-aeroplane will be well noted.

'The lessons we have learnt yesterday are that all too little encouragement has been given to maritime aviation, and that therefore our constructors have not been able to contest the foreign rivalry.

'The English supremacy which showed itself at Monaco yesterday is quite as important as that shown by the Germans in capturing the world's duration and height records.'

The writing was on the wall for all to see: the next four and a half years were to show that the writer of the article in *Le Temps* had more than a casual appreciation of the aviation scene in that peaceful Spring of 1914.

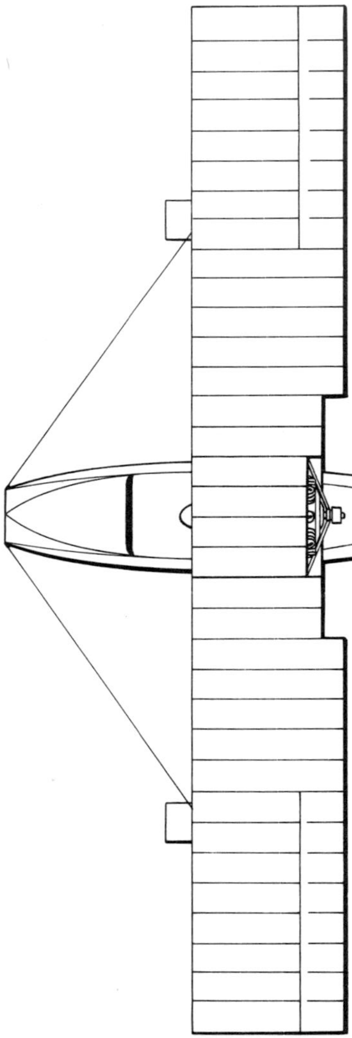

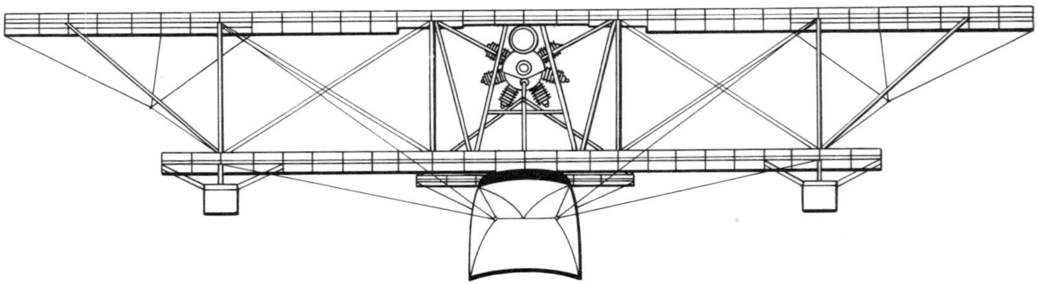

FBA (1914)

Wing Area: 279·8 sq. ft (26·0 m^2)
T-O Weight: 1,036 lb (470 kg)
Max Wing Loading: 3·70 lb/sq. ft (18·06 kg/m^2)
Horsepower of Power Plant: 100 hp

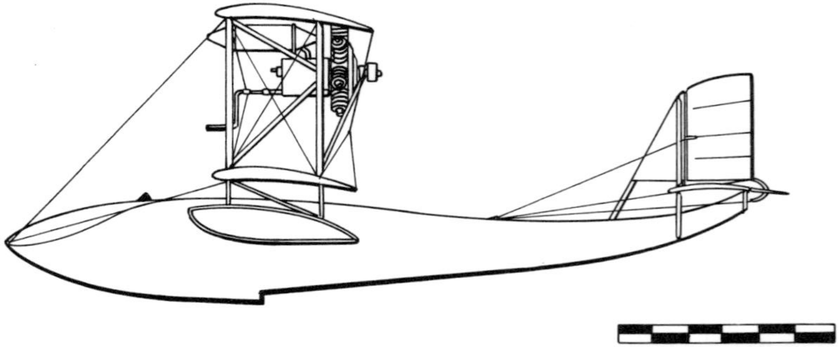

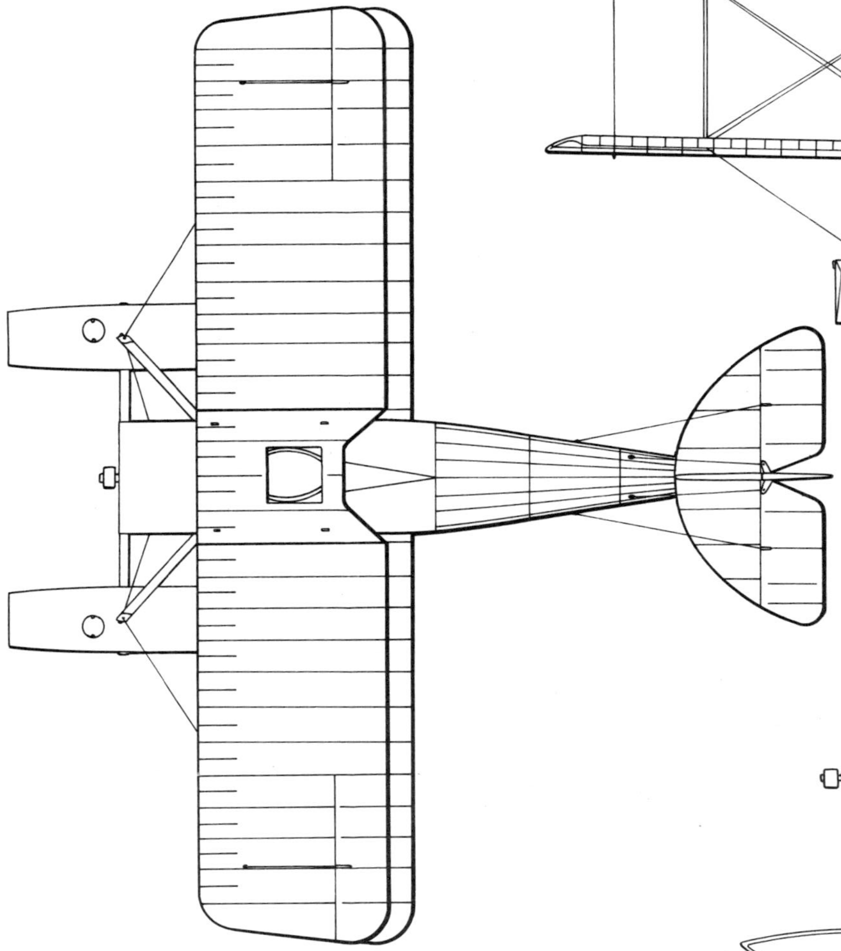

Sopwith Tabloid (1914)

Wing Span: 25 ft 8 in (7·82 m)
Length Overall: 22 ft 10 in (6·96 m)
Wing Area: 241 sq. ft (22·38 m^2)
Weight Empty: 1,220 lb (553 kg)
T-O Weight: 1,700 lb (771 kg)
Max Wing Loading: 7·05 lb/sq. ft (34·42 kg/m^2)
Horsepower of Power Plant: 100 hp

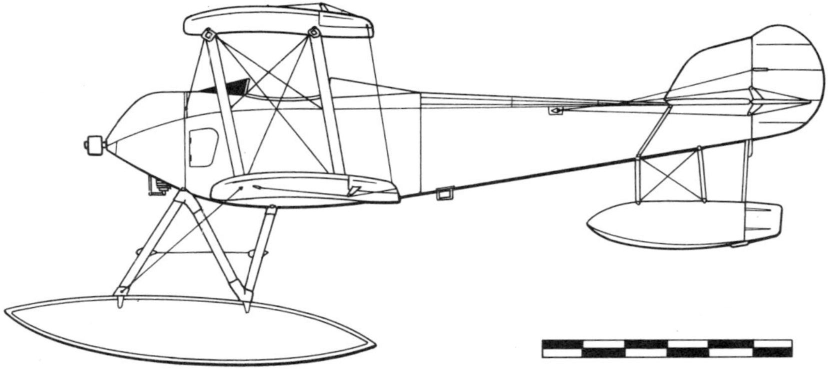

4

Fiasco in the fog

1919

The 'war to end wars' had dragged to a weary victory for the Allies after four and a quarter years: years in which the carnage on the Western Front had taken an appalling toll of human life. And during that same period, the aeroplane had developed from the frail body of an unwanted child into robust adult health. New attributes, such as reliability, increased range and scope, had been forged in the searing flame of a bitter conflict.

It has been said, frequently, that the first World War was responsible for revolutionary development of the aeroplane. This is not strictly true. It had advanced from being merely the toy of wealthy sportsmen to an important military weapon. But on the other hand, there had been little real advance in airframe constructional techniques. Improved performance stemmed rather from the development of more powerful and more reliable engines.

At the war's end, biplane aircraft still dominated the scene. The British ban on monoplane construction had been of extremely short duration, but had come at a time when the industry was gearing itself up for mass production of aircraft to meet military requirements. Few, if any, manufacturers seem to have been aware that the ban had been lifted and, even if they had, there were problems in plenty without a change in mid-course from biplane to monoplane configuration. Far more important in the early stages of the war was a need to cope with the demands for ever-increasing numbers of inherently stable aircraft, required to meet the reconnaissance role. This was the only task that military brass hats then considered within the capabilities of the new-fangled and noisy machines, and the biplane lent itself particularly well to such a requirement.

The primary power plant of Allied aircraft in the early stages of the war was the Gnome rotary, which had already proved reliable with its resolution of the overheating problem. But when it became necessary to develop agile fighter aircraft instead of reconnaissance plodders, it took little time to discover that the rotating mass of the engine had a gyro effect which was enemical to the highly desirable characteristics of response and manoeuvrability unless, of course, the pilot was attempting to turn in opposition to the direction of rotation, when a burst of throttle could whip him round very neatly. Furthermore, the high fuel and oil consumption of rotaries meant the type was unsuited to power long-range aircraft. The final straw came when the need arose for engines of considerably greater power output: constructional materials then available and the unusual configuration of the Gnome (as well as other engines of similar type) meant that 150 hp per unit was about the practical maximum.

The alternatives were radial and in-line engines. The former then suffered from the overheating problems which had given birth to the Gnome, and the first serious attempt to remedy this took the form of the Salmson (Canton Unné) water-cooled radial. Whilst permitting increased power output without overheating, this engine suffered the head-resistance penalty of all radials, plus the added weight of the water-cooling system. It is interesting to record, in passing, that the 200 hp 14-cylinder Salmson was a most unusual engine. This had two banks of cylinders, one behind the other, and each cylinder had an angle of 25·71° between it and those adjacent. The resulting firing order was (F: front; R: rear): 1F, 2R, 4F, 5R, 7F, 1R, 3F, 4R, 6F, 7R, 2F, 3R, 5F and 6R, which meant that three revolutions of the crankshaft occurred before each cylinder had fired. Thus, each piston had to make two idling strokes between exhaust and induction.

During the course of the war the air-cooled radial engine evolved gradually as a reliable power plant. The fact that its cylinders were sited in the full airstream meant that a cooling potential was readily available. Engine designers soon learned how to achieve acceptable cylinder temperatures coupled with increased power output. It needed far more careful attention to cylinder design, especially with regard to improved fins to dissipate the heat more rapidly, and the provision of suitable baffles to ensure the air flow was carried completely around the cylinder.

For military aircraft the radial engine offered certain definite advantages. It was easier to maintain and had no water-filled cooling system vulnerable to enemy fire. Additionally, the fact that the radial disposition of the cylinders allowed the use of a single crankpin—and consequently of a short, rigid crankshaft—meant that these power plants were less likely to suffer the mechanical failures resulting from crankshaft 'whip' that plagued many of the early multi-cylinder in-line engines.

When the liquid-cooled in-line engine had started its life in the aviation industry, it had already benefited from considerable development to power the motor car. For the latter application it had not mattered that it was big or heavy, and many early aviation engineers argued that the very much reduced frontal area of the in-line layout more than offset these shortcomings. Over the years, as lightweight, higher-powered engines were developed, this was to prove correct, but ignored the weight penalty and vulnerability of the cooling system, an engine less easy to maintain, and the parasite drag induced by coolant radiators.

To overcome one of the structural problems, that posed by the long crankshaft of six and eight-cylinder engines, the Vee type was evolved. Viewed from the front, the two banks of cylinders formed the shape of a letter V. Usually, 8-cylinder engines had the two banks of four separated by an angle of 90°, while a 12-cylinder engine had two banks of six separated by an angle of 60°. This almost halved the length of the crankshaft, reducing the number of bearings, the tendency to whip, and made for far greater reliability.

There is another wartime change to record: the hydro-aeroplane had acquired the more comfortable title of seaplane, a name bestowed reputedly by Winston Churchill. Thus, the two categories of maritime aircraft available at the war's end were seaplanes, if mounted on floats, while those with a boat-type hull retained their original appellation of flying-boats.

Landplanes had grown in size from the diminutive types which had flown somewhat tentatively to the front in 1914 to the large strategic bombers which appeared as the war progressed. Germany's Zeppelin Staaken R.VI, for example, spanned over 138 ft (42·06 m), had four 260 hp engines in tandem pairs and 18-wheel landing gear to cater for its maximum take-off weight of 25,265 lb (11,460 kg). Britain's largest bomber, the Handley Page V/1500, materialised too late to see operational service, but spanned 126 ft (38·40 m), had four 375 hp Rolls-Royce Eagle VIII engines in tandem pairs, and a maximum take-off weight approaching closely to that of the German 'giants' at 24,700 lb (11,204 kg).

Despite this kind of progress, the war had not brought comparable development in maritime aircraft. The small number of seaplanes in operational use were little more than slightly improved versions of aircraft which had competed in the 1914 Schneider Trophy contest. A requirement for long-range maritime patrol aircraft meant there had been some progress in the development of flying-boats, and the most significant of these was the Felixstowe F.2A/F.3 evolved by Squadron Commander John C. Porte, commander of the RNAS station at Felixstowe, Suffolk. Based on the American Curtiss H.12, they proved invaluable in a reconnaissance/bomber role, and were to set the design trend of British military flying-boats for the next two decades.

With the war ended, the time had arrived to re-start the Schneider Trophy contests. It came as something of a surprise to learn there would be no Gordon-Bennett races in 1919, but the British Royal Aero Club, designated organisers of the first post-war Schneider contest as a result of Howard Pixton's win at Monaco in 1914, received a request from the FAI at the end of May 1919 to press on with arrangements for a race to be held in that year.

It was assumed there would be very considerable interest in the resumption of this event which, in 1914, had shown the first real stirrings of international rivalry. This was confirmed when Belgium, France, Italy, Spain and the United States promised to contend Britain's tenure of the Trophy. Unfortunately, four months was all too short a time for many of the manufacturers to construct new or modify existing aircraft to compete, and it was not long before Belgium, Spain and the United States decided to withdraw. This left Britain, France and Italy to fight it out, and there was little doubt that the home team were firm favourites.

Anticipating a large British entry, the Royal Aero Club let it be known that a committee had been formed to supervise eliminating trials—leading to selection of three competitors for the race—and that the closing date for applications was 31 July. In early August it was announced that Wednesday, 10 September, had been chosen as the day of the contest and Bournemouth as its venue. This was an ideal choice from a spectator's point of view, but showed at an early stage that the organising committee had little appreciation of the competitor's needs. Although a delightful seaside resort, it was devoid of a harbour and any facilities suitable for the operation of seaplanes. Its narrow beach, well endowed with bathing huts, was of little use for the erection, maintenance and operation of aircraft.

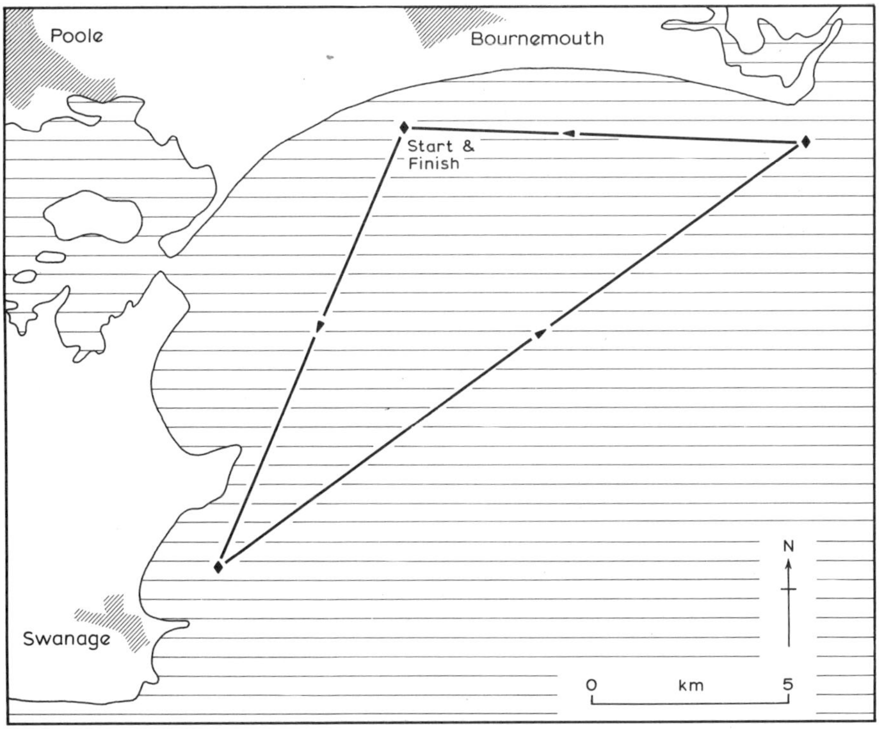

2. Schneider Trophy Contest Course: Bournemouth 1919

It seems strange, in retrospect, that the protected waters and adequate facilities of Poole Harbour were not utilised, for this would not have prohibited the use of the planned course, covering ten laps each of twenty nautical miles (37·06 km). Starting and finishing point was off Bournemouth pier, with a S.S.W. leg of 6 nm (11·11 km) to a turning point off the Old Harry rocks in Swanage Bay, then a stretch of 9 nm (16·68 km) almost due N.E. to a second marker boat anchored off Hengistbury Head, near Christchurch, with the final 5 nm (9·27 km) of the course almost due west back to Bournemouth.

Since it is easy to see both turning points from the cliffs that lend much to the attractions of Bournemouth, it was clear that in this one respect, at least, the organisers had selected an ideal site. Fortunately, there were others with a rather nicer appreciation of the problems involved in handling the aircraft competing in the race. In particular, there was S. E. Saunders Ltd of Cowes, Isle of Wight, who generously offered the use of their facilities to accommodate the competing aircraft. Little did they know what they had let themselves in for, and the Royal Aero Club were quick to accept the suggestion for, after all, the short overwater distance from Cowes to Bournemouth was unlikely to cause any serious inconvenience.

On 3 September the British entrants, a disappointing total of four, presented themselves for the eliminating trials. However, all had been specially prepared for the race and made an interesting collection. Of primary interest was the Sopwith Schneider, a much improved aircraft from that which had carried Pixton to victory in 1914. It was the only British entry to benefit from a long development period, its operational use as a seaplane extending throughout the war.

Registered G-EAKI, the Schneider was very different to its honoured ancestor, and had acquired many detail refinements. The biplane wings, with a gap of 4 ft 6 in (1·37 m), had slight backward stagger and sported ailerons on both wings. The fuselage structure had gained a number of lightweight stringers to improve streamlining, and the base of the fin had become an integral part of the fuselage. The forward fuselage, extending back to the cockpit, was covered with sheet aluminium and the remainder in fabric: the pilot's headrest was faired by a small turtleback. The plain, non-stepped floats were carried on four tubular-steel struts, braced with wire, and extended sufficiently far aft to eliminate the under-tail float that was seen on Pixton's mount.

Most significant change was in the power plant, the 100 hp Gnome Monosoupape replaced by a 450 hp Jupiter nine-cylinder radial air-cooled engine. This engine, a product of the Cosmos Engineering Company of Bristol, had been designed by Roy Fedden and L. F. G. Butler. Subsequently, when Cosmos went into voluntary liquidation in February 1920, Roy Fedden complete with Jupiter and Lucifer engine designs were to form the nucleus of the Bristol Aeroplane Company's Aero-Engine Department.

Beautifully turned out, the Sopwith Schneider is ready for the 1919 contest at Bournemouth

Reminiscent of more peaceful days, the Avro 539 in tow off the seafront at Bournemouth

The Jupiter mounted in the Sopwith Schneider was very neatly cowled, its streamline appearance enhanced by a large spinner covering the boss of the two-blade tractor propeller. Having demonstrated a maximum speed approaching 170 mph (273 km/h) during flight tests, it seemed that the Schneider in Harry Hawker's experienced and capable hands would prove sufficient to ensure that the trophy remained in the British bag.

Vital statistics of the Schneider were as follows: wing span (both) 24 ft (7·32 m); length overall 21 ft 6 in (6·55 m); height overall 10 ft (3·05 m); wing chord 5 ft $1\frac{1}{2}$ in (1·56 m); wing stagger 0 ft $2\frac{1}{2}$ in (6·35 cm); wing area slightly over 222 sq. ft (20·62 m^2); and maximum take-off weight 2,200 lb (998 kg).

Next entrant, of particular interest to aviation historians, was a Fairey IIIA (G-EALQ), which was specially modified by the company to compete in the event. It had been the original prototype of the Fairey III, the second of two experimental seaplanes built by the company in 1917, and had started its life as a two-seat patrol aircraft. Powered by a 260 hp Sunbeam Maori II liquid-cooled in-line engine, it was then an ugly machine with two radiator blocks mounted externally, one on each side of the engine cowling. Its two-bay biplane wings could be folded, and incorporated Fairey's Patent Camber Gear.

At the end of 1917, it had been modified as a landplane, gaining a simple Vee landing gear and tail skid instead of the floats, becoming re-designated Fairey IIIA. A total of 50 IIIAs were built for and saw service with the Royal Air Force, including the prototype, which was bought back by the Fairey company on post-war disposal for use in an experimental role.

Its use was not long delayed, and soon began to take new form, being converted back to a seaplane. The wing span was first reduced from 46 ft 2 in (14·07 m) to make a single-bay biplane of 28 ft (8·53 m) span, and the Patent Camber Gear was retained. This consisted of trailing-edge flaps on both wings, extending from centre-section to ailerons, and was considered likely to prove valuable in improving take-off and landing performance. Provision of floatplane landing gear presented no difficulty, being similar to the original twin-float with under-tail float configuration of the prototype, but differed by having the main floats carried on a four-strut mounting with bracing wires.

As with the Sopwith entry, it was clear that more power was necessary, and the Maori engine was removed and replaced by a 450 hp Napier Lion. This was another interesting engine, designed by A. J. Rowledge for Montague Napier in 1916. Napier's had concentrated upon motor car construction prior to the outbreak of war, but in 1915 received a government contract to build aero-engines to specification. This was the beginning of Napier's interest in the aviation industry, and at the war's end a decision was made to specialise in the design and construction of aero-engines.

Known as a double Vee or 'broad arrow' engine, the twelve cylinders of the Lion were arranged in three banks of four which, from the front of the engine, appeared in the form of an inverted arrowhead, the two outer banks of cylinders being inclined at 60° to the central, vertical bank.

In this design, Rowledge had aimed at reducing the length of the crankshaft to a minimum so that he could arrive at a high-powered but compact liquid-cooled engine that would not be plagued with crankshaft failures. To make doubly sure, the latter component was machined from a solid steel forging and supported by five roller bearings, with one plain bearing at the forward end of the crankcase.

This engine appeared too late to have any significant use during the war period, but was to prove a reliable and important engine in the ensuing years, for it was not only economical in operation, but produced 18·7 hp per litre of swept volume, which was a very considerable achievement at that time.

Unlike the Sopwith entry, the speed potential of which had been fairly accurately assessed, the Fairey IIIA—to be flown by Lieutenant-Colonel Vincent Nicholl—was something of a dark horse. However, with its big decrease in wing span and an engine of comparable power to that of the Schneider, it seemed likely to offer spirited opposition.

Third on the list of British contenders came an entry from the A. V. Roe stable, to be flown by Captain H. A. Hamersley. It was of particular interest because it was designed specially for the contest and was, in effect, the smallest practical biplane which could be built around its 240 hp Siddeley-Deasy Puma 6-cylinder in-line liquid-cooled engine.

Beginning life as the Avro 539, its progress through the works at Hamble was somewhat hectic in order that it should be available in time for the eliminating trials on 3 September. How touch-and-go this situation was is made clear by the fact that the 539 was not launched from the Hamble slipway until 29 August for Captain Hamersley to make the maiden flight.

Its general configuration was similar to that of the Sopwith machine, namely a single-bay biplane mounted on twin floats, but far less consideration had been given to streamlining. In contrast to the functional and neat-looking spinner/cowling arrangement of the Schneider, the 539 had a large frontal radiator through which the propeller shaft projected. The engine was neatly cowled in aluminium, however, with only cylinder heads and short exhaust tubes projecting slightly.

The biplane wings were of unequal span, with two interplane struts on each side, and the landing and flying wires were augmented by bracing wires and centre-section struts. Only the shorter-span lower wing was given dihedral, but ailerons were fitted on both wings. Four streamline-section steel tubes united the airframe with its two single-stepped floats, which were strut- and wire-braced, and being 14 ft (4·28 m) in length supported the aircraft without need for an under-tail float.

Henri Biard aboard the Supermarine Sea Lion

A Savoia S.13 flying-boat, the type with which Guido Janello delighted the crowds at Bournemouth

Specification of the Avro 539 included wing span (upper) 25 ft 6 in (7·77 m); wing span (lower) 24 ft 6 in (7·47 m); length overall 21 ft 4 in (6·50 m); wing aspect ratio, nearly 6; wing area 195 sq. ft (18·12 m²); float track 7 ft 0 in (2·13 m) and maximum take-off weight 2,119 lb (961 kg).

Last but by no means least was an aircraft named the Sea Lion (G-EALP), to be piloted by Squadron Leader Basil D. Hobbs. This had been evolved for the contest by a young recruit of the Supermarine company, named Reginald J. Mitchell, who only a year later was to become the company's chief designer.

This aircraft, too, was an unknown quantity, modified by Mitchell from the company's N.1B Baby single-seat fighter flying-boat, which had been the first British aircraft in this category. It was a fairly conventional single-bay biplane with a mahogany hull of the Linton-Hope type, had wingtip balancer floats and was powered by a single engine with pusher propeller.

The Baby appeared too late in the war to enter production, but powered by a 200 hp Hispano-Suiza engine it had demonstrated a maximum speed at sea level of 117 mph (188 km/h). For the Schneider contest Mitchell had substituted a 450 hp Napier Lion engine, and it was anybody's guess what sort of speed it might put up as a result of refinements to airframe plus the availability of more than double the horsepower of the original power plant. However, many of the self-styled experts considered that a flying-boat with pusher propeller installation stood little chance of success against the lighter seaplanes with tractor propellers.

If they had hoped to learn all the answers at the eliminating trials on 3 September they were unlucky. When the Avro 539 was making its take-off run, a float was damaged by contact with some floating object, and Captain Hamersley was unable to complete the test. Although the remaining three aircraft were all that were needed to form a British team, it was decided to give the Avro machine another chance on 8 September, allowing five days for repairs to be effected.

When it duly appeared for test it carried the registration G-EALG, had acquired a horn-balanced rudder and larger fin, and had thus become re-designated as the Avro 539A. But despite these changes it failed to eliminate the Sea Lion which had been in third position at the end of the original trials. Although the Avro was slightly faster, the Supermarine 'boat had a margin of points gained by superior water performance, so Avro and Hamersley had to be satisfied by being delegated as reserve.

France had no problems with elimination trials as only three entries had been received, two Nieuports and one SPAD. The latter, to be flown by the well-known pilot Sadi Lecointe, was a specially modified version of the SPAD XVII, bearing a fairly close resemblance to the SPAD XIV twin-float seaplane of which a number had been built for wartime service with the French Forces. In fact, Sadi Lecointe used one of these latter machines to train at Monaco in preparation for the contest at Bournemouth.

The SPAD XVII had been designed by Louis Bécherau, and it had been intended to build in 1918 a variant under the designation SPAD XXI. This did not materialise, and the designation went instead to the machine built for the Schneider contest and designed by Béchereau's successor, André Herbemont. Despite the intention, this aircraft was generally known as the SPAD-Herbemont. It was a much cleaner-looking machine than the Type XIV seaplane, with wing span reduced, single streamline I-type interplane and two centre-section struts on each side, braced by flying and landing wires. The float installation was similar to that of the Type XIV, consisting of two single-stepped floats, with Vee bottoms fore and aft of the step, extensively strutted and braced. Power plant comprised a 340hp Hispano-Suiza liquid-cooled engine, neatly cowled, and having a frontal radiator through which projected the shaft for the tractor propeller.

Shipped to Cowes, the SPAD arrived safely and was soon erected and prepared for flight testing. As a result of early flights, Herbemont, who had accompanied the SPAD team, decided on a further reduction of the wing span in an attempt to gain more speed.

Meanwhile, the Nieuport entries, variants of the standard Nieuport 29, had run into trouble. Flown by Lieutenant Jean Casale and Henri Malard, both had been damaged seriously during flight tests on the Seine, and the factory went all out to prepare two new machines in the shortest possible time. Immediately the first was ready, on 7 September, Casale took off from the Seine and flew direct to Cowes. He arrived in failing light and, having noted that the sea was running fairly high, decided to attempt a landing on the Medina River. All went well until the moment of contact, when his floats hit a mooring buoy and were wrecked, the machine nosing over and becoming stranded with its tail high in the air.

Fortunately, Casale was uninjured and was rescued quickly. The Nieuport had not been so lucky: when brought ashore it looked a hopeless, soggy mess, and general opinion eliminated it pretty quickly from the provisional list of starters.

Henri Malard was even less fortunate. Leaving Paris in the second machine on Monday, 8 September, there was very considerable concern when he failed to arrive at Cowes that same day. When, by the following morning there was still no sign of him, it was assumed that he was delayed in France by engine trouble. A telephone call showed this to be incorrect, and that Malard had set out across the Channel. In due course it was discovered that he had been forced to land in the sea, clinging to his aircraft which remained afloat until he was picked up a very long twenty-four hours later. Thus, the French challenge was reduced to a single aircraft.

There remained only the single Italian entry, an SIAI (Societa Idrovolanti Alta Italia) Savoia flying-boat, generally similar to the company's standard S.13, which was a two-seat reconnaissance/bomber. Converted to single-seat configuration, and with wing span reduced to increase speed, it was powered by a 240hp Isotta-Fraschini in-line liquid-cooled engine with frontal radiator, driving a pusher propeller.

So far as France was concerned, general opinion had not counted upon the British sportsmanship, typical of those happier days, which induced Samuel Saunders to put his employees hard at work in an attempt to get Casale's sorry-looking machine repaired in time for the contest. It was a mammoth task with only two days available, for floats, supporting struts, wings, fuselage and tail unit all needed varying degrees of attention, and a new engine was an essential. While this and new floats were en route from France, the Saunder men worked like beavers to carry out extensive repairs and the complete re-erection of the Nieuport. They made it, just, by working almost non-stop for forty-eight hours, making a superb contribution to the *entente cordiale*.

Meanwhile, the British contingent were able to view all this activity in a glow of assured calm, for short of utter calamity it was virtually certain that as daylight faded on 10 September the Schneider Trophy would be theirs for the second time. They had failed to take account of the British weather and the utter incompetence of the over-organised organising committee.

As daylight began to colour the rooftops on the day of the third Schneider Trophy contest, early risers soon discovered that Bournemouth and its surrounding area were blanketed in sea mist. This was not unusual in the late Summer following a warm day, and officials, contestants and would-be spectators comforted one another with assurances that the sun would soon burn off the cloying fog. Why, any of the local weather experts could confirm, and did, that this was all quite normal at that time of the year. There was nothing to worry about.

By ten o'clock they were not quite so complacent, for there was practically no change in the situation. They began to perk up a little about an hour later when Hengistbury Head was thought to be seen towards the east. Certainly there was no sign of the Old Harry rocks at Swanage, but the TSY *Ombra* loaned to the Royal Aero Club for use by the committee, and anchored off Bournemouth pier to mark the starting and finishing point, was definitely becoming visible.

Another hour passed, with slow but steady improvement in the visibility and the crowds of spectators who were beginning to assemble thrilled to the roar of an engine overhead. It proved to be Nicholl in the Fairey IIIA making a trial flight, and he was soon seen to touch down on the completely calm surface of the sea, taxying to the beach east of the pier.

About twenty minutes later two more aircraft came lower over the pier, heading off in the direction of Swanage; minutes later they returned and skimmed the surface of the sea. They proved to be the SPAD and the Savoia flying-boat, the latter narrowly missing collision with a rowing boat. This was the first clear indication that the committee had wasted little time in real organisation, and was confirmed a few moments later as the SPAD was seen to be taxying precariously among delighted bathers as it sought a mooring buoy east of the pier.

The Savoia, after landing, was first towed to the *Ombra*, then to the shore where it was beached and surrounded immediately by such a vast and enthusiastic crowd that their very mass threatened the safety of the aircraft. When a Supermarine representative complained to the Royal Aero Club committee of the lack of facilities and security for the European competitors, he was informed rather pointedly that they did not consider this their responsibility.

Meanwhile, the crowds were roused to excited chatter as the Sea Lion passed overhead, heading for a look-see over Swanage, followed almost immediately by the reserve machine, the Avro 539A, which Hamersley brought near the shore. As the hubbub over his arrival died down, there was a new fluttering among the crowd as the Sea Lion was seen coming in to land.

The time was then about 1 p.m. and things were happening fast. The scene was brightening, and it could be seen that thousands of spectators were lining the cliff top from Poole Head to Hengistbury. Already the rumour was spreading that the race was about due to start, the committee were only waiting for the Schneider and Nieuport to arrive.

'It's sinking', came a somewhat exaggerated shout from the crowd near the pier. They referred to the SPAD, which certainly presented an odd wing-down appearance, a clear indication that one float was taking in water. In a flurry of action it was towed to the shore and beached rather unceremoniously, causing more float damage in the process. Herbemont raised his hands in despair and could be excused any number of Gallic oaths as he fought to get men and materials through the crowds to begin the necessary repairs.

Excitement reached fever pitch when it was announced that the race would begin at 2.30 p.m., and a few minutes later Hawker was seen approaching very fast in the Schneider, making a perfect touch down before beaching his machine skilfully near the pier.

The hands of countless watches and clocks crept towards the 2.30 zero hour, and although the Nieuport had not arrived the Fairey IIIA was started up and Nicholl taxied towards the *Ombra*. This was it. No it wasn't, for a motor boat approached the Fairey machine, signalling it back to shore. There came a new surge of anticipation among the crowd as another aircraft was heard approaching: yes, it was the Nieuport, which landed smoothly and taxied towards a mooring buoy. Clearly, this was what the starter had been waiting for.

There had been so much to occupy the attention of the spectators during the last few minutes that it was with something of a shock that, with a moment to gaze around, they discovered that the sea mist was thickening again. Hengistbury Head and the Old Harry rocks had already disappeared.

Even those most anxious to see the contest agreed that it was impossible to begin the race under such conditions, and were not surprised at the announcement that a postponement until 6 p.m. had been ordered by the committee. Indeed, many began to question why they had not decided to cancel the event for that day. There was a last little bit of excitement for the crowd near the pier when it was seen that the newly-arrived Nieuport was taking on a list. It was beached quickly and attempts began to try and discover the leak in the float.

It became a yes-no afternoon of weary waiting as, time and again, a breeze would stir the gossamer veil to reveal the entire scene in sparkling clarity, only to die away and drop the grey curtain back into position. But then, when it began to appear hopeless, and the crowds were already beginning to drift homeward, a minor miracle slid the mist away completely to show a clear blue sky overhead. True, Swanage was still obscured, but it was then approaching 5 p.m., and with a sinking feeling that things were unlikely to get any better, the committee suddenly reached the bold decision to start the race. This brought a howl of complaint from the French competitors, who said they could not possibly be ready before the earlier-announced starting time of 6 p.m. The committee dealt with this quite easily by ignoring them.

Despite a general belief among the pilots that the weather was still not suitable for flying, Nicholl started up, taxied out in the Fairey IIIA and lifted cleanly off the water at 4.50 p.m. He should have been followed by Casale, according to the race order, but the Nieuport was not ready and Hawker, next in line, declined to go. Hawker was to be followed by the Sea Lion, so Basil Hobbs started up and was airborne quickly with little fuss.

This action convinced Hawker that, despite any misgivings, he had to have a go, so the Schneider's engine was brought to life and he taxied out to the start position. The fact that he arrived out of order unhinged the starter, who seemed undecided what to do with his flag. Hawker made the decision for him, roaring off with throttle full open and disappearing in the direction of Swanage. Last away was Janello in the Savoia, who waited patiently at the correct point until he received the starter's signal and made a faultless take-off.

Barely had the note of his engine died away before another aircraft was heard approaching from landward. It proved to be the Fairey IIIA, for Nicholl had decided to call it a day after one look at conditions in the Swanage area. Another aircraft was heard approaching: this should be the Sea Lion which had followed Nicholl into the air but, to everyone's consternation, it proved to be Hawker in the Schneider. Judging by the uneven tempo of his engine he was coming in to land because of some trouble; but then it settled down into a more even note, and Hawker banked away and was soon out of sight. A couple of minutes later he was back, made a neat landing and taxied quickly to the beach.

He and Nicholl were soon abroad the *Ombra*, trying to persuade the committee that conditions at Swanage were bad enough to represent a dangerous hazard. They insisted that the race should be abandoned for that day but, despite voices raised in anger, it was decided to allow things to continue for the present.

There came the sound of another aircraft approaching: this must be Hobbs in the Sea Lion. But no: it was Janello in the Savoia, who landed off Boscombe pier as prescribed by the rules for the first lap, took off again and made his second ordained landing off Bournemouth pier. He was completely confused to see the Fairey and Schneider beached: had the race been abandoned? Looking around he spotted an official boat, who's occupant was energetically waving him on, so he pushed open the throttle and was off the water quickly, heading for Swanage again.

Meanwhile there was mounting concern for Hobbs and the Sea Lion. Then came news that he had been seen making a landing on the sea near Boscombe pier, and that immediately after what appeared to be a perfectly normal touch-down the Sea Lion had up-ended and was still afloat, tail in air.

Launches raced to the rescue, and their occupants were soon to learn that conditions being so bad at Swanage, Hobbs had been uncertain of his position in relation to the cliffs. He decided to make a sea landing, hoping that visibility might be better on the surface and enable him to pinpoint the main hazards of cliffs and rocks. Unfortunately it was still too thick to see anything, but as there didn't appear to be any ominous shadows near at hand, he set a compass course for Christchurch and took off again. Just before the little flying-boat lifted clear of the surface there was a tremendous bang from beneath the hull. Hobbs was pretty certain that he had hit something fairly substantial floating on the surface, but could only cross his fingers and hope the hull was sound.

Soon he was clear of the fog and ahead of him could identify the Hengistbury Head marker boat without any difficulty: he decided to press on and make his first lap compulsory landings and have at least one more attempt at locating the Swanage turn. When he touched down off Boscombe, sea water deluged the gaping hole torn in the hull at take-off, up-ending the Sea Lion and throwing Hobbs into the sea.

Now there was only Janello left!

Despite the conditions, the Italian pilot began to pile up the laps steadily, his times remarkably consistent. The spectators who had decided to stick it out to the bitter end soon began to warm towards Janello who, after all, was the only competitor making a determined effort to give them their money's worth. Among them, only Tom Sopwith had some niggling doubts that all was not right. The lap times suggested that either the Savoia was travelling very much faster than it appeared to be, or that Janello was flying a reduced lap. The puzzling factor was the regularity with which he passed overhead.

Finally, in fading light, and to generous applause from those whom Janello had entertained, the Savoia came in to a smooth landing after the completion of eleven laps. This was permitted so that a total of ten in-flight laps could be used to establish a 200 nm speed record for seaplanes, and the Italians had elected to do this. But despite all that had gone before, Lorenzo Santoni, president of the SIAI company, went out by launch to meet Janello and request 'just one more lap', to ensure that the full distance had been covered. Janello protested that he had insufficient fuel, but Santoni was in a position to insist, so off went Janello again, only to have his engine splutter to a stop before he had completed the circuit.

In deteriorating conditions of visibility it was some time before the Savoia could be found and towed back to Bournemouth, by which time the committee had heard from the observers of the marker boat at Swanage that they had seen no sign of Janello all afternoon. This unfortunate pilot arrived to learn that he had been disqualified and the raced declared void.

When his initial shocked protests died a little, he was asked to point out on a map the position of the Swanage market boat: unhesitatingly he indicated a point in Studland Bay. A red-faced committee remembered suddenly that they had anchored a spare marker boat there, and that it was this which Janello had mistaken for the Swanage turning point.

Not surprisingly there was an uproar, culminating in an official letter of complaint from Lorenzo Santoni, insisting that Janello had complied with all the rules and conditions. He itemised three points:

(1) Janello made 11 circuits, and each time had seen the marker boat.
(2) Observation from below might have been obscured by the mist.
(3) The pilot insisted that the marker boat at Swanage was decorated exactly the same as the one at Christchurch. If the former was a third similarly-marked boat anchored short of Swanage, then it was the organisers who were at fault.

It was by no means the only protest. The aviation press described the event as a greater fiasco than had been necessary, despite the weather, if proper management had been exercised. It was clear, they stated, that too many officials had tried to be too officious without any appreciation of flying conditions. They had not even had the intelligence to request a trial circuit to be flown before ordering the race to begin. Under the conditions that prevailed the race should have been abandoned.

Comments of this nature echoed and re-echoed. Finally, at a later date, it was reported that the Royal Aero Club had recommended to the FAI that Janello should be awarded the trophy.

On 24 October 1919, at a meeting in Brussels where all the evidence was carefully considered, the FAI decided finally that Janello could not be awarded the trophy. By way of consolation to the Italians, they invited the Aéro-Club d'Italia to organise the 1920 contest. Understandably this was a bitter pill for them to swallow, but while accepting gracefully the FAI ruling they were resolute in their determination to show Britain, or any other nation for that matter, that they were more than capable of organising properly the next Schneider Trophy contest. Time was to prove the accuracy of their belief.

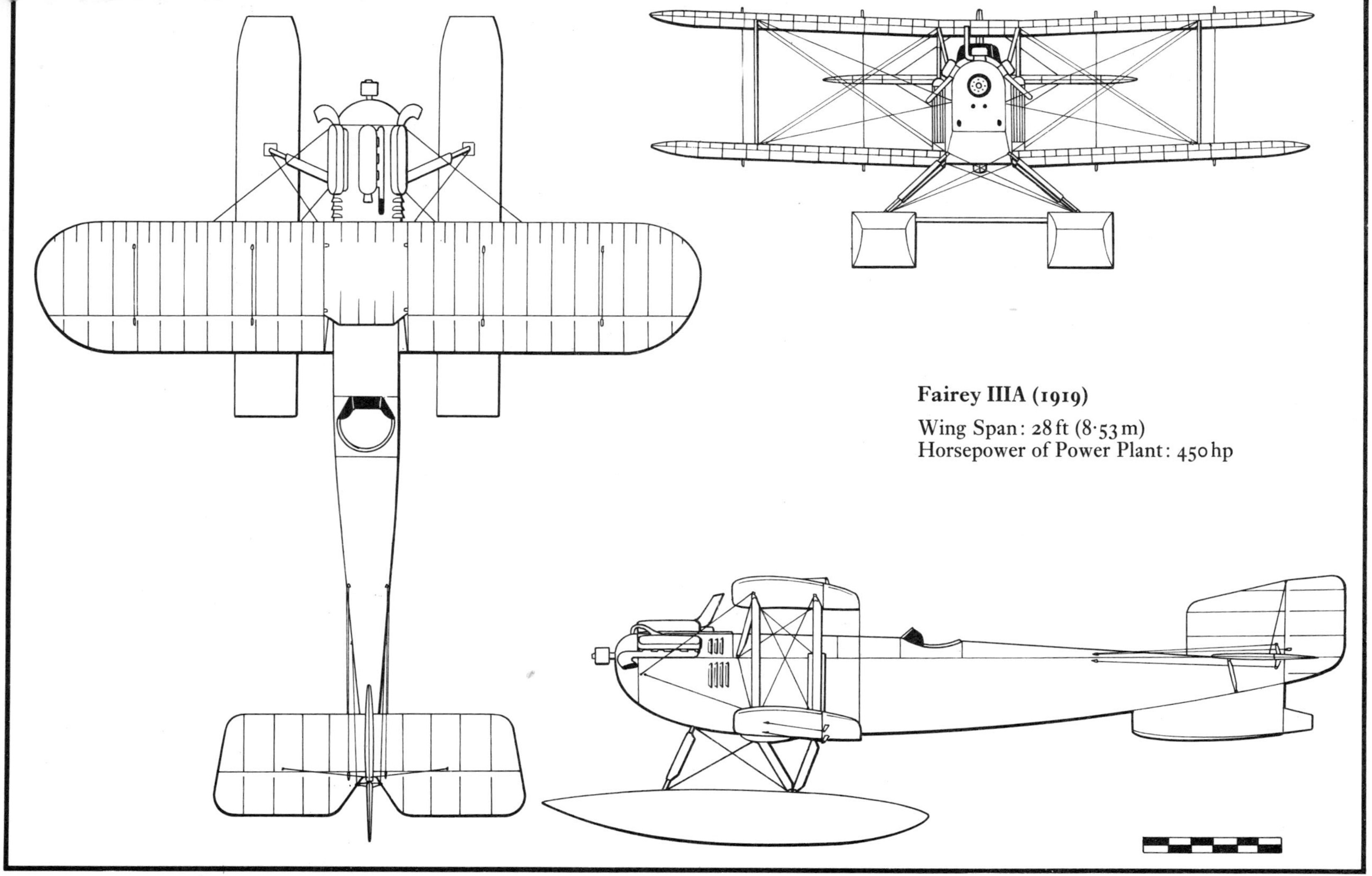

Fairey IIIA (1919)

Wing Span: 28 ft (8·53 m)
Horsepower of Power Plant: 450 hp

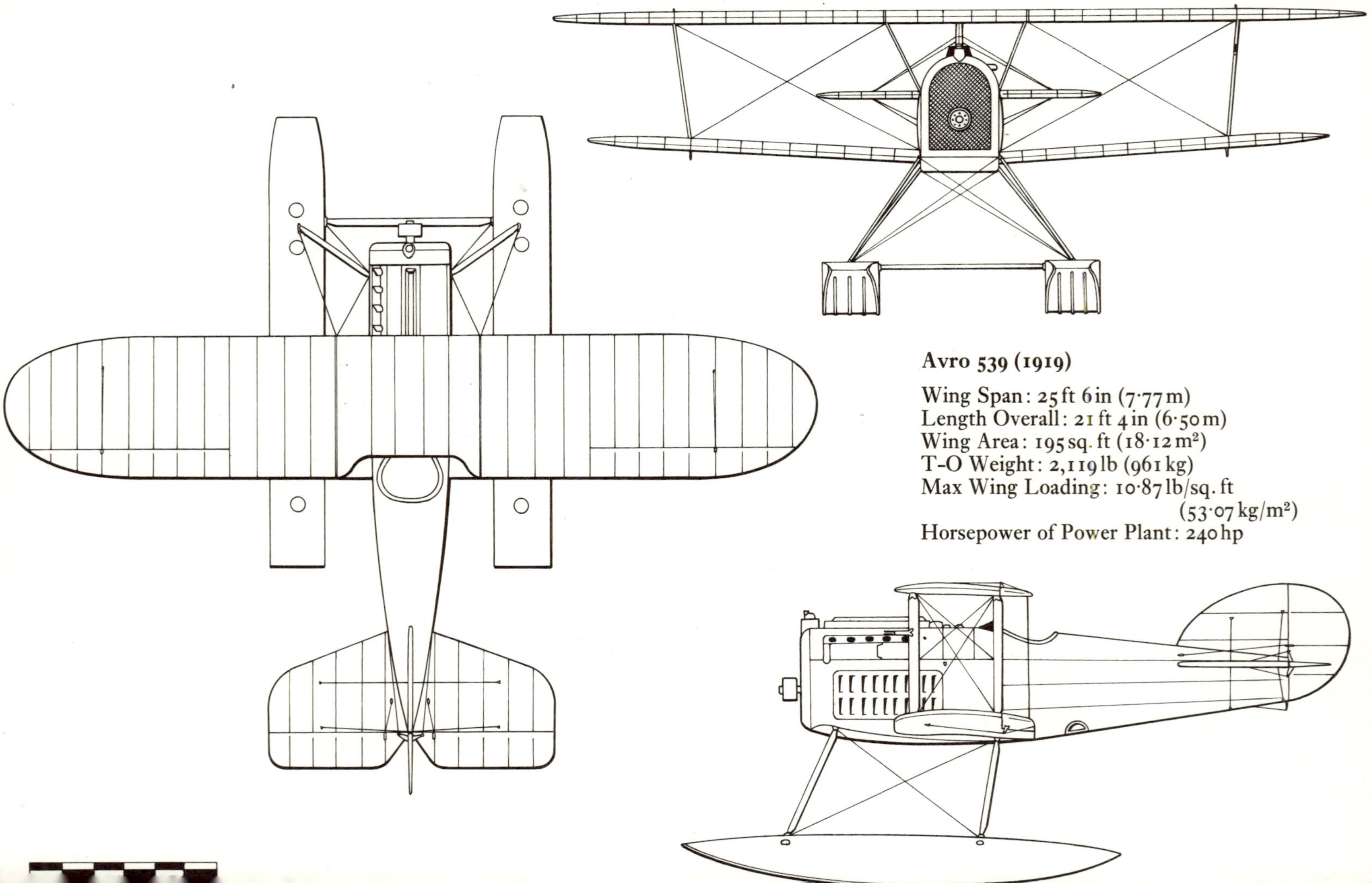

Avro 539 (1919)

Wing Span: 25 ft 6 in (7·77 m)
Length Overall: 21 ft 4 in (6·50 m)
Wing Area: 195 sq. ft (18·12 m²)
T-O Weight: 2,119 lb (961 kg)
Max Wing Loading: 10·87 lb/sq. ft (53·07 kg/m²)
Horsepower of Power Plant: 240 hp

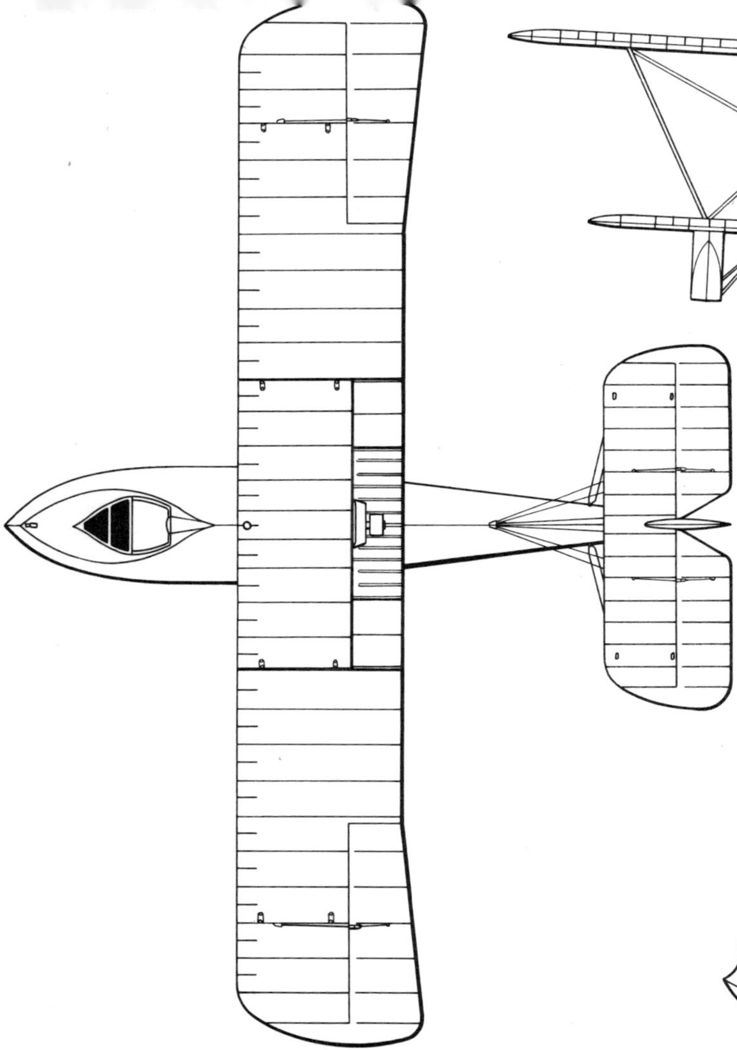

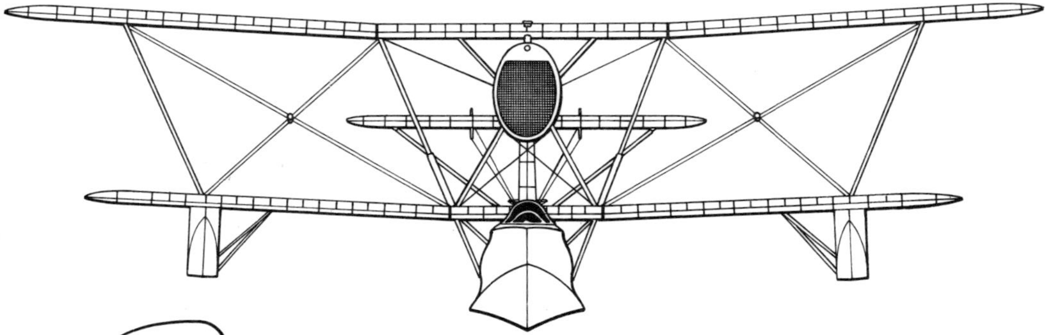

Supermarine Sea Lion (1919)

Wing Span: 35 ft (10·67 m)
Length Overall: 24 ft (7·32 m)
T-O Weight: 2,900 lb (1,315 kg)
Horsepower of Power Plant: 450 hp

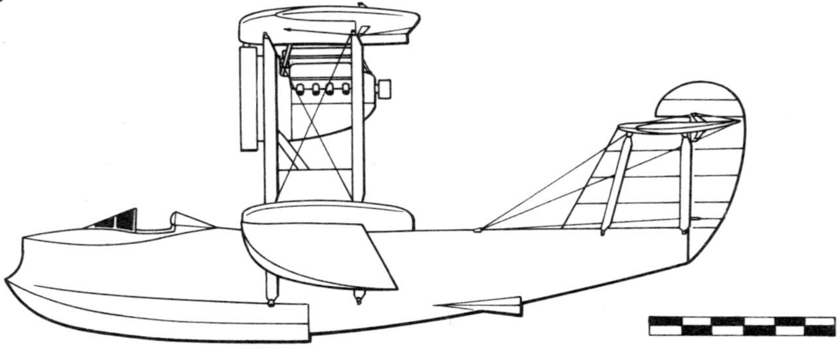

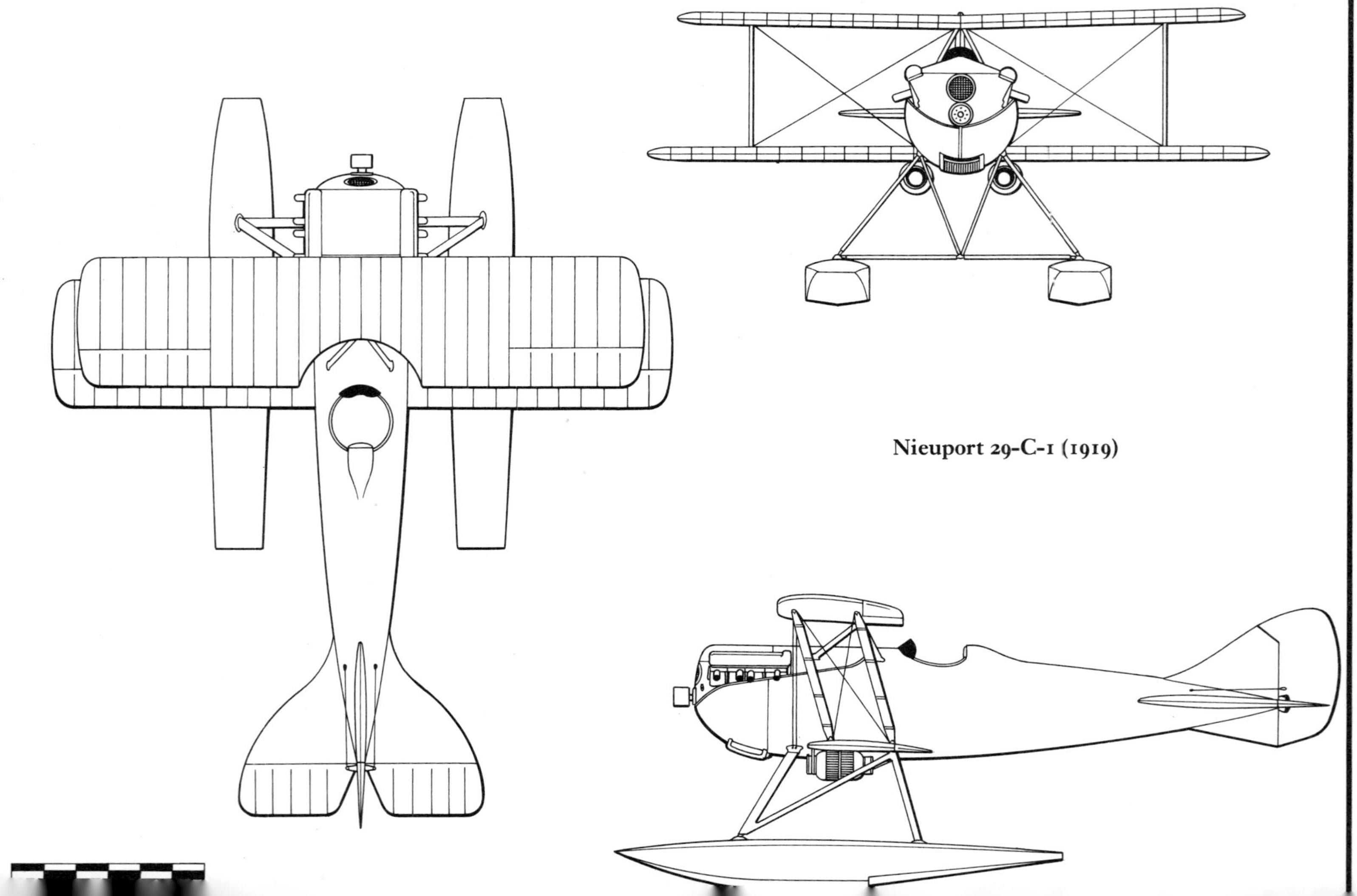

Nieuport 29-C-1 (1919)

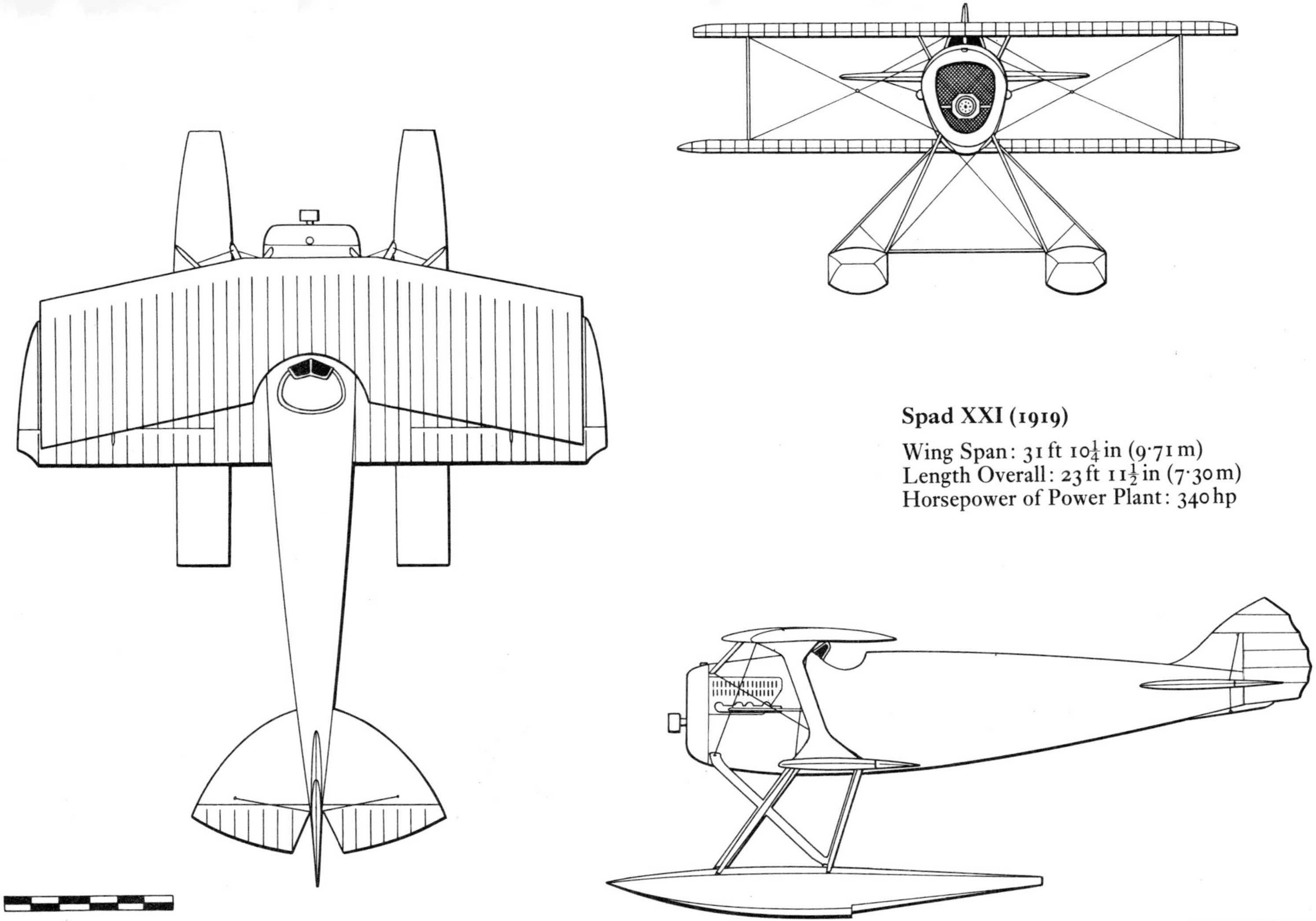

Spad XXI (1919)

Wing Span: 31 ft $10\frac{1}{4}$ in (9·71 m)
Length Overall: 23 ft $11\frac{1}{2}$ in (7·30 m)
Horsepower of Power Plant: 340 hp

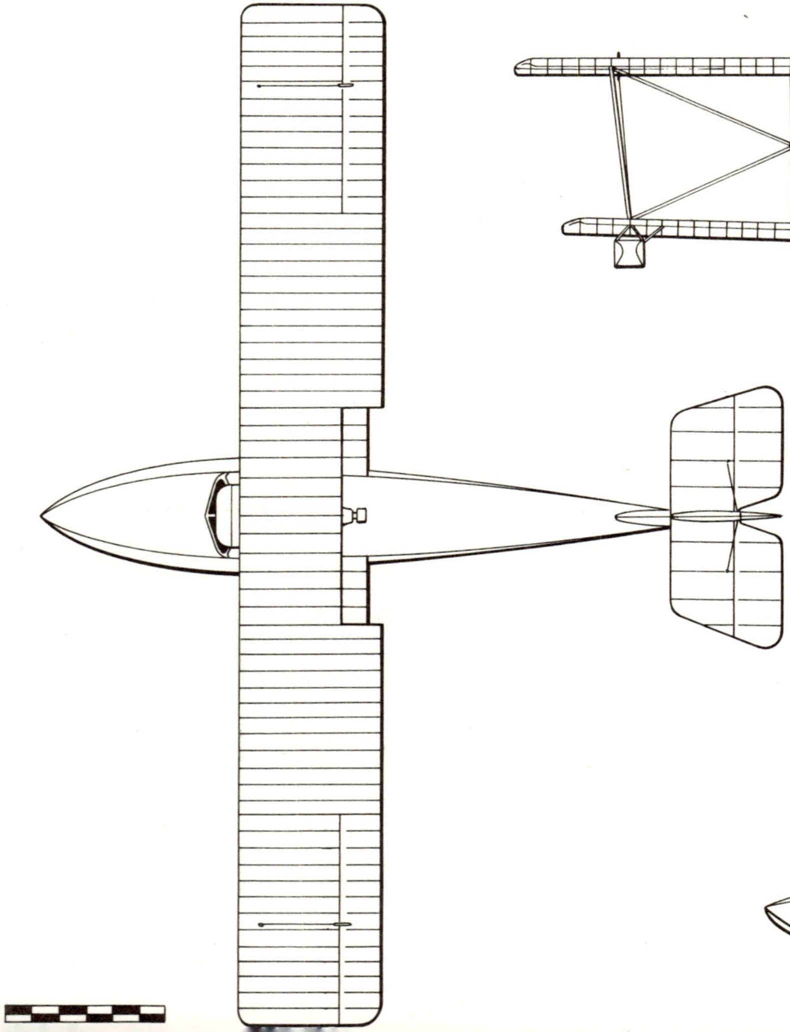

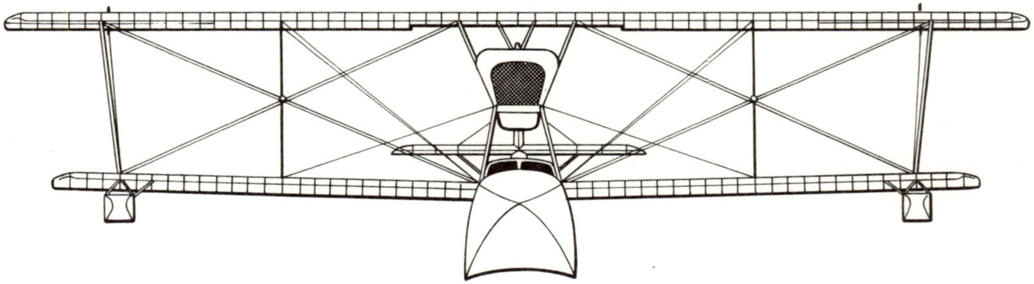

SIAI Savoia 12 (1919)

Wing Span: 38 ft 4 in (11·68 m)
Length Overall: 29 ft $6\frac{3}{4}$ in (9·01 m)
Wing Area: 495 sq. ft (45·98 m²)
Weight Empty: 3,500 lb (1,588 kg)
T-O Weight: 4,784 lb (2,170 kg)
Max Wing Loading: 9·66 lb/sq. ft (47·16 kg/m²)
Horsepower of Power Plant: 250 hp

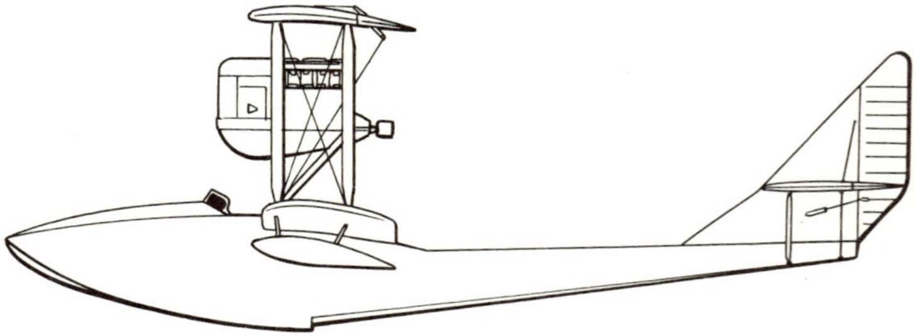

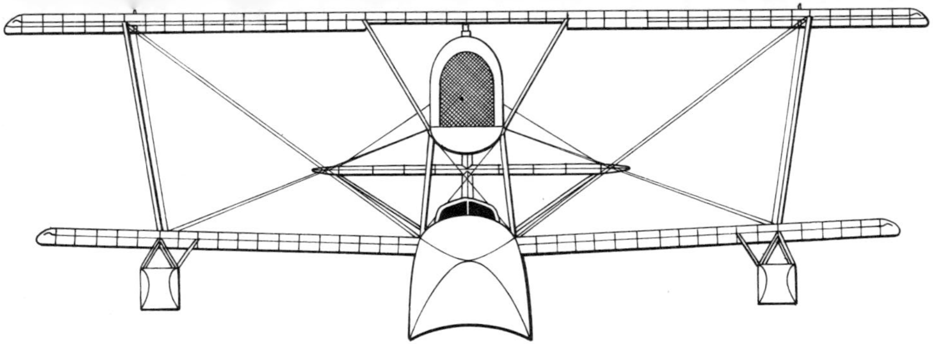

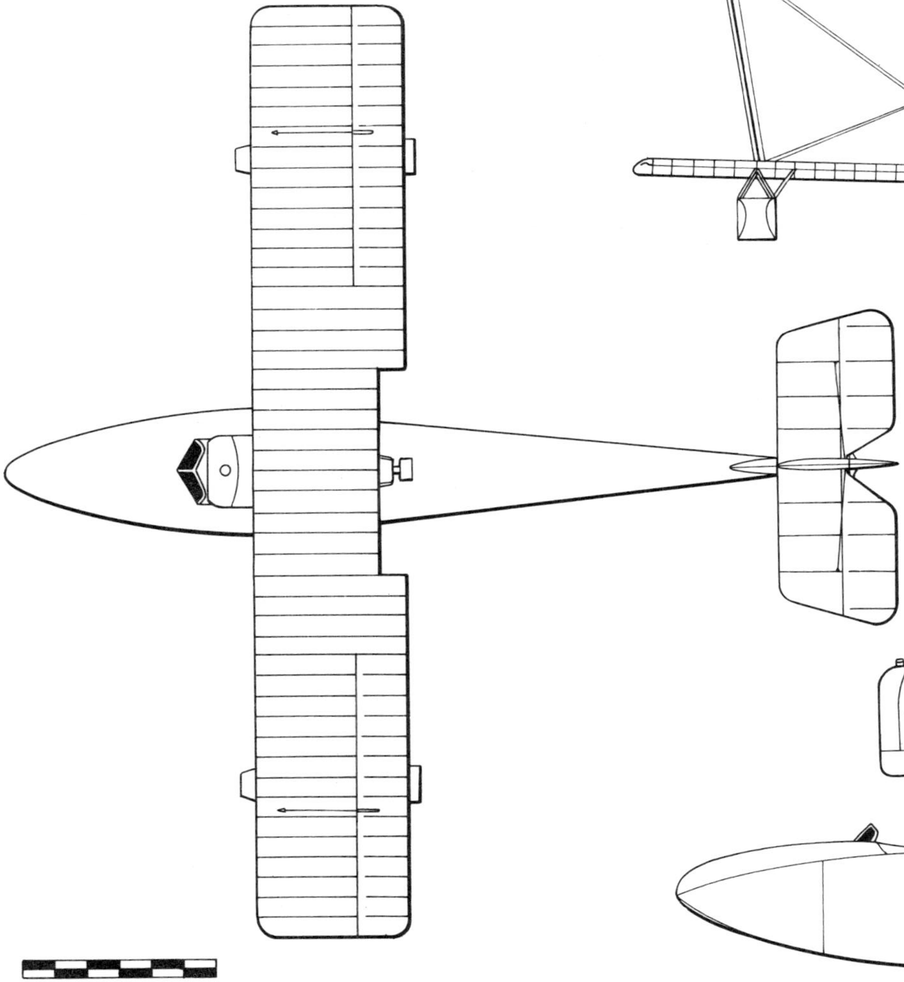

SIAI Savoia 13 (1919)

Wing Span: 26 ft 6 in (8·08 m)
Length Overall: 27 ft 2 in (8·28 m)
Wing Area: 211 sq. ft ($19{\cdot}60\,m^2$)
Weight Empty: 1,610 lb (730 kg)
T-O Weight: 2,075 lb (941 kg)
Max Wing Loading: 9·83 lb/sq. ft
($47{\cdot}99\,kg/m^2$)
Horsepower of Power Plant: 250 hp

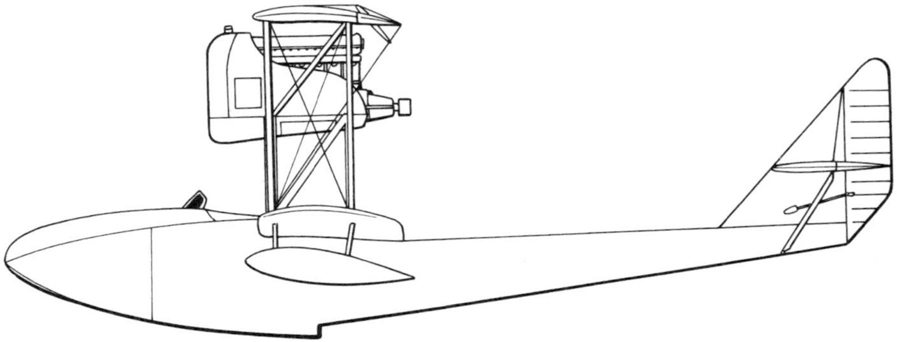

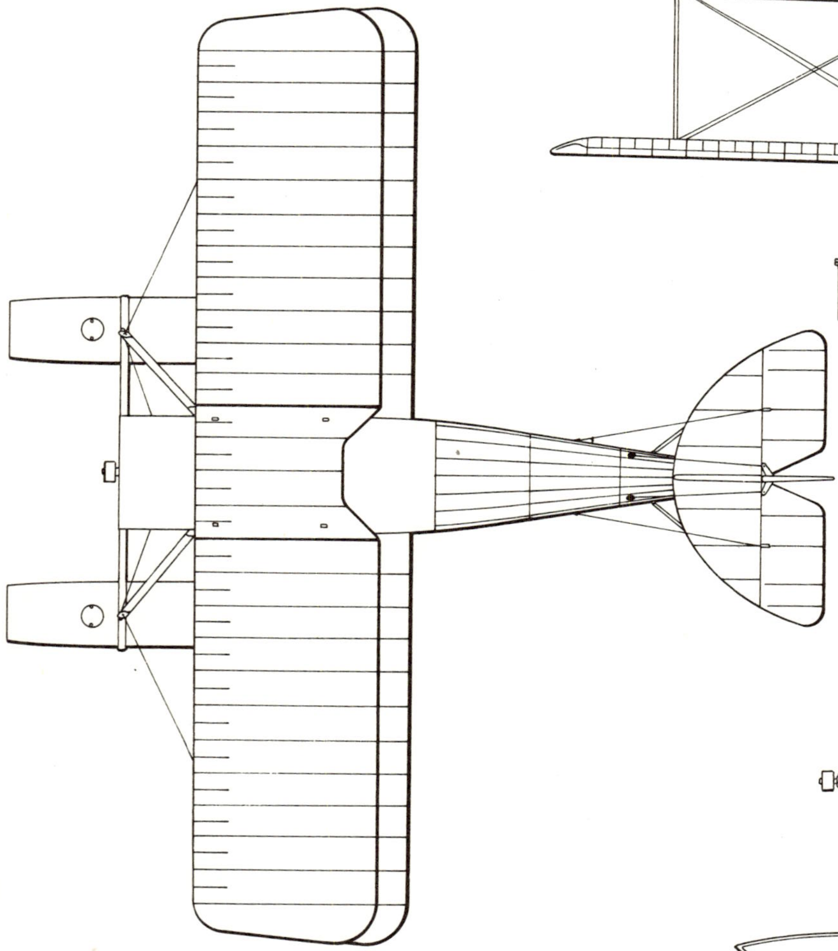

Sopwith Schneider (1919)

Wing Span: 24 ft (7·32 m)
Length Overall: 21 ft 6 in (6·55 m)
Wing Area: 222 sq. ft (20·62 m²)
T-O Weight: 2,200 lb (998 kg)
Max Wing Loading: 9·91 lb/sq. ft (48·38 kg/m²)
Horsepower of Power Plant: 450 hp

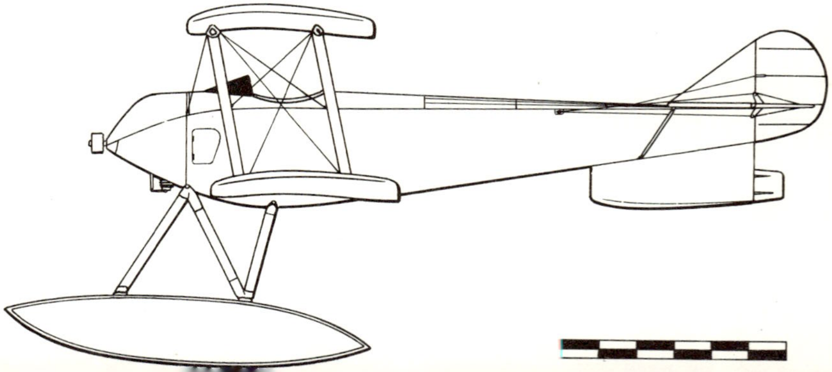

5

Beneath Italian Skies

1920–22

In early 1920 the Aéro-Club d'Italia, responsible for organising the Schneider Trophy contest of that year, issued its first lengthy mandate. There was little doubt they intended to do things properly and that any would-be competitor need have no uncertainty of what was expected of him.

As before, the course was to be of at least 200 nm (370·6 km), but a new requirement was that each competing aircraft must carry 661 lb (300 kg) of non-consumable ballast. It has been suggested that Italian representations to the FAI for inclusion of this weight penalty was intended to load the scales in favour of their own aircraft, which were all of the flying-boat type. True or not, it certainly posed a considerable handicap and ensured the elimination of all aircraft of marginal lifting capability.

The rules for the Navigability test were detailed and specific:

(i) Each machine, together with its load of ballast, was required to fly a course of several nautical miles. The length of this would be finalised by the organising committee, and might be all or part of the circuit for the contest proper.

(ii) Each machine was to be taxied over the starting line, take off, and subsequently alight at a position marked by a buoy. A distance of 984 ft (300 m) was then to be covered, taxying on the surface until, reaching the second marker, the pilot could take off again and complete the circuit. Landing was to be made before reaching the finishing line, and the aircraft taxied across this.

(iii) All competitors were required to complete the test satisfactorily during the week preceding the contest. If the officials were dissatisfied with any individual performance, then the pilot concerned would be required to complete the test again without delay.

(iv) Each aircraft taking part in the contest proper must be in exactly the same configuration as when it took the navigability trial. In the event of any damage to the aircraft during or subsequent to the trial, repair was allowed provided the aircraft remained the same, in all respects, as when it began the trials.

Not only were the Aéro-Club d'Italia determined that all instructions should be clear cut and completely unambiguous, they hoped that following the fiasco at Bournemouth there might be considerable interest shown in the 1920 contest. For their part, they were certain they could make a better showing than their British counterparts in 1919, and it was reasonable to assume that the weather of the Adriatic coast would be more co-operative.

They were to be greatly disappointed, primarily because most of the likely competing countries were feeling the effects of the severe financial pinch which had followed the end of the first World War. Obviously, the home team was in the strongest position, free of what could amount to quite considerable transport costs to get the competing aircraft to and from Venice, the chosen venue for the 1920 contest. Furthermore, would-be competitors could neither afford, nor get financial backing, to prepare special aircraft to take part.

Thus, American participation was clearly out and, following the Versailles Peace Treaty, Germany was unable to compete. It was reasonably certain that both Britain and France would field teams for, after all, with Germany out of the running, these two countries were most likely to produce a winner, drawing upon the experience gained in the construction of many types of aircraft during the course of the war. There was also rumour of an entry from Switzerland.

The Swiss challenge failed to materialise; not a single British competitor indicated the slightest interest and only two French entries were received, a Nieuport and a SPAD-Herbemont, the latter to be flown by Jean Casale. In the final analysis the Nieuport entry proved to be founded on rumour, while the SPAD was withdrawn.

Why oh why no British competitor? In an endeavour to enthuse some manufacturer or individual to challenge the Italians, the Royal Aero Club offered prizes of £250, £150 and £100 to the three who might form a team. These prizes would go to the first, second and third British competitor to complete the course, irrespective of their positions in the contest proper.

It was certainly a gesture of the right kind for money, or rather lack of it, was the determining factor. Unfortunately, the bait was not big enough: the cost of preparing a special aircraft, the cost of competing and of transport to and from Italy was very different in 1920 to that involved in the pre-war hydro-aeroplane meetings in the south of France. Try as it might, the British aviation press could whip up no interest from any source. 'What is the matter with our seaplane and flying-boat constructors?', asked Stanley Spooner. 'Have they got "cold feet" or are they suffering from a sense of injury on account of the unfortunate *contretemps* which disfigured the last race for the cup?' 'Cold feet' was not the right epithet: 'frozen purse strings' would have been far more accurate.

The Aéro-Club d'Italia pressed on regardless, announcing that the navigability test would be held on 18 September and the actual contest two days later. The course was triangular, beginning off the Porto di

Lido with a SSW leg of 5·9nm (11km) to a point just off the Porto di Malamocco; then 7·0nm (13km) almost due east to a marked position in the Adriatic, the final NW leg of 7·1nm (13·117km) leading back to the Porto di Lido. All turning points were to be indicated by captive balloons flying at a height of 164ft (50m). No false markers here! The circuit was thus near enough 20nm (37·117km), of which ten laps had to be completed, and the competitors were to be sent off at five minute intervals.

The rules for the navigability test received a final polish: 'Competitors must taxi over the start line at not more than 10 knots, take off, fly to and land ahead of a clearly marked buoy, taxi 300m at not more than 10 knots to a second buoy, take off, complete a reduced circuit marked by captive balloons, land before the finishing line and taxi over it at a speed not exceeding 10 knots.'

Clearly, the committee were doing their utmost to ensure that the confusion which had reigned at Bournemouth should not be repeated: it is regrettable that under such clear-cut conditions no outside challenge was made.

Consequently, as the day of the tests drew near, there remained only the four Italian entries. These consisted of two S.I.A.I. Savoia flying-boats

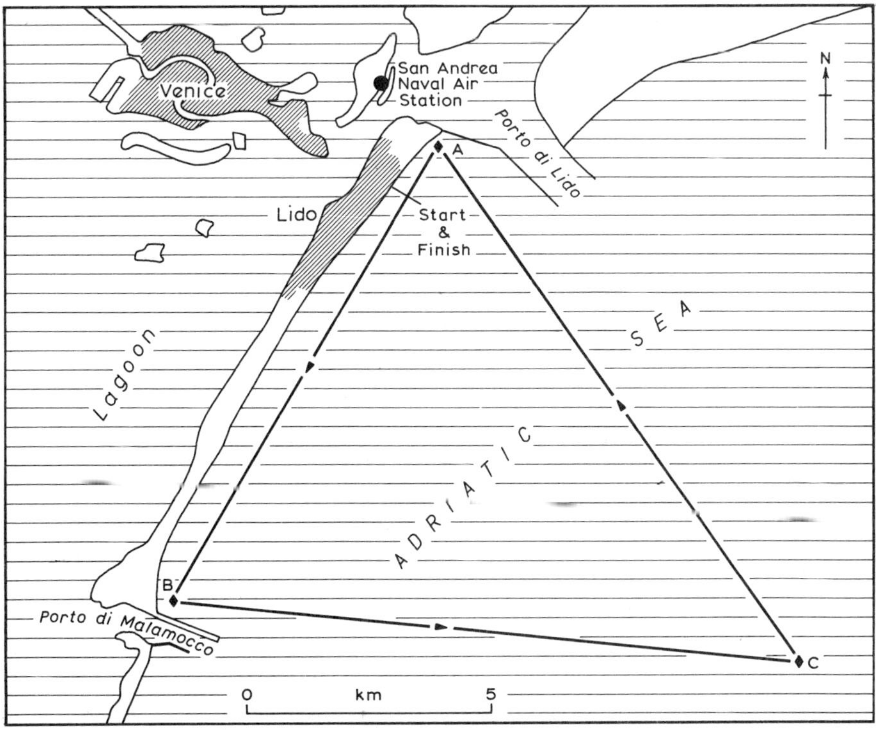

3. Schneider Trophy Contest Course: Venice 1920

to be flown by Lieutenant Luigi Bologna and Sergeant Guido Janello, and two Nieuport-Macchis with pilots Arturo Zanetti and Giovanni de Briganti.

The Savoia designs had stemmed from the S.8, a clean-looking two-seat single-engine reconnaissance/ASW flying-boat developed during the war. Bologna's mount was virtually a standard S.12, of biplane configuration, with the 550 hp Ansaldo San Giorgio 4E-284 12-cylinder in-line liquid-cooled Vee engine mounted on the fuselage centre-line between the biplane wings, and driving a two-blade pusher propeller. Balancer floats were mounted just inboard of the wingtips of the lower wing, and the tail unit was well upswept to keep it clear of spray thrown up during take off and well within the effect of the slipstream.

Janello's mount, designated S.19, had been specially prepared for the contest. Although generally similar to the S.12, its Ansaldo engine had been mounted so that it could drive a tractor propeller and, consequently, was expected to have the edge over the S.12 so far as maximum speed was concerned.

The Macchi entries, more accurately known as Nieuport-Macchis, originated from the Società Anonima Nieuport-Macchi which, in 1912, had first entered the aviation field to build Nieuport designs under licence at Varese. Towards the end of the war this company had started to build a series of flying-boats, the design of which had been inspired by a captured Austrian Löhner, resulting in the M.5 and M.7 military flying-boats which gained a high reputation for their performance and reliability.

The M.12, to be flown by de Briganti, was basically the standard three-seat reconnaissance/bomber aircraft first built in 1918, and which was powered by a 450 hp version of the Ansaldo 4E-28 engine driving a pusher propeller 9 ft 10 in (3·00 m) in diameter. Mounted on streamline-section struts from the 'boats hull, the engine was immediately below the upper wing, and centre-section struts extended from the engine mounting. In other respects it was remarkably clean, a single bay biplane with only two streamline interplane struts at about two-thirds span and a pair of landing and flying wires on each side. Balancer floats were mounted beneath the lower wing. Wing span was 55 ft $9\frac{1}{4}$ in (17·00 m), length overall 35 ft 4 in (10·77 m), height overall 12 ft 0 in (3·67 m) and wing area 656·6 sq. ft (61 m^2). Maximum level speed at sea level was approximately 118 mph (190 km/h), so reliability rather than speed was its trump card.

Zanetti's machine, however, was a two-seat version developed specially from the M.7 to cater for the new non-consumable payload condition imposed by the Committee. Designated M.19, it had a Fiat Type A14 12-cylinder in-line liquid-cooled Vee engine, developing a maximum of 700 hp, and this was mounted on the fuselage centre-line. Carried on six massive struts, it was faired into the centre-section of the upper wing. Wing interplane struts increased to three pairs per side which, viewed head-on, took the form of outward-sloping *N*s, and an additional pair of struts were carried from beneath the wings to each side of the hull. A far less elegant tail unit was extensively wire-braced.

As is so often the case with newly developed types, the Macchi M.19 and Savoia S.19 both suffered teething troubles. Coupled with labour unrest in Italy at that period it proved sufficient for both to be withdrawn from the contest. The same unrest had created also transport problems which, together with bad weather, eliminated the Macchi M.12. Consequently, when the Committee gathered to supervise the navigability trials they were able to concentrate their undivided attention upon the only remaining competitor, the Italian Navy's Luigi Bologna flying the Savoia S.12.

On 18 September he completed the trial successfully and, with no other competitors involved, it was decided that he should attempt the speed course on the following day. Despite long held beliefs that the Adriatic would at least be hospitable in respect of flying conditions, the weather clerk decided to throw in his lot to enhance the general feeling of anti-climax, producing an intensity of storms that prevented any attempt before 21 September. On that day, despite indifferent weather, Bologna lifted the Savoia off the water, flying rather cautiously so as not to overtax his machine. He completed the full distance of the course in 2hrs 10mins 35secs, to record an average speed of 107·22mph (172·55km/h).

However indecisive, Italy had won the 1920 contest and was once again responsible for organisation of the next event. In due course it was announced that this would again take place at Venice, provisionally towards the end of September.

There were some changes in the regulations, including elimination of the penalty of carrying non-consumable ballast, and it was disclosed that two trials would have to be completed successfully before the contestant could take part in the speed event.

First came a navigability trial, much the same as in previous years, with the requirement to fly a course of 5–10nm (9·2–18·5km) during which two stretches of water taxying of at least a half nautical mile (0·93km) each had to be made.

This was to be followed by a water tightness test, requiring that immediately after the navigability trial the machine should ride at anchor for six hours with a full load of petrol and oil. This was not quite so innocent as it might at first appear, for it meant that serviceable water-tight hull or floats were absolutely essential. It was introduced to encourage the development of really seaworthy craft, rather than lightweight 'keep-floating-if-we're-lucky' racing machines. This test, first imposed in 1921, was to remain in force until after the 1929 event.

Other changes included the provision that two attempts would be allowed at the navigability test; that a deposit of 5,000fr was required as an earnest of good faith (in addition to the nominal entrance fee), and was returnable provided that the contestant took part in the event; last but not least, any repairs needed after the contest had started must be carried out at sea. As with previous rules governing repairs, they must not be considered to have modified the aircraft in any way. It was also reported that any water seepage into hull or floats during the water tightness test could not be drained off prior to taking part in the speed event, but it has not been possible to confirm whether or not this was a regulation imposed by the Committee. All in all an increase in problems for would-be contestants and, however well intentioned, tending to discourage entries in what were then very difficult times.

For the organisers this must have been just about the most depressing period of the entire series of contests. There was little enough money to spare for the development of aircraft to spread the communication links of civil aviation, started so enthusiastically in the immediate aftermath of the war. Many manufacturers who had ended their wartime contracts with reasonable bank balances and high hopes were soon to find there was little or no demand for their products. Instead they turned to the manufacture of consumer goods to keep the factories solvent. Hence, there should really have been little surprise at the disappointing reaction to the announcements relating to the 1921 contest.

The British aviation press was not quiescent, arguing that waterborne aircraft represented the best possible long-term investment towards development of the nation's intercontinental air routes, and that Britain should ensure that it lead the world in such progress. However frequently or pithily put, it was a plea that fell on deaf ears.

Entrants for the 1921 contest had been required to apply by 1 June, but even though this date was extended it failed to change the situation in any way. So it was that an Italian team had to be selected by competitive elimination from a grand total of sixteen, challenged by a single French entry. The latter machine was a foretaste of things to come, for the French were not slow to appreciate that, without some form of backing, rising prices had put the cost of participation in such a competition far beyond the pocket of individuals and most flying clubs.

The course chosen for the 1921 event differed considerably from that of the previous year and was, in fact, the longest race of the series. Sixteen laps of a 13·3 nm (24·6 km) course had to be flown, giving an overall distance of 212·8 nm (393·6 km). With spectators in mind the Committee had retained the first leg of the 1920 course, shifting the first turning point marginally west. An acute-angled turn sent the competitors back on a near-parallel course as they raced towards the second turning point, off the Porto di Lido, giving a final NW leg of only 1·3 nm (2·4 km).

Another change related to the course for the navigability trial. It had a common starting point, but immediately struck due west across the Lido to a first balloon-marked turning point in the Laguna. An obtuse-angled turn onto a SSW heading crossed the Lido again, a final very acute turn headed back to the starting point to give a lap of approximately 8 nm (15 km).

This course was to prove too much for Sadi Lecointe's Nieuport-Delage, powered by a 300 hp Hispano-Suiza engine, when he took part in the navigability trial. At his first compulsory landing he hit the smooth water of the Laguna heavily, buckling the structure that united floats and fuselage and putting his machine out of the contest. Once again organisers and spectators were faced with an Italian fly-over.

But first it was necessary to select an Italian team from the mass of contenders. These comprised five Macchi M.7s, two Macchi M.18s, one Macchi M.19, six Savoia S.13s, one Savoia S.21 and one Savoia S.22.

As mentioned earlier in this chapter, the Macchi M.7 was one of the basic types from which the company's series of flying-boats had been developed. Spanning only 32 ft $7\frac{3}{4}$ in (9·95 m), with an overall length of 26 ft $6\frac{3}{4}$ in (8·10 m), height of 9 ft 8 in (2·95 m) and wing area of 286·3 sq. ft (26·6 m^2), it was powered by a 260 hp Isotta-Fraschini V6 6-cylinder liquid-cooled in-line engine, driving a two-blade pusher propeller. Extensive

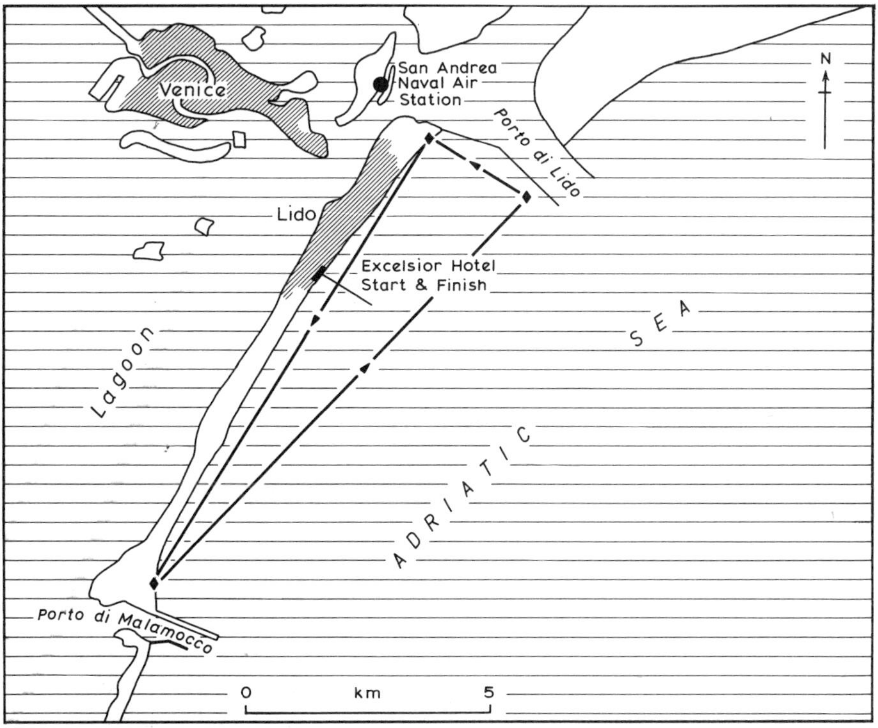

4. Schneider Trophy Contest Course: Venice 1921

Macchi M.19, the flying-boat flown by Arturo Zanetti in the 1921 contest

The Supermarine Sea King, or Sea Lion II, during early tests. Biard won the 1922 contest in this machine at Naples

service had eliminated the gremlins that plague new types, but with a maximum level speed of only 130 mph (210 km/h) at sea level, it was expected to be eclipsed by later derivatives and the specially-built Savoias.

The Macchi M.18 was something of a compromise between the M.7 and M.19, an attempt to arrive at a standardised design of the nine very similar flying-boats built previously by the company. Its description is generally similar to that already given for the M.19, except that its single power plant was installed as in the other versions, that is just below the upper wing. It comprised a 250 hp Isotta-Fraschini V6 engine. However, the M.18 had been intended primarily as a passenger-carrying 'boat, with accommodation for a pilot and three passengers and was, consequently, hardly likely to offer sparkling performance as a racing machine. This was made clear when it demonstrated a maximum speed of only 106 mph (170 km/h) and both of the M.18s were withdrawn before the eliminating trials. The Macchi M.19 differed only in detail from that which was entered in the previous year.

The Savoia S.13s were also much the same as that flown by Janello at Bournemouth in 1919, but two new machines designated S.21 and S.22 had been prepared specially for the contest.

Most unorthodox in appearance was the S.21, a biplane flying-boat of which the lower wing had considerably greater span than the upper. Interplane struts and bracing wires were reduced to an absolute minimum and the power plant, mounted immediately beneath the upper wing, was carried on the hull by six robust struts. An attempt had been made to streamline the engine, leaving a somewhat reduced entry to the frontal radiator of the 300 hp Ansaldo San Giorgio engine, which drove a four-blade pusher propeller. Comparatively small, with a maximum take-off weight of 1,984 lb (900 kg), it promised to be fast. This was borne out in trials when it demonstrated a maximum level speed at sea level of about 162 mph (260 km/h).

The S.22 represented a completely different approach and, with an empty weight of 3,527 lb (1,600 kg) and maximum take-off weight of 5,512 lb (2,500 kg), may well have been designed originally to cater for the carriage of non-consumable payload before announcement of the fact that this restriction had been eliminated for the 1921 contest.

A single-bay biplane flying-boat, spanning 44 ft 3¼ in (13·5 m), the S.22 had two pairs of interplane struts on each side, plus landing and flying wires. The power plant comprised two engines mounted in tandem, sited just below the upper wing, supported by massive struts. Each engine was a 260 hp Isotta-Fraschini V6, the forward engine driving a tractor and the rear engine a pusher propeller. Both propellers were four-bladed and of remarkably small diameter. Not surprisingly, in view of its size, it had nowhere near the performance of the S.21, with a maximum level speed of only about 137 mph (225 km/h) at sea level.

Prior to the trials to select the Italian team the S.22 crashed and was written off: the tiny S.21 was withdrawn as its intended pilot, Luigi Janello, was sick and no other pilot had sufficient experience to handle this odd-looking but fast machine. With the M.18s already out of the contest, it left only the Macchi M.7s and single M.19 and the Savoia S.13s from which to select a team.

In the trials all of the S.13s were eliminated, and of the M.7 contingent only Giovanni de Briganti and Piero Corgnolino qualified. Zanetti, in the M.19 powered by its 700 hp Fiat engine, proved to be by far the fastest and was clearly favourite to win the contest.

Inevitably the race, held on 7 August, was almost devoid of interest since it was merely a fly-over. True it was not without drama for the national spectators for the favourite, Zanetti flying the M.19, was soon proving that his machine had a turn of speed that should put him across the finishing line way ahead of his compatriots. But he had completed only a few laps when a crankshaft failure of the Fiat ruptured the crankcase and, within seconds, the engine was in flames. Fortunately, Zanetti was able to make a safe landing with the dead engine and escaped without injury.

This left the two M.7s to fight it out and, since both machines were fundamentally the same, some interest was aroused as it became clear that the race would almost certainly go to the most skilful pilot. The eliminating trials had suggested that this was Corgnolino, and as his M.7 gained steadily on that of his rival the surmise was confirmed. As he banked at the Porto di Lido to begin his last lap it seemed inevitable that he would take the honours for 1921. With the finishing line in sight, elation turned to despair as the engine began to misfire. Within seconds it was lifeless, starved of fuel, and Corgnolino made the second dead-engine landing on the Adriatic's waters.

Alone in the sky remained the M.7 of Giovanni de Briganti, who crossed the finishing line almost simultaneously with Corgnolino's landing, after 2 hrs 4 mins 29 secs in the air, to win the contest at a speed of 117·8 mph (189·6 km/h). The Trophy was Italy's for the second time. Only one more win was now needed within the next three years to make it their permanent property.

Realisation of this truth at last spurred Britain and France to prepare for the 1922 contest, while the British aviation press worked itself into a frenzy, declaiming the nation's inglorious role in the contests since Pixton's solitary success in 1914.

But no matter how much ink was spilt to generate the necessary enthusiasm, only a single British company was prepared to involve itself in the cost of fielding a contender. This was the Supermarine Aviation Works whose managing director, Hubert Scott-Paine, and his co-director Commander Bird, ex-RAF, decided to finance the venture with a fair degree of co-operation from other sectors of British industry. Napiers agreed to provide the engine, Shell the petrol, Wakefields the lubricants, while the General Steam Navigation Company promised to transport the aircraft to and from Naples, the venue chosen for that year's event.

The Aéro-Club d'Italia announced that the contest would take place late in August, that rules similar to those for the 1921 contest would apply, and that the speed course would consist of 13 laps each of 15·385 nm (28·5 km) to give a total of 200 nm (370·5 km). They had certainly chosen a delightful setting for the event and the Bay of Naples, dominated on the east by Mount Vesuvius, promised excellent facilities both for spectators and competitors.

Starting and finishing point was just west of the harbour and a short leg of 1·88 nm (3·5 km) headed SSW to the first turn at Cabo di Posillipo. Ahead, across the bay, ESE, was the longest side of the triangular course, 7·02 nm (13 km) to an acute turn at Torre del Greco, putting the competitors back on a NNW heading of 6·49 nm (12 km) to the starting point.

The competition promised to provide the excitement lacking from the two previous years for, in addition to the single entry from Britain, there were to be two from France and five from Italy. And since the entries of the two Continental countries were state-subsidised there was an expectation of new and interesting aircraft.

France had put her money on the products of a new company, Chantiers Aéro-Maritimes de la Seine (C.A.M.S.). If the choice of an untried company was surprising, it began to make sense when one discovered that its leading lights were Lorenzo Santoni, formerly managing director of the Italian Savoia company, together with Signor Conflenti, the Savoia designer.

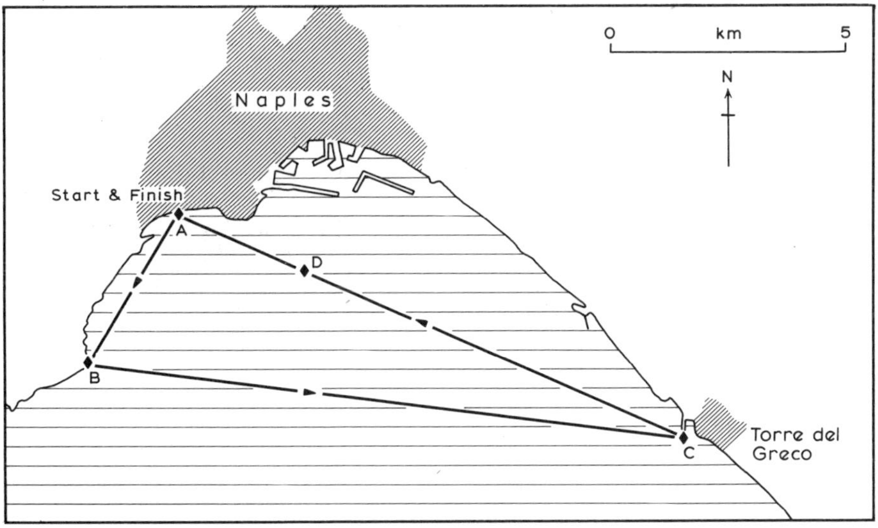

5. Schneider Trophy Contest Course: Naples 1922

Consequently, there was a distinct similarity between Savoia aircraft and the products of the new company, which included initially single-seat and two-seat utility flying-boats, as well as the C.A.M.S. 33 which eventually entered service with the French Navy.

The two aircraft built to take part in the 1922 contest were based upon the C.A.M.S. 31 single-seat flying-boat, which had a single engine driving a pusher propeller. To make them more suited for a speed contest they were modified extensively, the wing span being reduced and a 300 hp Hispano-Suiza engine being mounted in a streamlined nacelle, carried on struts between the two wings, and driving a tractor propeller.

The short-span wings were of single-bay configuration with a single I-shape streamlined interplane strut each side, and N-shape centre-section struts attached to the engine mounting. Balancer floats were mounted beneath the lower wing, directly under the interplane struts, and ailerons were fitted only to the lower wing.

Wing span of the C.A.M.S. 36 was 28 ft 2½ in (8·60 m), length overall 25 ft 5 in (7·75 m), height overall 9 ft 3 in (2·82 m), and wing area 215·3 sq. ft (20 m^2). Maximum take-off weight was 2,205 lb (1,000 kg) and flight tests showed that they had a maximum level speed at sea level of about 162 mph (260 km/h). Unfortunately, they were withdrawn from the contest, thus leaving it a simple battle between the lone British entry and the team of Italian machines.

Supermarine's entry was to be a modified version of the Sea King Mk II, a single-seat amphibian flying-boat of robust construction which had been designed originally as a high-performance scout/fighter. Powered by a 300 hp Hispano-Suiza engine, driving a four-blade pusher propeller, it hardly seemed a potent contender for Schneider honours, especially as its maximum take-off weight was 2,850 lb (1,293 kg) and maximum level speed around 125 mph (201 km/h).

At that time the company's chief test pilot was Henri Biard, and when asked by Scott-Paine to fly their entry in the contest, his enthusiasm at the honour of representing Britain must have been considerably dampened when he realised that his mount would be little more than a modified version of the dependable but slow Sea King. He had not reckoned with the skill of R. J. Mitchell, briefed by Scott-Paine, and set the task of boosting the Sea King to a maximum level speed of around 160 mph (257 km/h).

Mitchell set about the task with the thoroughness and attention to detail that were to characterise his whole association with the company. The heavy amphibian landing gear was removed, wing span reduced from 32 ft (9·75 m) to 28 ft (8·53 m), all superfluous fittings removed to reduce weight to a minimum, and the Hispano-Suiza engine replaced by the 450 hp Lion supplied by the Napier company. Mounted on solid-looking streamlined struts, the engine was located just below the upper wing, driving a large-diameter four-blade pusher propeller. Work on modification of the aircraft, which was given the name Sea Lion II, went ahead at a pace that would allow plenty of time for test, adjustments and general cleaning up to gain the absolute top speed. The big question of course was 'how fast?', for it was known that Italy would be making determined efforts to win the contest and retain the Trophy for good.

In fact, that country's main hopes for success lay in two new designs emanating from the S.I.A.I. company, designed by Ing Marchetti. These were the S.50 seaplane and S.51 flying-boat, and when the former crashed on test, killing its pilot, it seemed that misfortune continued to dog every effort of this company.

However, the S.51 with its gracefully streamlined hull looked every inch a winner. Its most unusual feature was the choice of sesquiplane configuration, which is basically a one-and-a-half-wing biplane, for we had not yet reached that period in aviation history when monoplane construction was pre-eminent.

It is interesting to digress a little and consider that when man sought to fly like the birds he at first copied them too slavishly, but eventually arrived at a monoplane structure for, after all, there are no birds with biplane wings. In arriving at the biplane configuration he was driven by the need to create lightweight, resilient structures with large lifting surfaces. But improving analysis of aerofoil surfaces showed that the biplane had an inbuilt disadvantage: the low pressure area above the lower wing tended to be destroyed by the high pressure area below the upper wing, a factor given the name of biplane interference. One way to reduce this was to increase the gap between the wings, but there is obviously an optimum point beyond which structural weight offsets any aerodynamic gain. Another way was to stagger the two wings in relation to each other, and the most efficient biplanes combined the optimum benefit of both these features.

The sesquiplane configuration was a compromise between monoplane and biplane construction, retaining sufficient lower wing to provide the integrity of the traditional biplane structure, yet ensuring that a large proportion of the upper wing could function aerodynamically as a monoplane, free from the problem of interference.

Returning to the S.51, the span of the upper wing was 32 ft 9¾ in (10·00 m), that of the narrow-chord lower wing only 13 ft 1¼ in (4·00 m), with two pairs of streamline section interplane struts on each side which, viewed from head-on formed a Vee, their base at the tip of the lower wing. Beneath each lower wingtip balancer floats were mounted, and ailerons were provided only on the upper wing.

Power plant consisted of a single 300 hp Hispano-Suiza engine, mounted in a beautifully streamlined nacelle, positioned so that the top of this formed the centre-section of the upper wing. The two-blade pusher propeller was faired at its hub by a spinner that complemented the lines of the nacelle

Looking somewhat ungainly on land . . .

. . . the Macchi M.17 appears far more graceful on water

and the chord of the upper wing, 6 ft 6¾ in (2·00 m), was such that a large cut-out was formed in the trailing-edge to allow clearance for the propeller.

Total wing area of the S.51 was 247·57 sq. ft (23 m²), length overall 26 ft 3 in (8·00 m) and height overall 8 ft 2½ in (2·50 m). Maximum take-off weight was 2,380 lb (1,080 kg), but the general appearance of the machine suggested that it would be fast.

Two Macchis completed the Italian team, an M.17 to be flown by Arturo Zanetti, basically similar to the tried-and-true M.7, and powered by a 260 hp Isotta-Fraschini engine; Corgnolino's mount was an M.7 with similar power plant. There was little doubt they would prove no match for the Savoia entry, but could be relied upon to complete the course if the new and untried S.51 should run into trouble.

At the beginning of August the Aéro-Club d'Italia announced that the preliminary trials would be held on 12 August, more than a week ahead of the anticipated date, which caused some consternation at Supermarines where the Sea Lion was not yet completed. A spell of round-the-clock working was essential to finish the machine, and spirits were at a low ebb when Biard had to make an emergency landing with a dead engine on his first flight test. Fortunately the trouble was of a minor nature, and on the following day he was able to demonstrate that the British contender was capable of at least 150 mph (241 km/h). In a flurry of hard work, last minute adjustment and refinements were made before the machine was crated for shipment from Southampton to Naples.

Understandably, the Italians were anxious to gain some knowledge of the capabilities of this sole challenge to their retention of the Trophy. They had learned, via the grapevine, that it was a variant of the Sea King II and knew that unless a minor miracle had happened it posed no real threat. Nonetheless, eyes and ears were constantly alert and Biard, using a little gamesmanship, ensured that during his air tests at Naples he never gave the Sea Lion its head. Adding A and B together, the Italians came to the conclusion that they need fear no danger from the British entry. This assumed, of course, that their S.51 came to the starting point without difficulty, for even if the airframe was unconventional, the Hispano-Suiza was a known quantity and could be relied upon to complete the course.

Their confidence met a severe setback during the seaworthiness test, for having sustained minor hull damage during the navigability trials, the S.51 took in water and capsized. Strictly speaking this should have eliminated it from the contest, but Scott-Paine, with typical British sportsmanship, raised no objection to its being salvaged, repaired and taking part in the contest. But for fate taking a hand, he might well have lived to regret that gesture.

The day of the contest dawned fair and calm, and as the hours progressed it became clear that, for once, the weather clerk had given his fullest co-operation. Blazing sun, blue sea and sky, lived up to one's mental impression of what an Italian coastal resort should be like in high Summer.

In fact, so high was the temperature that it was decided to delay the start until 4 p.m., by which time the fierce heat of the sun would be reduced considerably. Biard could hardly contain himself throughout the day, his feelings a blend of nerves and impatience, as he had won the draw for starting position, with Corgnolino, Zanetti and Passaleva to follow in that order. Hour by hour he worried about this and that, primarily race tactics, and it must have been with considerable relief that, with shirt sleeves rolled up and flying clothing cast aside, he squeezed himself into the cockpit of the Sea Lion and awaited the starting signal. At that moment his only happy thought was that he was first away and would not be baulked by other aircraft.

At six minutes past the hour came the long-awaited signal: Biard opened the throttle and lifted cleanly off the water, and with the Lion engine developing its maximum power he found himself at the first turn almost before he had time to draw breath. Determined to shave off every fraction of a second he came perilously close to the marker balloon, realising at once that he must exercise some degree of caution throughout the remainder of the race if he was to avoid disqualification.

By the time that he had finished his first lap, which proved to be his best of the race by just over seven seconds, Corgnolino and Zanetti had joined the circuit. Meanwhile, the Italians had wasted little time in calculating that the Sea Lion had completed its first lap at over 150mph (241 km/h), which meant that the Macchis were no match for it. All depended on Passaleva in the S.51, who took off while Biard was on his second lap.

But Passaleva had problems of his own. The ducking in the sea which the S.51 had suffered had affected the glue bonding the laminations of the wooden propeller. As these separated slightly at the tips unacceptable vibration was set up, and Passaleva could only contain this within what he considered safe limits by throttling his engine back below its maximum revolutions. In fact, they were far too low for the task ahead of him, for it was clear that with this imposed limitation on his maximum speed the British machine would be able to forge ahead. He could only concentrate on flying meticulously, pushing as hard as he dared, in the hope that Biard might make an error or that his engine would prove unequal to the strain.

It proved to be an exciting race for competitors and spectators alike. The latter, unaware of Passaleva's problem, knew only that there was very little between the Sea Lion and the S.51. Those who were keeping lap times were to find that in the closing stages of the race Passaleva was gaining on the British machine: would he be able to scrape home in the lead? For the less dedicated spectator there was the thrill of machines racing for lap after lap, the roar of their engines echoing and re-echoing in the natural and beautiful ampitheatre of the Bay of Naples.

In the air the Italians began to employ tactics designed to slow down the lone British machine, bunching together so that it would prove extremely difficult for Biard to overtake without a loss of valuable seconds. Biard tried again and again, but in the melee of aircraft at the turns it was far too risky: accident or disqualification could result from the slightest error of judgement.

Eventually, he managed to squeeze past and, with throttle wide open, attempted to create a lead of such proportions that he would need have no further fear of the Italians. He certainly gained a worthwhile lead, but fearful that he might overtax his engine he eased back on the throttle. It was at this stage of the contest that Passaleva's lap times began to equal, and then better, those of Biard. Could he snatch enough precious seconds to gain him the lead. Unfortunately, no. At every attempt to coax a few extra revolutions from the Hispano-Suiza engine, the immediate and dangerous increase in vibration caused him to throttle back again, for it was better to end a close second than face elimination from the race.

One hour, 34 mins and $51\frac{3}{5}$ secs from the start it was decided as Biard taxied in first; 2 mins $2\frac{3}{5}$ secs behind him was Passaleva, with Zanetti and Corgnolino third and fourth respectively. Britain had regained the Trophy, at an average speed of 145·7 mph (234·48 km/h), but by what good fortune was not then appreciated.

Ill luck had dogged the Savoia company time and time again in the contests to date. That their S.51 could easily have captured the Trophy for Italy, without the misfortune of the damaged propeller, was demonstrated a few months later. On 22 December the S.51 captured the world speed record for seaplanes, ratified at 174·08 mph (280·16 km/h) by the FAI.

There was little doubt that the Italians were still favourite to gain permanent possession of the Trophy in the 1923 contest, which would take place in British skies. Supermarine had much to think about in the ensuing months.

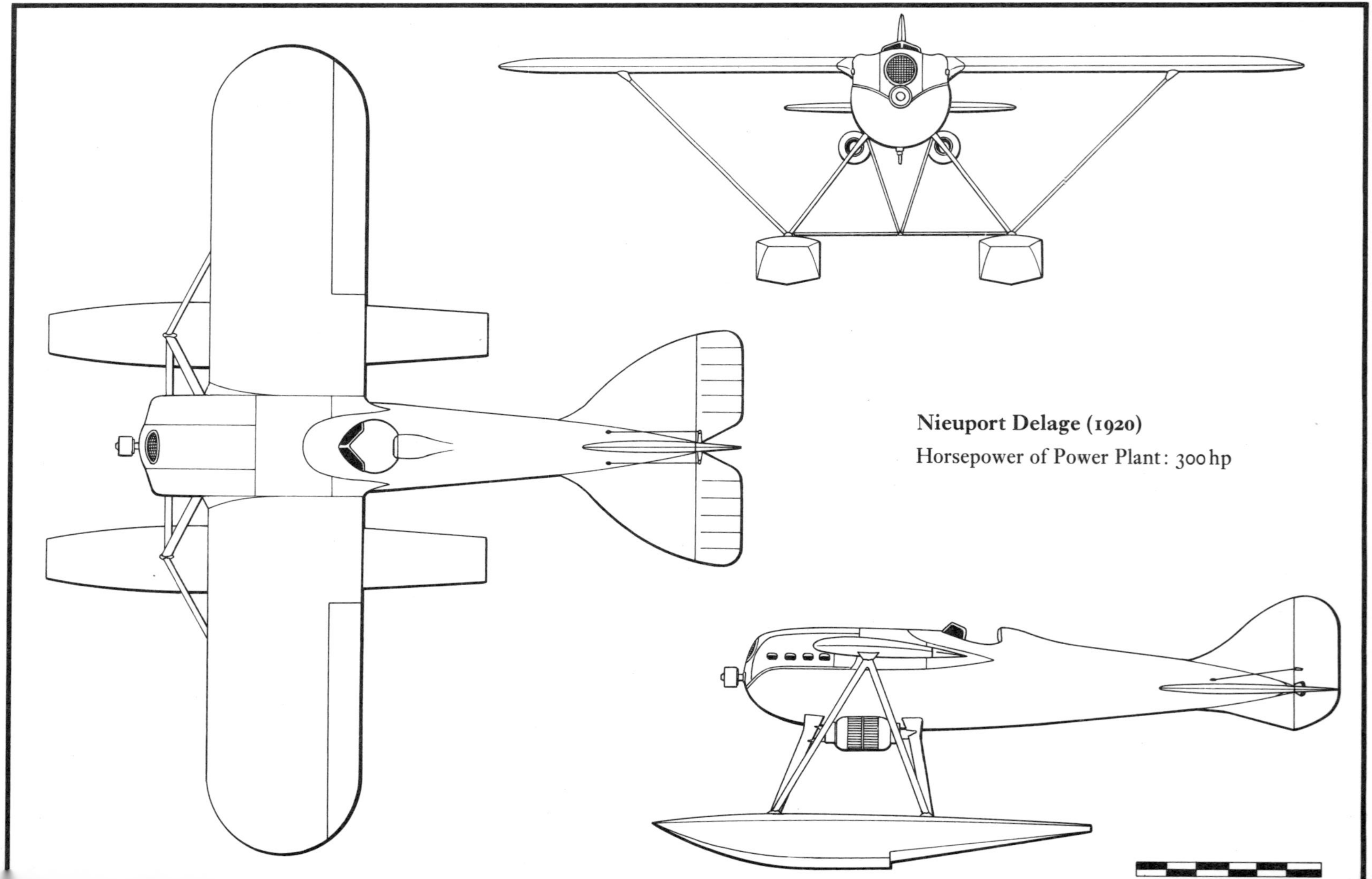

Nieuport Delage (1920)

Horsepower of Power Plant: 300 hp

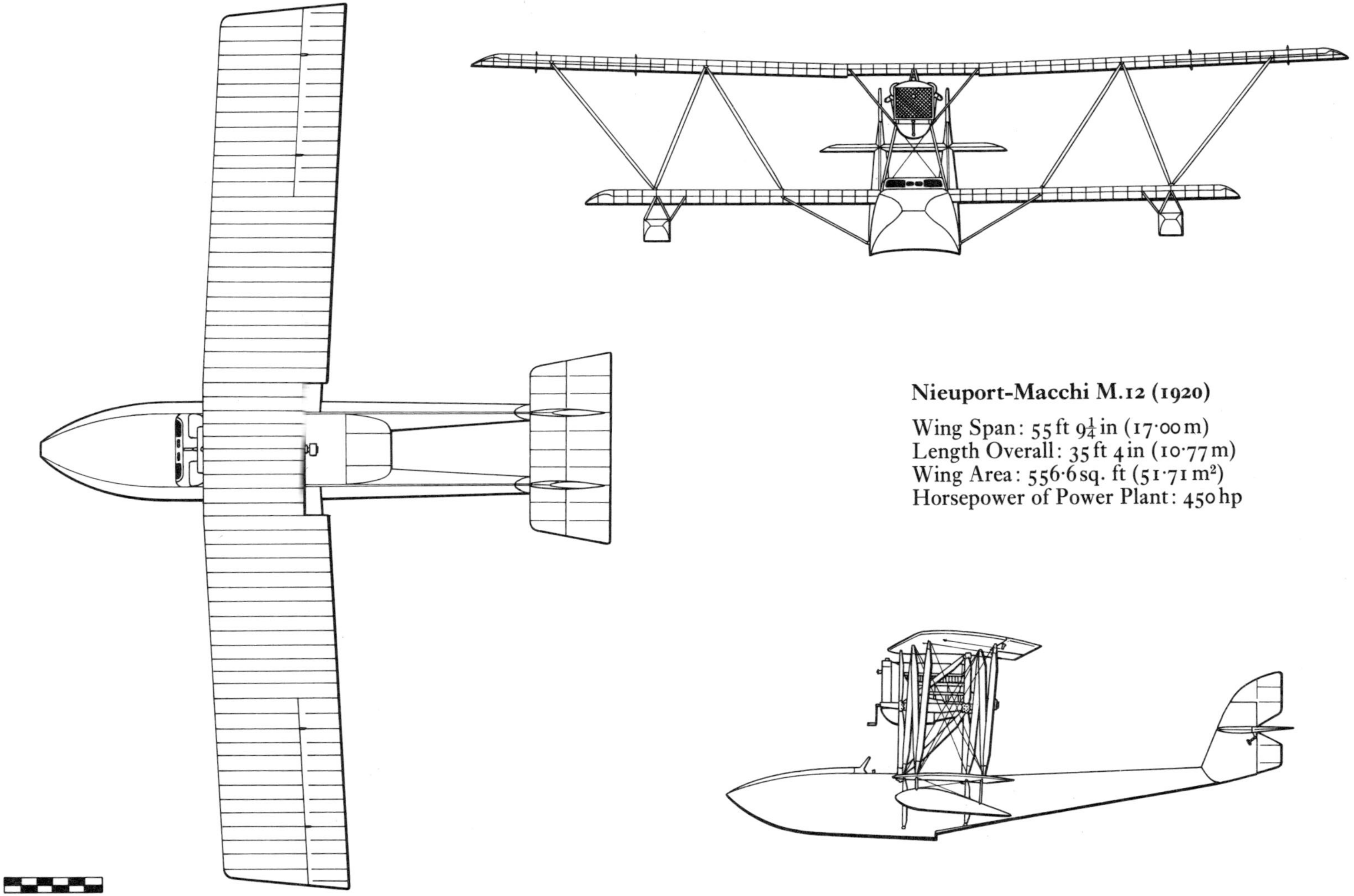

Nieuport-Macchi M.12 (1920)

Wing Span: 55 ft $9\frac{1}{4}$ in (17·00 m)
Length Overall: 35 ft 4 in (10·77 m)
Wing Area: 556·6 sq. ft (51·71 m²)
Horsepower of Power Plant: 450 hp

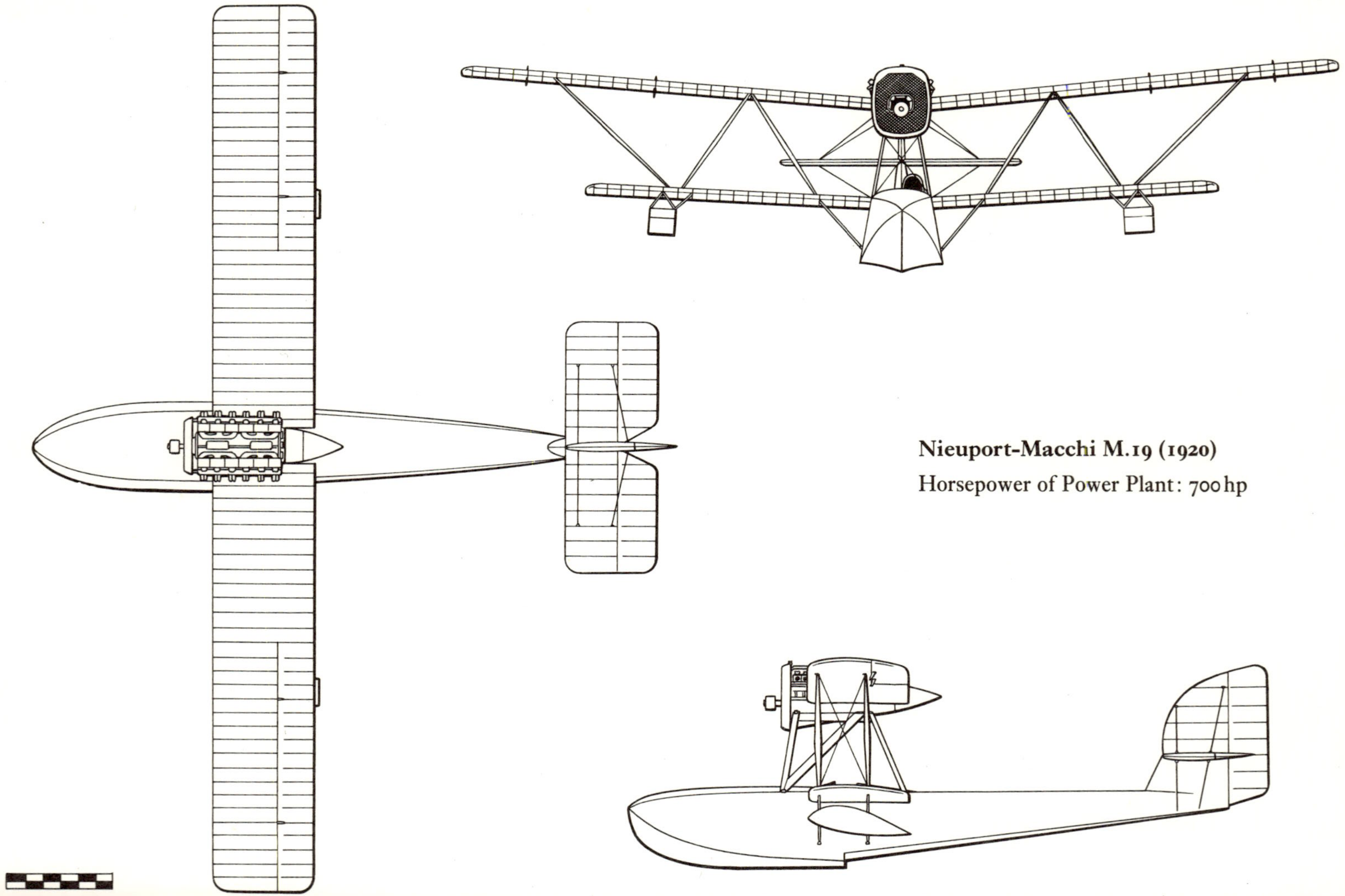

Nieuport-Macchi M.19 (1920)

Horsepower of Power Plant: 700hp

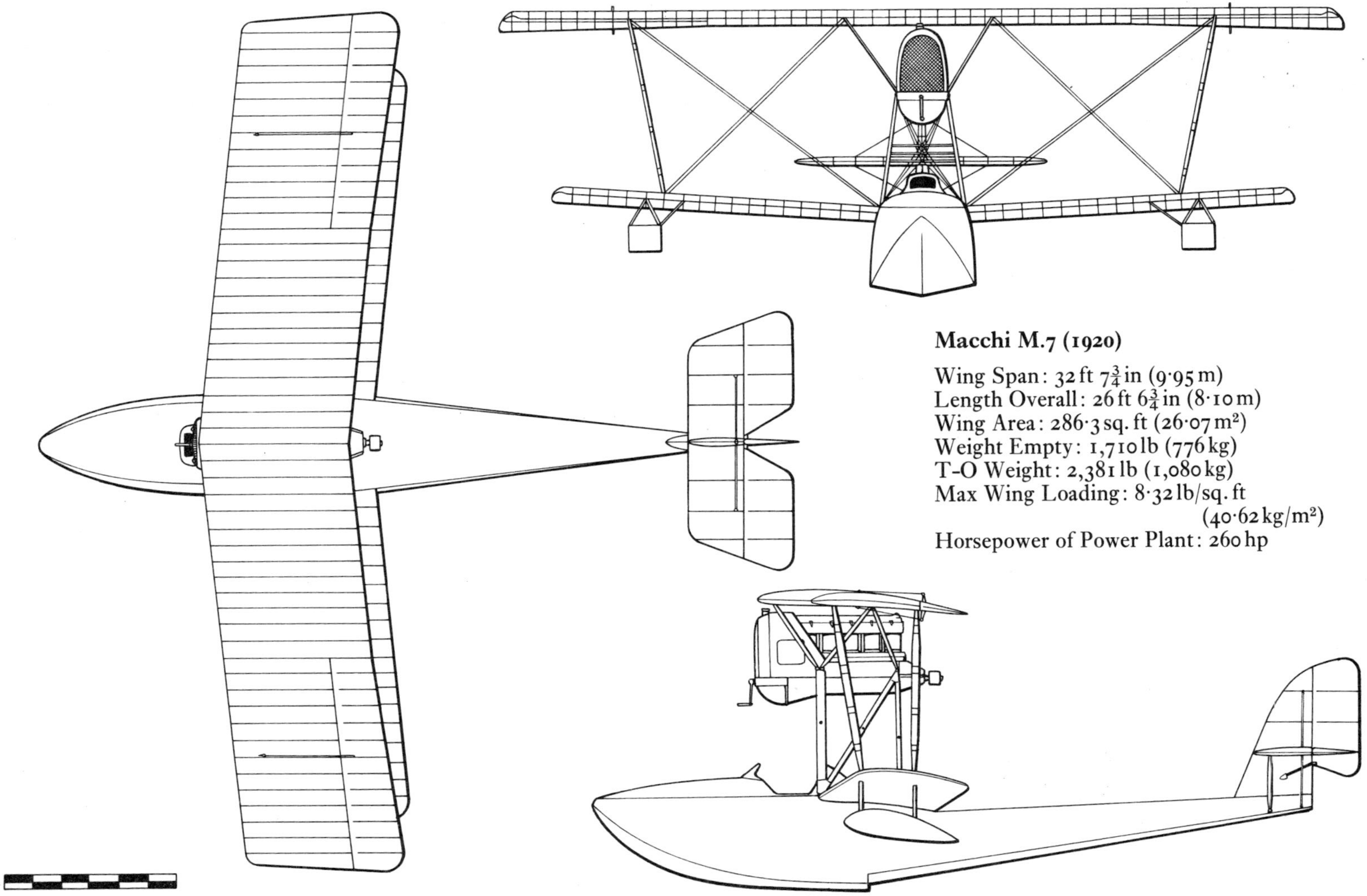

Macchi M.7 (1920)

Wing Span: 32 ft $7\frac{3}{4}$ in (9·95 m)
Length Overall: 26 ft $6\frac{3}{4}$ in (8·10 m)
Wing Area: 286·3 sq. ft (26·07 m^2)
Weight Empty: 1,710 lb (776 kg)
T-O Weight: 2,381 lb (1,080 kg)
Max Wing Loading: 8·32 lb/sq. ft (40·62 kg/m^2)
Horsepower of Power Plant: 260 hp

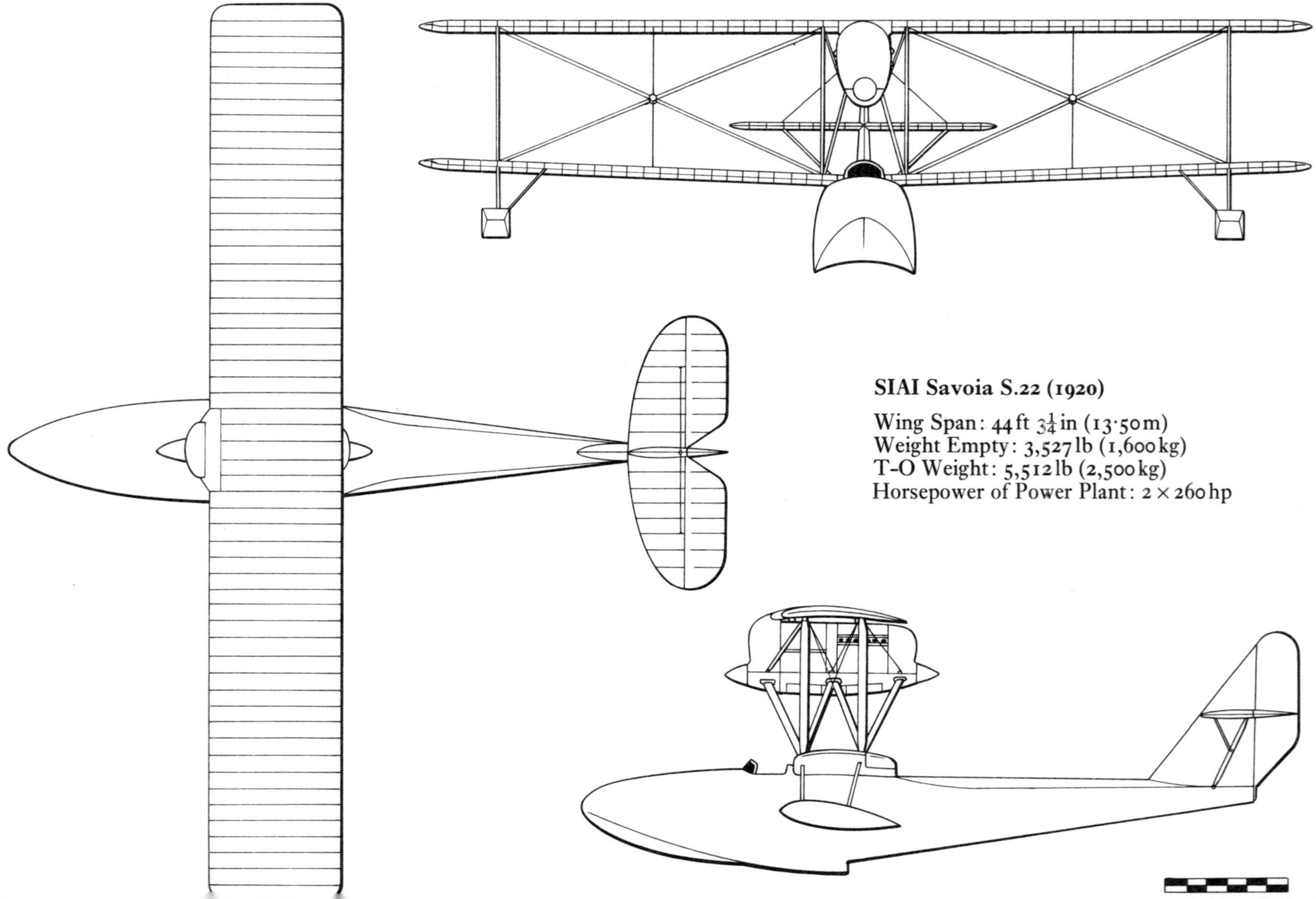

SIAI Savoia S.22 (1920)

Wing Span: 44 ft $3\frac{1}{4}$ in (13·50 m)
Weight Empty: 3,527 lb (1,600 kg)
T-O Weight: 5,512 lb (2,500 kg)
Horsepower of Power Plant: 2 × 260 hp

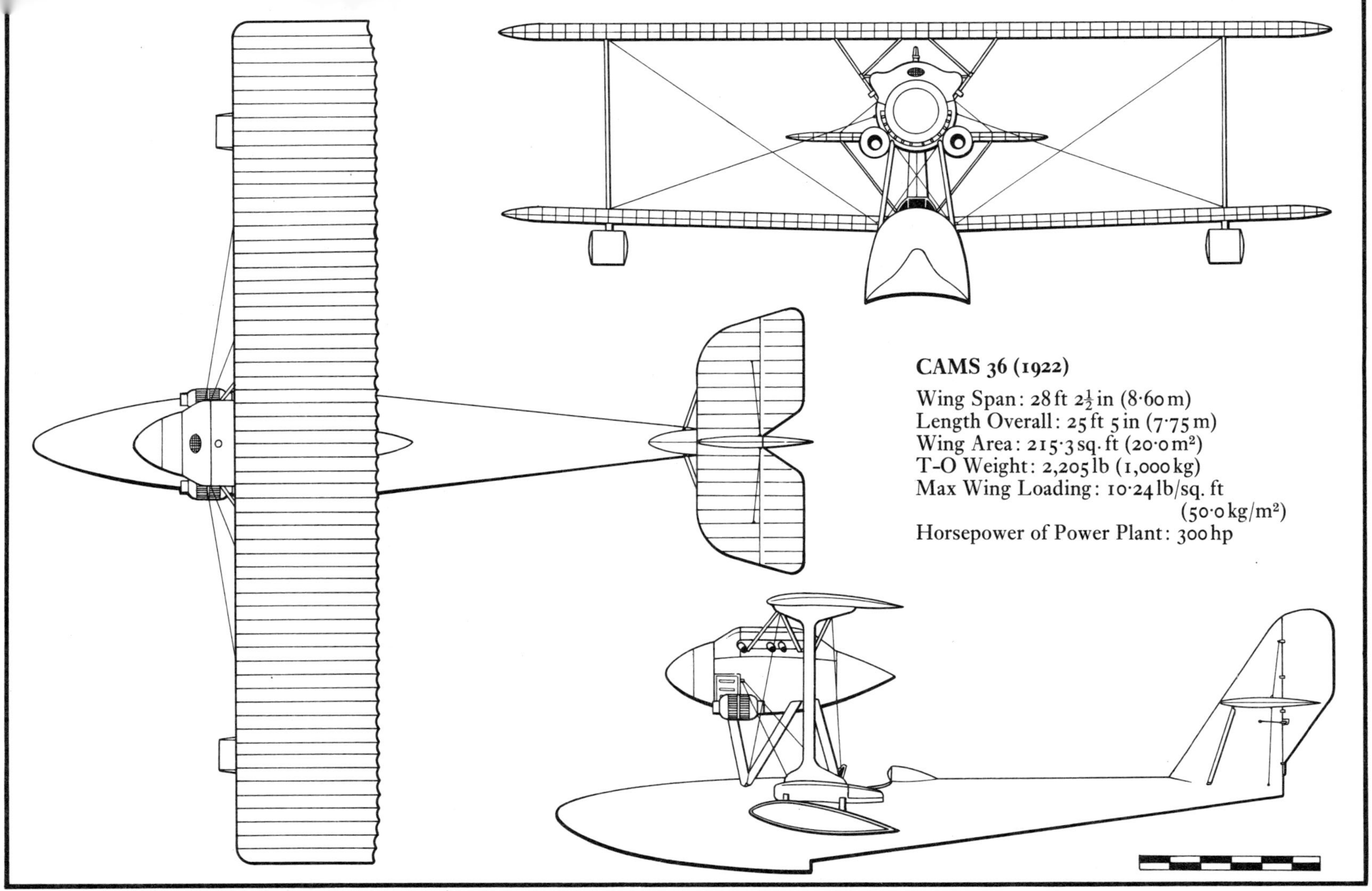

CAMS 36 (1922)

Wing Span: 28 ft $2\frac{1}{2}$ in (8·60 m)
Length Overall: 25 ft 5 in (7·75 m)
Wing Area: 215·3 sq. ft (20·0 m^2)
T-O Weight: 2,205 lb (1,000 kg)
Max Wing Loading: 10·24 lb/sq. ft (50·0 kg/m^2)
Horsepower of Power Plant: 300 hp

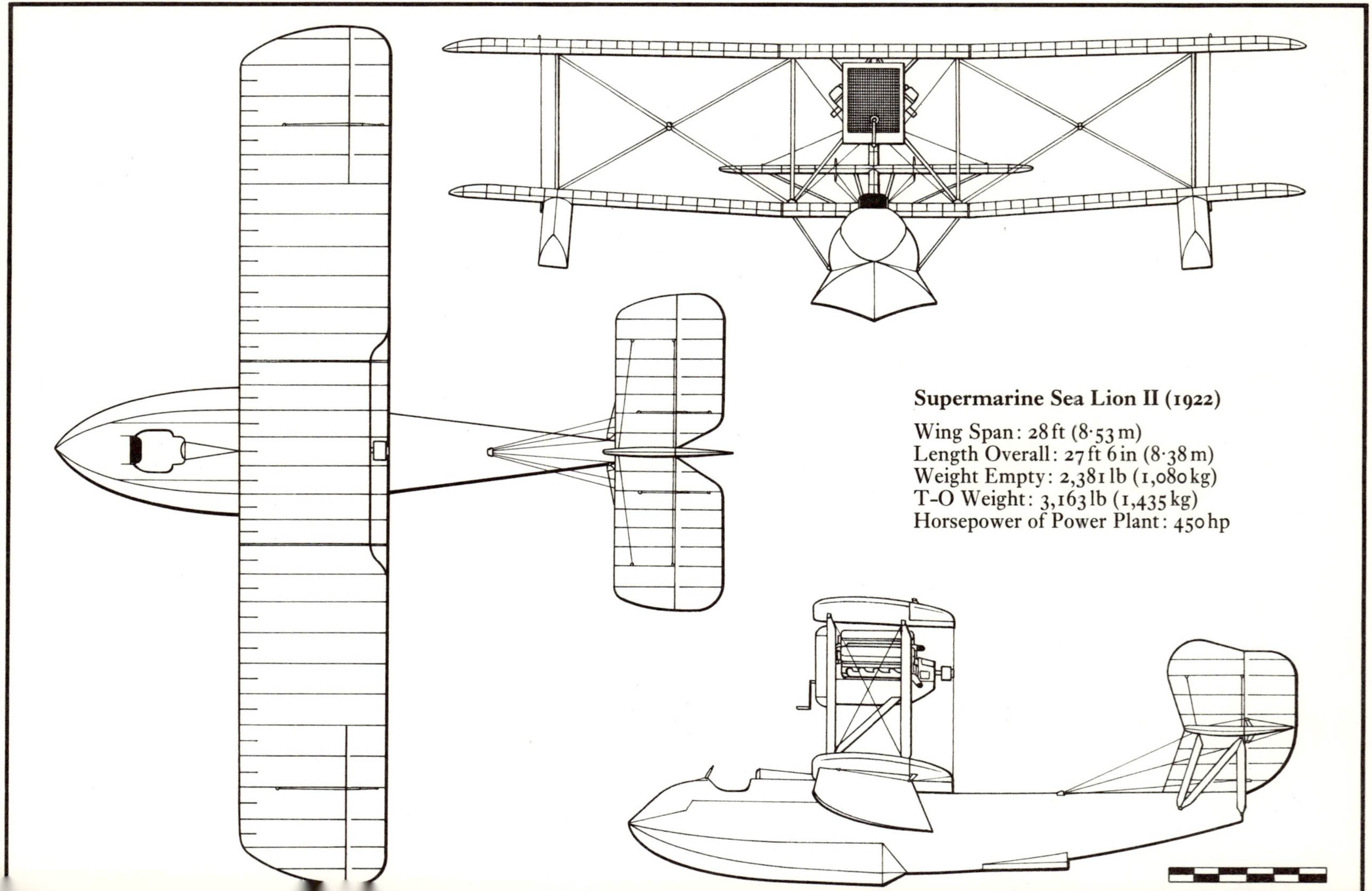

Supermarine Sea Lion II (1922)

Wing Span: 28 ft (8·53 m)
Length Overall: 27 ft 6 in (8·38 m)
Weight Empty: 2,381 lb (1,080 kg)
T-O Weight: 3,163 lb (1,435 kg)
Horsepower of Power Plant: 450 hp

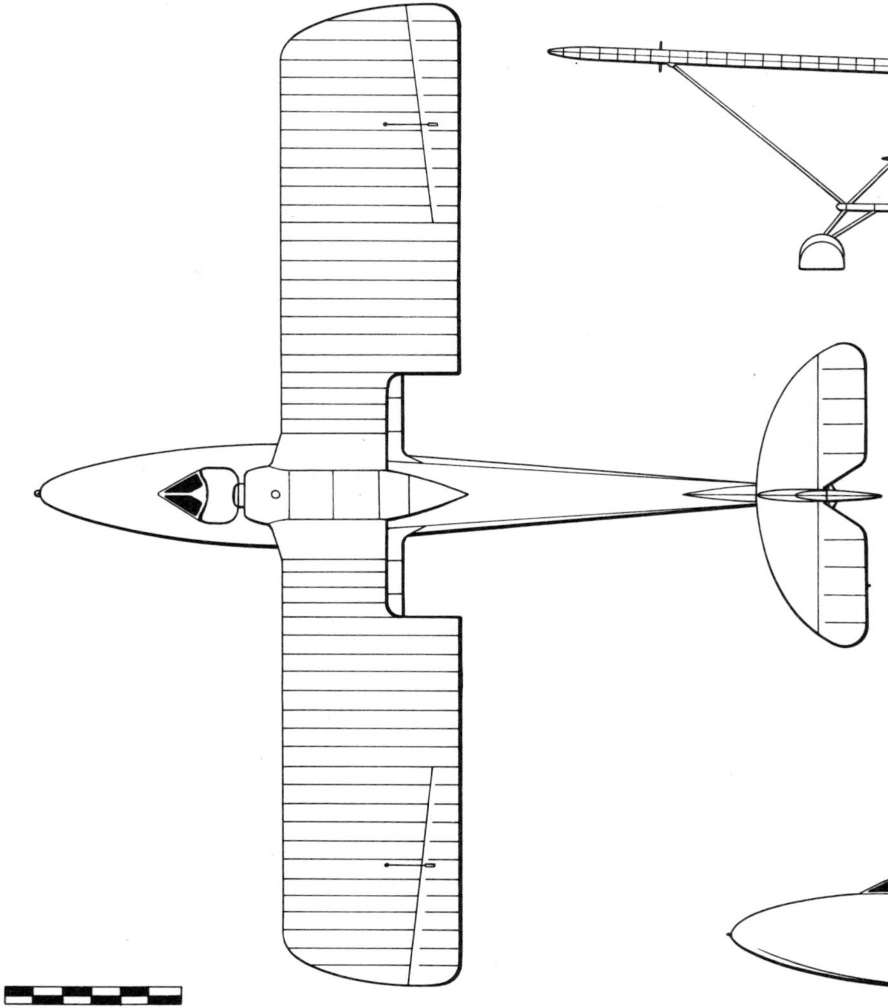

SIAI Savoia S.51 (1922)

Wing Span: 32 ft $9\frac{3}{4}$ in (10·0 m)
Length Overall: 26 ft 3 in (8·0 m)
Wing Area: 247·57 sq. ft (23·0 m^2)
Weight Empty: 1,716 lb (778 kg)
T-O Weight: 2,381 lb (1,080 kg)
Max Wing Loading: 9·61 lb/sq. ft
(46·92 kg/m^2)
Horsepower of Power Plant: 300 hp

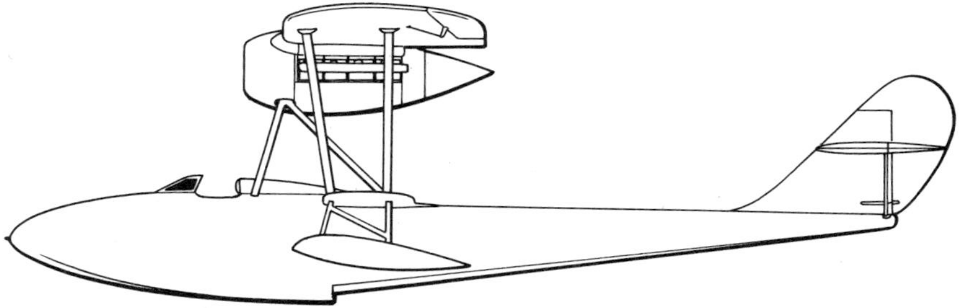

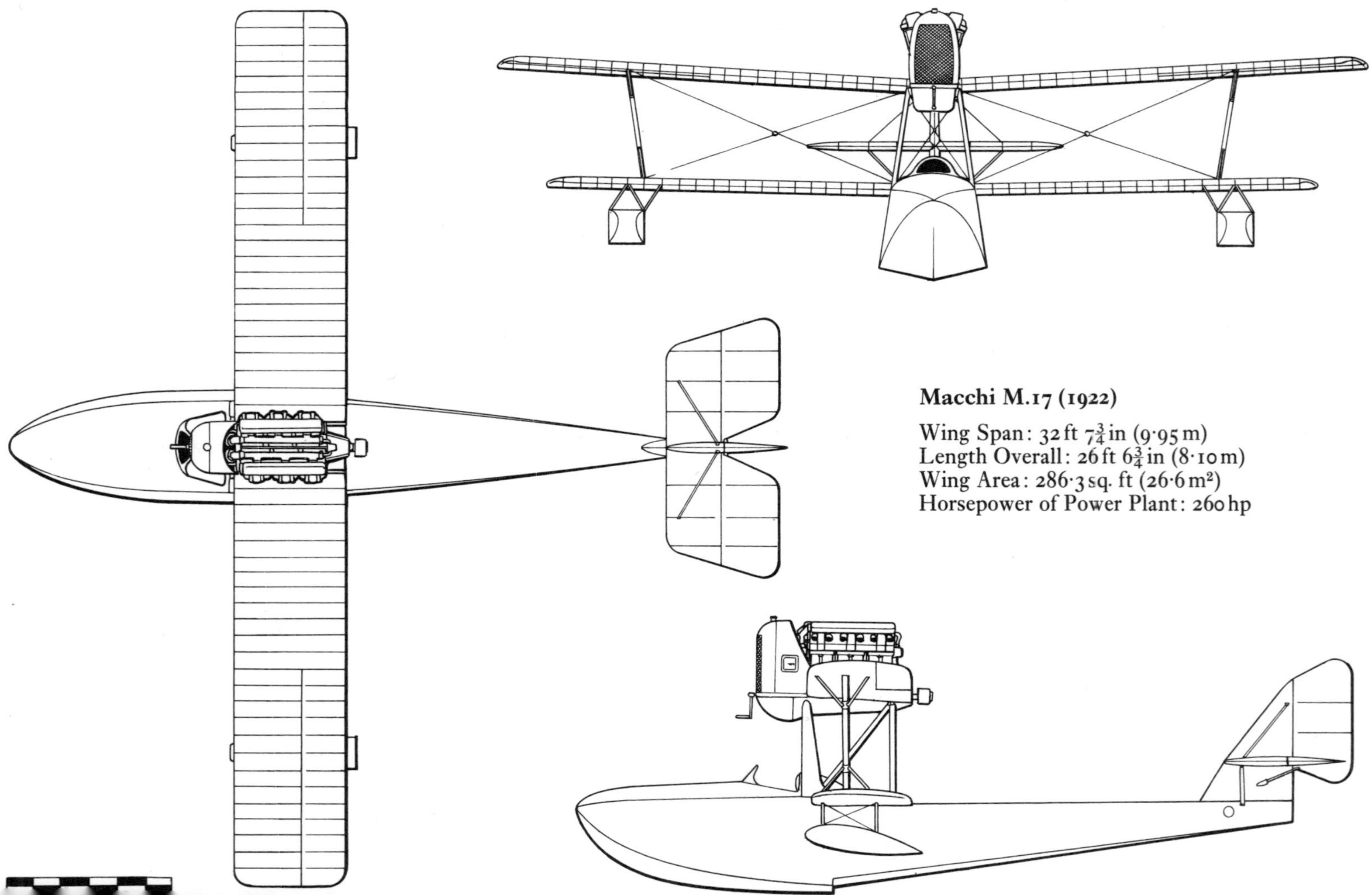

Macchi M.17 (1922)

Wing Span: 32 ft $7\frac{3}{4}$ in (9·95 m)
Length Overall: 26 ft $6\frac{3}{4}$ in (8·10 m)
Wing Area: 286·3 sq. ft (26·6 m^2)
Horsepower of Power Plant: 260 hp

6

Interlude at Cowes

1923

With Britain due to stage the 1923 Schneider Trophy Contest, as a result of Biard's win at Naples, it was inevitable that some people would retain memories of the fog-bound course and brain-fogged Committee of the Royal Aero Club which, together, had caused so much bitter argument during and after the 1919 contest.

Perhaps with a view to ensuring, so far as possible, flight conditions rather better than those often inseparable with Britain's south coast in late summer, the Editor of *Flight* made an early proposal that it might be well worth considering a triangular course of more international form. He suggested a cross-Channel race with, say, two turning points off the English and one off the French coast. Safety for the competitors could be ensured by British and French naval vessels policing the route. But however desirable from a pilot's or aircraft-proving point of view, such a course would have provided little for shore-bound spectators to see.

In the event, when the Royal Aero Club made their preliminary announcement regarding the 1923 contest, they stated that the starting and finishing point would be at Cowes, Isle of Wight where, once again, 'Sammy' Saunders, apparently undeterred by the difficulties experienced during the 1919 event, had offered the excellent facilities of his factory for all competitors. The contest, said the Aero Club, would take place towards the end of August, and entries must be received by 1 March, accompanied by a £10 entrance fee and a 'good intent' deposit of 5,000fr. The rules would be the same basically as those which had applied at Naples, differing only in that water taxying in the navigability test would be at a minimum speed of 12 knots (22·2km/h) and that no repairs, beyond a propeller change, would be allowed during the navigability or water tightness tests. During the speed contest, which would take place on a day to be appointed between 1 July and 15 November, landing for repairs at sea would be permitted. The course would be about 200nm (370·5km), plus or minus 10 per cent, and competitors would be sent off at intervals, their order of despatch being decided by lottery.

It began to appear that the Aero Club's organisation had benefited from the example set by the Italians during the three previous years. This was as well, for early information of three American, six French and three Italian entries, plus an extensive hoped-for home contingent, would require first-class arrangements to cope with as many as twelve aircraft competing in the speed contest.

By the closing date of 1 March no British entries had been received, and with a magnificent gesture of 'impartiality' it was announced that the closing date for British contenders had been extended to 1 August. Even this appeared to stimulate little interest from British manufacturers, and it was not long before the matter was brought to the floor of the House of Commons.

'What,' asked Lieutenant-Colonel Sir F. Hall, 'are the respective inducements offered by the governments of Great Britain, France, Italy and the United States?' In reply, Sir Samuel Hoare stated that America was sending three government-owned aircraft, but that he had no knowledge of what assistance, if any, the French and Italians had offered their competitors. The best his government could do, he stated, was to offer to purchase the winning machine, if British, for £3,000 less engine.

If the House of Commons was satisfied with such a reply, the aviation press could not be appeased so easily. Stanley Spooner devoted an Editorial in *Flight* to argue the urgency of Britain making determined efforts to win the 1923 contest. If we could not afford to field a strong team this year, and the Americans were to take the Trophy back across the Atlantic, what chance would we have of competing the following year when we would have to face the expense of sending a team to the United States? He went on to point out that America intended to send four aircraft and four pilots, ensuring that they arrived in Britain some weeks ahead of the contest date so that they would have every opportunity of becoming acclimatised to conditions. By comparison, the British government's efforts were footling and, for example, the French government considered international prestige of such importance to the commercial prospects of her aviation industry, that they had offered only recently the sum of 100,000fr to any national pilot/aircraft combination that could regain for France the world height and speed records.

This was all to no avail. The chance to compete in home waters might not occur again, but the government could not be moved to step-up their offer in light of the economic situation prevailing. They were, apparently, insufficiently far-sighted to appreciate the benefits to British aviation if a national aircraft could win in 1923, and retain the same initiative in 1924.

In mid-July the Royal Aero Club announced that the course, starting and finishing at Cowes, would have its first turning point at Selsey Bill, then head back towards Cowes along the south coast, with a gentle bank at a marker boat off Southsea pier to put the aircraft on a direct heading for the turning point at Cowes.

There was then still no signs of a British entry, and it came as something of a relief at the eleventh hour when it was learned that there was to be at least one British contender: the same combination of Supermarine, Napier and Biard that had brought the Trophy back to England in 1922.

A little later, apparently with a further slight 'stretch' in favour of British entries, two more contenders were announced and reported as coming from the Blackburn and Hawker companies.

This proved sufficient encouragement to prompt the Royal Aero Club to announce the final details for the contest. The circuit was to consist of five laps of a 37·2nm (68·93km) course, giving a total distance of 186nm (344·6km). It comprised a west–east leg of 18·52nm (34·32km) from Cowes to Selsey, with an east–west return of 10·23nm (18·95km) from Selsey to the marker boat at Southsea, and a final stretch of 8·45nm (15·64km) back to Cowes. The starting line must be crossed on the surface, the finishing line in flight. Repairs at sea would be permitted during the race, but these had to be completed without outside assistance or supplies. Refuelling was allowed only if surplus fuel in portable containers was carried on board the competing aircraft. The turning points would be identified by two marker boats at Cowes, some 900ft (274m) off Victoria pier; a white cross on the ground near to the windmill on Selsey Bill; and a single marker boat anchored off the South Parade pier at Southsea.

All competing aircraft were required to be at S. E. Saunders works by 20 September and erected for inspection by 26 September, at which time the 'good intent' deposit would be refunded. Navigability and water tightness tests would take place on 27 September, the speed test on the following day. The team for each country would take off together, separated by an interval of fifteen minutes, with Italy first and the United States, United Kingdom and France following in that order.

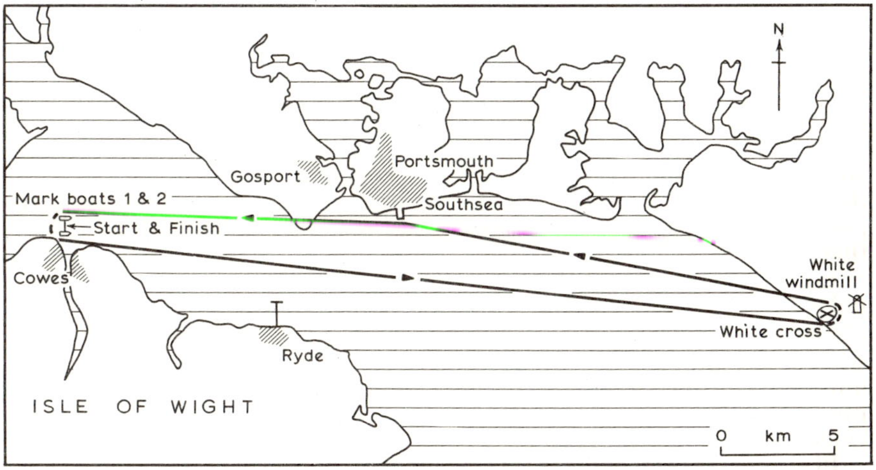

6. Schneider Trophy Contest Course: Cowes 1923

In late August the American contingent arrived at Cowes, and were soon settled in at their base at S. E. Saunders. Little time was lost in erecting their machines and they were quickly in the air, familiarising themselves with the course, water conditions and the regulations, especially those relating to the two tests prior to the speed event. This latter factor was particularly important as it would prove a major disaster to have crossed the Atlantic to compete, and then for any of the machines to be eliminated by failing to comply with a minor regulation.

Great interest was shown in the performance of their aircraft, both on the water and in the air. All were seaplanes, and showed a distinct tendency to porpoise even under good water conditions. With a fair degree of lop on the water they might well prove unmanageable.

Rumour suggested that the Curtiss machines might be capable of 175 mph (282 km/h), but this was regarded as something of an overstatement. True, there was little knowledge in Britain of American landplane racing in recent years, but those who had done their homework knew that the 1921 Pulitzer Trophy Race had gone to a Curtiss machine at 176·7 mph (284·37 km/h) and the 1922 Trophy Race to an improved Curtiss at 205·8 mph (331·37 km/h). It was assumed that the large floats required by the seaplane versions could be counted on to reduce the speeds by anything from 30–40 mph (48–64 km/h) and so, naïve to the last, the British 'experts' concluded that 175 mph was more boast than fact.

The trouble was that those whose knowledge of the Americans had been gained during the first World War were ready to write off all representatives of that nation as braggarts and show-offs. Had they been able to work alongside the US Schneider Trophy team at Cowes they would have needed to make a rapid revision to those opinions, for pilots and mechanics proved to be modest, hard-working and full of good humour.

Nonetheless, their aeroplanes certainly seemed pretty fast in the air and stop-watches could reveal only part of the story. It was unlikely that the American pilots would demonstrate their maximum speeds during practice. Unless Britain's designers had something fairly remarkable up their respective sleeves, the best ally might well prove to be the weather.

In fact, Britain's three entries held but a single aircraft of completely unknown capability, a product of Blackburn Aircraft at Brough, Yorkshire. Like most of Britain's manufacturers, Robert Blackburn was aware that success in what was fast becoming a prestigious competition could generate much-needed sales, quite apart from the more altruistic hope that it might prove possible to keep the trophy in England. Unfortunately, not all could afford to field a specially-built aircraft.

Blackburn's first association with waterborne aircraft had come with design and construction of the Type L seaplane, to compete in the 1914 Circuit of Britain seaplane race sponsored by the *Daily Mail*. The outbreak of war had prevented the race from taking place and all the contending aircraft were commandeered by the Admiralty. The Type L had been followed by the TB (Twin Blackburn) and the Blackburn GP, a general-purpose anti-submarine patrol bomber, prior to design of the company's first flying-boat, the N.1B. The beautifully proportioned hull of this latter machine was of Linton-Hope construction, and it had been intended that the wings should be of sesquiplane configuration and power provided by a single 200 hp Hispano-Suiza engine. But in November 1918, when contracts for the N.1B were cancelled, the company had completed only the hull of a single machine (N56), and this had been put into storage for some future occasion.

Robert Blackburn's private venture to contend the 1923 Schneider contest involved the N56 hull, and work went ahead to design suitable wings and tail unit, plus the installation of a 450 hp Napier Lion engine. As it began to take shape at Brough its clean appearance suggested a formidable contender. The single-bay wings were of unequal span and mounted directly on top of the hull, their narrow gap separated by streamlined V-shape interplane struts. N-shape centre-section struts supported the engine, which was mounted on top of the upper wing centre-section. A well-streamlined nacelle housed the Lion, which had a large two-blade wooden tractor propeller with spinner. To eliminate the parasite drag of a conventional radiator, flush-fitting surface radiators were mounted on the under surface of the upper wing. Span of the upper wing was 34 ft 0 in (10·36 m), lower wing 29 ft 6 in (8·99 m), length overall 28 ft 7 in (8·71 m) and height overall 10 ft 8 in (3·25 m). Maximum take-off weight was 2,800 lb (1,270 kg), and it was estimated that the maximum level speed would be around 160 mph (257 km/h).

Allocated the civil registration G-EBHF, and named the Pellet, it was not until early September that the machine was ready for the company's test pilot, Lieutenant-Commander R. W. Kenworthy, to settle himself in the cockpit when the little 'boat was launched for the first time on the muddy waters of the River Humber. Those who have experienced the vagaries of the ferry that shuttles from New Holland to Kingston upon Hull will be aware of the devilish tide race that can develop with varying conditions of wind and tide. It was one of those days, and before Reg Kenworthy could do anything about it the tide had taken charge: the starboard balancer float was sucked down into the silt-laden water, followed by the lower wing tip. Slowly, but inexorably, the whole machine turned turtle and sank, while Kenworthy made a hasty exit.

Determined that the Pellet should compete at Cowes, Robert Blackburn wasted no time in salvaging the aircraft, which was taken back into the works and stripped. Obviously the buoyancy of the balancer floats was suspect, so while Napiers busied themselves with a rapid overhaul of the waterlogged engine, larger floats were fitted. It was not until 23 September that the Pellet was once again in airworthy condition, but with the need

The unfortunate Blackburn Pellet being man-handled on land . . .

. . . and taking off with Reg Kenworthy at the controls

for it to be available for inspection at Cowes only three days later there was no time left for an air test. It was crated hurriedly and consigned by rail to Southampton.

Ill-fortune had also befallen another of Britain's team of three, the Sopwith/Hawker Rainbow (G-EAKI). We have already made acquaintance with this aircraft, the Sopwith Schneider of 1919. Acquired and re-built by Hawkers in landplane form and re-named, it had competed in the 1923 Aerial Derby and in which, piloted by Flight-Lieutenant W. H. Longton, it had come second to the Gloster I at a speed of 164·02 mph (264 km/h). Hawkers had endeavoured to clean up the airframe of the Rainbow and it was hoped that despite a reversion to seaplane configuration for the contest it might show a sufficient turn of speed.

It was not to be. Following some adjustments to the Rainbow, Walter Longton took off from Brooklands on a test flight. In the area of Burgh Hill golf course the engine decided to call it a day, giving up the ghost so rapidly that the spinner was catapulted from its mounting.

Unfortunately, there wasn't a clear area within gliding distance. Immediately below was a dense wood, leaving only the golf course within range, and it was liberally strewn with poplars. Longton decided quickly that the latter offered the most hospitable haven, and calling on every scrap of flying skill at his command began to bank and slide between frightening-looking trees. With a sigh of relief he scraped through, only to find that with nowhere left to go but down, a solid-looking and unavoidable tree stump was directly ahead. In a last desperate attempt to scrape over it he almost pulled the stick from its sockets, but the Rainbow had had enough and stalled in.

The landing gear hit the tree stump, which proved to be the classic immovable object, whipping the machine over on to its back. Seconds later a somewhat bedraggled pilot made his exit through the side of the fuselage, miraculously unhurt, as an irate golfer came bursting through the trees to discover that rather more than a handicap was in shreds.

The third of the British entrants was the Sea Lion which had secured the Trophy at Naples. Since that time it had been acquired by the Air Ministry, but was loaned to Supermarine for participation in the contest for, no matter how enthusiastic, that company could not afford to develop a more worthy contender at its own expense. Knowing that they would have little chance of beating the Italians unless the performance of the Sea Lion in 1922 could be improved, Mitchell had done his utmost to squeeze the very last mile per hour from what was obviously an outdated machine.

His work consisted mainly of reducing drag to a minimum. The nose of the hull was modified, fairing pieces added behind the steps, and new balancer floats of much-reduced head-on profile were mounted beneath new wings of improved design. Napiers had worked on the Lion, con-

Henri Biard at Cowes with the Supermarine Sea Lion III; although completing the course it was completely outclassed by the American CR-3s

R. J. Mitchell in close attendance as the engine of the Supermarine S.4 is tested

juring from it an extra 100 hp, and Mitchell had improved the streamlining of its cowling, reducing to the smallest acceptable size the entry to the frontal radiator. In this form the Supermarine 'boat was redesignated Sea Lion III, and carried the registration G-EBAH.

As regards the Italian aircraft industry, they considered it imperative that they should win the Trophy at Cowes and make it their permanent property. Like the British, they were anxious to ensure that it should not cross the Atlantic, for the single factor of distance might prove sufficient to prevent them from competing again. As it was, there was no help to be had from their government, bedevilled by economic and political problems. For the 1923 contest it seemed that their sole hopes must rely upon the Savoia company and the S.51 which had made such a good showing in the previous December.

But Savoia's Ing Marchetti, having kept himself informed of the progress made by American landplane racing aircraft, was reasonably certain that his company would be throwing money away unless quite a few more miles per hour could be got from the S.51. There was no scope for aerodynamic improvement of the airframe: increased speed must come from a more powerful engine. With no suitable power plant available, Savoia had to withdraw. There was to be no Italian challenge.

France, still very conscious of the fact that their nationally-inspired Trophy had been won by them only on the occasion of the first contest, in 1914, were determined to see it housed at the headquarters of the Aéro-Club de France after this year's contest. Every possible aid was given to field a strong team of flying-boats, comprising initially two C.A.M.S., two Lathams and one Blanchard.

Pride of Santoni's factory was the C.A.M.S. 38, to be flown by Maurice Hurel, a development of the C.A.M.S. 36 with much improved hull, biplane wings of slightly reduced area, modified tail unit, and powered by a 360 hp Hispano-Suiza engine driving a two-blade pusher propeller. Retaining the same overall dimensions as the C.A.M.S. 36, wing area was reduced to 202 sq. ft (18·77 m^2), increasing maximum wing loading to 13·6 lb/sq. ft (66·4 km/m^2).

The C.A.M.S. 36, to be flown by Pelletier d'Oisy, was basically the same as that entered for the 1922 contest, but the 300 hp Hispano-Suiza engine and tractor propeller had been replaced by a 360 hp version of the same engine. In this form it was re-designated C.A.M.S. 36*bis*.

The two Latham flying-boats, built by the company of that name whose factory was at Caudebec-en-Caux, were known as Twin Tandem Lathams. This name derived from the two 400 hp Lorraine-Dietrich 12-cylinder in-line liquid-cooled engines mounted in tandem between the biplane wings, but the correct company designation was Latham L.1. The broad-beam hull had three steps and the lower wing was mounted directly on the hull. Single-bay biplane wings had an I-shape interplane strut, plus flying and landing wires each side, and the balancer floats were mounted directly beneath the lower wing without struts or bracing. The tail unit was conventional but well upswept, and the tailplane braced by a hefty strut on each side. To carry the weight of the twin-engine installation there was a motley collection of large struts from hull to nacelles and from nacelles to the upper wing centre-section.

Seaworthiness rather than speed would appear to be the main qualities of the Lathams and, in fact, their entry was based on the belief that they would make a good showing in heavy sea conditions.

Last, and most massive of the French entries, was the Blanchard C.1, to be flown by Captain Teste. The Blanchard company had been founded in January 1923, so there was little enough time for them to produce an aircraft to contend in a contest that year, despite which they set about the formidable task of preparing their flying-boat. M. Blanchard had previously designed aircraft for the French companies of Georges Levy and the Farman Brothers, so he was no newcomer to the industry.

His C.1 was of parasol-wing monoplane configuration, massive N-shape centre-section struts being necessary to support the engine which, in a streamline nacelle, was an integral part of the wing centre-section structure. From mid-span two wide-chord streamline struts braced the wing to the hull. The tail unit was also unusual, with two fins. One of these was a dorsal fin, faired from the hull, and the tailplane, braced with five struts, was mounted at its top. Above the tailplane a second fin extended from the tailplane leading-edge back to a large-area rudder. With no lower wing from which to hang balancer floats, these were carried on struts mounted on each side of the hull.

Power plant comprised a 400 hp Bristol Jupiter, built in France under a licence acquired by the Gnome-Rhone company in 1922. It drove a two-blade tractor propeller, but the large frontal area of the radial engine configuration, plus the robust construction of the airframe, suggested that the C.1 would not prove very fast. Wing span was 40 ft (12·19 m), length overall 31 ft 10 in (9·70 m), height overall 9 ft 10 in (3·00 m) and maximum take-off weight 2,816 lb (1,277 kg).

When tested its maximum level speed was found to be about 150 mph (241 km/h) which, clearly, was nowhere near fast enough, and it was withdrawn. A second machine was under construction and it was decided to hasten its completion and install a more powerful Jupiter engine. This had the misfortune to crash during flight testing, so Blanchards were out of the contest.

It had been intended that the four remaining French entries should be shipped to Cowes aboard two French naval vessels. When the time came only one, the *Verdun*, was available and this took on board the two crated C.A.M.S. machines as deck cargo. The two Latham L.1s were flown over by Benoist and Duhamel on 25 September, in appalling weather conditions.

The engine of Benoist's mount decided to play up as they were almost at their destination and, unable to make headway against a full gale, he turned north to find shelter on England's south coast. With engine power failing rapidly, he was compelled to make a landing in shallow water, where a combination of wave damage and enthusiastic rescuers proved sufficient to eliminate him from the race.

On 26 September, the day before the navigability and water tightness tests, Blackburn's new machine on which many British hopes were centred took the water for her first test since being stripped and provided with new balancer floats at Brough. This took place at Hamble, in Southampton Water, where the Pellet had been erected at Fairey's works.

It did not take Kenworthy long to get her into the air, but it was clear to him at once that the machine was far from ready to compete in the Schneider, or any other, contest. In the first place the Pellet was so nose-heavy that it required almost all his strength to keep her level, and by the time he had crossed Southampton Water, heading towards Cowes, the cooling system of the engine had reached boiling point. There was nothing for it but to land without delay, and in short time he was down safely on the water. Eventually, the Pellet was taken in tow by a Saunders motor boat and, on arrival at Cowes, was hurried to the sheds so that work could start on getting the machine ready to compete in the tests on the following day.

Correction of the aircraft's trim presented no insuperable problem, but so far as the overheating was concerned it was reasonably certain that the area of the surface radiators on the upper wing was inadequate. The only solution possible within the time available was to by-pass this, and Saunders' men worked throughout the night to install a large Lamblin radiator amid the centre-section struts beneath the nacelle. At the same time, the two-blade wooden propeller was removed and replaced by a Leitner-Watts metal propeller.

No Italians, two French and one British machine eliminated. How were the Americans fairing?

Rather better, in fact, for the entire set-up was virtually a military operation. All four pilots were from the US Navy, commanded by Lieutenant Frank Wead, the other three being Lieutenants A. W. Gorton, R. Irvine and D. Rittenhouse. Their aircraft comprised two Curtiss CR-3 racing seaplanes, a Navy/Wright NW-2 seaplane and, for practice, a Naval Aircraft Factory TR-3A.

Most formidable of these, potentially, was the NW-2 of which two landplane versions had been built by the Wright Aeronautical Corporation to contend in the 1923 Pulitzer Trophy Race, plus a seaplane version for the Schneider Trophy Contest.

All three were of biplane configuration, having wings of cellular structure with ailerons, plywood covering and surface radiators on both. N-shape centre-section struts and N-struts from fuselage to about one-third span, plus I-shape interplane struts, landing and flying wires, made for a robust structure. Fuselage and tail unit were of welded steel-tube construction, with sheet aluminium skin from nose to forward of the pilot's cockpit. The remainder of the fuselage and tail unit were fabric covered, and light-weight wood stringers in the aft fuselage maintained the fabric in a good streamline form. The two long V-bottom floats, of the type developed and favoured by the US Navy, were strut-braced to wings and centre-section of the lower wing.

Power plant of the NW-2 was a 650–700hp Wright T-3 Tornado 12-cylinder in-line liquid-cooled engine which, at that particular time, made the NW-2 the highest-powered single-engine seaplane in the world. This drove a three-blade tractor propeller, the blades of which were of forged duralumin, each locked to the forged steel hub by a screw and wedge device. Although NW-2 was not quite so clean in appearance as the Curtiss CR-3s, there was little doubt that the extra horsepower available must make it strong favourite.

The CR-3s were superb-looking machines by any standard. Known originally as Curtiss Navy Racers, one (A6081) won the Pulitzer Trophy Race at an average speed of 176·7mph (284·37km/h) and on 3 November 1921 had established a world speed record of 197·8mph (318·32km/h). By the time they were entered in the 1922 Pulitzer race, A6080 had become designated CR-1 and A6081 CR-2. The former still had Lamblin radiators, but A6081 had acquired new wings and surface radiators. Both had Curtiss CD-12 direct-drive engines, vertical tail surfaces of increased area and minor improvements. This time they came 4th and 3rd respectively, at 187mph (300·95km/h) and 193mph (310·60km/h).

To help offset the drag of the large floats needed for the 1923 Schneider contest, CR-1 acquired surface radiators, and both aircraft had increased vertical tail surfaces. Improved Curtiss engines were installed, in which the cylinder bores had been increased by $\frac{1}{8}$in (0·32cm) and compression ratio pushed up from 5·3 to 5·8, enabling them to demonstrate an output on test of 507bhp at 2,300rpm. In this new form, both aircraft were re-designated CR-3.

Of particular significance was the Curtiss D-12 engine/Curtiss-Reed propeller combination. *Jane's All the World's Aircraft* of the period was quick to appreciate that the engine was something bordering on the revolutionary. Designed by Arthur Nutt, it was the world's first wet-sleeve monobloc aero-engine, the carbon steel sleeves being externally threaded at their closed end and screwed into the monobloc. Valve ports were machined out at a subsequent stage of manufacture. *Jane's* concluded their brief description of the engine by commenting that it 'is notable for its extremely compact arrangement and clean outline. It is of abnormally small frontal area, and could be built into a fuselage of a cross-section too small to contain a normal pilot.' Perhaps the compiler might have chosen the words average size in place of 'normal'.

Sadly, the significance of the propeller had escaped the writer of the above comment, for it was dismissed somewhat off-handedly as 'merely a sheet of metal twisted to suitable shape'.

The point is that steadily increasing engine power output meant that larger-diameter propellers were being employed to give greater tractive effort. But with this increase in diameter blade tip speeds began to approach the speed of sound, which brought a considerable loss in blade efficiency, for it must be appreciated that about one-third of each blade—at the hub end—produced no tractive effort whatsoever. It had been discovered that forged duralumin blades of thin aerofoil section suffered less loss of efficiency at speeds approaching those of sound, and that by reducing their diameter they could turn even faster, developing comparable or better tractive effort than that of a larger diameter, slower-turning, heavy wooden propeller. It can be seen that by use of the Curtiss-Reed propeller it was possible to eliminate an engine reduction-gear; a reduced-diameter propeller allowed a reduction in landing gear height and, of course, the smaller-diameter thin-section blades were lighter in weight. All represented very significant weight savings.

There was a third important component of the CR-3s power plant system, namely the efficient surface radiators which had been developed. Quite deeply ribbed to offer a maximum heat transfer surface, they were nevertheless sufficiently malleable to be formed to the wing section and consequently caused no appreciable drop in the aerodynamic efficiency of the aerofoil section. They created no parasite drag, whereas conventional radiators mounted in the slipstream had been shown to create sufficient drag to absorb as much as ten per cent of available engine power.

First man in Britain to appreciate the full implications of this power plant in its entirety was Richard Fairey, and he lost little time in acquiring an engine and propeller, plus licence rights to import and/or build the engine in Britain. Around this power plant he evolved a day-bomber of clean aerodynamic form and of such outstanding performance that, when demonstrated to Air Chief Marshal Sir Hugh Trenchard in 1925, an order for a complete squadron of the aircraft was forthcoming immediately.

A total of 28 of these aircraft, named the Fairey Fox, were built for the Royal Air Force, and all were used by No. 12 Squadron. When introduced into service they proved approximately 50 mph (80 km/h) faster than their predecessor, the Fairey Fawn. This does not sound a very exciting increase in this day of Mach speeds, but it becomes more significant if you understand that it represented almost a 50 per cent jump over the Fawn, and that 12 Squadron's Foxes were able to outpace any contemporary fighter. So agile and fast was this aircraft that, in the period 1926–31, they were able to penetrate mock-battle defences with embarrassing ease. As a result the Squadron's badge, approved by King George VI in 1937, bears a fox's mask and the motto 'Leads the Field'. Not all of the Fairey Foxes were powered by Curtiss engines throughout their service career, for some were later re-engined with Rolls-Royce Kestrels.

I make no apology for this digression because it is particularly important. Here we see the first real sign of Schneider Trophy contestants having a significant influence on the development of military aircraft.

So far as the CR-3 airframes were concerned they gave the impression that, if deprived of their massive floats and related struts and bracing, they represented the ultimate in biplane development. Single-bay biplanes, they had N-shape interplane struts, two centre-section struts, plus landing and flying wires. A neat wire-braced tail unit blended smoothly to the sleek fuselage contours and, of course, the Curtiss D-12 ensured that these elegant lines were maintained from fore to aft. So small was the fuselage in fact that there was no room for adequate fuel storage and, in consequence, the fuselage tank was supplemented by an 8 US gallon (30·27 litre) auxiliary fuel tank in each float.

A reporter was to mention these float tanks in illustrating the efficiency of the American team. He told how after the tanks had been filled, hand holes in the upper surface of the float were covered with doped fabric patches and that, when they had dried, a second coat of finishing dope was applied and polished to the same high standard as the aircraft's general finish.

Wing span of the CR-3s was 22 ft 8 in (6·91 m), length overall 25 ft 0 in (7·62 m), height overall 10 ft 9 in (3·28 m), wing chord 4 ft 0 in (1·22 m) and wing area 168 sq. ft (15·61 m^2). Maximum take off weight was 2,747 lb (1,246 kg).

Last of the American aircraft types to round off the 1923 Schneider team was the Naval Aircraft Factory TR-3. Intended to be used also as the reserve in case of dire disaster, it warrants a brief description if for no other reason than that it was the first US carrier-based biplane fighter specifically designed for that purpose.

In the US Navy it served in both wheeled and floatplane form, under the designation TS-1, 32 of them being built (28 by Curtiss). Two TS-2s with 240 hp Aeromarine engines and two TS-3s with 180 hp Wright-Hispano Type E engines followed. The second TS-3 (A6449) was first modified to compete in the 1922 Curtiss Marine Trophy race, and finally was modified extensively to provide a high-speed trainer for the 1923 Schneider team. A far from handsome biplane in original form, with 200 hp Wright or Lawrence radial engine, it looked completely different in the TR-3A configuration with thin-section wings, reduced interplane strutting, and surface radiators on the upper wing to cool the 265 hp Wright in-line liquid-cooled engine, driving a two-blade tractor propeller.

All of the American aircraft had proved particularly trouble free in practice. Two factors caused them a little concern: firstly that heavy seas might make their machines difficult to handle; second, that 'Jake' Gorton, pilot of the NW-2, felt that his machine had a greater speed potential than it was showing in practice. After an exchange of messages with the engine builders, it was decided to fine-off the pitch of the propeller to allow the engine to develop maximum rpm.

With this change made, comparatively simple in view of the screw and wedge method of securing the propeller blades, Gorton took NW-2 out on flight test. Benefiting from the finer pitch setting and maximum engine rpm, the seaplane rocketed off the surface, and it was immediately apparent to Gorton that he had found the answer to the sluggish performance of the NW-2. As he banked at Selsey he knew that his speed should prove sufficient to win the race, and as he dived the aircraft towards Southsea his ASI showed a speed approaching 220 mph (354 km/h).

His elation was short lived. With a sudden explosion of sound bits of engine came hurtling past his head and almost before he could take breath NW-2 hit the water, catapulting him clear of the cockpit at something like 200 mph (322 km/h). Unbelievably he was quite uninjured and rescued quickly, but it was believed generally that the method of fixing the propeller blades was suspect and that this, rather than engine failure, was responsible for the accident.

Such was the situation on 27 September when, in ideal weather conditions, the aircraft assembled for the navigability and water tightness tests. Only the Pellet was missing, still in the Saunders sheds where it was almost invisible beneath a host of willing helpers, all doing their utmost to get what was believed to be Britain's best hope into the competition. It was touch and go, and there were only minutes to spare before closing time for the navigability test when Kenworthy was able to clamber aboard and taxi away from the Saunder's slipway, positioning himself in the River Medina for take-off.

The moment had come. With the engine giving a hearty roar the little machine began to gather speed. Ahead, dangerously close to his track, was a rowing boat and Kenworthy applied a little rudder to steer him clear. Immediately, the Pellet began to porpoise violently, its hull hitting the water with resounding thumps. It was obviously becoming a case of shut down or get up and Kenworthy, presumably utterly frustrated by all that had gone before, must have decided to adopt the latter course. The Pellet became airborne in a semi-stalled condition and, pushed to starboard by propeller torque, the wingtip touched the surface and the aircraft heeled over and went beneath the surface like a stone.

Poor Kenworthy's troubles were far from over, for he found himself unable to free himself from the cockpit. A sixty-one second nightmare elapsed before, finally, his head bobbed clear of the surface. The near-disaster ended happily with his speedy rescue, but Britain's hopes now rested solely on the Sea Lion III.

C. G. Grey's was the most telling, and surely the most humorous comment on this sad event: 'This was Mr Kenworthy's second bath in the "Pellet", which after its double diving demonstration may as well be known in the future as the "Plummet".'

The Pellet was the only aircraft to fail out of those which took part in the navigability test, so with two American, three French and one British machine to enter, and survive, the water tightness test, the speed contest promised an exciting spectacle. Not surprisingly, potential spectators hoped for good weather on the following day and, for once, their prayers were answered. Sun, blue sky and calm water greeted the morning of 28 September, with pilots and mechanics busying themselves to ensure that their aircraft were ready for the fray.

Long before race time thousands of spectators lined every vantage point on both shore lines, revelling in the warmth of the late September sun and quite unconcerned that the conditions favoured the Americans. Predominantly British, they were there to enjoy the spectacle. If the race went to an English pilot, jolly good show. But if it was an American or Frenchman who took it, their traditional attitude of sportsmanship was such that their pride would suffer no hurt.

A few minutes before the appointed starting time of 11 a.m., Rutledge Irvine and David Rittenhouse in the CR-3s taxied out and positioned themselves to await the starter's signal. With a minute to go they started moving slowly towards the line which, with practiced assurance, they reached within seconds of the smoke and cone signals for which everyone had been waiting.

Gaining speed, but holding their machines down so that they crossed the line on the surface, they were soon into the air and making opposing 180° turns to set them back on course to Selsey. This had been necessary as the wind, which had increased somewhat during the morning, was blowing almost due west.

The Americans roared away, soon mere specks in the distance, and at Selsey, Rittenhouse was seen to be slightly in the lead. Turning widely, he levelled out, heading towards Southsea, with Irvine close behind.

Meanwhile, Biard had positioned the Sea Lion III for take-off. As he was about to begin his run he was staggered to see the two American machines flash by overhead. A lap in around fifteen minutes suggested a speed well beyond the capability of his craft, but determined to do his best he pushed the throttle wide open, anxious to get into the air as quickly as possible.

This was almost his undoing, for the flying-boat bounced along the surface so violently that, as he crossed the starting line, official observers insisted that he was airborne and therefore disqualified. The Royal Aero Club Committee once again found itself embroiled in noisy verbal conflict: those who opposed the disqualification insisted that the Sea Lion had been lifted into the air by a wave, and had made several more bounces subsequently before becoming airborne.

The argument as to the definition of being airborne, so far as a seaplane or flying-boat was concerned, was to rage for long after the contest. Fortunately, the Royal Aero Club Committee reversed their decision after only brief argument: Biard was back in the race but he, of course, was unaware that he had ever been out of it.

Meanwhile, with the approach of 11.30 a.m., the French contestants were manoeuvring into position. They had already been reduced to two, for as the surviving Latham L.1 was being started one engine backfired, shearing a magneto drive and effectively eliminating it from the contest. So far as France was concerned, everything now depended on the two C.A.M.S. machines. No, one; for d'Oisy in the 36*bis* managed to contest the right of way with a steam yacht. It, being of considerably more robust construction, survived the impact with only a scrape on its gleaming paintwork. The flying-boat had a damaged hull and was out of the race.

Maurice Hurel in the C.A.M.S. 38 was soon off the water, but the Hispano-Suiza was not running smoothly and developing far below its normal rpm. A first lap of nearly twenty minutes showed that his chance of a place was very slender, and even this was ruled out completely during the second lap. Approaching Selsey, the engine's power fell to a point where there was no alternative but to make a forced landing. This Hurel accomplished safely, but no doubt he was suffering the extremes of frustration for, as a general rule, the Hispano-Suiza was a most reliable engine.

Long-range observers with telescopes or binoculars confirmed that Hurel was down on the sea; at a secondhand level of communication he was down *in* the sea, and with a steady progression—or should it be retrogression—of reports, there was general belief that the machine had disintegrated, its pilot no more.

So far as the result of the race was concerned this might just as well have been so. Only three aircraft were left racing around the circuit, the roar of the fast-revving Curtiss engines adding to the atmosphere of excitement. But to even the most ignorant spectator it was clear that, barring accidents, the result was a foregone conclusion. The Schneider Trophy would soon be en route to America.

Optimistically, if unrealistically, intending to provide its readers with a rapid means of calculating lap speeds, *Flight* featured in its current issue a specially-prepared graph. By checking the lap time of a machine, reference to the graph would show its speed in miles per hour. Unfortunately, the Americans were displaying no spirit of co-operation, for with the exception of the first lap all of their times were completely off the graph.

Its upper limit had been set at 170 mph (274 km/h), but when Rittenhouse brought his CR-3 triumphantly over the finishing line, he had taken first place at an average speed of 177·38 mph (285·47 km/h). Close behind came

Irvine, with an average speed of 173·46 mph (279·16 km/h). Despite Biard's skill as a pilot, the Sea Lion was completely outclassed, gaining third place at 157·17 mph (252·94 km/h).

Clearly, the British 'experts' had failed completely to appreciate the progress made by America's aviation industry. Would it be possible to develop a racing seaplane fast enough—and soon enough—to bring the Trophy back to Britain? Or was it already too late; would it now rest forever far across the Atlantic?

Such questions were then unanswerable, but unless adequate finance was forthcoming to enable manufacturers to build more advanced high-speed seaplanes there seemed every chance that Jacques Schneider's Trophy had crossed the Atlantic for the last time. It was reasonably certain that the Americans would not allow the grass to grow beneath their feet before the next contest.

C. G. Grey closed his report on the 1923 contest in the following words: '. . . there was a certain amount of emotion to be got from seeing the lean grey form of the Curtiss racer come sliding down to the finishing line at something very close to 200 mph—the fastest seaplane in the world by quite a tidy margin.'

This was the problem facing would-be competitors for the 1924 event.

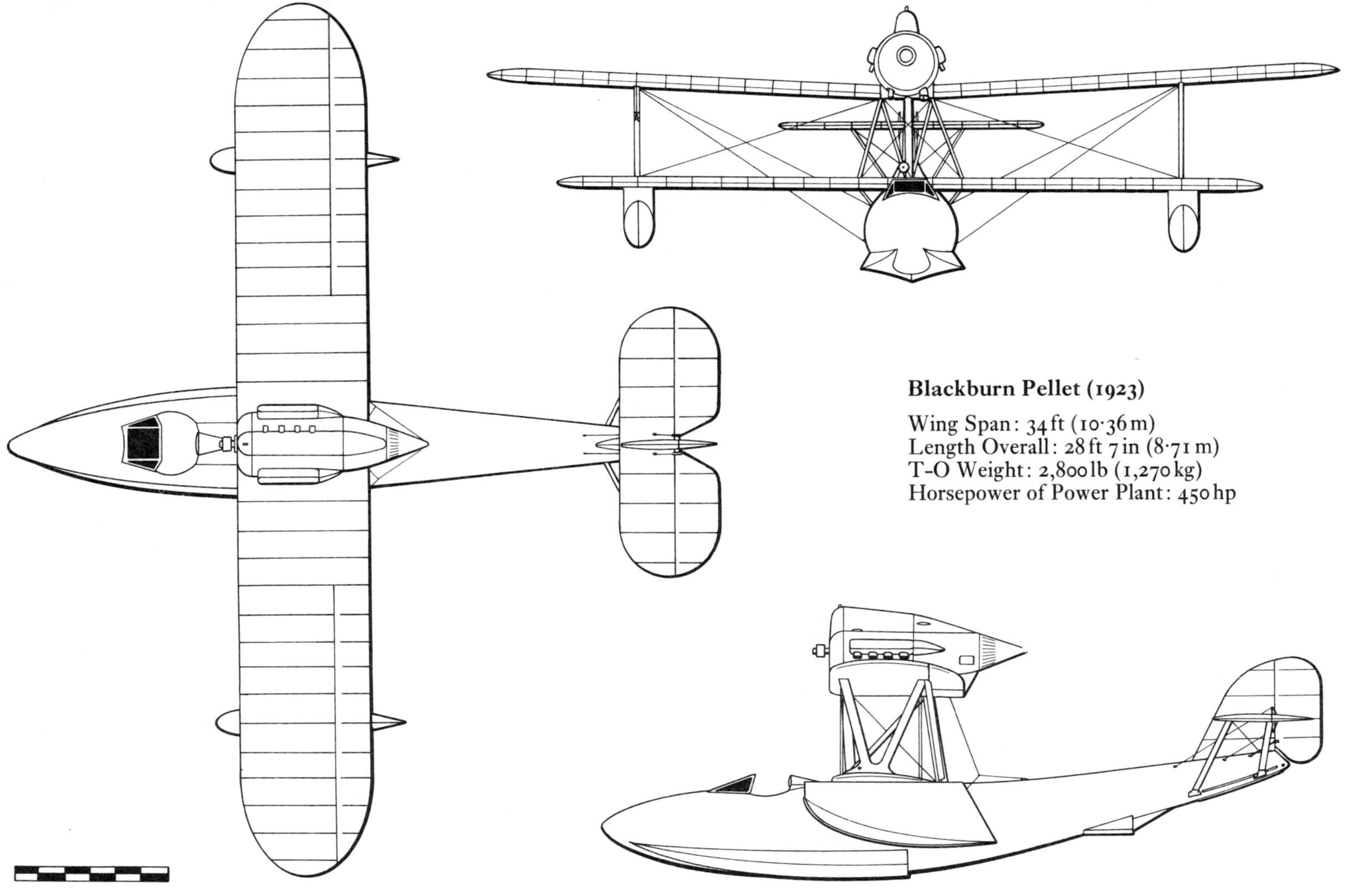

Blackburn Pellet (1923)

Wing Span: 34 ft (10·36 m)
Length Overall: 28 ft 7 in (8·71 m)
T-O Weight: 2,800 lb (1,270 kg)
Horsepower of Power Plant: 450 hp

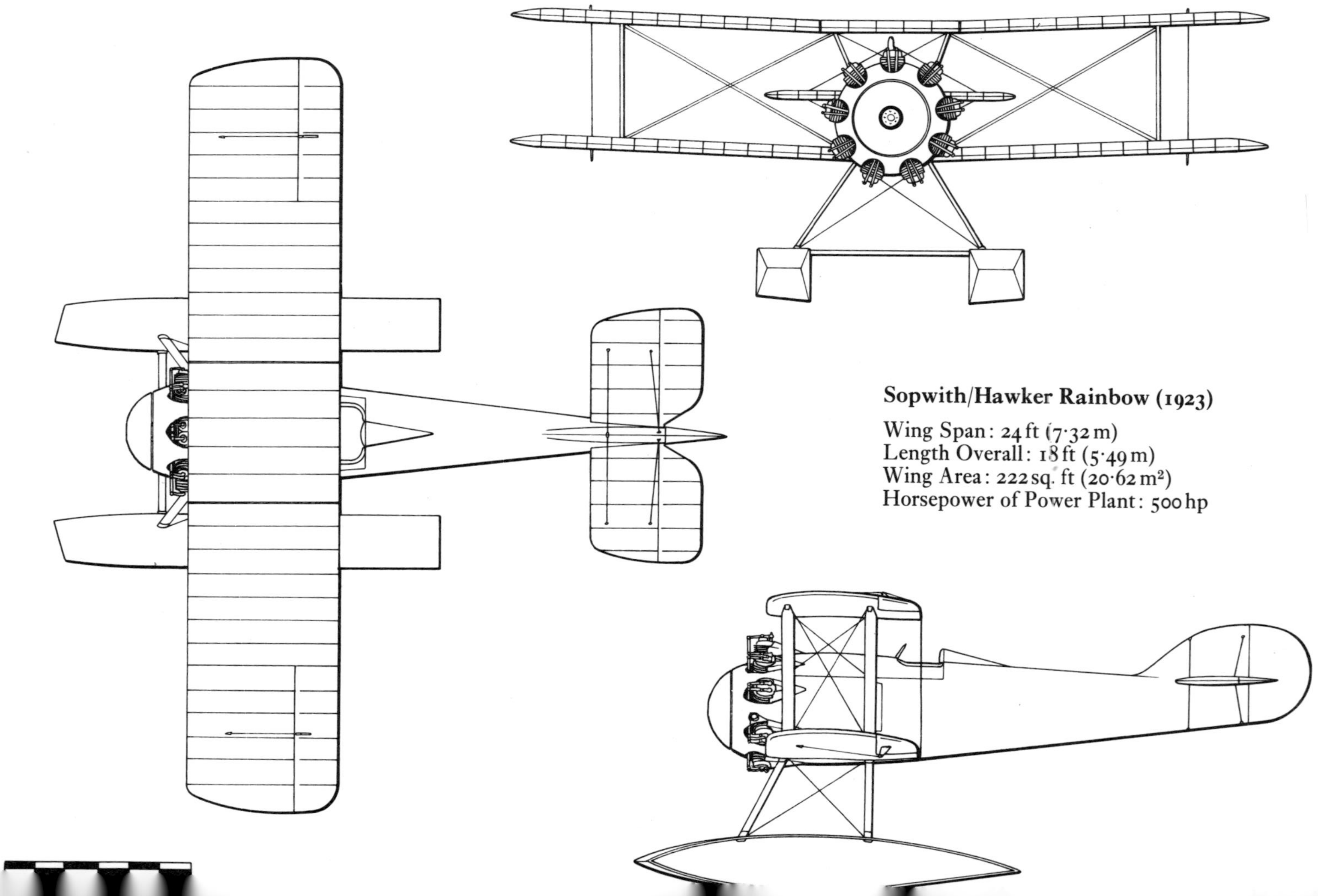

Sopwith/Hawker Rainbow (1923)

Wing Span: 24 ft (7·32 m)
Length Overall: 18 ft (5·49 m)
Wing Area: 222 sq. ft ($20{\cdot}62\ m^2$)
Horsepower of Power Plant: 500 hp

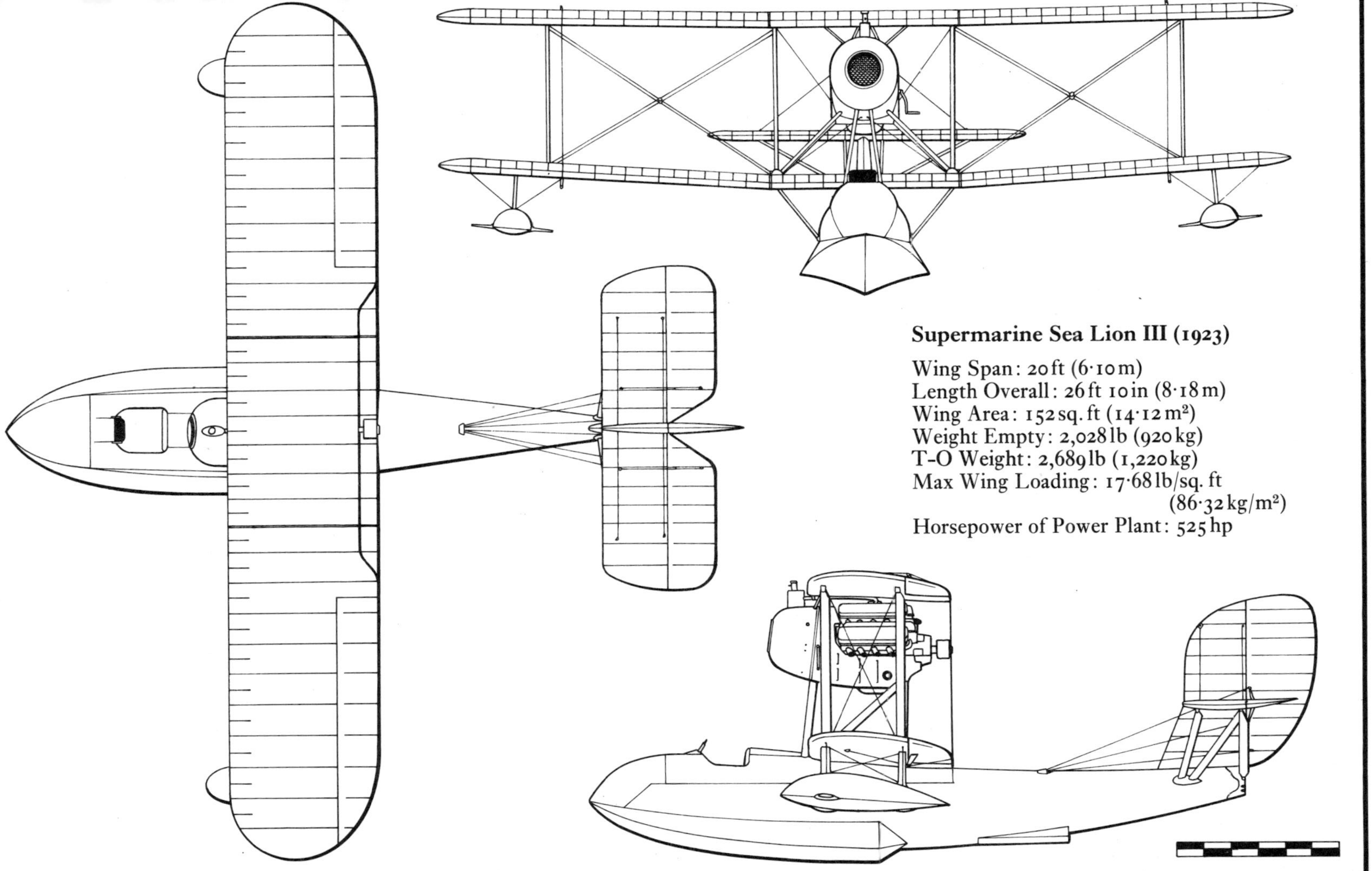

Supermarine Sea Lion III (1923)

Wing Span: 20 ft (6·10 m)
Length Overall: 26 ft 10 in (8·18 m)
Wing Area: 152 sq. ft (14·12 m^2)
Weight Empty: 2,028 lb (920 kg)
T-O Weight: 2,689 lb (1,220 kg)
Max Wing Loading: 17·68 lb/sq. ft (86·32 kg/m^2)
Horsepower of Power Plant: 525 hp

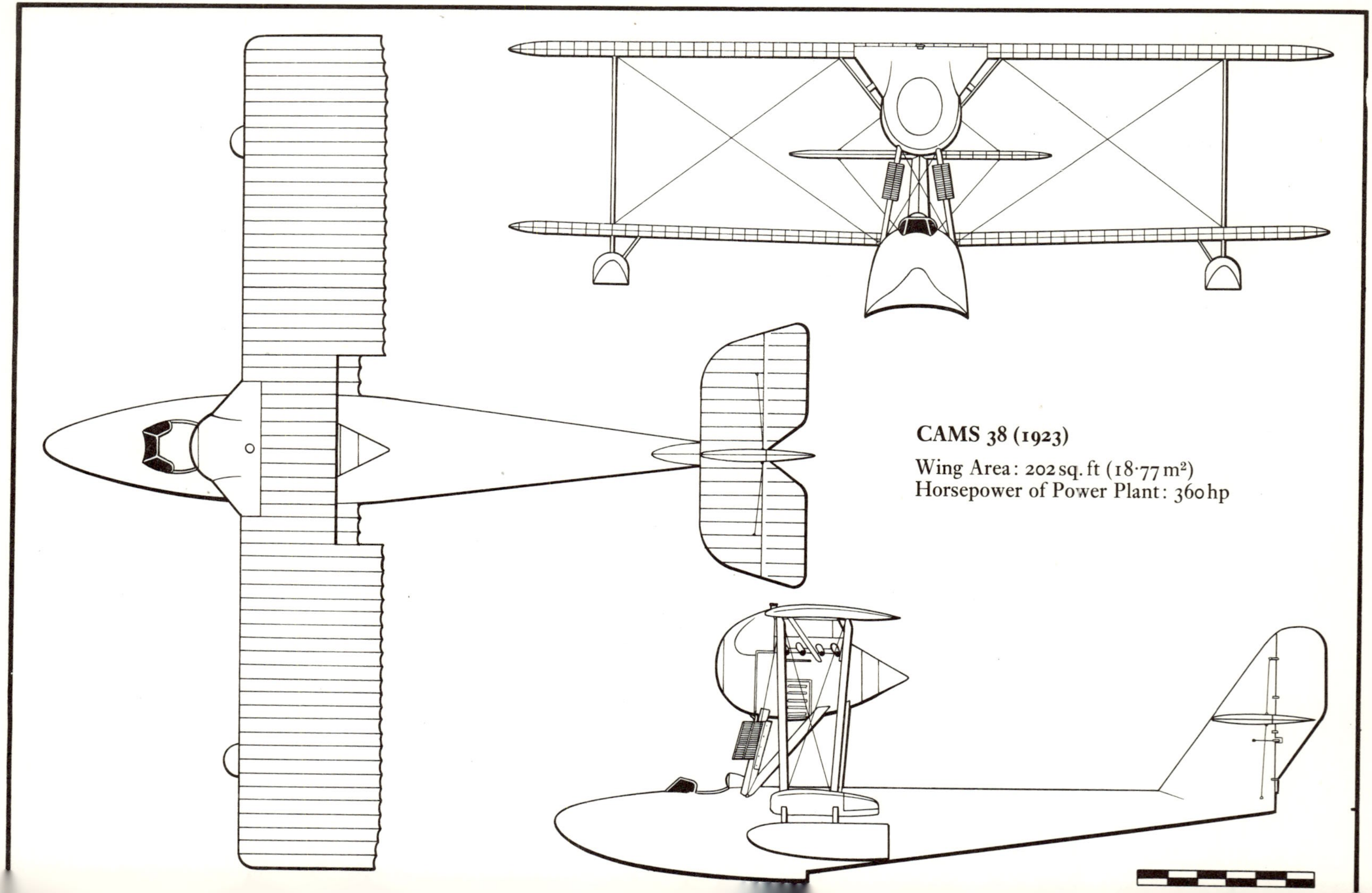

CAMS 38 (1923)

Wing Area: 202 sq. ft (18·77 m^2)
Horsepower of Power Plant: 360 hp

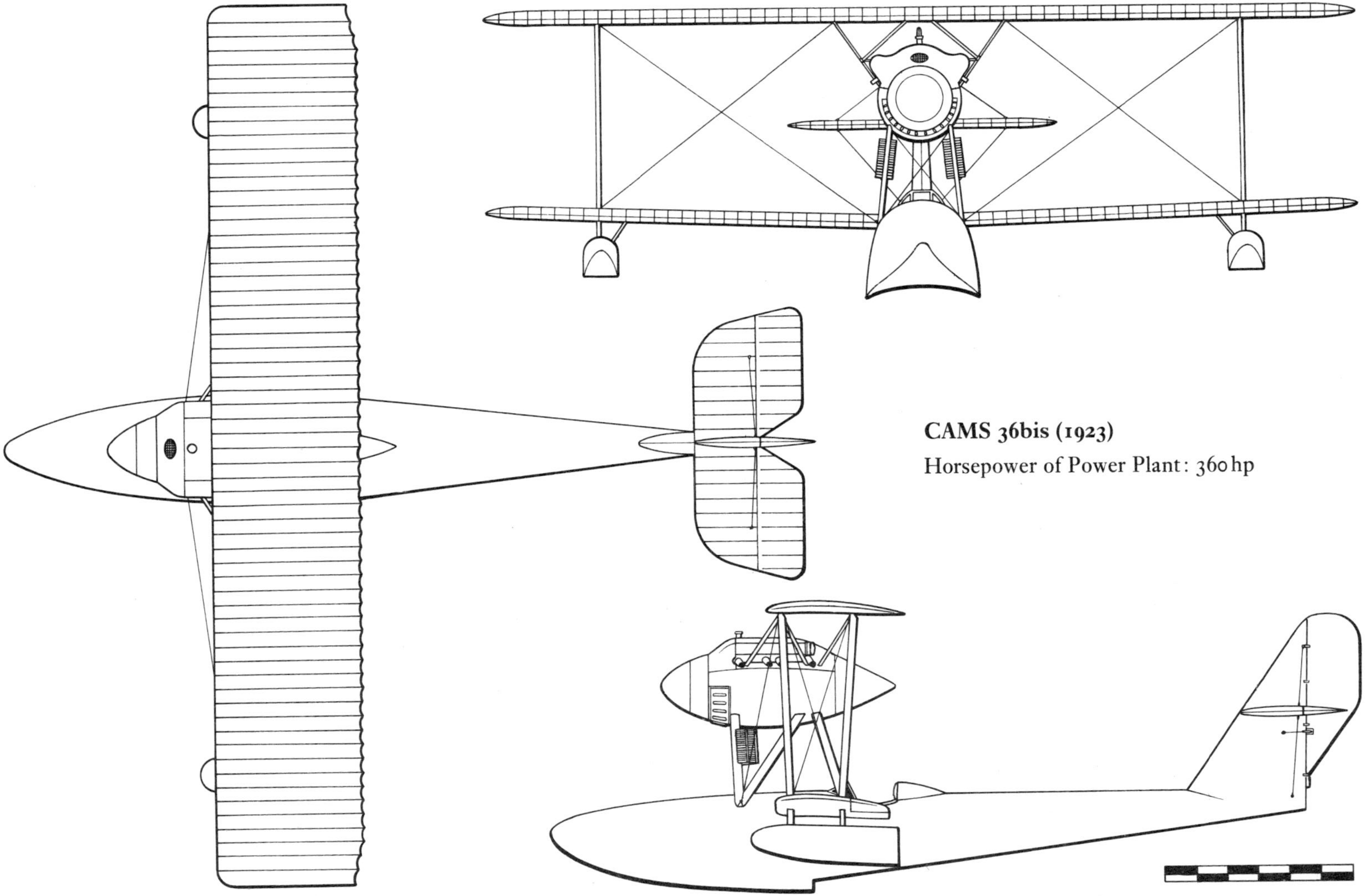

CAMS 36bis (1923)
Horsepower of Power Plant: 360 hp

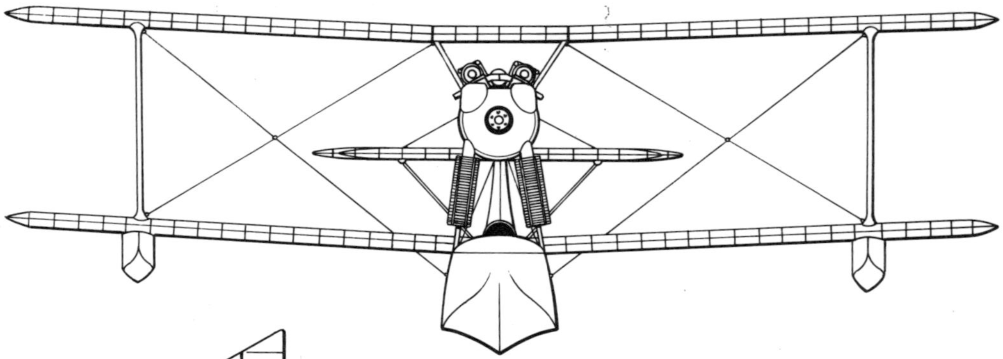

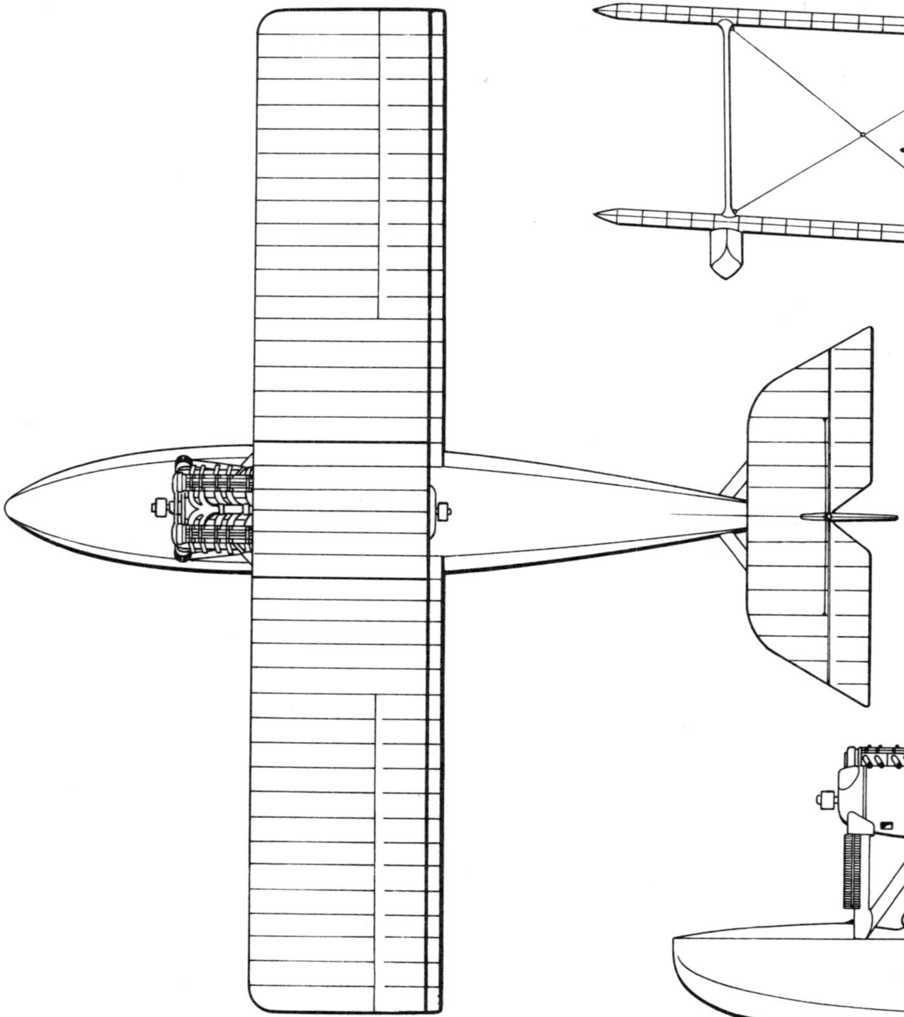

Twin Tandem Latham (1923)

Horsepower of Power Plant: 2 × 400 hp

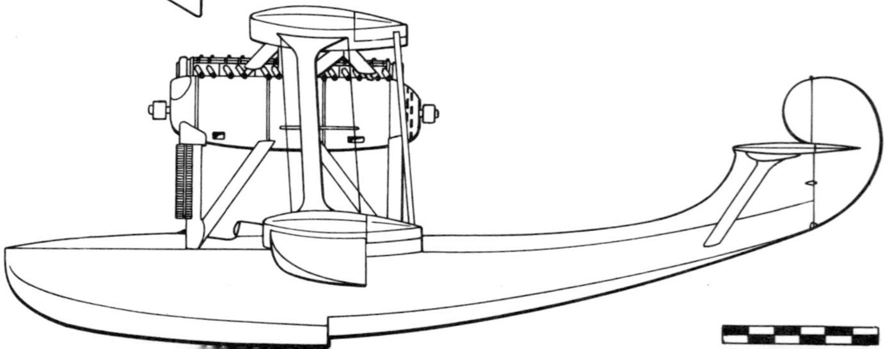

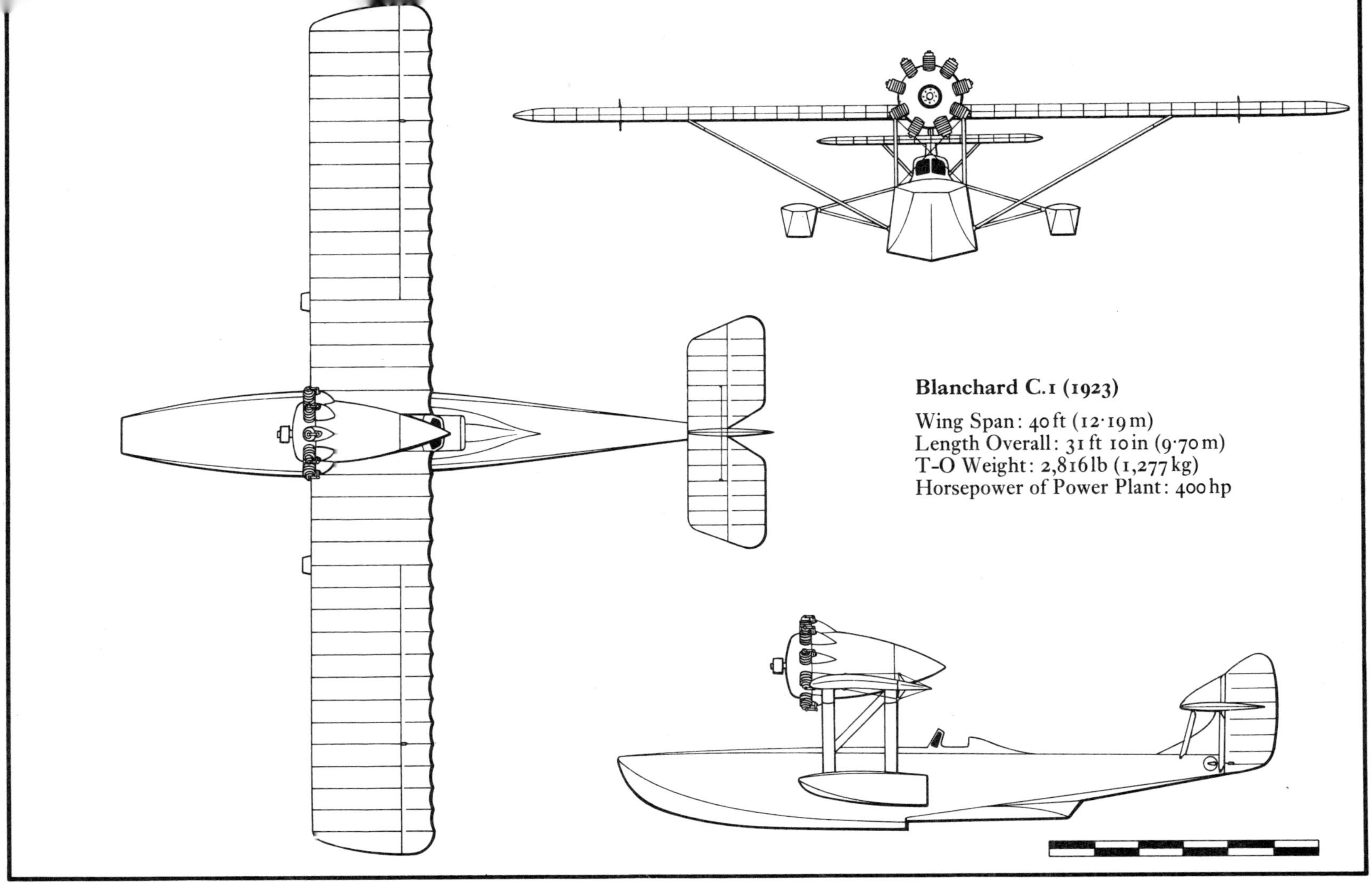

Blanchard C.1 (1923)

Wing Span: 40 ft (12·19 m)
Length Overall: 31 ft 10 in (9·70 m)
T-O Weight: 2,816 lb (1,277 kg)
Horsepower of Power Plant: 400 hp

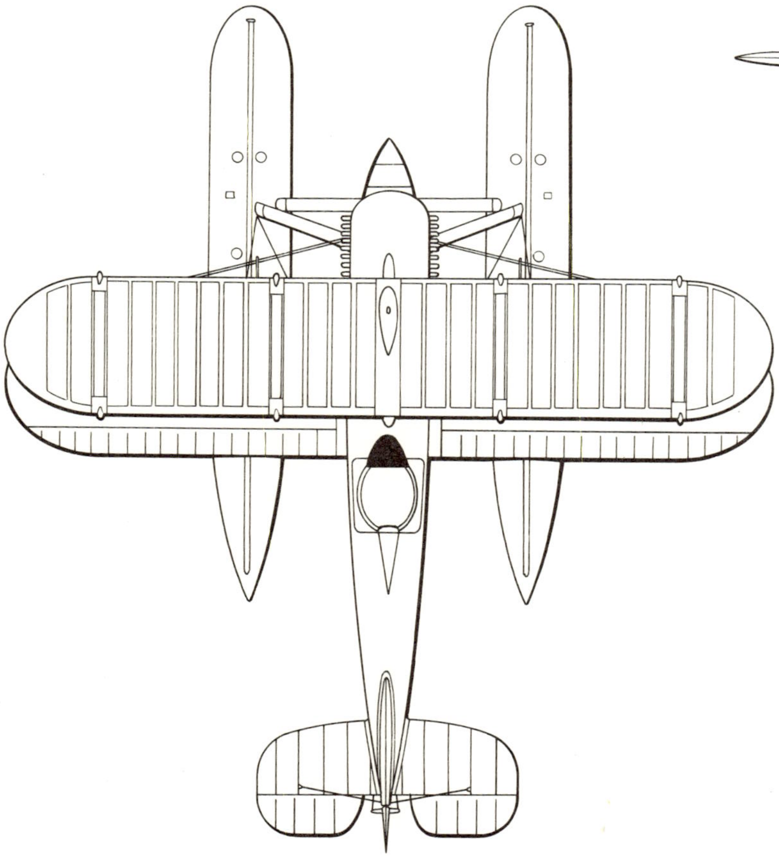

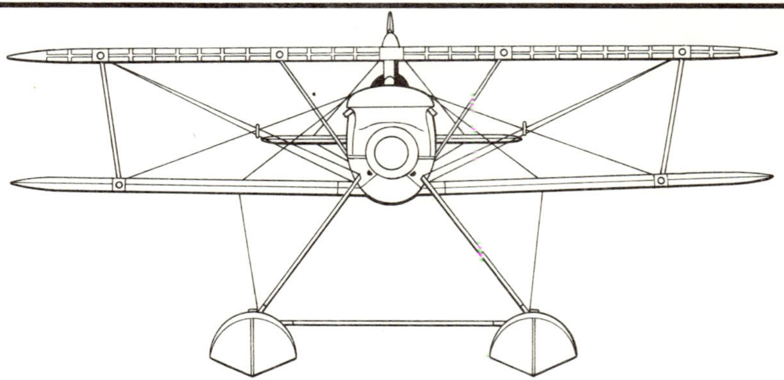

Curtiss CR-3 (1923)

Wing Span: 22 ft 8 in (6·91 m)
Length Overall: 25 ft (7·62 m)
Wing Area: 168 sq. ft (15·61 m²)
T-O Weight: 2,747 lb (1,246 kg)
Max Wing Loading: 16·35 lb/sq. ft (79·83 kg/m²)
Horsepower of Power Plant: 465 hp

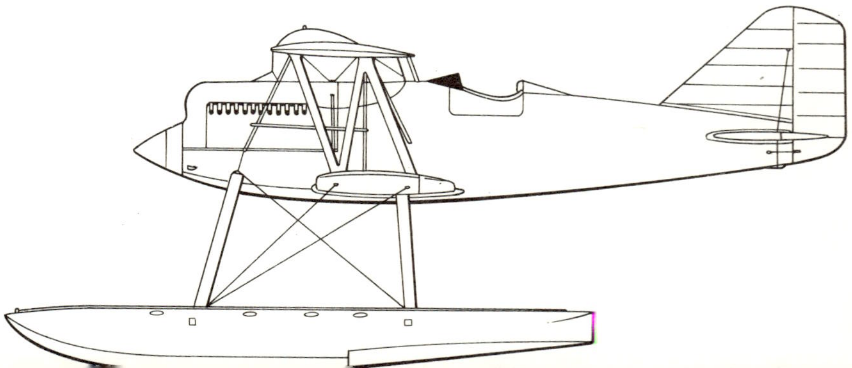

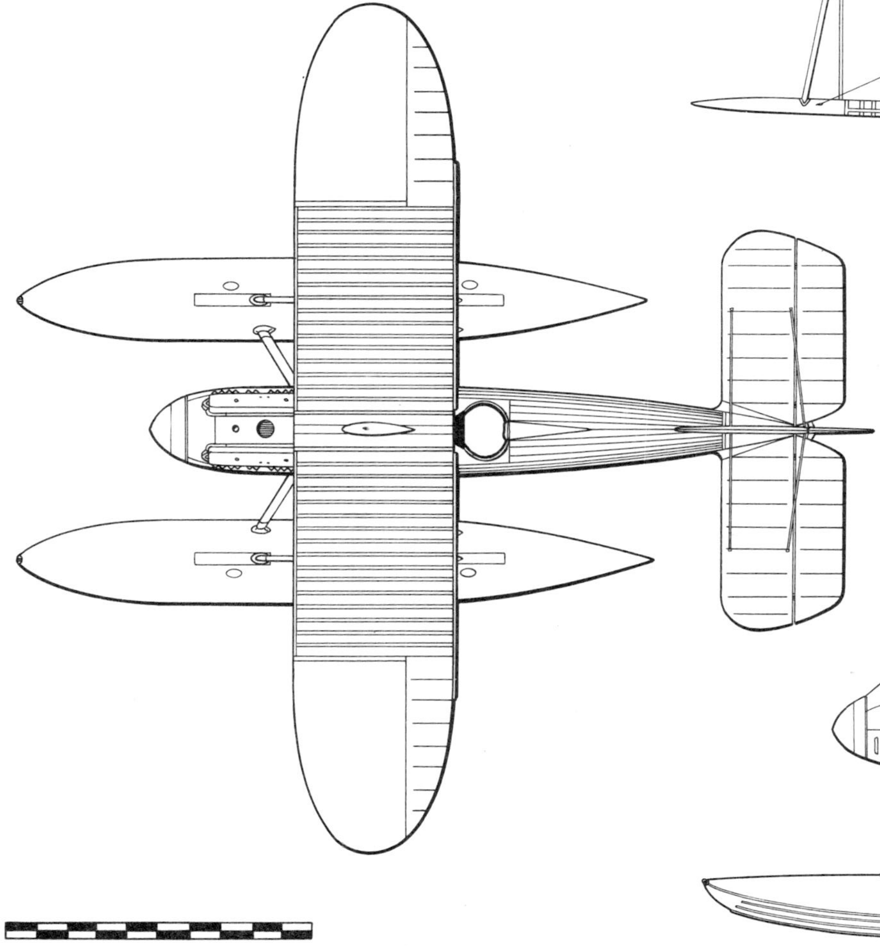

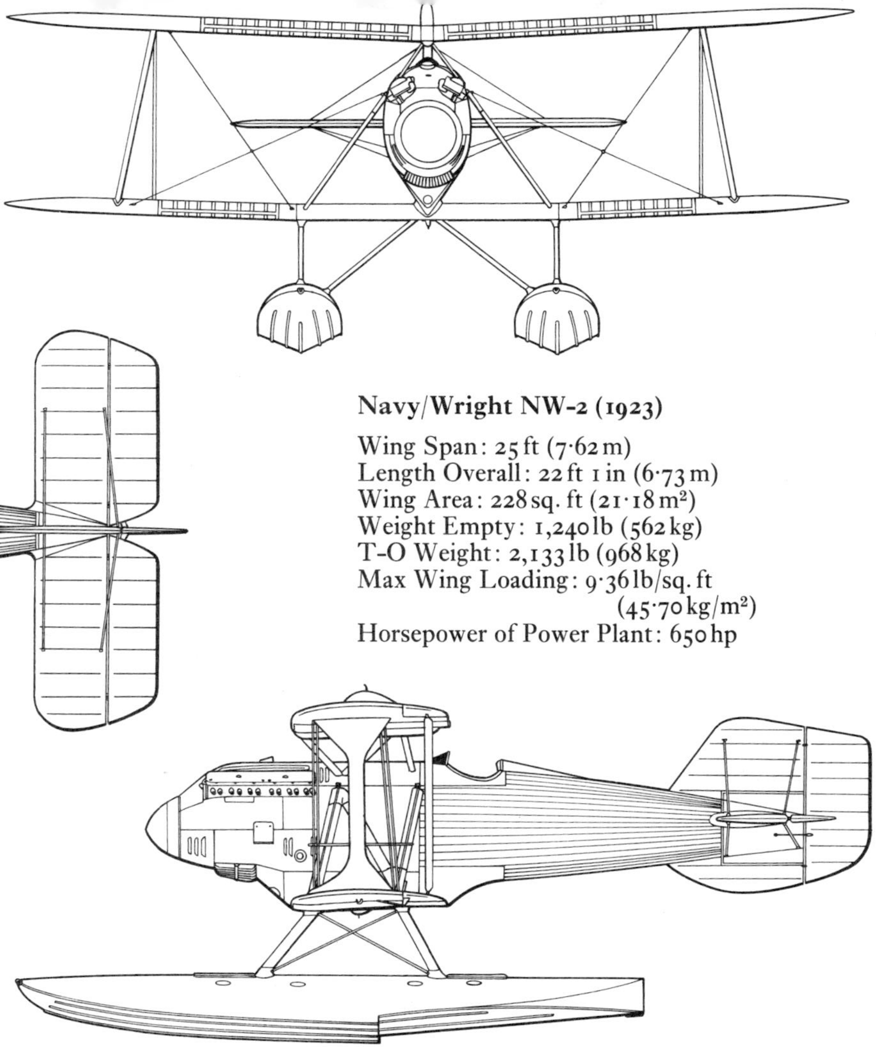

Navy/Wright NW-2 (1923)

Wing Span: 25 ft (7·62 m)
Length Overall: 22 ft 1 in (6·73 m)
Wing Area: 228 sq. ft (21·18 m²)
Weight Empty: 1,240 lb (562 kg)
T-O Weight: 2,133 lb (968 kg)
Max Wing Loading: 9·36 lb/sq. ft
(45·70 kg/m²)
Horsepower of Power Plant: 650 hp

7

At Baltimore, Maryland

1924–25

The initial announcement regarding the Schneider Trophy Contest for 1924 came from the FAI, which stated that the regulations would be the same as those which had applied at Cowes in the previous year. The Royal Aero Club followed by advising that British entries would have to be received by 1 April, the entrance fee being £10, accompanied by a £500 'good intent' deposit.

In due course, the National Aeronautic Association (NAA) of the United States announced that it had selected Baltimore, Maryland, as the site for the contest, and that the navigability and water tightness tests would take place on 24 October, the speed contest on the following day.

Despite a statement from the Royal Aero Club in late April to the effect that they had formed a committee to assist would-be British competitors in finalising their arrangements to compete so far from home shores, it was soon apparent that there was little danger of the committee being overworked.

Only a single entry was forthcoming, this from the Gloucestershire Aircraft Company (GAC), which at a later date was to substitute the more phonetic Gloster as the first component of this famous company name. Perhaps Gloowsestershire was something of an off-putting mouthful for potential overseas customers. The post-war policy of GAC was to concentrate its efforts on building high-speed aircraft for competition purposes, believing that success in this field might encourage the Air Ministry to look in their direction when much-needed military contracts were in the offing.

The changing fortunes of the aviation industry in the early 1920s had brought the transfer of H. P. Folland to GAC, when the company with which Glosters had been associated during the war—the Nieuport and General Aircraft Company at Cricklewood—closed its doors. Harry Folland was a designer of great ability: his activities at Farnborough before joining Nieuport and General Aircraft had brought early recognition of this fact, for the S.E.4, 4a, 5 and 5a owed much to his flair for detail design, the latter being one of the most successful fighter aircraft of the first World War.

Folland's first project at GAC was the Mars I racer, evolved from the Nieuport Nighthawk and with which, on 17 July 1921, the company's test pilot—J. H. James—won the Aerial Derby and Handicap Cup at a speed of 163·3 mph (262·32 km/h). With extensive modifications, which included reduction in wing area, a changed cooling system for its Napier Lion engine, fairing aft of the landing wheels and other detail attention to streamlining, it established a new British speed record of 196·4 mph (316·07 km/h) in late December 1921.

When this aircraft had won the 1921 Aerial Derby it had done so under the name Gloster Bamel, a name deriving from Folland's comment to Hugh Burroughes, when the prototype was under construction, that it was 'half bare—half camel', Bamel evolving and enduring. It subsequently reverted to the official name of Gloucestershire Aircraft Mars I, but by the time that it had been further modified to compete in and win the 1923 Aerial Derby—with new wing section, fuel tank located in the fuselage, revised tail unit and installation of a 530 hp Lion engine—it had been redesignated Gloster I. Eventually this aircraft became Royal Air Force property, with the serial number J7234 and, referred to usually as the Bamel, it served as a high-speed floatplane trainer at RAF Felixstowe from May 1925.

In this brief summary is given the parentage of the Gloster II, the seaplane racing aircraft developed by Folland to contend for the 1924 Schneider Trophy contest. Early in 1924 the company had received an Air Ministry order for two aircraft to compete in America. Folland chose as their basis the Gloster I, but great care went into refining the design to achieve what was then considered a most advanced degree of aerodynamic efficiency. To this end, emphasis went into careful fairing of the engine, elimination of all external pipework, and the use of Lamblin strut radiators mounted on the forward float struts. Even though the pilot's forward visibility was almost completely obscured by a fairing that encased the centre-section struts, it was felt that the potential speed gain from this feature was more vital than that the pilot should have a more-or-less unobstructed forward view.

Napiers were again chosen to provide the power plant, for a developed version of the Lion, the Mk VA, was then producing a maximum output of 585 hp. In the Gloster II it was put to work to drive a Fairey-Reed two-blade metal propeller with spinner.

In general appearance this aircraft was a remarkably clean single-bay biplane, with single I-shape interplane struts, flying and landing wires each side, and the narrow-gap wings slightly forward-staggered. Ailerons were fitted only to the lower wings. A wire-braced tail unit was conventional in form, save for a small dorsal fin which complemented the lines of the rudder. Single-step V-bottom floats of very small frontal area were carried on four streamline struts, strut-braced to each other and wire-braced to wings and fuselage. Wing span was 20ft 0in (6·10m), length overall 26ft 10in (8·18m), height overall 11ft 0in (3·35m) and wing area 165sq.ft (15·33m^2). Maximum take-off weight was 3,100lb (1,406kg) and maximum level speed at sea level estimated as 225mph (362km/h).

On 12 September the prototype, which had the RAF serial number J7504, was transported by road to Felixstowe. There, a week later, it was rigged and ready for its first test flight at the hands of Captain Hubert S. Broad, at that time chief test pilot of the de Havilland company. Those were days long before the performance of a prototype was reasonably predictable, and as soon as Broad was airborne he discovered the Gloster II to be excessively tail heavy. As a result he contented himself with a few circuits at moderate power before coming in to land. This was judged to a nicety, but unfortunately there was a considerable lop on the water. Almost immediately the floats touched the machine began to porpoise, the resulting stress proving too much for one of the forward struts which collapsed. Down beneath the waves went the Gloster II, Hubert Broad and the combined hope of Gloster and Britain for 1924. Happily, Broad managed to free himself from the cockpit without too much difficulty, and was soon picked up, but the aircraft was a complete loss. Britain was out of the 1924 Contest.

Italian hopes to compete had fared no better. Their problem was still one of finding a suitable power plant and, with the outstanding performance of the Curtiss D-12 engines in the 1923 Contest in mind, they had acquired two of them from America. One was allocated to Cantieri Riuniti dell' Adriatico, a company founded in 1923 which was a subsidiary of a well-known Italian shipbuilding company. They were to build a machine specially designed for the 1924 Schneider Trophy by General Guidoni, but this failed to achieve even the limited success of the Gloster II, for it sank before taking to the air.

The second of the D-12 engines was loaned to Società Anonima Piaggio, a shipbuilding and engineering concern which, during the war, had built aircraft of Caproni design. In August 1923 the company was re-established as an aircraft constructor, having acquired the assets of Pegna-Bonmartini of Rome, but with their very limited design experience it was not surprising that their venture failed to materialise. Consequently, Italy was also out of the 1924 Contest.

France, the only other country likely to enter, was never really among the contenders. There was a suggestion that a somewhat revolutionary cantilever monoplane designed by a company known formerly as Société d'Avions Adolphe Bernard might appear. Whether or not this was conjecture is uncertain, but later in 1924 the Ferbois-Bernard Racer, an all-wood aircraft built by the company under its new name of Société Industrielle des Métaux et du Bois, captured the world speed record for France at an average of 278·5mph (448·17km/h). Powered by a new 450hp

Hispano-Suiza 12-cylinder broad-arrow in-line liquid-cooled engine, mention of this machine warrants inclusion in this history as it is believed that its cantilever construction was to have some influence on R. J. Mitchell's ideas.

Only America was ready to field a team of aircraft at Baltimore. But due to the withdrawal of all foreign competition, the NAA decided to declare the contest void for that year, thus allowing a period of twelve months in which overseas competitors could prepare. It was an unparalleled sporting gesture, for if the Americans had followed the Italian example in 1920 and 1921, they could have flown over the course at their leisure to take the Trophy for a second time. This would have put them in a very strong position to retain the Trophy for all time, by needing only one more win on their home waters in 1925.

Their decision when conveyed to the Royal Aero Club brought spontaneous response. The British club cabled its warmest appreciation of this noble and sporting gesture—undoubtedly without the foresight of future decisions. It is particularly interesting to conjecture how much Britain, and the western world, owes to America's National Aeronautic Association. If America had flown over the course to take the Trophy in 1924, and retained it under pressure, as she did in 1925, would we in Britain have had the Supermarine Spitfire in time to play its vital role in the Battle of Britain?

Early in 1925 came provisional details for that year's contest, which was scheduled to be held at Baltimore, between 24–29 October, with rules unchanged. British contenders were required to file their entries by 23 March, accompanied by an entry fee of £10 and a deposit of £100.

At long last there were signs of determined efforts by Britain to regain the Trophy, for the Gloster and Supermarine companies both received orders from the Air Ministry to go ahead with the design and construction of high-speed racing seaplanes for 'technical development purposes'. If on completion they were considered acceptable after thorough examination, then they would be loaned to their respective manufacturers to take part in the Contest.

Supermarine had been busy during the previous year evaluating a somewhat revolutionary design. This concerned an aircraft of flying-boat configuration, with its engine in the hull and a geared drive to the propeller. However, problems developed in connection with the shaft drives and gearing and, as a result, the project was abandoned in early 1925.

Instead, R. J. Mitchell came up with a completely new design for a seaplane and this proposal, tendered to the Air Ministry, received approval on 18 March 1925. The company lost no time in proceeding with its construction under conditions of great secrecy, and so it was not until 25 August, when it flew for the first time, that the very advanced ideas introduced by Mitchell were seen by Press and public.

Designated as the S.4, it proved to be a small, clean monoplane with cantilever wing, tail unit and floats, completely free from the struts and bracing wires that produced so much drag. A reporter was to comment 'One cannot help feeling a certain amount of surprise that a British designer has had sufficient imagination to produce such a machine.'

This was hardly fair comment, for it was the first time that Mitchell or any other designer had had the opportunity to design a seaplane from scratch to compete in the Schneider Trophy Contest. Prior to that, it had been the usual custom to try and squeeze the maximum performance from an existing—and by comparison with other countries—outdated machine. In fact, so many new features were introduced by Mitchell that it was an almost fantastic achievement for the S.4 to make its first flight only just over five months from the go-ahead for its construction.

The one-piece two-spar monoplane wing, mounted in mid-wing configuration, was of all-wood construction, and covered with plywood skins that increased gradually in thickness from wingtip to centre-section. Ailerons extended from the wingtips to approximately mid-span of the wing trailing-edge. Between ailerons and fuselage were wing trailing-edge flaps, a feature which Mitchell was to delete from subsequent racing seaplanes. Their use on the S.4 shows the advanced ideas boiling in Mitchell's mind, for flaps and ailerons were interconnected, the latter being operable independently or in conjunction with the flaps.

The fuselage was of monocoque construction and this, apart from metal fittings and two tubular-steel A-frames, was all-wood, the fin and tailplane forming an integral part of this structure. Plywood skins covered the entire fuselage, except for aluminium cowlings around the power plant bay.

The tubular-steel A-frames served a three-fold purpose: the wing passed between them and was secured to them; the forward frame carried the engine bearers; and the lower extremities of the frames served as mounting for the single-step wooden floats which had an undersurface of pronounced Vee form. Between the floats were two small-diameter bracing struts, and aluminium shells provided streamlining for the main struts.

Power plant consisted of a Napier Lion VII engine which, in a continuing stage of development involving higher compression ratios and detail refinement, was then able to produce a maximum output of 700 hp. The useful life of such an engine was limited, but more than adequate for race purposes. Radiators mounted on the wing undersurface provided for cooling of the engine, and the oil cooler was sited in the underside of the fuselage, with only its fins exposed to the airstream. The two-blade metal propeller was of the Fairey-Reed type, its hub faired by a spinner that maintained the seaplane's elegant lines. Being entirely free from struts and bracing wires, it was almost certainly the most handsome of the seaplanes to emanate from R. J. Mitchell's drawing board.

The experienced Henri Biard was to pilot this new machine, and one can imagine the ripple of excitement as it was launched and many saw for the first time those breathtaking cantilever wings. How could they stay put? Mitchell certainly had no doubts of their structural integrity, for a complete wing had been sent to Farnborough and tested to destruction, confirming the amount of punishment it could take.

Biard apparently had some doubts about the unbraced monoplane wing, though whether they were in retrospect is uncertain. He was to write in his book* *Wings* that from the first moment he sat in the cockpit he felt some misgivings. Perhaps this stemmed from the wing position in relation to the cockpit, which just about cut off all forward visibility when the S.4 was taxying on the surface of the water.

But despite his feelings, Biard found that the machine got off the water cleanly on the first flight and proved extremely fast. So fast, in fact, that it was decided to make an attempt on the world speed record for seaplanes without any unnecessary delay.

On 13 September, over a 3 km straight course extending along Southampton Water, Biard flew the little seaplane at an average speed of 226·752 mph (364·92 km/h) to capture the record by a comfortable 38·7 mph (62·28 km/h) from the US Navy's George Cuddihy. The fastest run of those used to arrive at the average had been at a speed of 231·406 mph (372·4 km/h). Naturally, there was great elation at this success, but even this moment of triumph was not sufficient to dispel completely Biard's disquiet. Occasionally, just occasionally, there had been minor periods of vibration which seemed to originate at the wingtips: nothing one could put a finger on, but a little disturbing for the pilot of the world's fastest seaplane.

Meanwhile, the Press was busy extolling the virtues of the S.4, which it was hoped would bring the Trophy triumphantly back to Britain. Last minute adjustments and fitting of an improved propeller absorbed the remaining time before the seaplane, which had been inspected and accepted by the Air Ministry on 17 September, was crated ready for shipment to America.

Brief specification of the S.4 includes wing span of 30 ft 7½ in (9·33 m), length overall 26 ft 7¾ in (8·12 m), height overall 11 ft 8½ in (3·57 m), wing chord at root 6 ft 0 in (1·83 m), wing chord at tip 4 ft 3½ in (1·31 m) and wing area of 139 sq. ft (12·91 m^2). Maximum take-off weight was 3,191 lb (1,447 kg).

Over much the same period of time the Gloster company had also found themselves up to their eyes in work. Their proposal had received Air Ministry approval a little earlier than that of Supermarine, but they had been awarded an order for two examples of a biplane seaplane designated Gloster III.

Detail design had been started without delay, but their machine was a logical development of the unfortunate Gloster II rather than a completely

*Hurst & Blackett Ltd, London.

new design. Like the S.4, power plant comprised the 700hp version of the Napier Lion, but the overall size of these two Gloster machines was such that they represented the smallest aircraft of their power built in the UK to that time.

Generally similar in appearance to the Gloster II, which had been built to take part in the previous year's contest, the new machines had considerable improvement in detail design. The single-bay wings were unchanged in span and retained fabric covering, but the fabric-covered fuselage of the Gloster II had given place to an all-wood monocoque structure with plywood skins. New duralumin single-step floats, built by Shorts, were mounted on four wire-braced slender streamline struts.

Folland had designed wing surface radiators to reduce drag from this source to a minimum, but as these were not ready when needed they were replaced by Lamblin radiators which extended to almost one-third span on each of the lower wing leading-edges. The oil cooler was mounted in the undersurface of the engine fairing.

In this form, taxying trials began at Felixstowe on 16 August, but it was not until four days after the S.4's first flight that, on 29 August, Hubert Broad took the first of the Gloster IIIs on test. This proved generally satisfactory except for some directional instability, but the time available allowed Folland only to make a modest increase in area of the dorsal and ventral fins, and with these modifications the aircraft was re-designated Gloster IIIA. Before Broad's machine—bearing the RAF serial number N194—was crated for transit to America, four more test flights were made at Felixstowe.

The second machine, N195, which had also the civil registration G-EBLJ, was flown only once before being prepared for shipment. Its pilot was H. J. 'Bert' Hinkler, test pilot of the Avro company and loaned for the contest. Then little known to the general public, Hinkler was later to earn international fame as a long-distance pilot.

Thus, with little enough time to spare, the British team and their aircraft assembled at Southampton and embarked in the SS *Minnewaska*, a vessel belonging to the Atlantic Transport Company who had offered free transit to and from America. In addition to the S.4 and two Gloster IIIAs, the Bamel was taken along to serve as a practice machine, but it had by then been discovered that, true to form, the Royal Aero Club had already limited Britain's chance of success by entering only two machines for the Contest instead of the permitted three. One of the Gloster IIIAs might be making the expensive trip for no purpose.

Colonel J. T. C. Moore-Brabazon had made the trip to Southampton to wish the team god-speed, emphasizing in his toast to them the importance of the occasion it being, he said, the first time that Britain had made a serious attempt to gain the Trophy.

With the usual flurry of activity the *Minnewaska* moved slowly away

Gloster III N194 in original form, with Lamblin radiators and small-area vertical tail surfaces

The Gloster IIIA at Baltimore. Note the increased vertical tail surfaces fitted as a temporary measure to overcome poor directional stability

from the dockside. The team, lining the deck rail, waved their goodbyes as the gap between ship and shore widened, each busy with his own thoughts and the hope of success. I wonder if anyone had noticed that they totalled thirteen men?

Italy had made equally strenuous efforts to gain success. On the same day that Britain's men and machines sailed from Southampton, the Italian team had left Genoa aboard the SS *Conte Verde*. But whereas the *Minnewaska* carried four aircraft, the Italian vessel had only two, both Macchi M.33s built by Aeronautica Macchi at Varese.

Designed by Ing Mario Castoldi especially to take part in the Schneider Contest, the M.33 proved to be the last flying-boat to be entered in these races. It was, in effect, the smallest possible single-seat flying-boat that he could devise, having regard to the duration required and the power plant available. Of high-wing monoplane configuration it was remarkably clean for, like the S.4, it had a cantilever wing entirely free from struts and bracing wires, save for those which carried and braced the small underwing balancer floats, mounted near to the wingtip.

The single-step shallow Vee-bottomed hull was extremely slender, terminating aft in a neatly upswept tail unit which, however, was wire-braced. Unfortunately, the fact that the M.33 was a flying-boat meant that the single engine power plant could not be streamlined into the hull. Instead, it was carried high above the wing with an N-arrangement of struts on each side, braced by streamline wires. Though the power plant was mounted in a clean nacelle, this installation spoilt the aerodynamic efficiency of the aircraft. Additional drag came from cooling radiators, mounted on each side of the rear of the engine, so that they were directly in the slipstream of the two-blade wooden tractor propeller.

The problem of suitable high-powered engines was still troubling Italian manufacturers, and although the Fiat company had carried out an enormous amount of research and development work they still had no production engine ready for 1925. Consequently, there were available only the two Curtiss D-12s which General Guidoni had obtained from America in the previous year, and these had suffered from continual testing and examination by Fiats, to the extent that it is rather uncertain what was their actual power output. Perhaps Macchi were a little optimistic when they labelled their airframe drawings to the effect that the power plant was a Curtiss D-12 developing 450 hp.

Selected to fly the Italian aircraft were the company's test pilots, Giovanni de Briganti and Riccardo Morselli, for this was a company effort, unaided by a government still in a state of turmoil. Although flight testing before despatch of the flying-boats was generally satisfactory, Dr Ermanno Bazzocchi of Aeronautica Macchi has commented in recent years that the cantilever wing of the M.33 had a tendency to develop slight flutter at speed.

Gloster IIIB N195, the Lamblins replaced by surface radiators. Bump on the upper wing surface is a coolant expansion header tank

A Macchi M.33, in a placid setting on Lake Varese, demonstrates that even flying-boats could have remarkably clean lines

Dimensions of these aircraft included a wing span of 32 ft 9¾ in (10·00 m), length overall 27 ft 4¼ in (8·34 m), height overall (propeller turning) 10 ft 6 in (3·20 m), and wing area 176·53 sq. ft (16.40 m²). Maximum take-off weight was 2,768 lb (1,255 kg).

From France no entry had materialised so, for 1925 at any rate, the contest would be fought out between three nations when the challengers from Britain and Italy arrived at Baltimore. In America, not surprisingly, there had been very considerable effort to ensure that the Trophy should stay on that side of the Atlantic.

Both the US Army and Navy had decided to enter for the Pulitzer Trophy Race and Schneider Trophy Contest of 1925, and had ordered new racing aircraft from the Curtiss Aeroplane and Motor Company, two for the Navy and one for the Army. Designated R3C-1 they were required first to compete in the Pulitzer Race and so were completed with wheeled landing gear and, in general appearance, were indistinguishable from the R2C which had represented the next stage of development of the CR series. It will be recalled that it was a CR-3 which had taken the Trophy to America in 1923.

The R3C-1s were, however, very different from the CRs, with the upper biplane wing faired neatly to the fuselage upper surface. There were, consequently, no centre-section struts, and the smaller-span narrower-chord lower wing was braced by a single I-shape interplane strut, plus landing and flying wires on each side. The contour of the engine cowling had changed considerably, being of much improved streamline form, while the tail unit had lost all bracing and there was a considerable increase in area of both tailplane and elevators.

With float landing gear attached for participation in the Schneider Contest these aircraft were re-designated R3C-2, and the discerning eye might have considered that a seaplane with a tail skid was a little incongruous. The fact was that this feature of the landing gear was integral with the rear fuselage and could not be removed.

Considerably more power was available, for the Curtiss D-12 had been replaced by the company's V.1400 engine which developed 610 hp. This had evolved from the D-12, but the bore had been increased to 4⅞ in (12·38 cm) to give a total capacity of 1,400 cu. in (22,942 cc). Improvements in design included bronze valve seats, the steel sleeves then becoming pure sleeves, that is to say open-ended, but still screwed into the monobloc head. The rear flange of the propeller hub was an integral machining on the crankshaft, only the front flange being detachable.

Bench testing of the new machine had begun late in 1924, and during which two problems had predominated. These concerned occasional failure of the ignition system and shearing of the stainless steel drive shaft to the water pump. It was not until 1925 that these faults had been cured satisfactorily and the engine had completed its fifty hour type test. Although this power plant was virtually untried in the air, it had been selected for the R3Cs because satisfactory conclusion of the type test gave some guarantee that this new and more powerful engine would, at any rate, be able to survive the comparatively short term demands of the Pulitzer and Schneider races.

The 1925 Pulitzer Race was to be held only just over two weeks prior to the Schneider Contest, and it being considered inadvisable to enter all three aircraft in the earlier race, one Navy machine (A7054) was held in reserve. Wise precaution though it was, it proved to be unnecessary, for the two Curtiss machines not only completed the race without suffering any problems, but managed also to take first and second places. The Army's Lieutenant Cyrus Bettis (aircraft number A6979) was the winner, at an average speed of 248·97 mph (400·68 km/h), the Navy's Lieutenant A. J. Williams (A6978) second at 241·7 mph (288·98 km/h).

Although the race had gone to the Curtiss machines, the result was more than disappointing. Bettis had put up a speed only just over 5 mph (8 km/h) greater than the 243·67 mph (392·15 km/h) recorded by the R2C-1 in the Pulitzer Race of two years earlier while Williams, who had won that race, was almost 2 mph (3 km/h) slower. The Americans gained a crumb of comfort from the fact that weather conditions had been pretty grim on the day of the Pulitzer Race and that, in addition, both pilots were unable to obtain maximum power from the new engines. Hopefully, the weather would be better for the Schneider, and there was still time to tune the engines to give their best.

If no greater speed could be got from these machines, then American hopes were far from rosy. Floats would knock about 30 mph (48 km/h) off their maximum, and they were aware that the S.4 had already flown at over 226 mph (364 km/h). It seemed at that moment that Britain might be in the strongest position to win the Trophy.

However, the Americans retained one ace up their sleeve, in the form of Lieutenant J. H. 'Jimmy' Doolittle of the US Army. A brilliant and self-analytical pilot, he had already demonstrated an average speed over two laps of the Pulitzer Trophy course of around 254 mph (408 km/h). Conditions had been ideal, the engine behaving, and Doolittle had put his very extensive experience into practice to find the best possible way of completing the turns of the closed circuit. Further practice might make it possible for him to clip a few more vital seconds from each of the twenty-one acute angled turns of the Schneider course.

The site for the race was in Chesapeake Bay, an inlet to the Susquehanna River, and well protected by land to east and west, promising good water conditions. The base of operations was at Bay Shore Park, some fourteen miles (22·5 km) almost due south-east of Baltimore. The course was to be triangular, with a first leg only slightly east of due south, heading over the inlet of the Patapsco River, a distance of 9·2 nm (16·72 m). Turning at a lighthouse about 1·6 nm (3 km) SE of Gibson Island, the next heading was ENE 7·73 nm (14·32 km) distant, to a pylon adjacent to the eastern limit of the bay. Finally, a turn to head NW gave a last leg of 10·22 nm (18·96 km) back to the start and finish line at Bay Shore.

The British team and their aircraft had been first to arrive there, on 7 October, allowing plenty of time for preparation and practice. They were to discover that the site was not ready, and that until the contractors had completed the erection of tents that would serve as hangars and workshops, as well as making some essential improvements to the launching facilities, it was impossible for them to make a start.

In fact, it was not until six days later that Hubert Broad skimmed the

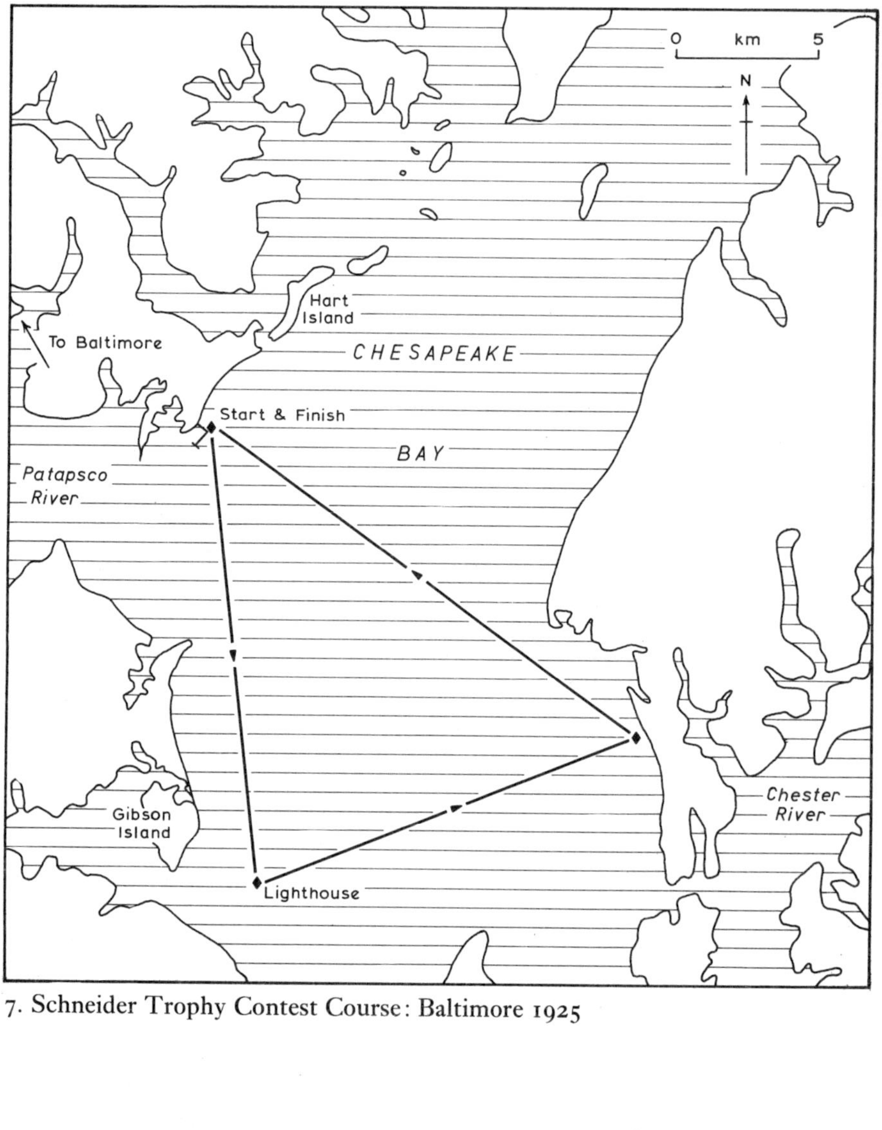

7. Schneider Trophy Contest Course: Baltimore 1925

waters of Chesapeake Bay in his Gloster IIIA, the first to take the air. Biard managed a couple of flights on the 16th, expressing himself satisfied with the performance of the S.4. The new propeller was undoubtedly an improvement and, although not pushing the machine to its limit, he considered that on the day of the race he would be able to show the Americans a clean pair of heels.

The latter viewed the S.4 with a fair degree of apprehension. Long before it had taken to the air its uniquely clean lines had suggested formidable speed, and this was confirmed to some extent by Biard's flights on 16 October. It was considered reasonable to assume that the British pilot was not giving the S.4 its head in practice. The Gloster IIA also caused some concern for the American team. Similar in configuration to their own machines, and with a more powerful engine, it might well provide some competition; but the favourite was undoubtedly the S.4. The Macchis were not thought to offer serious opposition. True, they might have some advantage under exceptionally bad water conditions but, in fact, if wind and water combined to produce a sea state that was bad enough to give a flying-boat significant advantage, then it was likely that—without showing any impartiality—the committee would postpone the speed contest until the weather had moderated.

At this moment of an expected British victory fate began to take a hand, pulling the sheets and blankets of a sick bed over the alternately shivering and perspiring Biard, stricken with influenza. Worse was to come, an autumn gale sweeping over the area and dismantling unceremoniously the tents erected a few days earlier. In the process a heavy tent pole fell across the tail unit of the S.4, causing considerable damage, requiring the Supermarine team to work hard to ready the seaplane in time for the navigability test, due to be held on Friday 23 October.

By that date Henri Biard was up and about again, even if a rather pale example of his real self. The British team leader, Captain Charles B. Wilson, suggested that if he didn't feel up to par it might be better for the reserve pilot, Bert Hinkler, to fly the S.4. Biard declined the offer, for Hinkler had never flown the Supermarine machine, and he felt certain that, although a little off colour, his own experience of handling the aircraft offered a greater chance of victory.

Accordingly, on the morning of 23 October it was Biard who squeezed himself into the S.4's cockpit. Ofstie, de Briganti and Broad had already taken to the air. With the Lion engine running to perfection, Biard was fast off the water, circling the tented area before heading for the judges' cutter.

Let *Flight* take up the story of events: '. . . coming back over the pierhead . . . at a height of about 800 ft (244 m) he was seen to make a steeply banked turn, which at first led the spectators to believe he was stunting, but it was soon realised that the machine was in difficulty and not under proper control . . . whatever the reason, Biard was obviously in trouble.'

Indeed he was, for within seconds the British favourite hit the water. Biard described that moment in his book *Wings*: 'A roar that seemed to shatter the world as my lovely monoplane hits the water and explodes on the impact like a bomb, an impression of green water, solid and hard as ice through which I am flung like a spear through snow, a horrible agonizing pain in all my limbs and through my body, and I regain consciousness thirty feet down under icy, motionless sea water, legs in the air, head and shoulders pinned down under awful, glue-like mud, scrabbling and dragging with broken finger nails and paralysed, frozen fingers at the safety-strap that still binds me helplessly to a splintered piece of what was formerly the cockpit.'

Biard won his fight against death, rising from the wreckage to paddle feebly on the surface, fighting for breath. First on the scene was Hubert Broad, who taxied across in the Gloster IIIA to fling a lifebelt to his team-mate. Soon a rescue launch was alongside, including among the anxious occupants R. J. Mitchell, torn with conflicting emotions. Relief that Biard had survived, dejection at the destruction of his creation.

The cause of the accident? Biard was to relate in his book that wing flutter was responsible, while many believed that he had misjudged the turn and stalled the aircraft. Perhaps it was inevitable that Biard should blame the aircraft but, of course, his belief may well have been correct. It is certain that we shall never know the truth. Dr Ermanno Bazzocchi told in later years that his extensive research relating to Schneider Trophy contenders suggested that the true cause of the accident was an inadvertent stall, but he expressed also the opinion that aileron flutter might have contributed to loss of control, leading to the stalled condition.

Henri Biard was lucky to have escaped with his life; as it was he suffered two broken ribs and severe injury to stomach muscles, and it was a pain-stricken and saddened pilot who witnessed the final twists of fate in what was, for Britain, an unhappy contest.

The loss of the S.4 meant that the reserve Gloster IIIA had to be prepared hurriedly to take part. There was to be considerable criticism of the team management at a later date, questions being raised as to why the reserve Gloster machine and the Bamel were not both in airworthy condition. It was shown that facilities at Baltimore were such that it had not been possible to get the second Gloster IIIA ready before this time and, in fact, the Bamel was never available for practice.

As the day of 23 October neared its end both of the Italians, the three Americans and Hubert Broad had all completed the navigability test satisfactorily, and their machines were anchored out in the bay for the water tightness test. A tremendous effort by the Gloster team had got their second string ready to essay the first of the compulsory tests, and Bert Hinkler climbed aboard and was soon airborne. Within no time at all he was seen coming in to land again, a broken flying-wire whipping dangerously in the slipstream. By the time it had been repaired the light was failing and Wilson, unprepared to endanger either Hinkler's life or the safety of the machine, waved aside the pilot's protests.

It seemed that Britain's reserve was out of the race also, but once again the all-pervading atmosphere of sportsmanship was to prevail. As the result of a unanimous appeal made by all competing pilots, the judges decided that Hinkler could make another attempt at the navigability test on the following morning. This he did, at first light, but found that the water offshore was too rough for him to take off. The Gloster machine was towed to shore and beached.

It was soon apparent that the weather was worsening, and as the wind whipped waves into white horses there came news that racing was postponed for the day. The decision had been inevitable, for in no time a full gale was blowing, collapsing tents and creating miserable conditions for everyone involved. So violent was wind and sea that seventeen Curtiss-designed Martin-built SC-1 seaplane torpedo-bombers, which had attended at Baltimore to wave the US Navy's flag, were torn from their moorings and wrecked: seven beyond repair.

Not until Monday 26 October were conditions considered suitable for the contest to proceed and, once again, Bert Hinkler took his place in the Gloster machine at daybreak to attempt the navigability test and complete the 6-hour water tightness test before race time. He should have known that twenty-six comprised two thirteens, that enigmatic number that plagued the British team in 1925.

This time Hinkler got his machine off the water without difficulty, heading for the beginning of the course where he had to alight and complete the first of the two compulsory taxi tests. Out in the bay the waves were still undulating from the storm, and as Hinkler got the seaplane down on the water they began to pound at the floats. This proved too much for the forward struts: as they collapsed the propeller carved its way through the duralumin floats, effectively eliminating him from the race. Britain's hopes now centred on Hubert Broad.

By race time conditions had improved still further, and the latest piece of information gave a little more confidence to the Americans: like Britain, Italy had only a single machine to contend the race. Morselli's M.33 had an unco-operative engine and had been withdrawn.

At 2.30 p.m. the roar of a Curtiss engine signalled the appearance of Jimmy Doolittle, who wasted little time in coaxing his R3C-2 into the air and setting course for the first turn at a cracking rate. Broad, Cuddihy, Ofstie and de Briganti followed in that order, all getting off without incident and joining the circuit.

Times for the first lap showed that Doolittle had recorded an astounding 223·15 mph (359·13 km/h) from a water take-off. For the first time in a

Lieutenant James H. Doolittle with the Curtiss R3C-2 with which he won the 1925 contest at Baltimore

USAF Museum close-up of the R3C-2 shows that designers had still a great deal to learn about clean finish

Schneider Contest the vast crowd could participate in such breath-taking information, for an excellent public address system and commentary kept them constantly aware of events. This oral communication was supplemented by notices, posted within a minute or so of lap completion, which gave last lap and average speeds for each competitor.

In the opinion of the crowd this was air racing at its best, especially with Doolittle flying like an inspired madman. Taking his turns low and tight, he thrilled the crowd near the turning points as he seemed almost to scrape the paint from the pylons. His second lap at a speed of nearly 234 mph (377 km/h) gave confidence that, barring accidents, the Trophy would stay in American hands.

Hubert Broad was doing his utmost to cut his lap times to a minimum, but the directional stability of the Gloster machine was still well below par and, try as he might, he found himself side-slipping out at every pylon into a wide-arc second-consuming turn. As a result he was averaging around 200 mph (322 km/h) for each lap and it seemed unlikely that he would be placed.

In the sole Macchi, de Briganti was showing that experience added to the superb manoeuvrability of Castoldi's trim flying-boat had so-nearly provided a worthy opponent. Unfortunately, the tired Curtiss D-12 was developing well below its maximum power; unless at least two of the competitors fell out of the race, it meant that his efforts would count for nothing.

So far as the Americans were concerned, Doolittle's team-mates were not making such a good showing. Both employed the flat, wide turns that had seemed so successful in the 1923 Contest, but which were giving them laps speeds around 20 mph (32 km/h) lower than those of the Army pilot, who was setting the crowd alight with a brilliant exhibition of flying skill. As the fifth lap figures were posted it seemed the result was certain, with Doolittle well in the lead and Cuddihy, Ofstie, Broad and de Briganti following in that order.

During the sixth lap came news that Ofstie had force-landed. This brought consternation to the Americans when it was known that he had suffered an engine failure. The more knowledgeable of the crowd began to wonder whether the pace was proving too hot for what was, after all, a comparatively new engine. They nodded their heads in wise confirmation when, during the last lap, Cuddihy's engine seized and caught fire, its oil supply exhausted. He, too, made a safe landing and, with fire extinguished, was towed disconsolately to the shore.

To the relief of the Americans, Doolittle's engine maintained the same high note of victory, driving him home the winner at an average speed of 232·573 mph (374·287 km/h), followed by Broad and de Briganti at 199·17 mph (320·527 km/h) and 168·44 mph (271·073 km/h) respectively. The winner had pushed the top speed up by over 55 mph (88 km/h) from the last contest, and even Broad's speed was almost 22 mph (35 km/h) above that of the 1923 Trophy winner.

Clearly, the seaplane had ousted the flying-boat from future contests; and once again the combination of engine, propeller and surface radiators that comprised the power plant system of the American aircraft had shown its superiority. Had the surface radiators which Folland had planned for the IIIA been ready in time, Glosters might well have captured the Trophy for Britain in 1925. Instead, as matters then stood, both Britain and Italy had a great deal to do in the next twelve months if America's firm grip on the Trophy was to be prised loose.

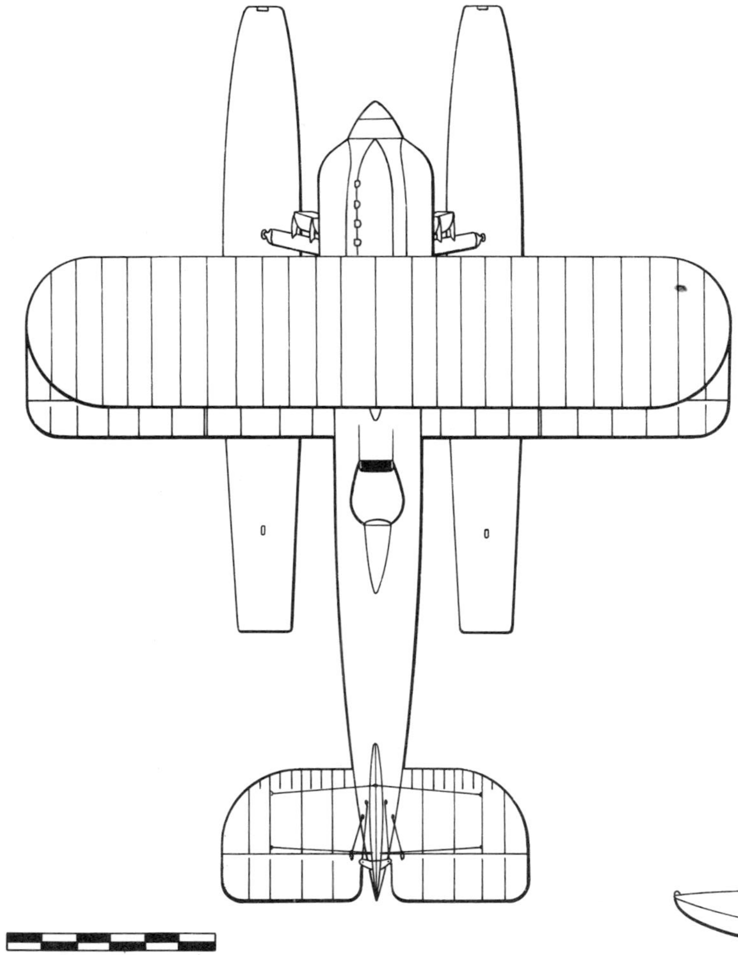

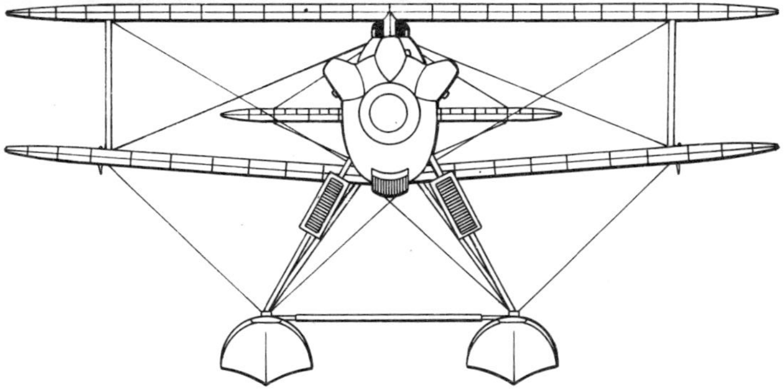

Gloster II (1924)

Wing Span: 20 ft (6·10 m)
Length Overall: 26 ft 10 in (8·18 m)
Wing Area: 165 sq. ft (15·33 m^2)
Weight Empty: 2,500 lb (1,134 kg)
T-O Weight: 3,100 lb (1,406 kg)
Max Wing Loading: 18·79 lb/sq. ft (91·74 kg/m^2)
Horsepower of Power Plant: 585 hp

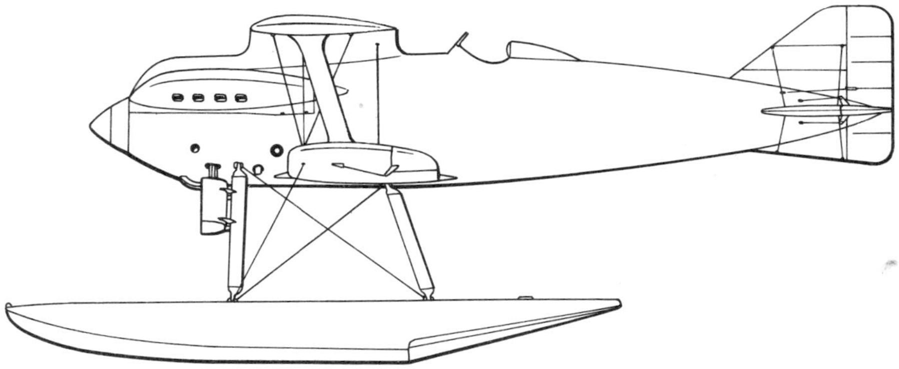

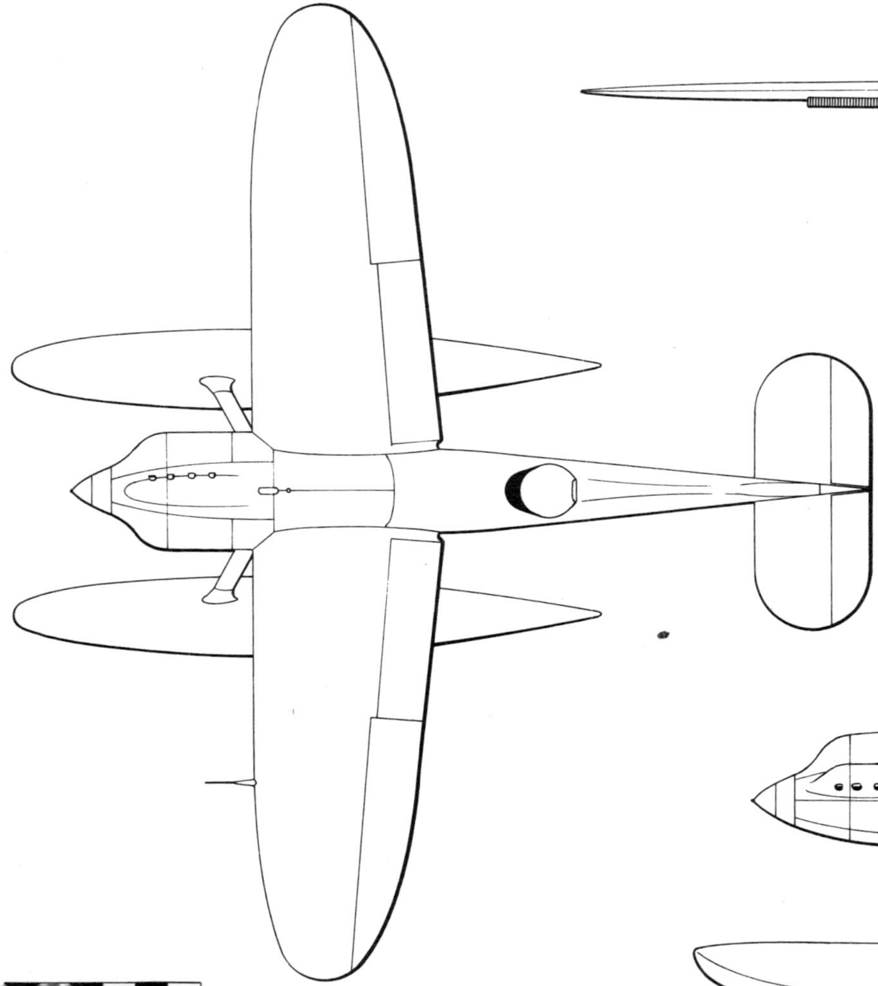

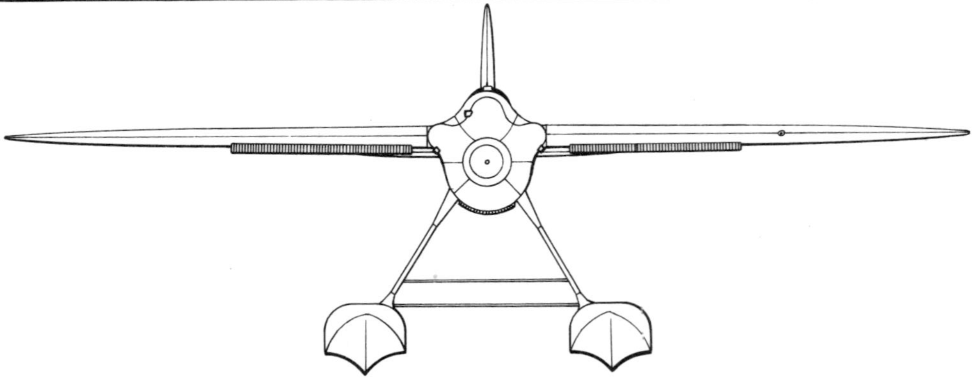

Supermarine S.4 (1924)

Wing Span: 30 ft $7\frac{1}{2}$ in (9·33 m)
Length Overall: 26 ft $7\frac{3}{4}$ in (8·12 m)
Wing Area: 139 sq. ft (12·91 m^2)
Weight Empty: 2,600 lb (1,179 kg)
T-O Weight: 3,191 lb (1,447 kg)
Max Wing Loading: 22·96 lb/sq. ft (112·10 kg/m^2)
Horsepower of Power Plant: 680 hp

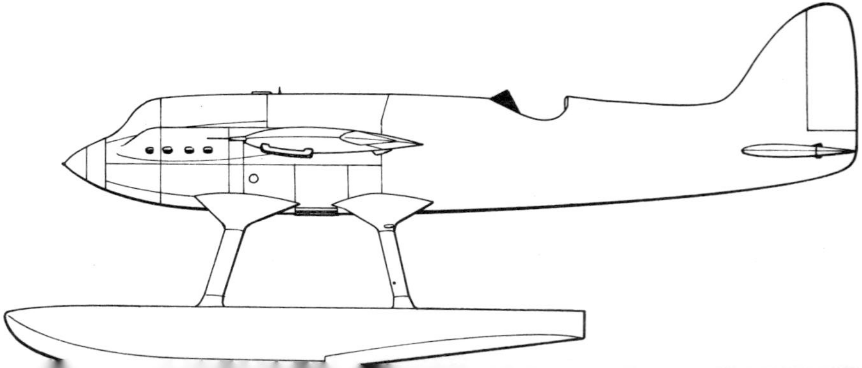

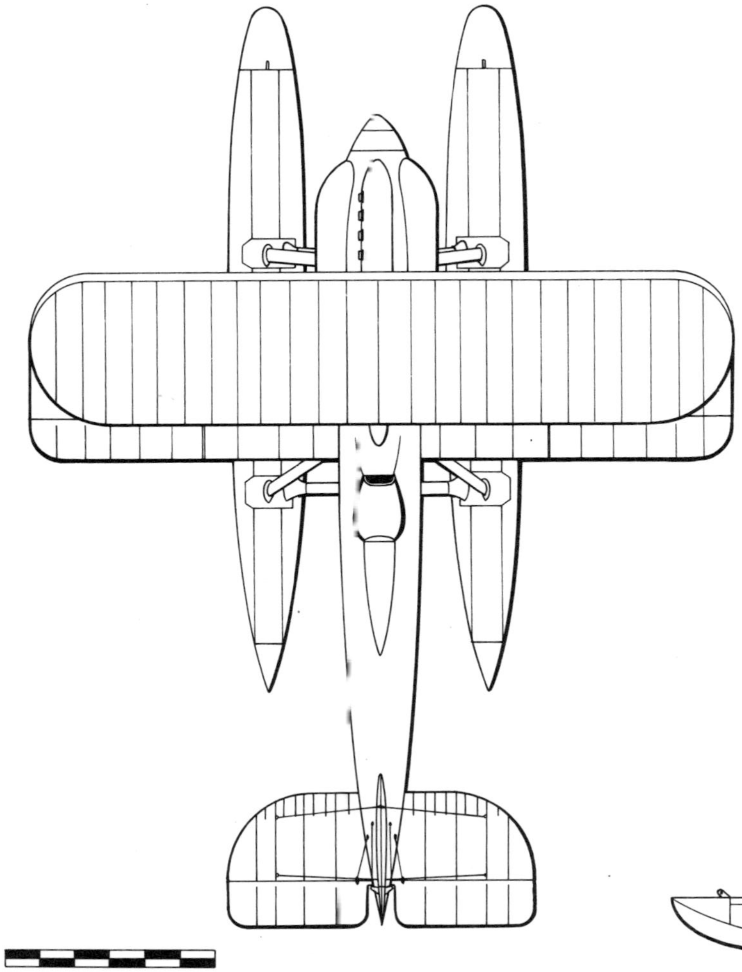

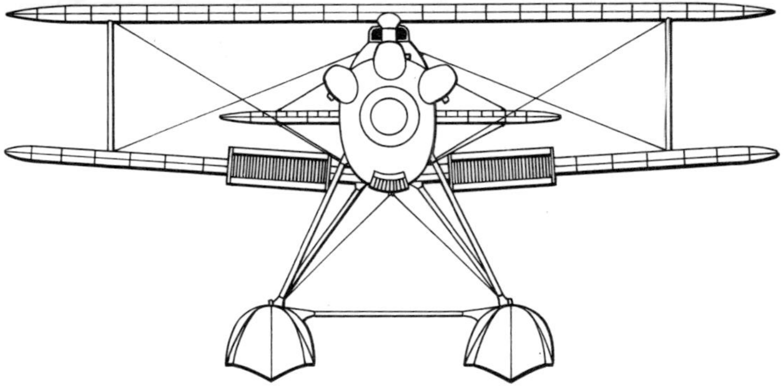

Gloster IIIA (1924)

Wing Span: 20 ft (6·10 m)
Length Overall: 26 ft 10 in (8·18 m)
Wing Area: 152 sq. ft (14·12 m²)
Weight Empty: 2,028 lb (920 kg)
T-O Weight: 2,689 lb (1,220 kg)
Max Wing Loading: 17·68 lb/sq. ft (86·32 kg/m²)
Horsepower of Power Plant: 700 hp

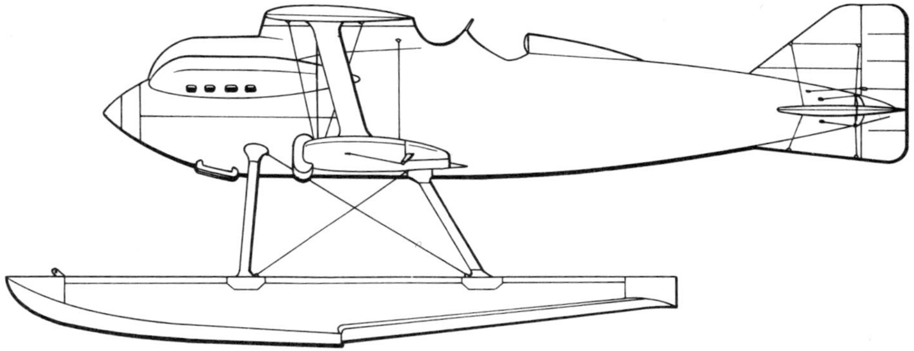

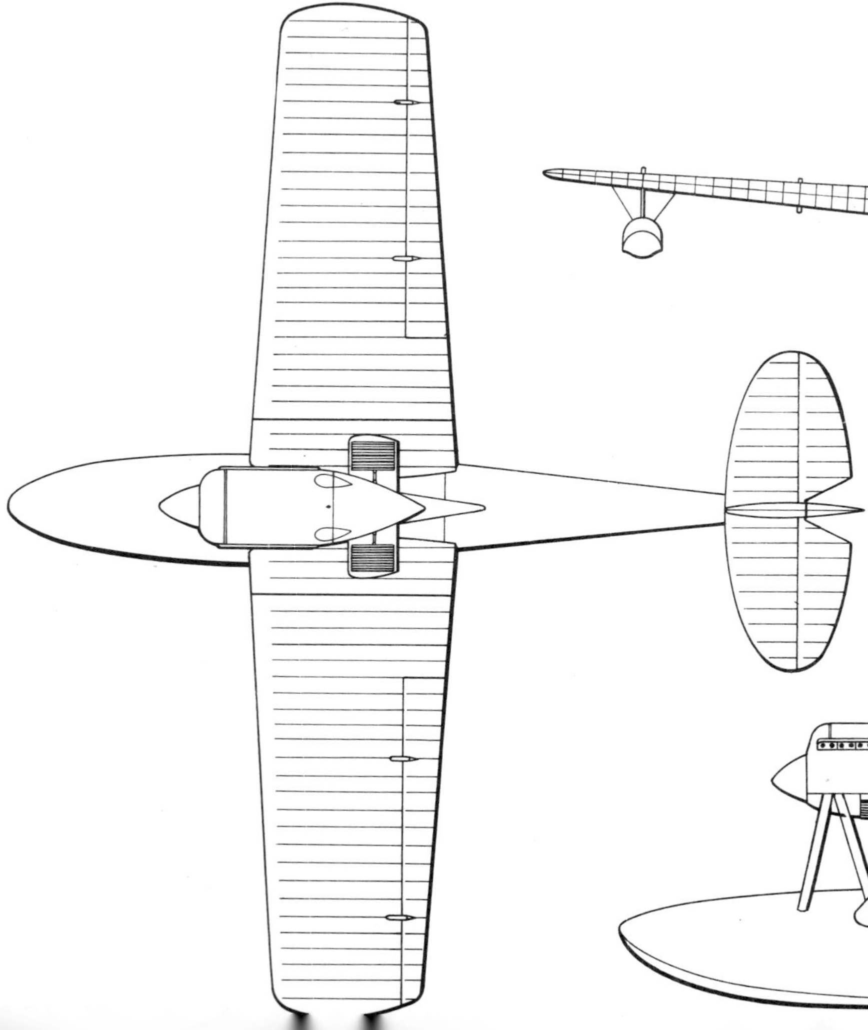

Macchi M.33 (1924)

Wing Span: 32 ft $9\frac{3}{4}$ in (10·00 m)
Length Overall: 27 ft $4\frac{1}{4}$ in (8·34 m)
Wing Area: 176·5 sq. ft (16·40 m^2)
Weight Empty: 2,149 lb (975 kg)
T-O Weight: 2,768 lb (1,255 kg)
Max Wing Loading: 15·63 lb/sq. ft (76·31 kg/m^2)
Horsepower of Power Plant: 450 hp

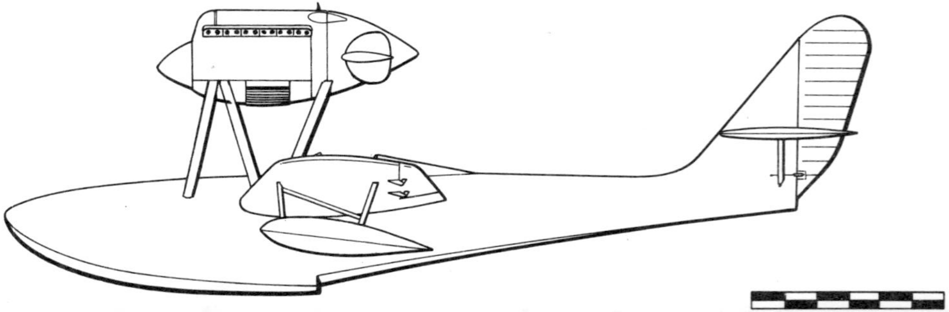

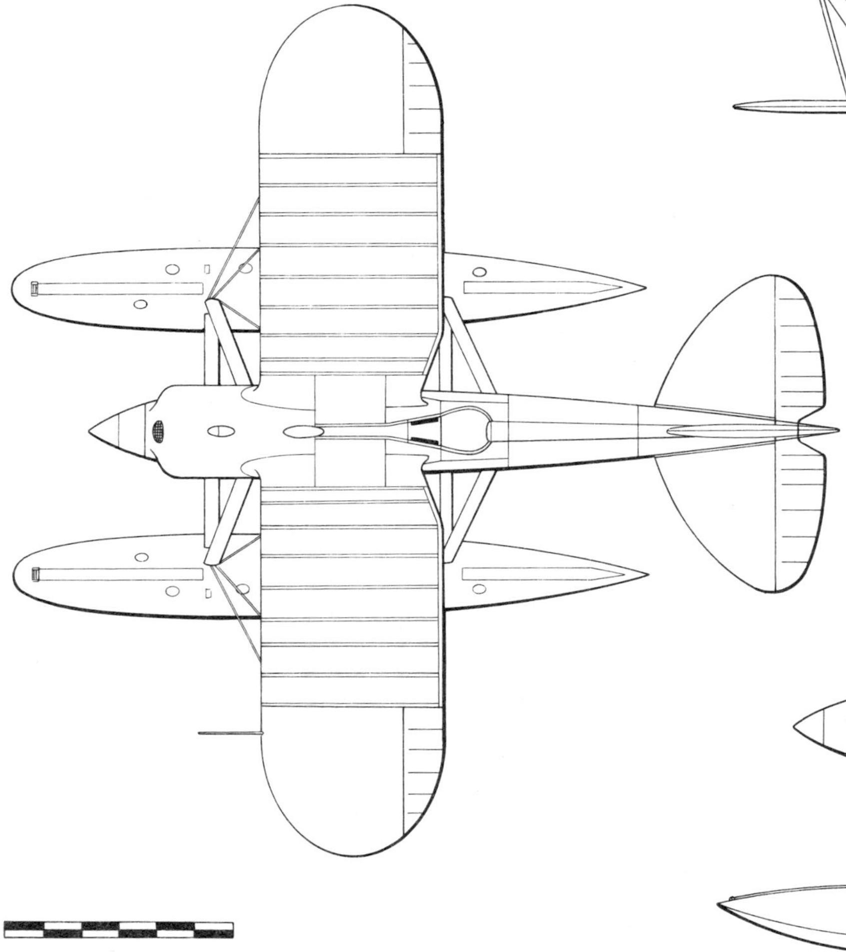

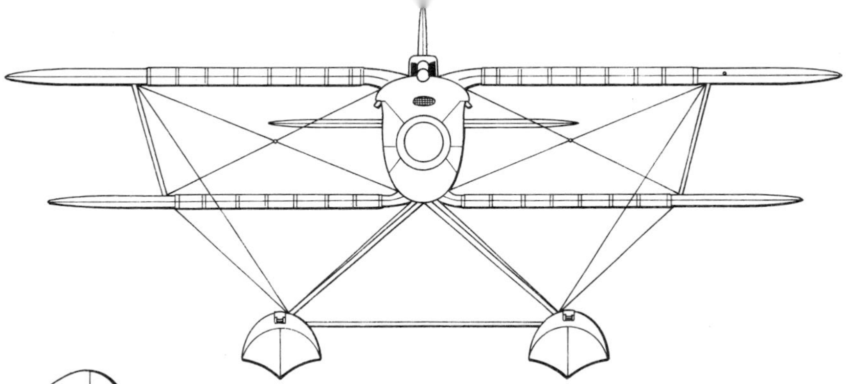

Curtiss R3C-2 (1924)

Wing Span: 22 ft (6·71 m)
Length Overall: 19 ft $8\frac{1}{2}$ in (6.00 m)
Wing Area: 149 sq. ft (13·84 m^2)
Weight Empty: 1,750 lb (794 kg)
T-O Weight: 2,768 lb (1,255 kg)
Max Wing Loading: 14·43 lb/sq. ft (70·45 kg/m^2)
Horsepower of Power Plant: 610 hp

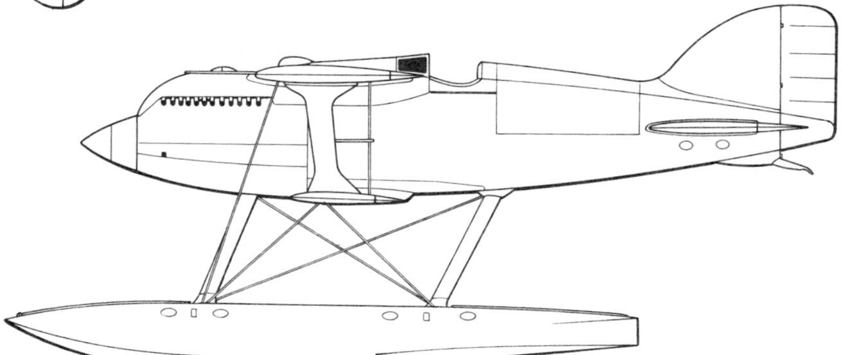

8

Italian victory in Virginia

1926

Following upon the pre-1925 contest comments of Colonel Moore-Brabazon to the effect that, for the first time, Britain was making determined efforts to win the Trophy, it was inevitable that there should be a spate of post-race questions. Why had Britain failed again? Was she no longer capable of producing competitive aircraft?

Heading the list was the destruction of the S.4. Why had it crashed? Did not its failure highlight, once again, the inherent weakness of a monoplane configuration? Indeed, had Mitchell stepped beyond the bounds of technological prudence? In answer to the latter question it was pointed out that Mario Castoldi had adopted a similar configuration. Whilst admitting this to be true, the 'experts' argued that the available engine power of the Italian machine was much lower than that of the S.4 and that, in consequence, it must be assumed its speed was lower as well.

In a paper read to the Royal Aeronautical Society on 21 January 1926, Colonel J. S. Buchanan, an Associate of the Society, did much to put the situation in proper perspective. He emphasised the lack of facilities at Bay Shore Park which, together with the appalling weather, had made it extremely difficult for the British team to prepare for the contest despite their early arrival. This had meant that Biard, Broad and Hinkler had far too little time in which to practice. By comparison with the experience of the US Army and Navy pilots, especially under racing conditions in earlier Schneider and Pulitzer races, our men had been able to accumulate only an hour or two in the air in their new machines, and under trying conditions. Confirmation of the difficulties under which they had worked was also to come in a letter from C. M. Keys, President of the Curtiss Company who wrote:

'At Baltimore conditions were a very severe test of both materials and men. The weather was execrable. Your men worked for ten days under very trying physical conditions. My own men were working under the same conditions, so that I have a rather intimate knowledge of them. Your representatives kept their good nature, their good manners and good sportsmanship and came out of the trying situation with a host of friends and no enemies.'

But with regard to the aircraft themselves, Colonel Buchanan pointed out that the US had a clear design lead in their combination of power plant, propeller and surface radiators. Only in float design could it be said that Britain held distinct superiority.

He detailed what he considered four vital points if Britain was to have any chance in the next Contest:

(i) Designers must concentrate on reduction of fuselage drag, by reducing fuselage size and improving aerodynamic efficiency.

(ii) Wing surface radiators were essential: the day of drag-inducing coolers of the Lamblin type was past so far as high-speed aircraft were concerned.

(iii) More emphasis should be placed on increasing propeller efficiency, to which end there must be ample opportunity for testing competing aircraft with various propeller combinations well prior to the race.

(iv) Last, but by far from least, it was absolutely essential to have pilots who had been trained for high-speed flight. The US pilots had all gained such experience as normal routine in their service training. Apart from a few isolated and short periods in the air the British pilots had no experience at speeds in excess of 200 mph (322 km/h).

In the discussion which followed the presentation of Colonel Buchanan's paper, Harry Folland gave his support in particular to items (iii) and (iv). There were, he said, indications that the Gloster machines had suffered from propeller inefficiency, the pitch of the blades being affected by straightening of the blade under centrifugal force. In this connection he pointed out that the tip speed of the propeller fitted to the Gloster machines was 1,120 ft/sec (341 m/sec), by comparison with only 950 ft/sec (290 m/sec) of those fitted to the Curtiss racers. He could, he said, see little point in evolving aircraft capable of much higher maximum speed if we did not have specially trained pilots capable of exploiting the full potential of such aircraft.

Problems there were indeed. There were those who thought them too many and too great. It was Colonel W. A. Bristow, a consulting aeronautical engineer, who put the whole matter into commonsense proportions when he commented: 'If all our difficulties are eliminated, there will be no need to run the race at all. Competitors will send models of their machines to an international wind tunnel, which could be set up at Locarno, and a year or two later the winner will receive a certificate signed by all the Prime Ministers of Europe.' To put it in another way, the difficulties inherent in all technological advance must be overcome by realistic research and development.

All of this, and much more, proved to be somewhat academic, for the Royal Aero Club had already said there was insufficient time for Britain to design, build and prepare suitable aircraft to contend in 1926 and, accordingly, asked the American NAA to postpone the race until 1927. This was the first suggestion that a period of twelve months was inadequate to evolve the special racing aircraft needed to take part in this international high-speed event, and though then a little premature, it was a proposal that was to be adopted at a later stage in the contests.

Not surprisingly, the Americans were not prepared to accept such a postponement. They had already won the event twice in three years, and with permanent tenure of the Trophy requiring only one more win they were determined to hold the event in 1926. They believed that with a further twelve months in which to continue the development of their Curtiss racers, they would still be in a position to retain their performance lead without recourse to completely new and costly designs. Why should they wait until another nation had produced a better aircraft? A comment in Britain's aviation Press put this even more pointedly: 'If the Americans do not fly over and claim the Trophy [in the absence of foreign competition] this year, they are better sportsmen than they need be and worse businessmen than they ought to be.'

Another proposed change in the regulations had been submitted to the FAI by both the French and Italian aero clubs. Differing slightly, they raised once again the question of non-consumable load, France suggesting that this should be 551 lb (250 kg), while Italy wanted this load to be 881 lb (400 kg) and proposed also a minimum control speed of 70 mph (113 km/h).

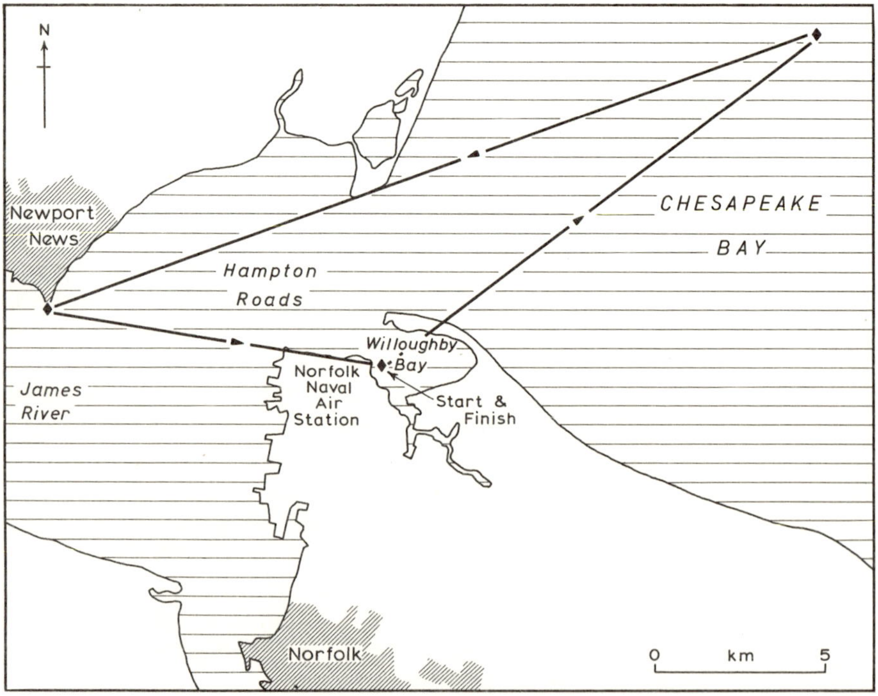

8. Schneider Trophy Contest Course: Hampton Roads 1926

It is worth considering that, in fact, these proposals were realistic and in keeping with the fundamental intention of Jacques Schneider; namely, to encourage the development of waterborne aircraft that would be capable of initiating safe and regular intercontinental air travel. The original emphasis on speed he had considered necessary to breed reliability, but one must appreciate that the lightweight, high-speed racing seaplanes which were then being developed for the annual contests were a far cry from the dream of ocean-crossing airliners, capable of carrying passengers across and around the face of the world.

Be that as it may, the FAI turned down the French and Italian proposals, and the Schneider remained a speed contest pure and simple.

However, Britain was not alone in her endeavours to bring about a postponement of the 1926 contest, for the Italians had similar feelings. They, too, did their utmost to influence the Americans to defer the next contest until 1927. It was to no avail, but both of these European nations believed that if no contenders were forthcoming it was unlikely the Americans would have the audacity to take the Trophy for all time by the anti-climax of a fly-over.

Despite all representations, including a personal appeal made in America by Sefton Brancker, the NAA remained adamant, duly advising that the contest would be held once more in the Chesapeake Bay. This time, however, the centre of organisation would be Norfolk Naval Air Station (NAS), Virginia, where facilities for the handling of seaplanes already existed. The contest was to be held during the week commencing 24 October.

This date provided adequate excuse for a new spate of protests, it being argued that the weather conditions at the end of October were unfavourable. Surely, there had been ample evidence of this the previous year, and better weather could be more or less assured by holding the event in the early summer. It would be appreciated, of course, that by bringing the contest forward to, say, June, it would not be possible for the British or Italians to produce suitable aircraft within this time scale. Postponement until the early summer of 1927 was, therefore, imperative. Needless to say, the Americans were not moved from their former decision by this rather strong-smelling red herring.

At this same time in Britain there was evidence of attempts to sway the Air Ministry into creating a pool of specially trained high-speed pilots. Among other campaigners, C. G. Grey proposed in *The Aeroplane* a Royal Air Force team comprising the best service pilots available from Farnborough and Martlesham. He suggested that in the absence of suitable racing seaplanes they could begin their training on fast aircraft, such as the Fairey Fox, converting to the Bamel for seaplane experience and following up on the Gloster IIIAs. By this means they would have acquired considerable experience by the time that more advanced aircraft became available to contend the Schneider contest.

To make certain, when the time came, that these pilots and their aircraft should compete under the best possible conditions, C.G.G. added that they should travel to America in an aircraft carrier. By this means they would have the best possible maintenance and facilities, and would be completely independent of the very difficult conditions with which they had had to contend at Baltimore. He concluded by emphasising the urgent need to win in 1926: 'No more muddling through,' he wrote, 'for if so we admit that our designers are inferior.'

No matter how many endeavours were made by the aviation and general Press to whip up some degree of enthusiasm, it was to prove a waste of effort. It did seem at one period that there might be two private venture entries from Britain, for rumour had it that Supermarine and Short Brothers were to build aircraft. This was a rather premature leak and none materialised. And if any confirmation of the task facing British and Italian manufacturers was required, it had already been provided by Jimmy Doolittle who, on 27 October 1926, had set a new world speed record for seaplanes in the Curtiss R3C-2 at an average of 245·713 mph (395·43 km/h).

As soon as it became completely clear that there would be no postponement of the contest, and that the Americans were determined to win the Trophy for all time in 1926—by making an unopposed fly-over of the course if necessary—Italy decided that despite all the difficulties and the minimal time available, she must make an all-out effort to ensure that the Trophy was brought back to Europe.

The decision was that of Benito Mussolini, the 'Duce', who had first attained power in Italy by a *coup d'état* in October 1922. The political, industrial and economic problems associated with the new regime were the prime reason why Italy had been unable to make a strong challenge for the Trophy since losing it to the British in 1922. Gradually, however, Mussolini had succeeded in transforming Italy into a totalitarian state, with himself as its Dictator, uniting the majority of the people in a common aim to work for better times.

Mussolini knew that to wrest the Trophy back from America would be first-class propaganda, emphasising both at home and abroad the growing potential of the country's aviation industry and, by inference, the strength of her war machine.

However eloquently phrased, Mussolini's first appeal to the aviation industry fell on deaf ears. There was no manufacturer who could afford to design and construct unaided an aeroplane sufficiently advanced to present a worthwhile challenge to the Curtiss racers. Furthermore, no suitable power plant was then available in Italy.

Such excuses meant nothing to Mussolini, determined to show the world what had been achieved by the 'miracle' of Fascism. His appeal became changed to an order: Italy was to win the Trophy at any cost, and the government would provide all financial backing and any other assistance required.

Only two Italian firms had the experience and ability to take on such a formidable task, Macchi and Fiat. Both had protested there was insufficient time available to design and develop the necessary hardware. But with a government unprepared to accept a refusal they found themselves elected.

Since there was no alternative, Mario Castoldi called to the workers in the Macchi factory for their assistance, enthusing them with the suggestion of what success might mean for the company if their machine could win. It was highly possible that a grateful government might well prove generous in the distribution of contracts for new, fast fighters to equip the Regia Aeronautica, and all would benefit from a new degree of prosperity.

For his part, Castoldi concentrated on producing a world-beater: when the drawings for the new machine were seen for the first time, they showed that he had arrived at a monoplane seaplane, combining lessons learned from those aircraft which had competed at Baltimore. A low-wing monoplane configuration had been chosen, primarily to enhance the pilot's view when on or near the water, and since the M.33 and S.4 had both hinted that their cantilever construction might be suspect to flutter—a phenomenon for which no explanation existed at that time—the new seaplane had a wire-braced wing. Designated M.39, the simple three-dimensional line drawings which had emanated from Castoldi's drawing board suggested immediately an aircraft of classic appearance. When presented in Rome the new design was accepted without delay. If Fiat could provide an engine that took an equally advanced step into the future, they would together form a formidable combination.

As detail drawings began to appear in the Macchi works, the team allocated to construction of the five examples (two trainers and three for competition) set about the task of component fabrication. So great was their enthusiasm and dedication that in mid-April 1926 the first machine was beginning to take shape on the factory floor.

The wide-chord monoplane wing was of all-wood two-spar construction, with surface cooling radiators on both upper and lower surfaces that extended almost to three-quarter span. Two streamline bracing wires on each side stretched from the upper longerons of the fuselage to the upper wing surface, and from beneath the wing to the top of the floats. Wide-span ailerons extended inward from the wingtips and occupied almost three-quarters of each wing trailing-edge.

The all-wood monocoque fuselage bore a resemblance to that of the Curtiss racers, differing primarily in that the area of the tailplane was considerably greater, and to enhance directional stability a large ventral fin swept down to align with a deep rudder. Single-step V-bottom floats, very similar to those of the Gloster IIIA, were carried on two streamline-section inverted Vee struts, strut-braced to each other.

The power plant installation was remarkably clean, the cylinder blocks within beautifully streamlined fairings and the short stub exhausts almost flush with the engine cowlings. The oil cooler was beneath the engine, and contoured to conform with the lines of the lower cowling. The Curtiss-Reed two-blade metal tractor propeller had a sharply pointed spinner.

What had Fiat done to provide a power plant worthy of installation in this aircraft which, apart from the encumbrance of floats, seemed to suggest aerodynamic perfection?

Their task was perhaps the most difficult, for the availability of a surplus of power could often make good any shortcoming in airframe design. Their problem, however, was one that was troubling engine designers around the world. It seemed that so far as the 12-cylinder in-line liquid-cooled engine was concerned, whether of Vee or broad arrow configuration, a platform of performance had been attained. Excursions into the field of greater power output were merely extending into new areas of difficulty. More power, however achieved, brought more heat to be dissipated, and unless temperature could be controlled to within certain limits carburation and ignition problems began to proliferate. There was also a conflicting weight penalty for, generally speaking at that time, more power came from bigger, heavier engines. These two factors, in conjunction with increases in fuel and oil consumption, frequently offset the limited power increase that was gained. The real need seemed to spell the word impossible: more power, less frontal area and reduced weight.

Benefiting from their tests and study of the Curtiss D-12, Fiat had evolved in 1925 a 12-cylinder Vee engine designated A.20, which had a nominal rating of 410 hp and maximum take-off rating of 455 hp. A slightly larger version, the A.22, had nominal and maximum ratings of 550 and 590 hp respectively. An even more powerful engine, the 750/800 hp A.25 was under development, but although then running on bench test its physical size was such that it was quite unsuited for installation in the Macchi M.39 without deforming the sleek lines of the aircraft.

It was clear to Fiats that within the time available it would be impossible to design, build and type test a completely new engine, and they elected instead to see what could be done to increase the power developed by the A.22, the overall dimensions of which made it the most suitable for installation in the new Macchi seaplane. This, then, was the basis of their new engine for the Schneider contest and which, in due course, acquired the designation AS.2. Put in the simplest form, the changes involved increases of bore and stroke, rpm and compression ratio, but a better comparison of the difference between these two engines is provided by the table opposite.

Thus, they achieved a significant gain in horsepower without any increase of frontal area. Of particular importance was the fact that the operating weight of the AS.2, complete with coolant and oil, was 62 lb (28 kg) below that of the standard production A.22 without coolant and oil.

	A.22	AS.2
Bore	5·31 in (13·5 cm)	5·51 in (14·0 cm)
Stroke	6·30 in (16·0 cm)	6·69 in (17·0 cm)
Compression ratio	5·3	6
Weight, dry	970 lb (440 kg)	783 lb (355 kg)
Weight, including water and oil	—	908 lb (412 kg)
Maximum horsepower	590	850
Maximum rpm	2,100	2,500

As the external dimensions of both engines were the same, it was possible to use the A.22 to power the practice machines, first off the factory floor, and these also had slightly increased wing span. The pilot's initiation to the new type was, therefore, of a more gentle nature than if he had been thrown into a symbolical deep end, represented by the new M.39 racer with a high powered engine.

Dimensions of the M.39 included wing span of 30 ft 4⅝ in (9·26 m), length overall 22 ft 1⅜ in (6·74 m), height overall 10 ft 0½ in (3·06 m) and wing area of 156·08 sq. ft (14·50 m²). Maximum take-off weight was 3,560 lb (1,615 kg).

The first of the trainers was ready in a remarkably short time, making its maiden flight in the hands of the company's test pilot, Romeo Sartori, on 6 June; but it was not until towards the end of August that he was able to fly the first of the competition machines.

There had been considerable speculation in America as to whether the Italians would be ready in time to compete in the contest, but the constructional progress being made in Italy was such that it was possible for the Aéro-Club d'Italia to confirm to the Americans in mid-August that they would be ready and able to take part on the appointed date.

Base for the team of Italian pilots training for the contest was at Schiranna Air Station on Lake Varese, conveniently situated to the Macchi works. Here assembled Major Mario de Bernardi, Captain Arturo Ferrarin and Lieutenant Adriano Bacula, with Commandant Vittorio Centurione as captain of the team, and with Captain G. Guasconi as reserve. All were experienced pilots, members of the Regia Aeronautica, and Ferrarin was already well-known for achievement in long-distance flights. As soon as their aircraft became available practice began, but it was soon clear that all was not well with the new Fiat engine. It was suffering from carburation problems, as had engines of other manufacturers attempting to obtain a quart from the proverbial pint pot. While Fiat's engineers did their best to minimise the fault, the pilots did their utmost to become acquainted with the new aircraft. They presented no serious problems in flight, proving to be fast and sensitive to the controls.

'Fast' is relative: it can be put in perspective by noting that de Bernardi recorded around 257 mph (414 km/h) over a measured 3 km stretch on 17 September. This was exactly the tonic the Italians needed, for the 1925 race had been won at just over 232 mph (373 km/h), and it seemed unlikely that the Curtiss racers could be pushed to much higher speeds. Understandably, this speed capability of the M.39 was maintained as a well-guarded secret.

Their new-found elation was destroyed just four days later when Centurione, flying one of the practice machines, stalled into the lake and was killed. This set-back, coupled with continuing engine problems, induced the Italians to ask the NAA to postpone the race for a short period. Sportingly, this was agreed, the new date for the Contest being changed to 11 November, a decision that was accompanied by a howl of protest from Britain's Royal Aero Club. What, I wonder, would the British Club have expected if they, and not the Italians, had been involved in similar circumstances.

These extra days of grace gave the Italian pilots and mechanics the breathing space they needed, allowing time for all of the team to put in some additional practice before, on 12 October, they and their aircraft sailed from Genoa on the SS *Conte Rosso*.

In fact, the situation in the United States was not quite so happy as might have been expected, and the gain in time resulting from the Italian application for a temporary postponement suited the Americans very well.

For 1926 their team was without US Army participation. Instead Lieutenant H. J. Norton of the US Marine Corps had been brought in, together with Navy pilots Lieutenants F. Conant and W. C. Tomlinson, as well as Lieutenant G. T. Cuddihy who had had the misfortune to suffer engine failure during the last lap of the 1925 contest.

There was to be little change in their aircraft. The Curtiss racers which had done so well in 1925 would defend the Trophy again, two of them being modified only to accommodate engines of greater power, while all three had improved single-step floats. That which retained the Curtiss V-1400 engine was the machine which had carried Doolittle to victory, still retaining the designation R3C-2 (A6979). With the installation of a Packard engine A7054 became re-designated R3C-3, while A6978 with a more powerful Curtiss engine became designated R3C-4.

The Packard Motor Company's Model 1A-1500 installed in the R3C-3 was a 12-cylinder in-line liquid-cooled engine of V form, and was provided with reduction gearing to allow increased engine rpm without detracting from propeller efficiency. The standard direct-drive engine developed 525 hp at 2,100 rpm with a compression ratio of 5·1. The standard geared engine developed 600 hp at 2,500 rpm with compression ratio of 6, but for the Schneider contest a special engine with compression ratio of 7·6 was prepared, this developing 700 hp.

The Curtiss engine, designated V-1550, represented a further stage in the development of the D-12. Its capacity had been increased by enlarging the cylinder bores to $5\frac{1}{8}$ in (13·0 cm) and that prepared for the contest had had its compression ratio raised to 7·5 so as to develop 708 hp at 2,600 rpm. Detail improvement in the design, such as the use of a single two-spark magneto to replace two separate magnetos, and a change in the spur gear drive for the camshafts had reduced frontal area, overall length and weight.

In addition to the three R3C racers, one of the first of the famous line of Curtiss Hawk fighters was allocated as reserve machine. The Navy had ordered nine of these aircraft, designated P-1, in March 1925 and these had provisions for float installation. Delivered as F6C-1s with 440 hp Curtiss D-12 engines, they were of biplane configuration with pronounced forward stagger to enhance pilot visibility. The single-bay wings were of wood two-spar construction, fabric-covered, with N-shape interplane and centre-section struts. Fuselage and wire-braced tail unit were of welded steel-tube construction, fabric-covered. It was one of these Navy aircraft which was allocated to the team for practice and as a reserve.

These aircraft, combined with a team of experienced pilots, gave the Americans every confidence of success, but when they began practice in early September they had quickly run into trouble. On 13 September Lieutenant Norton flying the CR-3 (A6081), the machine which had won the 1923 contest and which had been made available for practice, stalled in a turn. The seaplane dived into shallow water and he was killed. This was bad enough, but when the team moved to Hampton Roads there was yet another tragic accident.

On 30 October Lieutenant Frank Conant took off from his unit at Anacostia en route to Norfolk, but while skimming low over the waters of Winter Harbour his aircraft hit an obstruction sticking out of the shallow water and he, too, was killed.

Replacements had to be hurried in: Lieutenant C. Frank Schilt of the USMC, an experienced fighter pilot, replaced Norton; Lieutenant C. C. Champion was brought in as the reserve. It was an inauspicious start, aggravated still further when the engine of the R3C-4 overheated during flight practice, the resulting detonation damaging the engine seriously.

Spirits were at low ebb, and the first sight of the Macchi entries when the Italian team arrived at Hampton Roads towards the end of October came as something of a shock. There was no doubt that they looked very advanced aircraft and with their engines of nearly 900 hp might provide unbeatable competition.

The first grain of comfort came when the Italians started flying, and the Americans discovered that they, too, were having problems with their engines. When de Bernardi made his first flight he had force-landed with his engine on fire. Both of the other Fiat engines were in trouble, one still plagued by carburation problems, the other needing two new pistons which had to be cannibalised from their reserve aircraft.

Designated R3C-4, one of the 1925 Curtiss R3C-2s re-engined with a 700 hp Curtiss V-1550 engine

It was this beautifully finished Macchi M.39, flown by Mario de Bernardi, which took the Trophy back to a temporary home in Italy

By then the appointed day for the navigability test, 10 November, was fast approaching, and neither team had a great deal of confidence in their machines.

The Americans had discovered an unexpected difficulty with the R3C-3, its geared Packard engine turning the propeller in the opposite direction to that of the direct-driven Curtiss engine. This meant that propeller torque was contrary to that of the Curtiss-engined aircraft with which the team had gained their racing experience. An attempt had been made to reduce the tendency of the starboard float to dig in by offsetting the fin, but the machine's speed on the surface was such that this had little effect. Consequently, the R3C-3 was something of a handful to get into the air.

Its pilot, Cuddihy, was highly experienced and soon mastered the differing technique required for a clean take-off, but flight tests had shown the R3C-4 to be the faster machine and, because of his experience, Cuddihy was ordered to fly this latter aircraft instead.

The course for the 1926 contest was one of 26·98 nm (50 km), to be covered seven times, with its starting point in Willoughby Bay, adjacent to Norfolk NAS. The first NE leg was of 8·58 nm (15·906 km) to a pylon out in Chesapeake Bay, an acute turn to a WSW heading would then put the competitors on the longest stretch of the course, 12·96 nm (24·021 km) to Newport News, the final turning point on to a course slightly south of due east, 5·44 nm (10·073 km) back to the starting point.

In the opposing camps there were alternations of elation and despair, brought about as first one and then the other side was seen to have an aircraft capable of breathtaking speed. There was always the underlying and enigmatic question as to whether the speed demonstrated was or was not studiously restricted. Only one factor was clear: there was every indication that the top speed of both American and Italian aircraft was very close and that, with good weather and well-behaved engines, it could be an exciting race.

Typically frustrating was the weather which, on 10 November, was at its most unco-operative, requiring a postponement of twenty-four hours before the navigability test could start. In fact, it was not until late afternoon of 11 November that conditions were good enough for de Bernardi to begin the test and, with failing light, it was decided that those who were not inclined to take the test that evening would be allowed to do so on the following morning. Schilt alone of the Americans decided to go that evening, but both of the remaining Italian pilots, Bacula and Ferrarin, followed de Bernardi into the air.

Fate was busy knitting a pattern of trouble for the Italians. De Bernardi landed after completing the test successfully but, in the poor light conditions, had a float holed by the boat that came out to tow him to the mooring for his water tightness test. Bacula landed without trouble, but of Ferrarin there was no sign. Much later it was discovered that he had force-landed in the seaway after an engine failure, in grave danger of collision with shipping, for his aircraft had no navigation lights. It was well over two hours later that he was located and towed back to Norfolk NAS.

The first quick glance at his aircraft was far from encouraging: rivulets of oil were dripping from the lower cowlings. With the cowlings removed the situation seemed hopeless, for jagged holes in the crankcase made it clear that at least one connecting rod had failed.

All through the night the Italians worked to get their two machines ready to complete their tests on the following day. The repair of de Bernardi's machine was not covered by the rules, but since it was a motor boat belonging to the organising committee which had dealt the vicious blow to the Macchi's float, it was only reasonable to allow the Italians to repair or replace it.

That was the least of their troubles. The main difficulty was that they had no spare engine, which meant that the already-cannibalised engine of the reserve machine had to be stripped completely, components from it and Ferrarin's engine being combined to produce one whole. It was a near-exhausted gang of men who, next day, had the reward of seeing both de Bernardi and Ferrarin qualify for the speed contest.

Meanwhile, the Americans had been having their share of trouble. Lieutenant Champion was confined to a sick bed and had been replaced by the reserve, Lieutenant Tomlinson. As he and Cuddihy came out on the morning of 12 November to begin the navigability test it was seen that Cuddihy took the Curtiss-engined R3C-4, Tomlinson the more-touchy R3C-3.

Both got away without incident, though poor Tomlinson found the opposite torque of the Packard engine/propeller combination rather more than he had bargained for, and staggered rather than flew into the air. Once airborne, however, he settled down well enough, and was seen to be handling the Curtiss racer with a fair degree of skill, taking time to become familiar with its differing handling characteristics.

But when the moment came for him to put the R3C on the water for his first landing he misjudged his height, the aircraft stalling in from only a few feet, but heavy enough and fast enough for it to cartwheel and end up on its back. A somewhat shaken Tomlinson was trapped in the cockpit, but recovered quickly enough and escaped, sitting on a float until rescued.

With only two machines left to compete against the three Italians it was considered essential to bring in the reserve. Consequently, later that day, a dried-out Tomlinson was tucked into the little F6C-1, in which he completed the test successfully. With a maximum level speed of around 150 mph (241 km/h) there was really little point in entering the Hawk, but barring disaster it could be relied upon the complete the course if, for one reason or another, all the other machines failed to get around the seven laps.

Saturday 13 November showed that even that late in the year it was possible for the weather to be kind, for sun, clear skies and calm water greeted the crowds that assembled to see if the home team could make the Trophy American property. As at Baltimore the facilities for communicating events to the crowd were good and, all in all, it promised to be an exciting day for the some 30,000 spectators occupying every convenient vantage point.

And so it was, from the word go, for with each team fielding three competitors there was scope for the exploitation of tactics. First away just after 2.30 p.m. was Adriano Bacula, impressing the spectators with his fast, smooth take-off. He was followed by Tomlinson in the F6C, it appearing more Dodo than Hawk by comparison with the spectacular performance of the Macchi.

Next to go, officially, was Ferrarin. But so that he could sit on the tail of Cuddihy, next away, he pretended some difficulty in starting the Fiat engine. As he had hoped, the American was waved off to begin his take-off, and immediately Ferrarin started and moved up to be next off. It was not long before the two remaining competitors, de Bernardi and Schilt were safely airborne, and the crowd began to bubble with excitement as they awaited the first lap speeds that would tell so much.

Slowest, as expected, was Tomlinson in the Hawk at a mere 137·31 mph (220·97 km/h), but the greatest shock came when Bacula in the Macchi was seen to have lapped at only 209·58 mph (337·29 km/h). If this was typical of the Macchis, then the Italians were clearly outclassed. And if any confirmation of this was needed the announcement of Cuddihy's speed made the situation startlingly clear. At 232·427 mph (374·04 km/h) he was almost 23 mph (37 km/h) faster than the Italian. American hopes soared.

Ferrarin's first lap brought them back to earth again, just over 2 mph (3·2 km/h) faster than Cuddihy, and de Bernardi staggered them with 239·44 mph (385·34 km/h); just over 7 mph (11 km/h) faster than Cuddihy. It was going to be a thrilling race.

In the air, as the race progressed, elements of the unexpected began to creep in. Ferrarin was first to find the situation becoming too much for him, the temperature of his hastily-assembled engine nearing danger point. As he maintained the chase after Cuddihy he left a dense wake of black smoke, a sure sign that the engine's life blood was seeping away. Three laps was all that he could manage, for during the fourth lap the slowly sinking oil pressure gauge had bottomed at zero. As he landed the engine gave up the struggle: a fractured oil pipe had defeated the all-night attempt of the Italian mechanics to ensure success.

His prime opponent, Cuddihy, could also see approaching trouble. His fuel contents gauge was reading alarmingly low and, pump as he might, the hand pump did not appear to be lifting life giving fuel from the auxiliary tanks in the floats.

But by then it had become a duel between Cuddihy and de Bernardi, the latter clearly ahead on time. But the Italian's lap times were slowing for he, too, was suffering from an overheating engine and was lapping at increased height in an attempt to keep going. As they entered the last lap it could have been anybody's race.

But for poor George Cuddihy the moment of truth had arrived. His engine spluttered and died, starved of petrol. For the second year in succession he had met bitter defeat in the last lap. de Bernardi stormed home the winner at an average speed of 246·496 mph (396·70 km/h), Frank Schilt second in the R3C-2 at 231·363 mph (372·34 km/h), Adriano Bacula third at 218 mph (350·84 km/h) and Bill Tomlinson last with a mere 137 mph (220·48 km/h). If Cuddihy and Ferrarin had kept going it would have been a nail-biting finish, for at the time they were forced to retire Cuddihy had averaged 239 mph (384·64 km/h) and Ferrarin 238·358 mph (383·59 km/h).

The Italians had lived to fight another day and it must have been with great pride that de Bernardi cabled Mussolini: 'Your order to win at all costs has been obeyed. We have won at a speed never before attained.' Back came the flowery reply: 'To you, to your fellow aviators, to all the personnel who have collaborated in the conquest of the dearly sought prize, Italy sends her greatest applause for the superb victory. This Italy, who has followed you and guided you in this perilous and difficult test, is today proud of the men who by their genius have created such powerful machines, and is enthusiastic of you, magnificent pilots, who have brought them to triumph.' It was signed simply, 'Mussolini'.

However laboured the wording of this cable, its meaning was clear enough: the 'Coppa Sneederr' was en route to Italy. 'We were overconfident', was the comment of the US magazine *Aviation*, '. . . the Italians won because their machines were faster, their pilots better trained.' They might have added also that it was the first confrontation of government-subsidised teams flown entirely by military pilots.

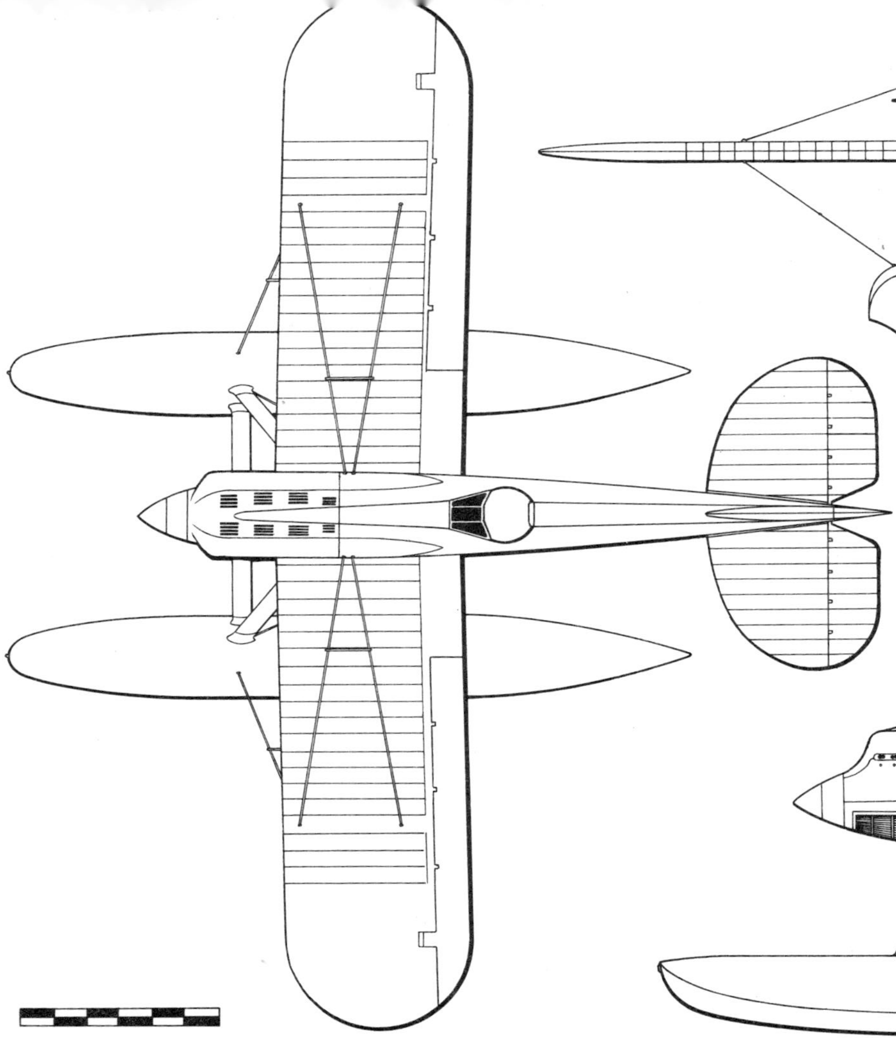

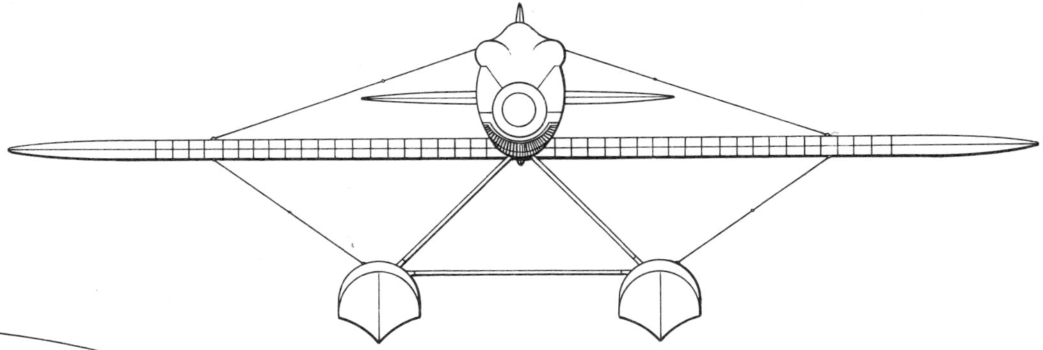

Macchi M.39 (1926)

Wing Span: 30 ft $4\frac{3}{4}$ in (9·26 m)
Length Overall: 22 ft $1\frac{1}{4}$ in (6·74 m)
Wing Area: 156·08 sq. ft (14·50 m^2)
Weight Empty: 2,778 lb (1,260 kg)
T-O Weight: 3,560 lb (1,615 kg)
Max Wing Loading: 22·81 lb/sq. ft (111·37 kg/m^2)
Horsepower of Power Plant: 880 hp

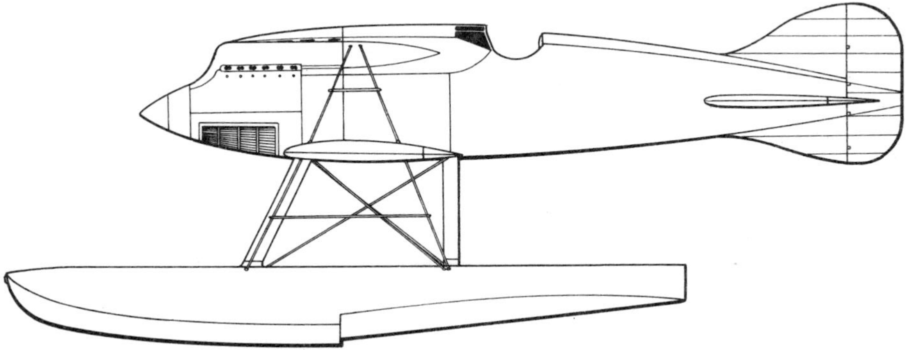

Curtiss R3C-4 (1926)

Wing Span: 22 ft (6·71 m)
Length Overall: 19 ft $8\frac{1}{2}$ in (6·00 m)
Wing Area: 149 sq. ft (13·84 m^2)
Horsepower of Power Plant: 700 hp

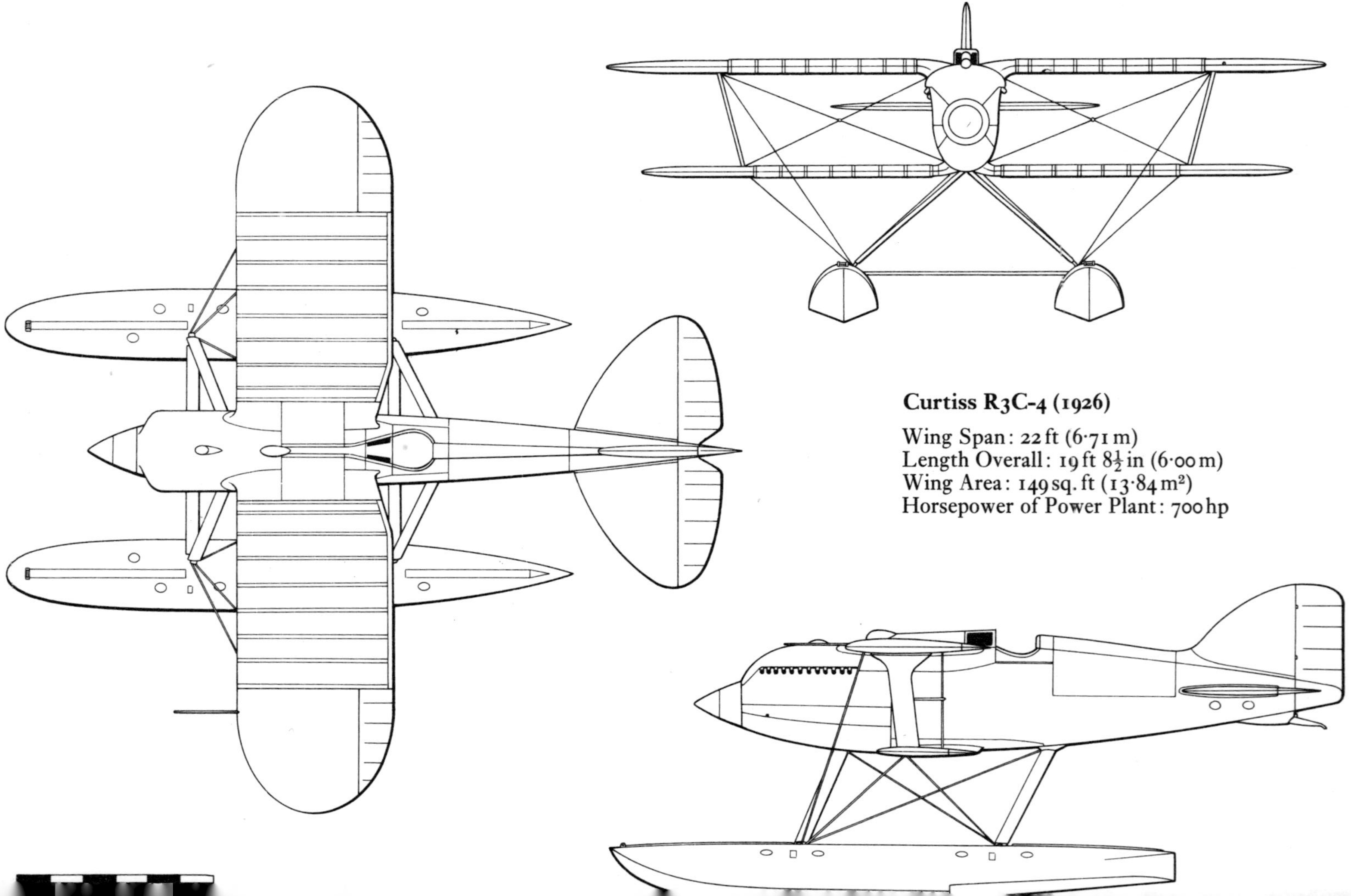

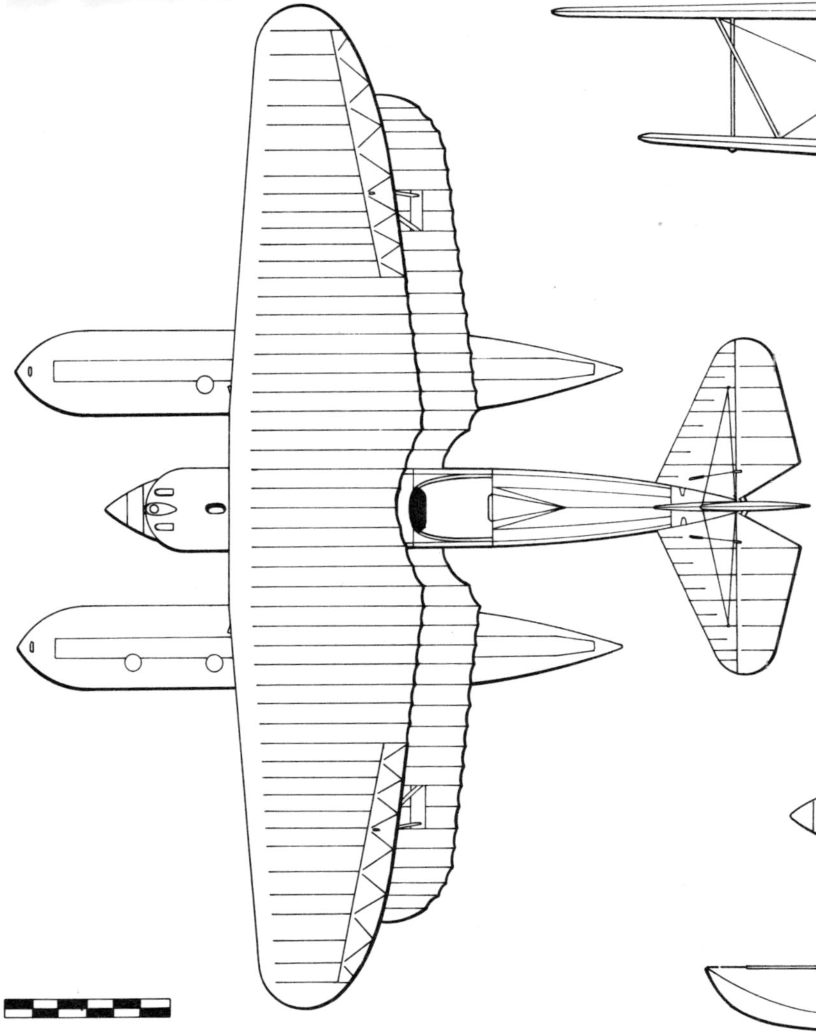

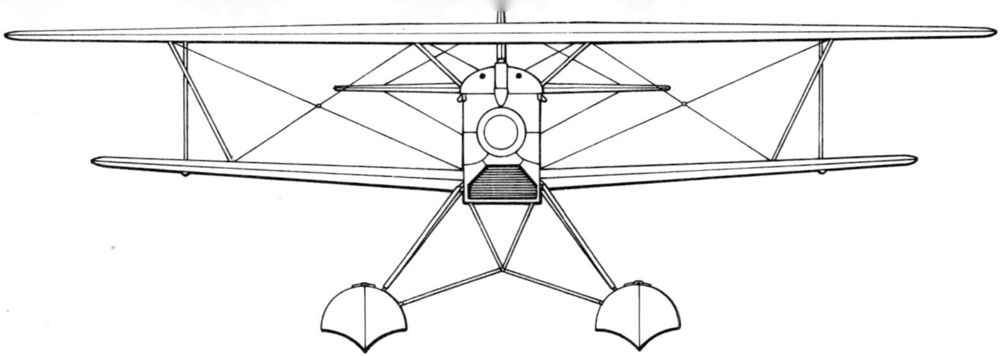

Curtiss F6C-1 (1926)

Wing Span: 37 ft 6 in (11·43 m)
Length Overall: 22 ft 6 in (6·86 m)
Wing Area: 252 sq. ft (23·41 m²)
T-O Weight: 3,171 lb (1,438 kg)
Max Wing Loading: 12·58 lb/sq. ft
(61·42 kg/m²)
Horsepower of Power Plant: 440 hp

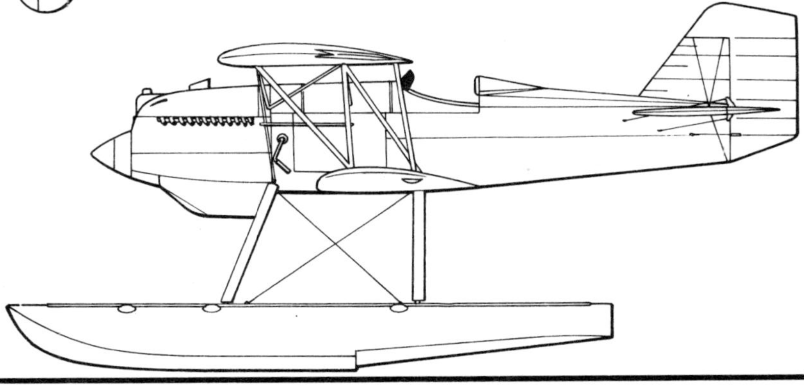

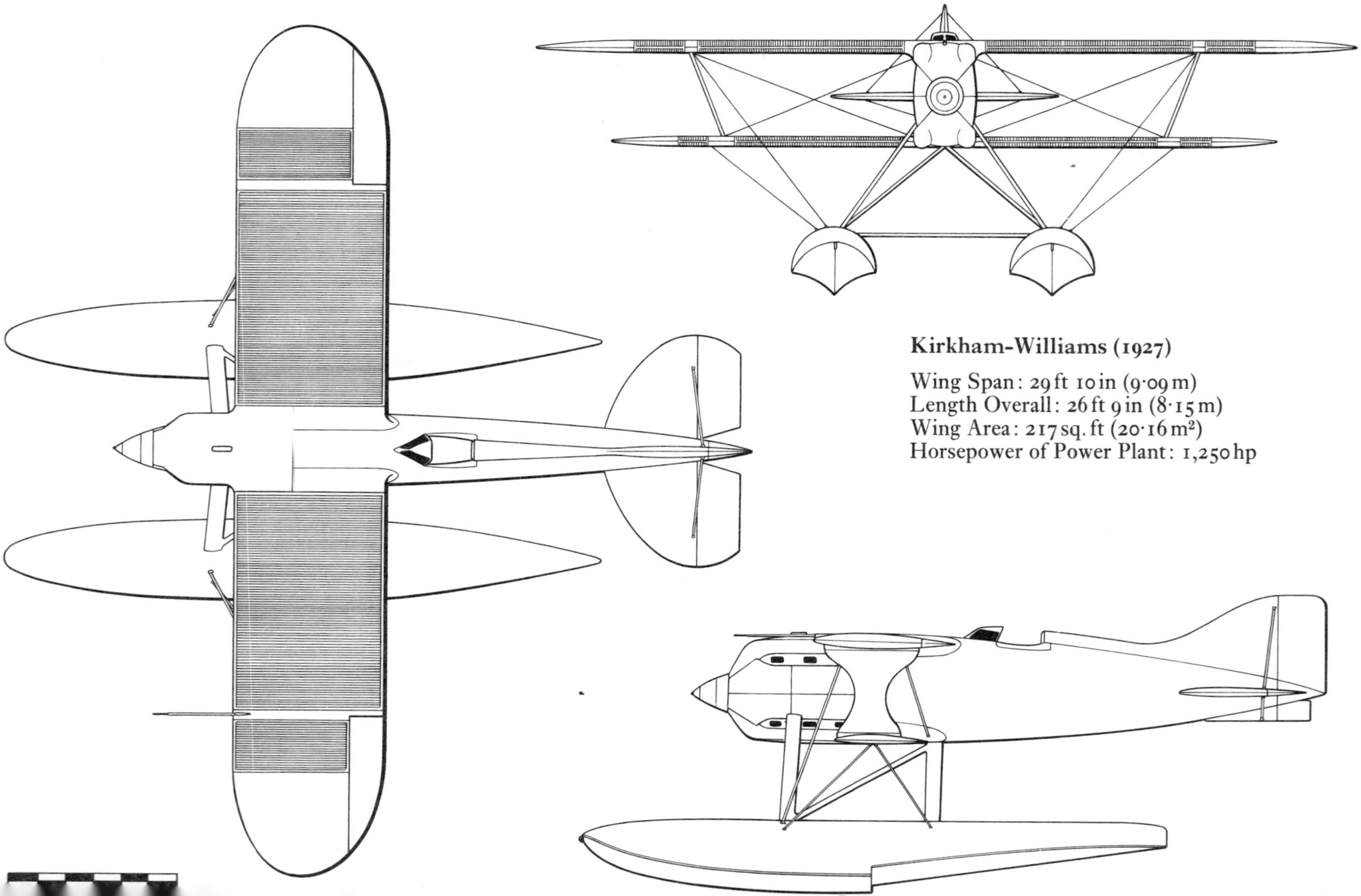

Kirkham-Williams (1927)

Wing Span: 29 ft 10 in (9·09 m)
Length Overall: 26 ft 9 in (8·15 m)
Wing Area: 217 sq. ft ($20{\cdot}16\ m^2$)
Horsepower of Power Plant: 1,250 hp

9

Excursion to Venice

1927

As an opener to the next Schneider Contest, the vexed question of annual or biennial events soon raised its head. In an attempt to resolve the matter the FAI called an extraordinary meeting in Paris on 25 January 1927, where the queries could be discussed in full, for it will be recalled that a previous decision had been made for biennial competition, with the next contest to be held in Italy.

Three countries were involved primarily, America, Britain and Italy, for there seemed little likelihood of participation by France. America favoured the biennial choice, but with little indication of continuing government support had only a weak hand to play. Italy, elated at their success in Virginia and by de Bernardi's new world speed record for seaplanes set at 258·87 mph (416·62 km/h), wanted to strike again while the iron was hot. They thought they held a considerable design lead with the Macchi M.39 and Fiat AS.2 engine, both of which they believed could be developed further to ensure victory in 1927, especially as they would be defending the Trophy at home.

Britain, which had not taken part in the 1926 contest, was quite happy to have a try for the Trophy in 1927, as development of her new seaplanes was progressing satisfactorily. Indeed, the guiding hands of the Society of British Aircraft Constructors favoured 1927. Their new aircraft, which could be pushed ahead for a confrontation with the Italians in that year, might well have been superseded by new developments if the contest was deferred until 1928.

This two to one vote was sufficient to sway the FAI into agreement for a 1927 contest, and it was announced accordingly that this would take place in Italy between 1 September and 15 November, with Venice as the chosen site.

The Royal Aero Club accepted the decision with a proviso: a British team would contend provided the event was not brought forward to a date earlier than 1 September, and duly advised that British entries must be received not later than 23 February, accompanied by a £5 entry fee and £50 deposit. It was stated also that the rules which had applied in America would remain unchanged.

Before that date came news that the US Navy would not be entering a team and that a decision whether or not to contend had not been reached by the US Army. Mid-February brought confirmation that Britain had entered a team of three aircraft, and by the closing date for British entries it was clear that France would not be taking part.

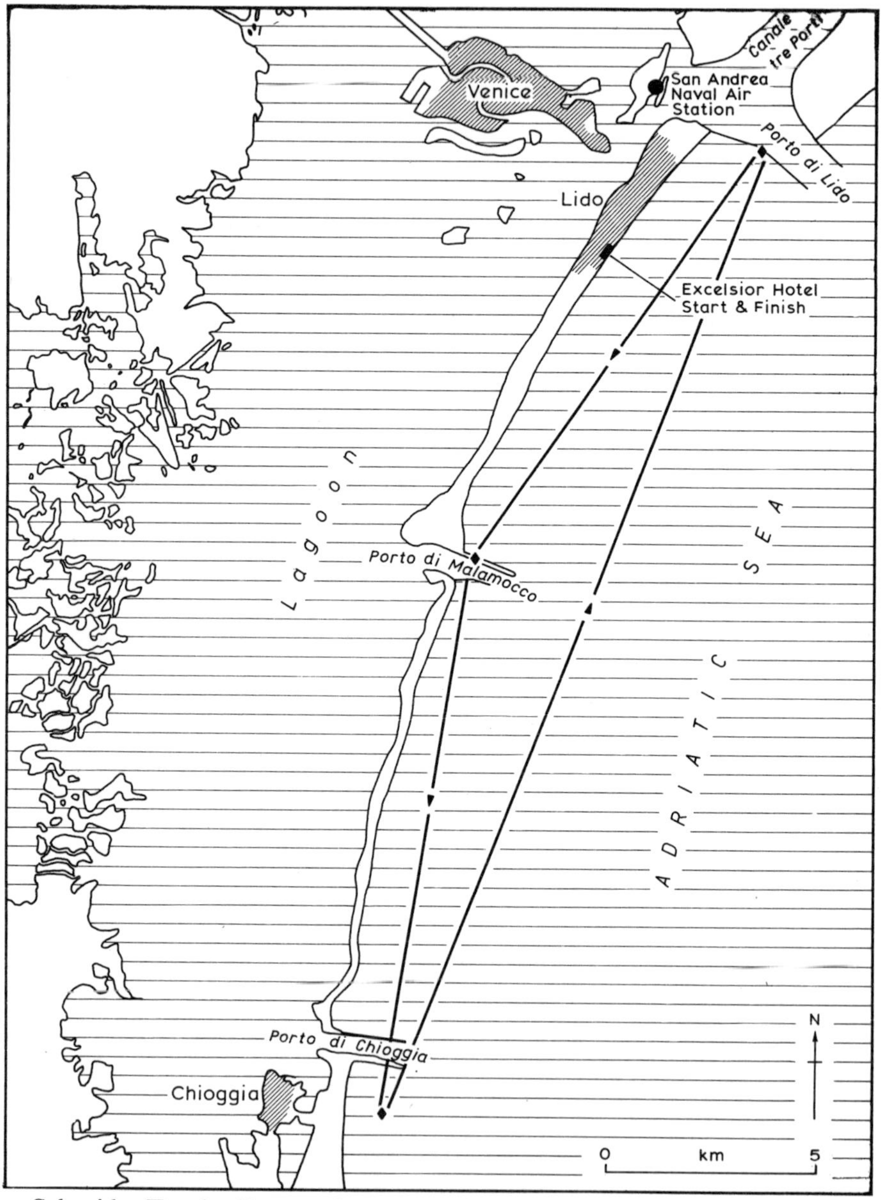

9. Schneider Trophy Contest Course: Venice 1927

The assumption was, therefore, that it would be a simple two-nation contest, for no service entry had been notified from America, although the NAA had wisely made a provisional entry for three aircraft in the event that later decisions might result in some competition being offered to the British and Italians.

In Italy there was a great flurry of activity. The Aéro-Club d'Italia were fully occupied with their preparations for the contest, simplified somewhat by the fact that Venice had been the scene of two earlier events and, consequently, its pros and cons were already well known.

They had, however, chosen a very different circuit for the speed contest. The first leg stretched from a pylon on the southern mole of the harbour entrance of the Porto di Lido, for 6·00 nm (11·69 km) to a pylon on the northern mole of the Porto di Malamocco, where a gentle port bank around the pylon gave a heading slightly west of due south to a third pylon 0·54 nm (1 km) from the beach at the Lido di Sottomarina, near Chioggia, 7·28 nm (13·49 km) distant. Round this acute turn the pilots would then head their aircraft back to the Porto di Lido pylon, a long straight run of 13·39 nm (24·82 km). This represented a course of 26·97 nm (50 km), which had to be lapped seven times. Starting and finishing line was opposite the Hotel Excelsior, on the Lido, which was about 2·15 nm (4 km) from the Porto di Lido pylon. It was announced that this year, for the first time, the competing aircraft would be airborne when they crossed the starting line.

With the contest to be held in 1927 it meant that no new and advanced design could be developed by the Italian aircraft industry within the time available. It was, however, considered that refinement of the Macchi M.39 could be achieved without too much difficulty and, of course, Fiat was expected to conjure additional horsepower from the AS.2 engine.

Mario Castoldi was able not only to effect some improvement of the design, but with the promise of more power could afford to reduce wing span and wing area, as well as the area of the horizontal tail surfaces, to reduce airframe drag. New features included a slight reduction in the fuselage hump and a moderate degree of sweepback on the wing leading-edges. The floats were reduced in length and volume to a minimum compatible with providing a sufficient margin of buoyancy. In this form, with the new Fiat engine, the Macchi was designated M.52, and had a wing span of 29 ft $5\frac{1}{2}$ in (8·98 m), slightly increased overall length at 23 ft 5 in (7·14 m). Wing area was 143·2 sq. ft (13·30 m²) and empty weight 2,618 lb (1,187 kg).

The quest for extra power from the engine, following what had then become almost conventional practice, involved another increase of bore and stroke to 5·7 in (14·5 cm) and 6·9 in (17·5 cm) respectively, and by pushing up the compression ratio from 6 to 6·7. This was expected to result in an increase of horsepower to almost 1,000. Frontal area was slightly reduced, and with the forward fuselage benefiting from this it was anticipated that the new Macchi might have the capability of exceeding 300 mph (483 km/h)

The Macchis for the 1927 contest at Venice were designated M.52. All three are seen here prior to the race

A close view of Ferrarin's M.52 shows clearly the sleek lines of the Italian monoplane

for the first time. The passing of this important milestone should prove more than adequate to defeat the British.

From America had come confirmation of no government-backed entry from either Army or Navy. This was a severe blow to national pride, for with two wins to their credit in three consecutive contests they needed only a victory in 1927 to secure the Trophy for the United States. There was, of course, considerable agitation in America in an endeavour to bring about a government change of mind. It was to no avail: Congress declined to provide funds for new aircraft, arguing that the very considerable sums of money for development of the Curtiss racers had already given a maximum technological return. Further expenditure on the scale required for participation in Italy was unlikely to give any worthwhile dividend of new knowledge.

But if the government had washed their hands of the affair, there was still one man determined to do his utmost as a private individual to wave the Stars and Stripes in Italy and, if possible, steal the Trophy back again. This was Lieutenant A. J. 'Al' Williams of the US Navy, winner of the 1923 Pulitzer Trophy Race, who added every available cent of his personal money to a fund raised by private individuals to ensure that America would be represented at Venice.

His mount became designated the Kirkham-Williams racer, evolved by Booth and Thurston, former designers of the Curtiss company, and built by the Kirkham Products Corporation of Long Island, New York, formed by another one-time Curtiss employee. The limited funds available could not possibly cover all the needs of such a project, and countless individuals donated funds, components, accessories and hundreds of constructional man-hours.

Almost inevitably the resulting aircraft bore a distinct resemblance to a Curtiss racer, being a single-bay biplane of sesquiplane configuration and of all-wood construction. Its large-span wide-chord upper wing, which seemed completely out of proportion to the rest of the aeroplane, was aligned with the top of the fuselage; the much narrower-chord lower wing was flush with the fuselage under-surface. Thus, there were no centre-section struts and only a single outward-canted I-shape interplane strut on each side. Dual streamline-section landing and flying wires were disposed on each side, the forward flying wires being attached to the floats in the seaplane configuration, or to the landing gear struts in landplane configuration. A conventional tail unit with large dorsal fin and rudder was also wire-braced. Surface cooling radiators of brass occupied most of the upper and lower surfaces of the upper wing, and the oil cooler was also of the surface type and mounted on the undersurface of the starboard wing. Large single-step V-bottomed floats were mounted on four large streamline struts, diagonally braced, but without any inter-float bracing.

The power plant, donated by the Packard Motor Company of Detroit, Michigan, was a new 24-cylinder X-shape in-line liquid-cooled engine, with a rated output of 1,200 hp at 2,600 rpm and with a maximum take-off rating of 1,250 hp at 2,700 rpm. Cylinder bore was 5⅜ in (13·64 cm), stroke 5 in (12·70 cm) and compression ratio 7·5. Its 8 ft 6 in (2·59 m) two-blade metal propeller was directly driven without reduction gearing.

Wing span of the upper wing was 29 ft 10 in (9·09 m) and its area 142 sq. ft (13·19 m^2). Area of the lower wing was 75 sq. ft (6·97 m^2) and overall length of the aircraft 26 ft 9 in (8·15 m).

News of this aircraft caused some concern to both British and Italian interests. Although its potential speed was an unknown factor, the Packard power plant was considerably more powerful than any being used by either of the European nations and if it was reliable it could, combined with the known skill of Al Williams, prove sufficient to put the Trophy back across the Atlantic once again.

Meanwhile, in Britain, progress was being made towards a determined effort to wipe away the defeats of the past. Ignoring, for the moment, the aircraft that were being developed, we find the beginnings of the organisation that earlier critics had demanded, but which had not been easy to realise.

It was readily appreciated that in the past there had been far too many fingers in the Schneider pie, and it was by more luck than judgement that on two vital occasions we had been lucky enough to pull out the plum.

Both America and Italy had demonstrated that success was most likely if the contest was mounted as a military operation, with government-subsidised aircraft being flown by well trained and disciplined service pilots. This was a lesson understood and appreciated by those concerned with arranging British participation at Venice. None believed that, however well intentioned, the Royal Aero Club had the ability or power to bring about an aircraft/pilot/organisational combination that would ensure success.

This had to be the prerogative of the Air Ministry, and none appreciated this better than Sir Hugh Trenchard. There was one snag: approval from the Treasury was needed to finance such participation. This was not forthcoming before very considerable representations had been made to argue the advantage—military, civil and economic—that could accrue, and it was not until 13 May 1927 that the Air Council finally received Treasury authority to get on with the job.

In fact, the starting gun had been anticipated in one respect, for an embryo High Speed Flight had formed at RAF Felixstowe on 1 October 1926, when Squadron-Leader Leslie J. Slatter had been posted there as its commander. Officially, the formation of such a flight was quite unconnected with the Schneider Trophy Contest. Its promulgated purpose was to provide a pool of experienced pilots to research the problems associated with flight at steadily increasing speeds. The fact that the aircraft available for their task were the Bamel and Gloster IIIAs was, perhaps, rather more than fortuitous.

Felixstowe was at that time the base of what was known as the Marine Aircraft Experimental Establishment (MAEE), and it was anticipated that its pilots, experienced in handling waterborne aircraft, would form the balance of the new flight. In fact, only Flight-Lieutenant O. E. Worsley of the MAEE was to become a full-time member of the team, and Flight-Lieutenant S. N. Webster and Flying-Officer H. M. Schofield were posted in, selected from a number of applicants who had volunteered for duty in the research flight.

However keen, they all suffered the same vagaries of East coast sea and weather, as well as aircraft unserviceability imposed by conditions experienced during the winter months, but all had gained some knowledge of seaplane operations before spring brought better weather. Then, with the news in mid-May that the 1927 Schneider Contest had fallen on to the RAF's plate, Slatter and his team could barely contain their patience as they awaited the arrival of the new and exciting aircraft that were to be the focal point of so much hope and endeavour.

Following British failure in America in 1925, the Air Ministry had drawn up specifications for three different high-speed seaplanes, the emphasis being on maximum speed at sea level. Following careful design appraisal by combined Air Ministry, RAE and NPL efforts, involving also wind tunnel and tank testing of scale models, the design proposals from the Gloster, Short and Supermarine companies were accepted. Contracts were placed for three Gloster and three Supermarine aircraft, plus a single example of the Short proposal which had what was then considered a somewhat unorthodox power plant for a racing aircraft.

Gloster's design represented a further stage in the development of the Gloster III, for although a monoplane configuration had won in 1926, and in so doing had raised the speed by some 14 mph (23 km/h) over the previous biplane victor, Harry Folland still favoured a biplane configuration, arguing that a well streamlined biplane could be both light and robust, ideal to face the stresses of high-speed races.

So evolved the Gloster IV, in which infinite care had been taken to reduce head resistance and increase propeller efficiency, and while all three were basically similar the resulting Gloster IV (N224), Gloster IVA (N222) and Gloster IVB (N223) had detail changes.

Their wings differed considerably from those of the Gloster III, being of sesquiplane configuration and having no stagger. The roots of the upper wings were downswept into a fairing behind the outer banks of the broad-arrow engine, giving a gull-wing appearance. The lower wing roots were upswept, meeting the fuselage at an angle of 90°. Of wooden construction, they had a multiple spar and rib structure, covered by two layers of spruce skinning. Very thin single outward-canted I-shape interplane struts were

N
222

N
224

machined from duralumin forgings. Landing wires were sited conventionally on each side, but the dual flying wires extended from the upper attachment of the interplane struts to the upper surface of the floats. Ailerons were provided only on the upper wing. To minimise control sensitivity at high speed, Gloster introduced their patented variable control system. For small control movements in high-speed flight this transmitted stick position changes at a ratio of 2:3. For large control variations in low-speed flight the ratio was changed to 3:2.

There was a difference in tail units. That of the Gloster IV was quite conventional, but the IVA and B had a deep ventral fin and corresponding rudder so that one could describe the resulting configuration as cruciform. The fuselage was of wood monocoque construction with lightweight formers and ash longerons, skinned with a dual layer of spruce strips laid diagonally. Forward of the wings and in other load-carrying areas, the skin was increased to a treble thickness.

One of the great disadvantages of all seaplanes were the wretched floats, each of them often almost as large as the fuselage. Their size was dictated by the need to provide adequate strength and buoyancy for rough-water landings, but being unnecessary appendages in flight it was essential to keep their weight and volume to an absolute minimum. Furthermore, their design was also of critical importance if the aircraft which they supported on the water was to be capable of stable control on the surface, conflicting somewhat with the ability to provide a quick take off. In an attempt to improve on the floats of their earlier racing aircraft, Gloster decided to design their own for the new machines. Considerable time was spent on this project, hydrodynamic and aerodynamic tests of many designs being required before final selection of the shallow V-bottomed single-step duralumin floats that were carried on two pairs of inverted-Vee struts. No horizontal struts separated the floats, their only bracing being a pair of streamline section wires.

Folland's genius was of no avail without a suitable power plant, and there was still no aero-engine in Britain that could better the performance of the specially-developed Napier Lions. Once again it had been urged to produce more power, by increasing maximum rpm to 3,000 and with a compression ratio of 10. Some reduction in frontal area had been made also, which was no mean achievement, and the direct-drive Lion VIIA developed 900 hp for a dry weight of 850 lb (386 kg), the geared-drive VIIB 875 hp for a dry weight of 930 lb (422 kg). The Gloster IV and IVA each had direct-drive Lion VIIAs, with propellers of 6 ft 9 in (2·06 m) and 7 ft 0 in

Opposite page: (*top*) The Gloster IV has the reputation of being the most graceful of the biplane racing seaplanes. This is not apparent in this photograph of the Gloster IVA (*centre*) but the head-on view tells a very different story (*bottom*) This shot of the Gloster IV N224 shows the tail unit adopted ultimately for both the IVA and B

(2·13 m) diameter respectively, while the IVB had a geared VIIB engine and a propeller of 7 ft $8\frac{1}{2}$ in (2·35 m) diameter.

More power meant more heat to dissipate, and surface radiators of unusual form were designed for these aircraft. Of corrugated copper, with brass leading- and trailing-edges, they were made in sleeve form and slid over the wingtip to the required position, where they were secured by brass ferrules. These, together with extra radiators mounted on the upper surface of the floats, between the mounting struts, provided a total cooling arca of 125 sq. ft (11·61 m^2). A combined tank and cooler for the lubricating oil was mounted in the undersurface of the engine cowling. The main fuel tank was in the fuselage, with a small gravity header tank immediately aft of the engine.

Folland believed that the improvement in aerodynamic efficiency coupled with increased engine power should provide maximum speeds considerably in excess of the Air Ministry's specified minimum of 265 mph (426 km/h) at up to 1,000 ft (305 m). Early testing of the Gloster IV had shown that the wings were very efficient, consequently the IVA and B each had their wing span and area reduced. Dimensions were, therefore, as follows: Gloster IV, wing span 26 ft $7\frac{1}{2}$ in (8·11 m), wing area 164 sq. ft (15·24 m^2), length overall 26 ft 4 in (8·03 m), height overall 9 ft 2 in (2·79 m). Gloster IVA, IVB: wing span 22 ft $7\frac{1}{2}$ in (6·90 m) and wing area 139 sq. ft (12·91 m^2), other dimensions as for Gloster IV. The engine and dimension variations gave differing maximum take-off weights, as follows: Gloster IV, 2,780 lb (1,261 kg); Gloster IVA, 3,130 lb (1,420 kg); Gloster IVB, 3,305 lb (1,499 kg).

In the Supermarine works there had been a similar eruption of activity to develop a worthy successor to the S.4 monoplane which had come to grief at Baltimore. It had, so far as the airframe was concerned, represented an aerodynamic ideal. But although Mitchell had a mind teeming with advanced ideas, he was a sufficiently realistic and practical engineer to appreciate that, on occasion, a degree of compromise was necessary.

By comparison with the fully cantilever wing of the S.4, that for the new machine was braced and moved to a low-wing position. This improved the pilot's view, was the best possible situation to require minimal bracing by means of streamline wires and, because it was braced, could be of more lightweight construction.

A conventional two-spar wing of all-wood construction, the spruce ply-wood ribs had wide flanges to provide good fixings for the plywood skins and surface radiators. In the outboard section of the wing structure a diagonal member was included to give improved rigidity.

The fuselage was an all-metal semi-monocoque structure, the forward section carrying the engine on cross-braced bearers. Aft of the engine bay was a main frame structure, to which were attached the wing spars, forward float struts and wire bracing. The aft section of the fuselage comprised close-spaced formers to which the skin was riveted without need for longerons. The fin formed an integral part of the rear fuselage structure, heavier gauge frames carrying the rudder post and tailplane spars. Tailplane, elevators and rudder were of conventional wooden construction with plywood skins.

The floats were of usual Supermarine construction with a single step and V-bottom, and were carried on four wire-braced streamline-section struts. The starboard float contained a steel petrol tank and that of the first machine (N219) was slightly longer than the port float in an attempt to offset propeller torque. Subsequent testing showed that this had no significant advantage and the floats of the other two machines, N220 and N221, were of equal size. All three aircraft had the starboard float offset 8 in (20·32 cm) further from the centre-line of the fuselage, also to assist in reducing the torque effect of the propeller.

There had been some discussion on the utilisation of a modified Rolls-Royce engine to power Mitchell's new creation, which had the designation S.5, but it was decided to use the Napier Lion once again, it being considered that the proven reliability of this engine outweighed the risk of experimentation with an unknown quantity. Consequently, N219 had a direct-drive Lion VIIA, the other two aircraft had the geared Lion VIIB.

As with their installation in the Gloster machines, strict attention to provide adequate cooling was essential, and copper surface radiators covered almost the entire upper and lower surfaces of the monoplane wing. Cooling of the lubrication oil was tackled differently, an 11 ft (3·35 m) long corrugated steel cooler being mounted along each side of the fuselage outer surface.

At a lecture given to the Royal Aeronautical Society after the 1927 contest, on 26 January 1928, R. J. Mitchell outlined the principal differences between the S.4 and S.5:

(i) Lowering of the wing.
(ii) Adoption of wire-bracing between wing, floats and fuselage.
(iii) Reduced cross-sectional area of fuselage and floats.
(iv) Wing surface radiators replacing Lamblins.
(v) Higher-power geared engine to improve propeller efficiency.

By these modifications he had anticipated the following changes in speed potential:

(i) A loss of 3 mph (4·8 km/h), but offered improved pilot visibility and a more rigid wing.
(ii) A reduction of 9% in structural weight, giving an increase of 3 mph (4·8 km/h).
(iii) Increases of 11 mph (17·7 km/h) and 4 mph (6·4 km/h) respectively by reduction of fuselage and float cross-sectional area.
(iv) An increase of 24 mph (38·6 km/h) resulting from reduced drag.
(v) An increase of 30 mph (48·3 km/h) from improved propeller efficiency.

Before the contest this information was known to only a very small number of people, but the S.4 having taken the world speed record for seaplanes at 226·75 mph (364·92 km/h), it suggested that the S.5 had a potential of close on 300 mph (483 km/h).

Dimensions of the S.5 included wing span of 26 ft 9 in (8·15 m), length overall 24 ft 3½ in (7·40 m), height overall 11 ft 1 in (3·38 m), wing chord 5 ft 0 in (1·52 m) and wing area of 115 sq. ft (10·68 m²). Maximum take-off weight of N220 and N221 with Lion VIIB engine was 3,242 lb (1,471 kg).

The last of the British contenders was that being built by Short Brothers, and known as the Short-Bristow Crusader. Colonel W. A. Bristow, an aeronautical consulting engineer, had been the driving power behind this project, the overall design being in the hands of W. G. Carter who had been with the Hawker Aircraft company.

It, like the S.5, was of braced low-wing monoplane configuration, the elliptical all-wood two-spar wing having spruce box-spars, spruce ribs and mahogany skin, covered overall with silk and doped.

The fuselage was a composite structure, the rear bay being an all-wood monocoque with spruce frames and stringers, skinned with two layers of diagonally laid mahogany strips finished, as the wings, with silk and dope, and terminating in a sharply-pointed tail cone. From aft of the cockpit forward to the engine mounting the structure was a strut-braced frame of high-tensile steel tubes, covered by detachable duralumin panels. This structure provided rigid attachment for the wing spars and the four tubular struts which carried the Short-designed low-drag duralumin floats. The wire bracing of wings to floats and to and between float struts presented something of a birdcage.

The tail unit was conventional, of all-wood cantilever construction, rudder and elevators being fabric-covered.

Most unusual feature of the Crusader was its power plant, a Bristol Mercury I 9-cylinder air-cooled radial engine. It could surely have been argued that a radial engined aircraft stood little chance in competition with the sleek in-line engined seaplanes. Either someone had a very persuasive line of sales talk, or the Air Ministry had decided to hedge its bets as widely as possible with the permutations on biplane, monoplane, geared and direct-drive in-line and radial engined seaplanes. At least it gave convincing proof that their interest was in high-speed aircraft rather than the capture of the Trophy—or did it?

The Mercury engine then in service use was rated at 500 hp, but a developed, supercharged version had demonstrated 960 hp on bench test, although flight testing had not proved so successful due to a succession of ignition troubles. The main problem was, of course, to minimise the head resistance of the radial engine's large frontal area and still provide an adequate supply of cooling air. Early attempts with fairings behind each cylinder had proved disappointing, and eventually individual helmets

Unmistakable in head-on view was the Short-Bristow Crusader . . .

. . . and this magnificent shot shows clearly the unusual wing configuration

were designed for each cylinder which gave the best compromise between streamlining and cooling. The main fuel tank was situated in the fuselage, and an auxiliary tank in the starboard float.

Dimensions of the Crusader included wing span of 26 ft 6 in (8·08 m), length overall 25 ft 0 in (7·62 m) and wing area 120 sq. ft (11·15 m²). Maximum take-off weight was 2,712 lb (1,230 kg).

It is interesting to mention one other aircraft that was designed for the 1927 contest but which, due to lack of financial support, failed to materialise. Designed by S. E. Saunders and Percy Beadle, this was a braced low-wing monoplane rather similar in appearance to the S.5 and which was to be powered also by the Napier Lion. Wing span was 26 ft 5 in (8·05 m), length overall 25 ft 6 in (7·77 m), height overall 9 ft 9 in (2·97 m) and wing area only 98 sq. ft (9·10 m²). Maximum take-off weight was estimated at 2,502 lb (1,135 kg).

First of the British machines to arrive at Felixstowe in late April was the Crusader, quickly christened 'Curious Ada' by the wags of the High Speed Flight. They were somewhat disappointed to find that its first flight was to be made by Bert Hinkler, but as the aircraft had only passed taxying tests at Rochester it was perhaps considered prudent that the first flight should be made by a civilian test pilot. It seems likely that Short's test pilot, John Parker, could well have been numbered among the disgruntled.

Nonetheless, Hinkler was elected, and he immediately expressed himself dissatisfied with the area of the rudder, which was increased before the maiden flight on 4 May. Power plant of the Crusader at that time was a Mercury de-rated to 650 hp, the ignition problems at higher powers still unresolved. Despite this, Hinkler took her off very cleanly and found that, apart from a tendency to yaw at high speed, the Crusader handled very well. On this first flight, timed by stop watch on opposing runs over a measured mile, he averaged 232 mph (373 km/h) which was considered encouraging with only about two-thirds of the expected power available.

Then came an immediate setback. As Hinkler came in to land he put the machine down port float first, the resulting snatch to port buckling the float struts. Gingerly it was towed back to the slipway and brought ashore.

Hinkler was first to admit that the snaking at high speed was due to excessive rudder area. When, with float struts repaired and rudder sized to the designer's original dimensions he flew it again, 'Ada' behaved perfectly. Perfectly, that is, except for the erratic behaviour of the engine.

Flight-Lieutenant Webster was the first service pilot to take the Crusader aloft. He, too, was to discover it pleasant to fly, apart from the engine's disconcerting habit of going on strike for no apparent reason and, as suddenly, reverting to full power.

Flying-Officer Schofield soon developed a love-hate relationship with 'Ada', known also as the 'Blind Wonder' because pilot visibility was not all that could be desired. He too was plagued with the supercharger/

ignition problems that were driving the Bristol engineers to drink. Schofield said that when the engine cut out at full power it was rather like hitting a brick wall, and hardly had you recovered from that shock before it cut in again with such violence that the seat back just about drove all the breath out of your body.

After one or two such experiences, it became automatic to heave the throttle back after the 'brick wall' effect, and while this left the pilot with an essential reserve of breath to curse the supercharger and all its designers, it was hardly the sort of performance to snatch the Trophy from the Italians.

Little, if any, progress had been made by the time the Crusader was crated for shipment to Italy, aboard a collier which carried also an S.5 (N219) and the Gloster IVA.

Progress of the Gloster machines had not been quite so far advanced, but they began to arrive at Calshot soon after the High Speed Flight, which had been transferred there in mid-July. First to arrive was N222, acquiring less than an hour's flight before being shipped to Venice, along with N223.

Flight-Lieutenant Worsley had flown the prototype S.5 (N219) in early June, and as the other two became available it was soon clear that they were faster than the Gloster IVs, hence the decision to send the three S.5s, two Gloster IVs and Crusader to Venice. In fact, the S.5s gave little trouble of any kind in the limited flights that were made at Calshot, once a tendency to tail-heaviness had been corrected. The biggest problem was in getting them off the water, for selection of floats with the absolute minimum cross-sectional area, and consequently minimum buoyancy, meant that propeller torque tended to make one float dig in badly as power was applied to the engine. The pilots soon learned how to overcome this by applying full opposite rudder, and at the same time trying to dodge the deluge of spray before the S.5 recognised a master's touch and got up neatly on her steps.

Clearly, this problem was related to propeller efficiency. A finer pitch improved take-off performance, but reduced maximum air speed: the ideal coarse pitch propeller that would hurtle the S.5 through the air at its top speed would be completely useless for take-off. Inevitably, much of the testing at Calshot was concerned with arriving at the most suitable propeller for the dual task: like so much aviation technology of that time it must needs rely upon the best compromise.

While these tests were being made, time melted away as if by magic, and on 27 August the two remaining S.5s and the Gloster IVB were shipped aboard the SS *Egyptian Prince* for transit to Malta, where they were to be transferred to the aircraft carried HMS *Eagle* which would deliver them to and attend upon them at Venice.

News from America had indicated that the President had authorised the shipment of the Kirkham-Williams racer to Venice aboard the cruiser

Trenton, but apart from this virtually nothing was known of the progress made in the construction or testing of this aircraft.

Confirmation of lack of progress came in late July when the Aéro-Club d'Italia received a request from the NAA for a thirty-day postponement. At the beginning of August the Italian organising committee met to discuss this request, under the chairmanship of General Balbo. Since it did not comply with the regulations they, in turn, asked the British Royal Aero Club if they considered that the Americans should be allowed sufficient time to bring their sole contender to Venice. The Royal Aero Club's committee were adamant against such an extension and, in the face of this, the Italians were forced to decline. In view of American sportsmanship in earlier years it is quite likely that the Italians were not too happy at having to send such a reply. And, in any event, they themselves would have regarded such a postponement as being rather more than useful, for they were suffering problems of their own with the new boosted Fiat engine.

In the face of such a decision Al Williams knew that he could not possibly be ready in time and withdrew his entry. An American commentator was to record 'Britain's action was far more exacting than America's would have been under the same circumstances.' Not for the first time Britain's sporting attitude in respect to this series of contests was to be seen as something less than impartial.

The Italian team, under the command of Colonel Tacchini, had begun their training at Varese in the early summer. The leading lights were again de Bernardi and Ferrarin and, adding to the problems being experienced with the new Fiat engine, there had been another fatal accident. Contemporary reports would suggest that an air of complacency permeated the team, and if this was the case it was probably because they believed that their aircraft were still markedly superior to those of the British. In retrospect, it seems more likely that their problem was one of frustration imposed by the unreliability of the new engine from which Fiats were attempting to gain an output of 1,000 hp, as well as a reduction in weight and size. Ermanno Bazzocchi was to comment that '. . . the quest for power at all costs soon revealed the limitations of the "souped-up" power plants: the reliable Fiat AS.2 was boosted to 1,000 hp and resulted in the treacherous AS.3'.

In fact, Fiat seems to have followed what had then become an empiric formula: increased bore, compression ratio and revolutions. All this was done without adequate research to ensure that the engine's components were capable of accepting the new and much higher stresses imposed on them. Worse still, in their attempts to reduce weight to a minimum, extensive use had been made of light alloy components and, at the eleventh hour, they had even substituted new and inadequately-tested light alloy pistons.

By the end of August the first members of the British team arrived at Venice, and once again they discovered that the Italians had spared no efforts to ensure that facilities for their competitors were of the highest order. Nothing was too much trouble, and the slighest request for assistance was met quickly and graciously.

Britain's team at Venice was under the overall command of Air Vice-Marshal F. R. Scarlett, and as the pilots and their machines assembled, little time was lost in preparing for practice. First of the aircraft to arrive were those consigned on the SS *Eworth*, an S.5, the Gloster IVA and Crusader, but it was not until 10 September that Squadron-Leader Slatter was able to fly the S.5 for the first time. A replacement in the team that had assembled at Felixstowe was Flight-Lieutenant S. M. Kinkead, a highly experienced pilot, and it was he who followed Slatter into the air in the Gloster IVA.

All went well, but it was not until the next day that the Crusader was ready for its first test after re-assembly. Schofield must have climbed aboard with some trepidation, for with memories of the stop-go Mercury engine the fact that a new fully-rated engine had now been installed could hardly have made for peace of mind. If it adopted the same tactics as its predecessor the brick wall/seat-in-the-back effect would be even more violent, and 'Curious Ada' could well get curiouser and curiouser.

With fuel tanks full to give him sufficient endurance for a complete run around the course, Schofield found the Crusader responding very sluggishly on take off. It was a very hot day and the tired air seemed reluctant to take upon itself the added burden of the heavily laden seaplane.

Hardly was he airborne than the port wing dropped sharply. Instinctive aileron correction did nothing to help, in fact the rate of roll increased and the Crusader plunged into the sea at an estimated 150mph (241km/h). Fortunately, the wood-constructed aft fuselage broke away at the cockpit, throwing Schofield clear. Though practically unconscious his sub-conscious mind dictated that he should swim for his life, and this he continued to do, non-stop, even after anxious rescuers had struggled to get him out of the water. He was lucky to escape with very severe bruising and slight concussion.

There was, naturally, much speculation as to the likely cause of the accident. An eye-witness stated at the time: 'It seemed as if he were well away and just about 15ft (4·57m) off the water when he did a half-roll, just as if he had tried to level the machine out against the engine torque and had only then discovered that his aileron wires had been coupled up the wrong way. That, of course, is impossible, but it was the impression the turnover of the machine gave to an experienced aviator.'

Impossible? Regrettably no. When the Crusader was salvaged about a week later it was found on investigation that during re-rigging at Venice the wrong halves of two turnbuckles had been connected together, crossing the aileron controls.

This setback for the British team was followed by a spell of bad weather which prevented any practice for a few days but, in the interim, the *Eagle* with her escorting destroyers arrived. Her cargo was soon unloaded, and the new machines rigged and prepared for practice as soon as the weather showed signs of improvement.

On 21 September the team were back in the air, but as Kinkead in the Gloster IVB came in to land the propeller spinner became detached. It received an almighty clout from one of the propeller blades, with resulting damage to the propeller shaft. More work for Napier's engineers, but sparing no efforts they managed to get it airworthy again for the navigability test on Friday 23 September.

The Italian team's Macchis did not arrive at Venice until 19 September, so they too had little enough time for practice over the course. Even when they took to the air the British contingent were unable to gain any real appreciation of their speed capabilities: one could only look at the very clean scarlet-painted machines and soak up the impression that they might prove very fast indeed. Time would tell, and there was little enough of that remaining.

The British team for the race was finalised as Webster, flying the S.5 N.220, Worsley in the S.5 N.219 and Kinkead with the Gloster IVB N.223 all, apparently, completing the navigability test without any problems. True, Webster became airborne by wave impact just ahead of the start line, but as no disqualification flag was raised in protest he carried on and completed the test in fine style. The Italian team, making a somewhat later start, all completed the test without difficulty and the keenly watching British team were impressed by the way in which the Macchis lifted cleanly off the water and, in the air, were clearly fast and responsive to the controls. Two of them had new Fiat AS.3 engines, one was equipped with the reliable AS.2 so that, if the new engines failed, there was reasonable assurance of one Italian machine completing the course, even if its speed proved inadequate to throw off the British challenge.

The six machines lined up at anchor for the water tightness test were a colourful sight: scarlet Macchis, dull blue and gold Gloster, and the pale blue and silver S.5s. All that was needed was fine weather on the Sunday, for the following day was a free day, allowing time for last minute checks and adjustments.

In late afternoon came a shock for the British team when it was announced that Webster had been disqualified for crossing the start line incorrectly. Fortunately the rules allowed a second attempt, and this he completed without incident the following morning.

Opposite page: (*top*) The Supermarine S.5, the first of Mitchell's finale of Schneider Trophy winners, which carried Flight-Lieutenant S. N. Webster to Victory at Venice (*centre*) Considered the 'poor relation' of Italy's 1929 team, Dal Molin's Macchi M.52R was to gain second place (*bottom*) By contrast, both of the new Macchi M.67s were forced to retire during their second lap

N
22

By then Venice had become invaded by throngs of spectators, all keyed up for the race on the following day. Taking a leaf from the Americans' book the Italians had arranged a good public address system, as well as a large scoreboard to record lap times of the contestants. The weather smiled on the idyllic scene and Leonard Bridgman—a later editor of *Jane's all the World's Aircraft*—wrote in *The Aeroplane*: 'For Venice one has nothing but admiration. Six-wheeled 'buses and pneumatic drills are unknown, but if one steps off the curb inadvertently one is precipitated into the dark romantic waters of the open sewer system.'

There was but one fly in this peaceful scene. On Sunday morning the weather once again decided to show its complete unconcern for the wishes of the assembled thousands, a strong wind making conditions so bad that a twenty-four-hour postponement was announced.

Monday morning was little better at first, but as the day advanced the committee decided that the race was on. Tension mounted steadily as starting time approached, and it was with a feeling of relief that Kinkead in the Gloster IVB pushed the throttle wide open as the starting gun broke the hush of expectancy, at exactly 2.29 p.m. on that Monday afternoon. He was followed by de Bernardi, but although the Italian machine was seen to be travelling very fast it was leaving in its wake such a dense cloud of black smoke that it seemed its engine had already lost much of its enthusiasm.

Webster was next away, and as he disappeared rapidly from the view of the crowds at the Lido, it was already apparent that something was amiss with the Italian recording of lap times. Fortunately, George Reynolds, official time keeper of the Royal Aero Club was present and on his toes, able to confirm that contrary to Italian belief de Bernardi had completed his first lap some 9 mph (14·5 km/h) faster than Kinkead.

By then the new boy of the Italian team, Captain Federico Guazzetti in the AS.2-powered Macchi was airborne, followed by Worsley and Ferrarin. The latter's participation was particularly short lived: as he crossed the starting line his engine made sounds of protest, followed almost immediately by a puff of smoke and a tongue of flame. Beating a hasty retreat, he made for the sheltered waters of the lagoon.

This was shattering for the Italians, for Ferrarin was not only a popular hero, but many considered him favourite of the Italian team. Even worse misfortune had already and unbeknowingly taken place, for de Bernardi had also been forced out of the race by engine failure. Picked up by a patrol boat from HMS *Eagle*, it was discovered that, in the words of C. G. Grey: 'A connecting rod had come out of his crankcase for a breath of fresh air.'

To add to the misery of the Italian spectators it began to rain. Their only glimmer of hope was centred on Guazzetti, who continued to lap steadily, but it needed no complicated calculations to show that he was completely outpaced by the British machines: their sole chance of a victory or a place depended upon his keeping going if all or some of the British machines failed to maintain the pace they were setting. It seemed over-optimistically remote, for the roar of the Lions was aggressively healthy: with five laps completed it appeared inevitable that Britain would be placed 1–2–3.

But fate decreed otherwise. During the sixth lap Kinkead believed that once again his spinner was working loose as violent vibration made it clear that, bitter though it was, prudence demanded he should throttle back and retire from the race. It was fortunate that he did, for subsequent examination of his machine showed that the propeller shaft of the Lion had a shear line extending for about three-quarters of its circumference.

This news brought a flutter of hope to failing Italian hearts: it was almost as quickly dispelled. As Guazzetti was on the point of completing his sixth lap a fuel line fractured, almost blinding the pilot as the slipstream whipped a stinging spray of petrol into the cockpit. Luckily, he managed to pull off a safe landing in the lagoon of the Alberoni. This was a national tragedy, and streams of sympathetic tears came from the Italian skies as spectators whose patriotism far exceeded their interest in aviation began to make their way home.

Two aircraft only remained in the circuit, one final quirk remaining to bring a degree of concern for the British team. As Webster crossed the finishing line he went racing on, clearly intent on completing another lap.

To guard against their pilots miscounting the number of laps completed, each British machine carried a 'Heath Robinson' board with holes covered by paper. By punching one out at the end of each lap the pilot would have a simple and foolproof means of keeping his lap score. Webster had duly punched out his seven holes, but a glance at his watch showed an elapsed time of only forty-six minutes out of an anticipated fifty-plus. Had he slipped up with his 'counter'? He could not be sure that he had not punched a hole at the beginning and end of one lap.

On the ground both Scarlett and Slatter were afraid that Webster would run out of fuel on this eighth lap, with the attendant dangers of an unpowered landing. It was with considerable relief that his approach was heard some minutes later, the Lion giving a roar of victory as it swooped over the finishing line. The S.5 had recorded an average speed of 281·65 mph (453·28 km/h), winning not only the Schneider Trophy but setting also a new world speed record for seaplanes and bettering the existing world speed record for landplanes by 3 mph (4·8 km/h). Close behind was Worsley with an average speed of 273·01 mph (439·36 km/h).

The combination of Supermarine, Napier and a team of highly trained pilots had paid off in a resounding victory, and the first to offer a vociferous shower of congratulations were the defeated but very sportsmanlike Italians. And as might be expected there was a hectic round of receptions and banquets before the British team were able to return home for another riotous reception in England.

A typographical error in a telegram delivered to *The Aeroplane* perhaps described more aptly and accurately than its originator intended a subsequent reception for the architects of victory, held at Southampton: 'Commander Bird, Mitchell and Ransom of AID received great ovation Sunday afternoon at West Station from Mayor, hundreds of townspeople and whole of Supermarine employees. Reception was hell in Mayor's Parlour.'

But in the same journal C. G. Grey was to provide a very necessary and cautionary reminder against the dangers of complacency if we were to win the next contest:

'We have an unfortunate tendency in this country when we have done anything good, to sit back and assume that we have done the very best that can be done, and that nobody else can do any better, instead of realising the plain cold fact that we have merely set a standard for somebody else to beat.'

Was it possible that this realistic piece of commonsense would percolate through to those called upon to make decisions before we would have to defend the Trophy a brief twelve months later?

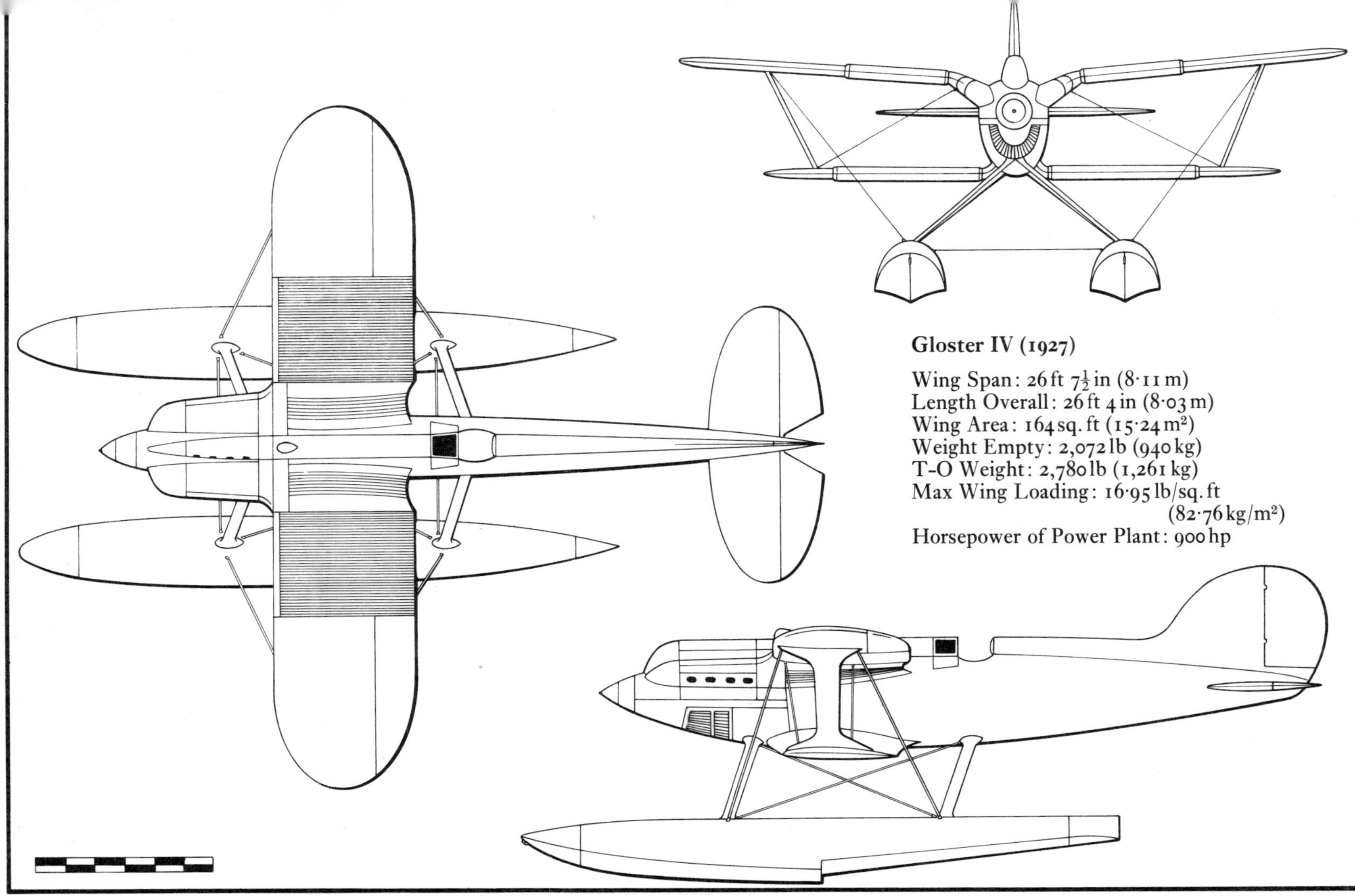

Gloster IV (1927)

Wing Span: 26 ft $7\frac{1}{2}$ in (8·11 m)
Length Overall: 26 ft 4 in (8·03 m)
Wing Area: 164 sq. ft (15·24 m^2)
Weight Empty: 2,072 lb (940 kg)
T-O Weight: 2,780 lb (1,261 kg)
Max Wing Loading: 16·95 lb/sq. ft (82·76 kg/m^2)
Horsepower of Power Plant: 900 hp

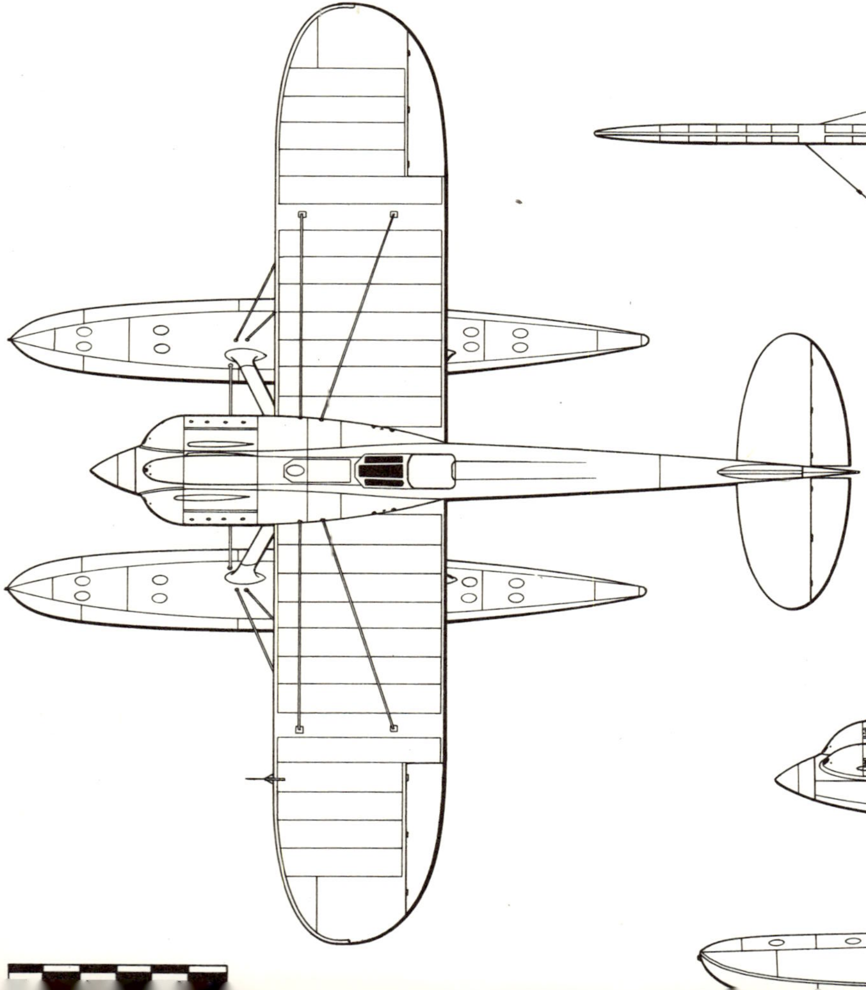

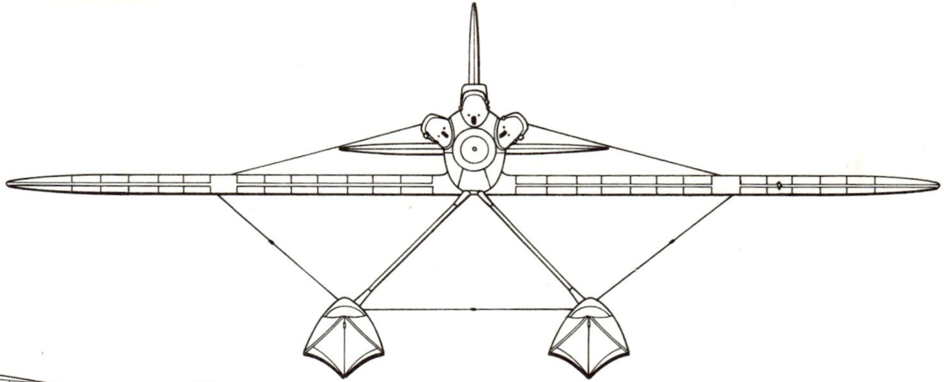

Supermarine S.5 (1927)

Wing Span: 26 ft 9 in (8·15 m)
Length Overall: 24 ft $3\frac{1}{2}$ in (7·40 m)
Wing Area: 115 sq. ft (10·68 m^2)
Weight Empty: 2,680 lb (1,216 kg)
T-O Weight: 3,242 lb (1,471 kg)
Max Wing Loading: 28·19 lb/sq. ft (137·64 kg/m^2)
Horsepower of Power Plant: 875 hp

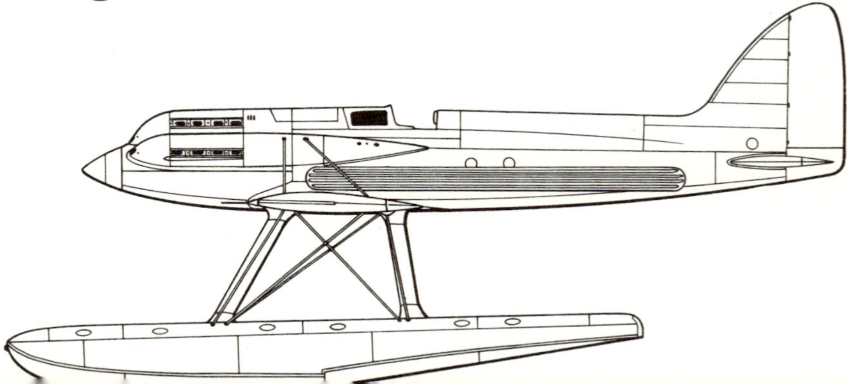

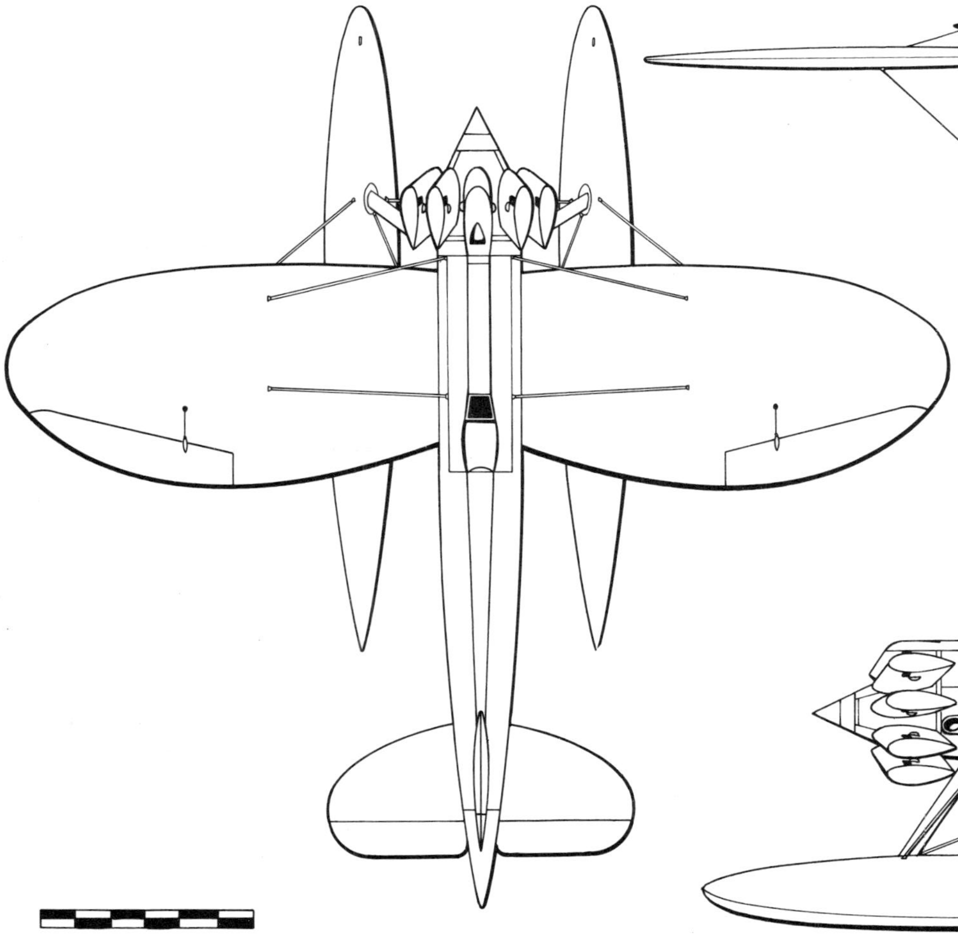

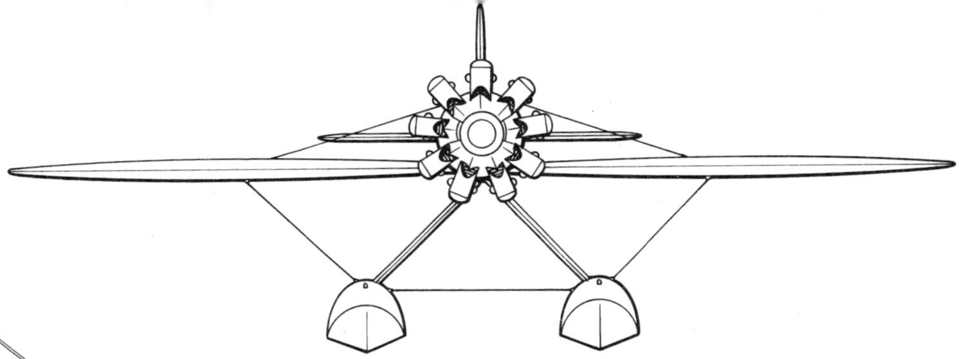

Short-Bristow Crusader (1927)

Wing Span: 26 ft 6 in (8·08 m)
Length Overall: 25 ft (7·62 m)
Wing Area: 120 sq. ft (11·15 m^2)
Weight Empty: 1,938 lb (879 kg)
T-O Weight: 2,712 lb (1,230 kg)
Max Wing Loading: 22·60 lb/sq. ft (110·34 kg/m^2)
Horsepower of Power Plant: 800 hp (approx.)

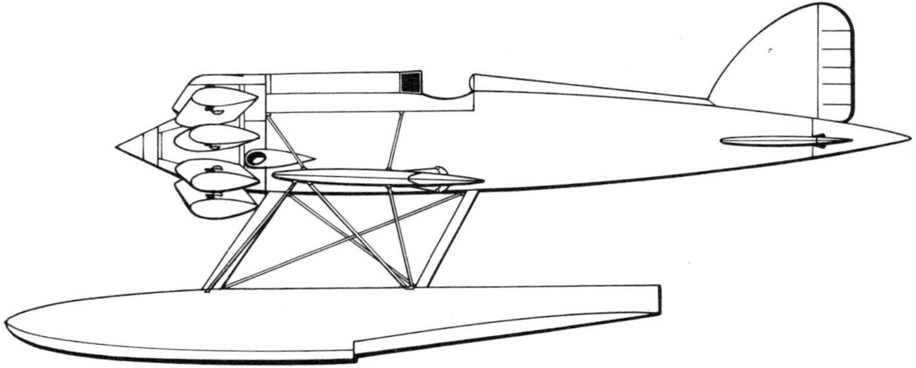

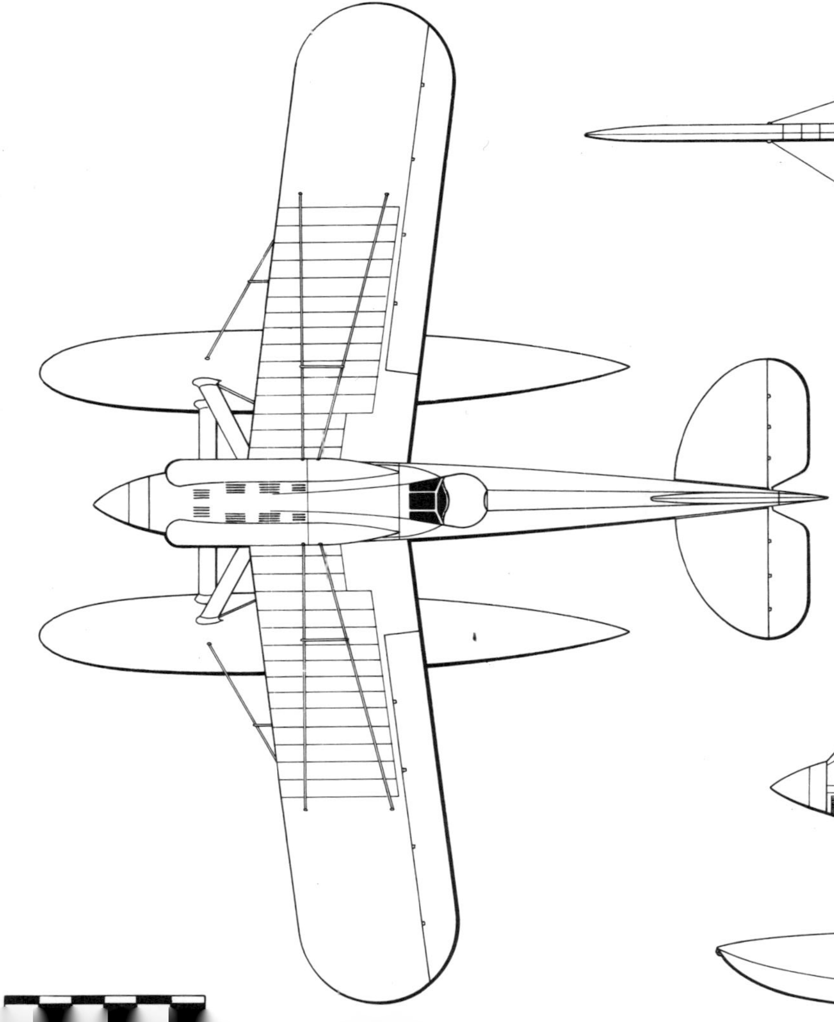

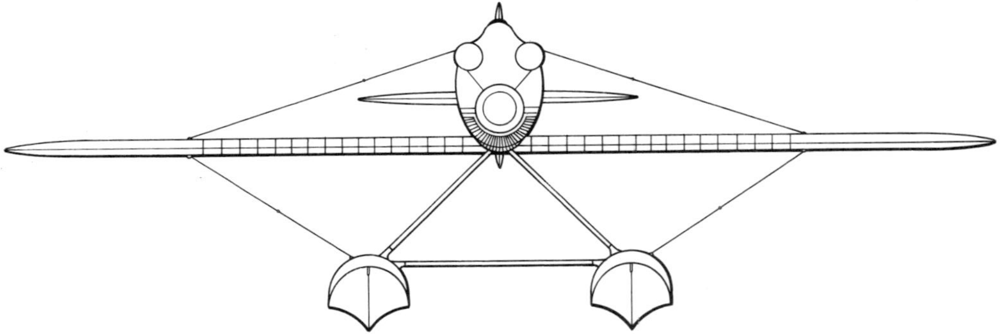

Macchi M.52 (1927)

Wing Span: 29 ft $5\frac{1}{2}$ in (8·98 m)
Length Overall: 23 ft 5 in (7·14 m)
Wing Area: 143·2 sq. ft (13·30 m²)
Weight Empty: 2,618 lb (1,187 kg)
T-O Weight: 3,340 lb (1,515 kg)
Max Wing Loading: 23·32 lb/sq. ft (113·86 kg/m²)
Horsepower of Power Plant: 1,000 hp

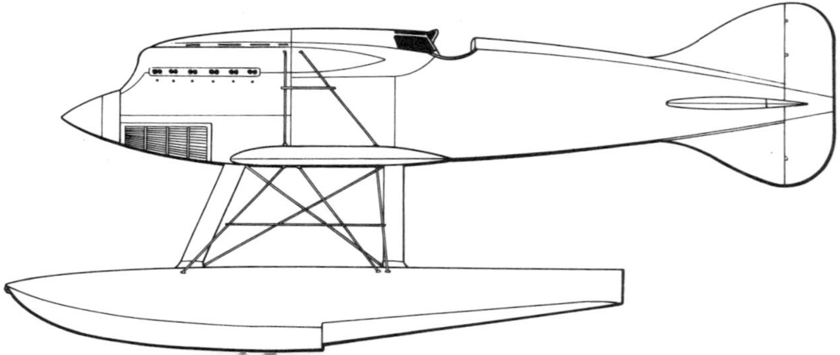

10

Intermission

A point has been reached where it is desirable to look around the aviation scene of that period and draw a comparison between military aviation and the high-speed aircraft which had been built to contend in the Schneider Trophy Contest. It is also worth underlining that this was the year in which Charles Lindbergh had made his superb solo west–east crossing of the North Atlantic: in a landplane!

The following table, covering several nations, will give some appreciation of the speeds being attained by single-engine military aircraft of the period:

Country	Aircraft type	Engine type	Horse-power	Maximum level speed
France	Dewoitine D 21	Hispano-Suiza 12 Gb	575	166 mph (267 km/h)
France	Nieuport-Delage 42	Hispano-Suiza 12 Hb	500	165 mph (266 km/h)
France	SPAD 61/2	Lorraine 12 Ew	450	174 mph (280 km/h)
Italy	Fiat C.R.20	Fiat A.20	400	171 mph (275 km/h)
Japan	Nakajima A1N1	Nakajima-built Bristol Jupiter	520	148 mph (238 km/h)
Netherlands	Fokker C.V-D	Hispano-Suiza	450	158 mph (254 km/h)
Russia	Polikarpov I-3	M-17	600/650	186 mph (299 km/h)
UK	Armstrong Whitworth Siskin IIIA	Armstrong-Siddeley Jaguar major	420/450	186 mph (299 km/h)
UK	Fairey Fox Mk.1	Curtiss D.12	480	156 mph (251 km/h)
UK	Gloster Gamecock Mk.1	Bristol Jupiter	425	155 mph (249 km/h)
USA	Boeing PW-9	Curtiss D.12	435	165 mph (266 km/h)
USA	Curtiss P-18 Hawk	Curtiss D.12	400	160 mph (258 km/h)

If the maximum speeds of these twelve different aircraft are averaged we arrive at a figure of around 166 mph (267 km/h), giving a fair picture of the state of the art.

In contrast, the S.5 had demonstrated a speed of just over 281 mph (452 km/h) in the 1927 Schneider contest which, by comparison with the above average, shows an increase of approximately 69 per cent in maximum speed. It was clear that such progress was of very considerable interest to those concerned with the procurement of military aircraft.

What accounted for this wide speed margin? Primarily, of course, because the S.5 and its contemporaries were stripped to the bare essentials and oriented solely for short-duration high-speed performance. They were very different creatures from the single-seat fighters of that era, capable of making fairly long patrols, carrying guns and ammunition, and built robustly to survive the vagaries of service life.

But surely there was scope for some compromise? More powerful engines were becoming available and the superior aerodynamic efficiency of the monoplane wing was being demonstrated adequately. Yet, so far behind was the development of military aircraft that even twelve years later, at the outbreak of the second World War, large numbers of slow, biplane aircraft continued to equip the air forces of the world.

At the moment in time when Jacques Schneider died, on 1 May 1928, an impartial analysis would have shown that:

(i) The primary objective of the Schneider Trophy Contest had failed. Instead of reliable long-range ocean-crossing waterborne transport aircraft, those which had been evolved to take part in the contests were lightweight, fast, single-seat seaplanes. They were flimsy, their water performance highly questionable, their life expectation and that of their engines bearing comparison with that of a mayfly.

(ii) To meet the demand for ever higher speed, power plant output had grown nearly tenfold, for the 100 hp engines of 1913 had given place to new developments capable of almost 1,000 hp. In the mid-range of this scale reliable engines were the rule, but so had been engines of very similar output soon after the end of the first World War. The much increased power of the racing engines had resulted from pushing existing designs very nearly to their limit: as a result they had only a very brief life expectancy.

(iii) The biplane versus monoplane controversy was still unresolved. In the main, airframe construction relied upon the skill of the cabinet maker rather than the metal worker.

Nevertheless, a vast pool of knowledge was being fed from countless streams of research. These, in the near future, would begin to have significant effects upon the development of both civil and military aircraft, and it should be remembered that much of this research stemmed from the need to find answers to questions which had been posed by the Schneider Trophy machines. Perhaps one of the greatest drawbacks of this contest had been that annual competition gave so little time for designers to make significant changes in fundamental design. Of necessity they had been forced to improve upon existing designs, rather than look ahead and experiment before turning drawing board dreams into hardware.

The forward-looking work of Mitchell and Castoldi had also been harassed by the needs to meet what were really unrealistic deadlines. The requirements were clear enough:

(i) Minimum drag and structural weight.
(ii) Greater propeller efficiency.
(iii) Structural integrity.
(iv) Engines of greater power and improved reliability.
(v) Successful systems integration.

The realisation of such ideals in a single aircraft needed considerable time.

That so much was accomplished is nothing short of miraculous. The sheer volume of work was staggering, especially in an age when no computers were available to process quickly and accurately the enormous mass of calculations needed to evaluate the results of wind tunnel testing of models.

Even the models and wind tunnels had not then attained a very high degree of sophistication, and before it was possible to arrive at a near-satisfactory configuration there stretched a seemingly endless succession of models, each with minute changes to fuselage form, wing section, or tail unit in an endeavour to attain the ideal. Each change needed more time-consuming tests, and the allied and inseparable manual calculation of aerodynamic efficiency and structural stress.

Much that we now accept unquestioningly as standard—indeed, we can hardly believe there was ever an alternative—was then a plunge into the unknown. It seems hardly credible today that anyone should have questioned whether a structure held together by snap head rivets was or was not aerodynamically more efficient than one which relied upon flush rivets. But ships had been built with snap head rivets from the first days of iron vessels, and the ability of such structures to survive punishment from the sea was well known. Perhaps it was logical that the floats of a seagoing aircraft should have similar construction.

Even the search for cooling efficiency was fraught with question marks. How big an area? Ribbed or flush? With or without fins? Every variation was a new step requiring, so often, a lengthy process of trial and error.

Even the long-enduring and preferred biplane configuration was loaded with problems so far as high speed flight were concerned. Were struts better than bracing wires? Which imposed the greater drag, and at what point was structural integrity of more significance than a minimal improvement in drag coefficient?

Slowly but surely progress was made, duralumin replacing wood and offering better strength/weight ratios. Bracing wires of high tensile steel and of improved streamline section worked to the same end. But even when it was clear that a bracing wire of a particular streamline section offered a significant reduction in drag, it might then be discovered that manufacturing techniques were then incapable of meeting such a requirement. This demanded time-consuming hand finishing.

Take just one other small point. Landing and flying wires have different functions, the former helping support the wing structure when the aircraft is on the ground, the latter when it is airborne. With the flying wire in tension and correctly aligned to give minimum drag, landing wires often lost tension and alignment, offsetting the gain of the former. Automatic tensioning devices were developed to overcome this problem, but in their turn added to structural weight and partially offset the hoped-for gain in efficiency.

As speeds increased factors of this kind became increasingly critical. A wing section that was ideal for high speed flight was far from being the most suitable for take off and landing. Even a half degree of error in the incidence of a rigged wing could produce a situation requiring full aileron deflection merely to keep the wings level. This was, of course, because the control surfaces of these high-speed aircraft needed to be small: if they were not their movement became so critical that the pilot tip-toed along one of the most critical tight-ropes ever created.

Compromise was always the guiding word. Structural strength was maintained at the expense of weight saving, with the accompanying effect of reducing speed not only by this factor, but often also through increased drag. Light weight offered speed, but increased the dangers that might result from a lack of structural integrity. And even though the airframes of these racing seaplanes had, in the main, a very limited life they were imposed to such great stresses that, for example, aileron loading on the S.5 was such that hinge-pin wear resulted after only a few hours of flight. As soon as this happened aileron flutter would develop.

Float design was something approaching a nightmare, for their size added greatly to the overall drag coefficient. They were quite superfluous for the primary requirement of the aircraft: high speed flight. Thus they had to be as light as possible, while retaining sufficient strength to cope with landings in bad water conditions. They needed to have as small a frontal area as possible, but could not be reduced beyond a width that would allow sufficient V-bottom to give directional stability on the water. Above all, there was a limit to their minimum volume, for they must provide adequate buoyancy in all water conditions for the fully laden aircraft.

It is hardly surprising, therefore, that almost as much effort went into float design as that expended on the airframe itself.

Propeller efficiency was another vital factor. The development of the

Curtiss-Reed propeller had done much to ease this problem, and initially the pitch of these propellers had been set by twisting a sheet of duralumin of suitable thickness to the required angle before machining it to the finished shape. This was fine at the beginning, but it was found that higher propeller speeds could produce sufficient stress to partially untwist the blades. The resulting finer pitch setting improved take-off performance, but was of little assistance in attaining the focal point of maximum speed.

The answer to this lay in taking a large billet of forged duralumin from which the requisite propeller was machined: thus, the resulting shape was virtually unstressed in its normal state. As a result, torsional loads did not tend to bring about changes in the pitch setting of the blades.

Where to house the fuel? That was another difficult problem. More power required more fuel; more fuel not only needed increased storage and added a weight penalty but could, if not disposed with great care, bring about significant and disconcerting changes in the aircraft's trim as the fuel was consumed in flight.

As the fuselage became smaller it was simultaneously less suited as a housing for the fuel tank or tanks. So why not put the fuel in the floats? An excellent idea so far as storage was concerned, but complicating the fuel system considerably. At one stage of this development it was found that high *g* turns proved too much for the lift of the fuel pump, causing the engine to cut through starvation. This was resolved by putting a small gravity header tank aft of the engine into which the fuel from the floats was pumped. More weight. More complication.

To ensure that the header tank was never over-pressurised a by-pass system was necessary to return surplus fuel back to the main storage in the floats. More pipes. More weight. And when engines developed a thirst that could down anything up to two gallons of fuel a minute, larger bore pipes and pumps of greater delivery rates were needed.

And what of the engines themselves? We have seen already that Fiats had run into serious trouble with their efforts in getting the AS.3 to produce around 1,000 hp. More power produced more heat, and the dissipation of this heat led to inevitable weight increases. More power usually needed also more engine weight, and it was the attempt to reverse this trend which had led Fiats into a completely new area of difficulty and unknowns by the use of lighter weight alloy materials for basic structure and components.

Heat had presented them with serious problems in the AS.2, and to ensure that the resulting expansion of internal components had not brought about engine seizure, excessive clearances had been allowed in final assembly. The sloppy fit of the pistons in their cylinder barrels accounted for the trail of smoke in the wake of the Macchis, but this was then the only practical means available to make sure that as engine temperature reached a maximum at full power, theoretical expansion of components would be just sufficient to ensure that the engine continued to run.

In Britain we had been fortunate that the original Napier Lion had such a great reserve of development potential. Thus, the 450 hp engine of 1919 had been urged to give almost double that power within just eight years, attaining what had long been considered an ultimate in engine design by producing just over one horsepower for each pound of dry weight.

It was clear, however, that the Lion had grown almost to full stature. It seemed unlikely that any significant increase of power was likely from that source and Supermarines began to look around for a successor.

The principal difficulty was that most engine manufacturers had followed the then conventional uprating technique by increasing bore, stroke and compression ratio. Additional rpm was beneficial, but apart from a mechanical limited imposed by the stress loads on reciprocating components, there was also the question of propeller efficiency to be taken into consideration.

We have already seen how the introduction of the Fairey-Reed propeller gave additional breathing space in this area, but it was not long before engine speeds had risen to the point where propeller inefficiency once again began to be of limiting importance.

An interim solution lay in the development of engine reduction gearing, this allowing the engine crankshaft to rotate at the desirable high speed while maintaining the propeller shaft at a lower speed that allowed the propeller to operate at its most efficient. But where energy is concerned it is impossible to gain such benefit without penalty. Those which have to be paid in this case are the additional weight of the reduction gear plus the power absorbed from the engine in driving this gear train. The nett result is an improvement, but is just another example of the compromise situation.

From where was additional power to be gained? To understand this a little better it is necessary to have a little knowledge of the inner workings of an internal combustion engine. We will look at only one aspect of a single cylinder engine. At the beginning of its operating cycle a valve between the cylinder and the induction system is opened: this allows the descending piston to suck in a volume of petrol/air mixture. At the bottom of the stroke the valve is closed and, as the piston rises again, this mixture is compressed. If, by the time the piston has reached the top of its stroke, the total volume has been reduced to half, then our hypothetical engine would be said to have a compression ratio of 2. If the volume had been reduced to one-tenth then the ratio would be 10.

This mixture which has been compressed should be in suitable proportions of petrol and air to form a combustible mixture, the burning of which is initiated by a sparking plug. It is the function of the carburettor to meter the petrol and maintain the desirable petrol/air ratio of the mixture drawn in by the piston. Too much fuel causes rich mixture; not only wasteful, but sooting up the sparking plugs and causing uneven running. Too weak a mixture causes overheating and damaging detonation. The engine runs correctly only when the petrol/air ratio is just right.

It is easy to see, therefore, that it was quite logical to increase cylinder volume by bigger bore and longer stroke so that more of this combustible mixture could be taken in to be available as a source of heat or energy. But this meant bigger, heavier engines, the last requirement of the airframe designer who was trying to reduce frontal area and overall weights to an absolute minimum.

There was one possible solution, already in common use by the motor racing fraternity. If the petrol/air mixture could be forced into the cylinders under pressure when the inlet valve opened, then the total volume of combustible mixture would be greater and, consequently, would produce more energy as it burnt. True, there would be more heat to dissipate, but this seemed to pose a far less difficult problem than charging the cylinder with abnormal quantities of a correctly proportioned fuel/air mixture.

The designers of racing car engines had been subjected to the same stringent power/weight requirements as those who developed power plants for aircraft. Thus a pump, called a supercharger—to super charge the cylinders—had been developed, significantly increasing power output but adding considerably to the engine's total weight. This proved to be the solution adopted by most aero-engine builders, who were soon busy experimenting with superchargers of different designs.

But a motor car engine did not have to operate at very differing altitudes, and the task for their designers was far simpler. At ground level the density of the air is reasonably constant. As height increases air density decreases, and so the whole business of supercharging aero-engines had to be tied in most carefully with mixture control. If not, the supercharger would provide sufficient air by volume, but since its density had decreased there was insufficient oxygen by weight to form an ideal combustible mixture as a result of the undiminished quantity of fuel introduced by the carburettor. This was an area of development which needed precious time in which to remove the bugs from the system.

The supercharger presented also a similar give and take penalty as imposed by reduction gears: it needed considerable power to drive it and also added to the weight and overall dimensions of the engine. More supercharging, or boost pressure, required more power to produce it and, in the early stage of the art, the gains were minimal. Only as techniques improved was the power gain of really worthwhile significance, far outstripping the penalties imposed by this new and increasingly complicated component of the fast-developing piston-engine.

At Derby, in 1906, had been established a company whose name would soon become a part of our language, used often to describe something luxurious, reliable or of superb quality: Rolls-Royce Limited. It was in their direction that Supermarine turned their gaze for in 1925 a new engine known as the F.10 had its origin. By June 1927 it had completed a 100 hour type test, developing 490 hp and having a dry weight of 760 lb (345 kg).

It was, in fact, the first of the famous line of engines that became named Kestrel, and which powered a host of military and civil aircraft of all nations.

This was followed in 1927 by a larger and more powerful engine, known originally as the Type H, but later to be named the Buzzard. This had a bore and stroke of 6in (15·24cm) and 6·6in (16·76cm) respectively, and was provided with a supercharger designed to produce its maximum output at ground level for the critical phase of an aeroplane's take off.

This engine then developed 955hp at 2,300rpm, had a dry weight of 1,540lb (699kg) and with its very compact frontal area seemed the most suitable power plant for Mitchell's new machine. This, of course, was true only if it could be developed to produce considerably more power for a short duration life and if—the biggest if of all—Henry Royce could be induced to build such a specialised engine.

This may seem strange to the reader of today, but it was then a strict company policy not to become involved in competitive motoring or flying events. The Rolls-Royce car and its engine, and the Rolls-Royce aero-engines were supreme in quality. It was not considered necessary for them to prove this in costly competition, and entry into such events might impose deadlines which could be met only by building an engine or engines that could fall below their very high standards of quality. This, they had always considered, was a procedure to be avoided at all costs.

Mitchell and Supermarines were faced with this seeming insoluble problem. It was resolved finally by a combined visit of Commander Bird of Supermarines and G. P. Bulman, an Air Ministry official responsible for the development of aero-engines, who called upon Henry Royce at his West Wittering home, on the Sussex coast.

It was, they knew, useless to bait Royce with the prospect of kudos for his company: it had already acquired an enviable worldwide reputation. Something a little more subtle was necessary: they decided to base their gambit on national prestige and the ultimate benefits to the nation's aircraft industry.

Henry Royce could hardly turn down such an appeal, and agreed that the Buzzard, which was then about to enter production, had the requisite development potential. For Britain a most significant train of events had been set in motion.

11

Confrontation at Cowes

1929

Barely had the excitement of Britain's win at Venice died down before there was another round of discussions as to whether, in the future, the contest should continue on an annual or biennial basis. It will be recalled that the former decision in favour of biennial competition had been revoked, with the result that the contest scheduled originally for 1928 had been brought forward to 1927.

The argument in favour of biennial competition was becoming more viable as month succeeded month. With constant emphasis on more power from the engine, more speed from the aircraft, designers and constructors were stepping into areas of new technology. This required time-consuming research and experiment to cope with the problems that began to proliferate out of all proportion to small gains in power or speed.

The question was resolved finally at a meeting of the FAI, held in Paris on 5 January 1928. It was a meeting attended by Jacques Schneider who, despite indifferent health, wished to be present to offer his congratulations to Britain's representatives on their country's win at Venice in the previous autumn.

The committee of the FAI needed no convincing that biennial competition made commonsense: they had heard all the views in favour expressed previously. This time came unanimous agreement and suitable amendment to the rules: 'The winner to be the country which shall have gained three victories out of five successive contests, the contests to be held every two years.'

With this matter settled, Britain's Royal Aero Club was able to make a preliminary announcement for the 1929 contest, following a meeting held on 29 February, and stated that this would take place between 24 August and 5 October 1929. The venue was not named, as there had been several alternatives suggested and these needed to be evaluated by the committee before a decision was announced.

Seven weeks after this meeting came news of the death of Jacques Schneider, on 1 May 1928, at Beaulieu near Monte Carlo. He had lived to see the winning speeds of the contest which he had founded climb from the 45 mph (72 km/h) set up by Maurice Prévost in 1913 to the 281 mph

(452 km/h) of Flight-Lieutenant Webster at Venice in 1927. In the month which had followed, on 4 November, de Bernardi of Italy had set a new world speed record of 297·76 mph (479·2 km/h). In so doing he demonstrated that Italian aircraft design was very much on a par with that of Britain and that, similarly, the main problem concerned the evolution of reliable high-powered engines.

Jacques Schneider died without knowing that Britain could become the final holder of his Trophy. Or without any awareness of the extent to which his attempt to advance maritime aviation would be responsible for a new generation of high-speed fighter aircraft of historic importance.

That was then all very much in the future. And, to the average person, so was a Schneider contest in the Autumn of 1929. But for those concerned with producing the aircraft which would compete there was by no means time enough.

The situation must have been rather different for the members of the High Speed Flight. After months of training they had achieved success and a new pinnacle of achievement. From the elation of Venice and the immediate return and receptions came a sobering return of everyday service routine as, temporarily at any rate, the team were disbanded and returned to their units.

It was not until early 1928 that it was reformed, with the primary aim of regaining for Britain the world speed record which de Bernardi had set in the previous autumn.

Flight-Lieutenant S. M. Kinkead had been elected to make the attempt, and he and the ground crew stood by at Calshot, practising in the S.5 N.221 whenever the weather would allow. Even when they considered the moment ripe the weather was far from reliable, and day after day they waited impatiently for suitable conditions under which to make the attempt.

On March 1928 the weather seemed about right, but a start was delayed from hour to hour in the hope that visibility and sea conditions might improve just that little bit more. It was not to be so, and as failure to seize the opportunity presented on that day could result in another frustrating period of waiting, it was decided to go ahead.

By then it was well into the afternoon, the water motionless and with a mirror surface. As Kinkead took off and began to position the S.5 for his approach to the measured strip a thin mist had formed close to the surface of the water. He turned on course, putting the nose down and opening the throttle wide: those who watched heard the Lion's roar first and then, in the distance, a speck that represented the little machine grew in size rapidly as it approached the starting line of the measured course.

Within seconds it was all over, the S.5 converted to splintered wreckage as, with the engine developing full power, the seaplane plunged into the water. Sam Kinkead, a brave, much respected and highly decorated pilot, was killed instantly. There were suggestions that a problem had developed with the aircraft's controls, but had this been so it is reasonable to assume that, at least, Kinkead would have throttled back the engine instinctively Eye-witnesses said there was no indication of any change in the engine's note and no one will ever know for certain the reason for this tragic accident. Air Commodore D. D'Arcy A. Greig told the writer that it was generally believed that under the prevailing conditions of light and water Kinkead completely misjudged his height and flew straight into the water at maximum speed. At that time Greig was a Flight-Lieutenant and as likely as anyone to know the true facts for it was he who, following a call for a suitable volunteer, was posted to replace Kinkead on 1 May 1928.

But in the meantime the Italians had not allowed the grass to grow beneath their feet. Fiat's had been working on the AS.3 engine and managed to ensure that its performance was far more reliable than when the Macchis had suffered such abject defeat at Venice. During the same period Mario Castoldi had made some refinements to the Macchi M.52. Most significant of the changes was a reduction in wing span to 25 ft 9 in (7·85 m), wing area falling to only 117 sq. ft (10·87 m^2). In addition, the horizontal struts bracing the floats to each other had been replaced by streamline wires.

In this form the M.52 was re-designated M.52R (sometimes referred to as the M.52*bis*), and on 30 March 1928, shortly after Kinkead's fatal accident, de Bernardi had flown this to a new world speed record of 318·57 mph (512·69 km/h). This not only demonstrated that Castoldi had been right in his original estimate that the M.52 should be capable of a speed of around 300 mph (483 km/h), but had also pushed the target a little higher for D'Arcy Greig, who was standing by to set a new record in the S.5 as soon as ideal conditions presented themselves.

When he made the attempt, on 4 November 1928, he managed to exceed the speed set up by de Bernardi, averaging 319·57 mph (514·30 km/h), which represented a new British speed record, but was not a sufficient increase over the Italian's speed to qualify as a new world speed record.

In early January 1929, Flight-Lieutenant A. H. Orlebar was promoted to Squadron Leader and posted to Felixstowe to command a new High Speed Flight which was to form there on 1 February 1929. Apart from the engineer officer, Flying-Officer T. H. Moon, the team was entirely new. It had been decided that year that previous experience of operation with waterborne aircraft was of lesser importance than proven flying skill and knowledge of flight in high-speed aircraft. In addition to Flight-Lieutenant D'Arcy Greig, Orlebar found himself responsible for the activities of Flight-Lieutenant G. H. Stainforth and Flying-Officers R. L. R. 'Batchy' Atcherley and H. R. D. Waghorn, more usually known as Waggon. .

Renewed participation in 1929 was a situation which had been unanticipated by the Air Council, for the Treasury had gone to some pains to make it absolutely clear in 1927 that their support in that year was not to be regarded as creating a precedent. In fact, the roles became reversed, the success in 1927 motivating the government to ensure that Britain should make a good showing on the home course in the next contest, the Air Ministry proving somewhat reticent to accept responsibility. Not surprisingly, it was the government that called the tune.

Once the decision to participate had been declared, the Air Ministry lost little time in getting down to their preparations. The High Speed Flight was re-activated at Felixstowe, their training concerned initially with familiarisation on seaplanes. Available for their use in this respect were several aircraft, including a Fairey Flycatcher amphibian and the Gloster IVs.

Meanwhile, the now-recognised suppliers of high-speed racing seaplanes, Gloster and Supermarine, were approached to develop new aircraft which would, undoubtedly, need to be capable of significantly higher speeds.

Soon after the successful conclusion of the 1927 contest, Folland began the design of a successor to the Gloster IV. He was firmly convinced, despite any evidence to the contrary, that the biplane configuration still maintained worthwhile advantages for racing aircraft. And despite the problems experienced with the Lion engines in the Gloster IVs, he favoured a continuing relationship with the Napier company, perhaps arguing that allegiance to the devil one knew was a safer bet than becoming involved with a completely new power plant of unknown quality.

Napiers had developed a new version of the Lion, the VIID, promising a power output of 1,320 hp at 3,600 rpm without increase of bore or stroke. This had been achieved by incorporating a supercharger, but as the frontal area was no bigger it seemed the natural choice for the new biplane design, designated as the Gloster V.

Inevitably, the provision of a supercharger for the new Lion had involved an increase in weight. This engine was some 240 lb (108 kg) heavier than the geared VIIB, and changes in wing position to allow for the resulting alteration in CG would have brought the upper wing directly above the cylinder blocks. This was quite unacceptable, for the pilot's visibility would have been limited severely. The Gloster V was stillborn.

Instead, in May 1928, Folland began the design of a new aircraft to utilise the Lion VIID engine, turning for the first time to a monoplane configuration, and received an Air Ministry contract in November 1928 for two examples of what became designated the Gloster VI.

A low-wing monoplane of composite construction, the multi-spar multi-rib wooden wings were of spruce. Two spruce skins were applied overall to this structure, with an additional skin in stress areas. These skins were made up and glued on formers of the same contour as the basic wing structure. When the glue had set the skins were removed from the formers and attached by screws to the leading and trailing-edges of the wing structure.

Most unusual feature of the Gloster VI lay in the design of these wings, with straight leading-edges, and trailing-edges which were swept forward so that wing chord reduced progressively from the outer panels to the centre-section. In addition, wing section was at its maximum thickness near the tips, reducing to almost half that dimension at the wing root. By the use of this design Folland hoped to combine the benefits of good low-speed lateral control with the advantages of a thin-section low-drag wing. Dual streamline landing wires extended from the upper fuselage to approximately two-thirds span, flying wires from two-thirds span to the top surface of the floats.

The fuselage was an all-metal semi-monocoque structure with oval formers, the duralumin skin secured by flush rivets. The tail unit was conventional and of cantilever construction.

Single-step V-bottom floats of Gloster design were generally similar to those of the Gloster IV in outward appearance, but both had integral fuel tanks from which the fuel was lifted by engine-driven pumps to a small header tank in the fuselage. Additionally, they each had three watertight bulkheads to reduce the risk of the aircraft sinking if the floats were damaged. They were carried on four tubular steel struts, which were streamlined by light alloy fairings, and were wire-braced diagonally and to each other by two streamline wires.

Power plant, as mentioned already, comprised the new Napier Lion VIID, this driving a Gloster two-blade metal propeller 7 ft 8 in (2·34 m) in diameter. The increased power of this engine involved greater cooling problems, and liquid cooling was effected by extremely thin copper surface radiators on the wings. So thin, indeed, that pressure from the thumb was sufficient to dent them, requiring the exercise of great care during maintenance work on the aircraft.

Aft of the pilot's cockpit a combined oil cooler/tank encircled the fuselage, flush with the surface, and the available cooling area could be supplemented by surface coolers on the upper surface of each float.

It was not until 12 August 1929 that the first of these aircraft (N.249) was delivered to Calshot, the second machine (N.250) following it five days later. When assembled and visible to the press they made a splendid sight. N.249 had a gold coloured fuselage and blue floats, earning it the name *Golden Arrow*, but because of its very slender fuselage the members of the High Speed Flight often referred to it as the *Golden Bodkin*. N.250 had an even more magnificent colour scheme, comprising gold wings, blue fuselage and white floats. One reporter was sufficiently moved to comment that they seemed: '. . . more the conception of an artist who can make and create his own lines by the stroke of a brush, than the work of a designer who is bound by the principles of engineering and the comparative inelasticity of metal and timber.'

Mitchell at Supermarine had also considerable problems to face, for he was involved in designing an aircraft to utilise the somewhat unknown power of a new and untried engine. Of course, he knew its dimensions reasonably accurately from the outset, since they would be much the same as those of the Buzzard. Likewise, he knew that he must cater for a dry weight of about 1,500 lb (680 kg). The power that this engine might provide was very much in question.

To Commander Bird's original enquiry, Henry Royce had suggested they might achieve about 1,500 hp, and Mitchell was to comment very much later how, in those early days, he had said to A. J. Rowledge: 'Of course you will get your horsepower as high as possible.' Later, he said, he had begun to regret that remark and that, in the later stages of development of the 'R' engine, he began to hate Mr Rowledge, by then reduced to the cautionary request to 'Go steady with your horsepower.'

The task taken on by Rolls-Royce Ltd in February 1929 was close on Herculean. The prototype Buzzard, which had developed 925 hp on bench test in July 1928, had now to be coerced into producing rather more than half as much power again to achieve Royce's suggested figure of 1,500 hp. This had to be achieved without significantly changing the engine's dimensions, and certainly with no increase in frontal area, while reliability coupled with fuel and oil consumption of the lowest possible order was essential.

The solution lay in a larger, double-sided centrifugal supercharger to give higher boost pressures, bigger carburettor, special fuel, higher engine revolutions, strengthening of components to accept new stress levels and the introduction of a special forward-facing air intake. This latter feature, which became patented, virtually supplied the supercharger with ram air and, at the aircraft's maximum speed, was responsible for a gain of more than 200 horsepower.

Despite these requirements, an engine was run on the bench about three months later, on 14 May, producing 1,545 hp at 2,750 rpm for a continuous period of 15 minutes. It was an auspicious start. By 23 July the engine had completed a one-hour endurance test producing 1,614 hp at 3,000 rpm, and raised again to 1,800 hp at 2,850 rpm which was maintained for 1 hour 20 minutes on 27 August. The final racing engines for use in the contest operated at a boost pressure of 12·25 lb/sq. in (0·86 km/cm^2) and at 2,900 rpm developed no less than 1,900 hp. The engine had a dry weight of only 1,530 lb (694 kg). Rolls-Royce had more than kept their word.

Meanwhile, Mitchell had been busy designing the airframe to contain this power plant of enigmatic output. With an engine that could conceivably mature with almost double the weight of the direct-drive Lion VIIA, it was inevitable that the airframe would have to be of increased size.

So satisfactory had been the basic configuration of the S.5 that it was decided that the new machine should be fundamentally an enlarged version. This time, detail design would have to be concentrated on weight limitation. To this end the S.6, as it became designated, was of all-metal construction, the two-spar wings having ribs with large lightening holes in their webs.

The surface radiators were built up from duralumin sheet and themselves formed the upper and lower surfaces of most of the wing. The tail unit was also an all-metal structure.

Floats were of Supermarine design and construction, both containing fuel tanks to cater for an engine that would have a bigger thirst than the Lion, and were also somewhat bigger in volume to provide additional buoyancy. Carried on four streamline struts, they and the wings were braced by streamline wires similarly to the S.5. To provide additional liquid cooling surface, the forward upper portion of each float had a surface radiator.

Oil cooling promised to be a more severe problem than with the Lion engine, and while retaining the external coolers on each side of the fuselage, additional cooling area was deemed necessary. Thus, the hot oil leaving the engine travelled down one side of the fuselage, was then carried to the top of the fin where it ran down the inner surface of the skin under the control of ribs and gutters, before collection in a tank and filter system at the base of the fin. From there it travelled back down the other side of the fuselage to the engine.

It was not until Monday 5 August, only a month from the contest date, that the first machine, N.247, was launched on the water for the first time.

Having taken a look at the progress of the Trophy's defenders, we must now see the extent of the competition ranged against the British. With Italy holding the world speed record it seemed certain that a strong challenge must emanate from that country. But there were also reports that America, France and Germany might all participate, so it was possible that the 1929 contest could be a truly international event.

The situation in America, however, was that the government no longer had any interest in the contest and, once again, it was left to 'Al' Williams to defend the country's honour. Again he had to rely upon the generosity of individuals to make possible the construction of a competing aircraft. A non-profit making company was floated, the Mercury Flying Corporation, to finance the construction of a seaplane which became designated as the Mercury. The US Navy took upon itself the task of designing the aircraft, the testing of scale models at the Washington Navy Yard, and construction of the aircraft at the Naval Aircraft Factory at Philadelphia.

A development of the Kirkham-Williams racer, the Mercury had followed the prevailing trend of change to monoplane configuration. Set in a mid-wing position, the wire-braced wing was of wooden construction with plywood skins, the ailerons being of light alloy. Fuselage and tail unit were of wooden construction, the tail unit comprising a large vertical fin and deep rudder so that its resulting configuration could almost be described as cruciform.

The typically-Navy very large floats were conventional in their single-step V-bottom duralumin construction. Their unusual feature was the siting of surface radiators on the float undersurfaces, to offer additional low-temperature cooling surfaces during taxying and take-off, when airflow over the wing surface radiators was at a minimum and providing the lowest cooling efficiency at a moment when the engine was delivering maximum power.

Power plant comprised the 24-cylinder X-form Packard that had been used in the Kirkham-Williams racer, with minor modification to improve maximum power rating for take-off. Unfortunately, this proved inadequate, for when it was found impossible to get the Mercury off the water, tests showed that the aircraft was some 400lb (181kg) over design weight. The only solution lay in the provision of more power, and plans were put in hand to utilise an up-rated Packard engine, reputedly capable of developing between 1,300 and 1,500hp.

France, who had not competed for six years, was determined to make special efforts to record a victory in 1929. This seemed essential, for since the war the nation's aviation industry had fallen far behind the capability of the leading European countries and needed a boost for its morale.

Accordingly, in early 1928 four racing seaplanes were ordered by the Ministry for Marine for competition in the Schneider contest, comprising two from Société des Avions Bernard and two from Société Anonyme Nieuport-Delage.

The two aircraft designed by the former company were basically similar, and having the designations HV.40 and HV.42 (HV: Haut Vitesse: high speed). The former was supposedly to be powered by a new Gnome-Rhone engine, reported as a 9-cylinder radial known as the Mistral, but as the maximum power output of this engine was only 550hp at 2,350rpm it seems hardly suited to the requirements of the Schneider Trophy Contest. If a Mistral engine was intended, it seems more likely that it would have been the 14-cylinder Mistral Major, which had a maximum rating of 800hp at 2,130rpm, but even this was rather far behind the engine power of likely competitors.

The HV.42 was a more realistic contender, relying upon another new power plant, the Hispano-Suiza 18R which was specially developed for the 1929 contest. This was an 18-cylinder in-line liquid-cooled engine of broad-arrow configuration, the 80° separation between each bank of cylinders giving it almost an inverted 'T' shape. The aim was high power output allied to light weight and, theoretically at any rate, this was achieved. Extensive use of light alloy was intended to control the weight factor, limiting the dry weight to only 1,144lb (519kg). Design power output at take-off was 1,680hp at 2,400rpm, but with a compression ratio of 10, no supercharger, and a carburettor for each pair of cylinders it promised, and proved to be, somewhat temperamental.

Oddest looking feature of the Bernard design for the airframe was the wire-braced monoplane mid-wing. The wing section at the root was so deep that it conformed with the contour of the fuselage, which meant that the one-piece wing formed an essential part of the fuselage structure. Because of the deep aerofoil at the centre-section its structure was multi-cellular. Vertical members of laminated plywood had spruce stringers top and bottom, these being skinned with plywood. Outer panels of the wing were of conventional two-spar construction, with metal ailerons hinged to a false spar.

The forward section of the fuselage was, essentially, the wing centre-section, the engine mounting being attached to its forward edge. Behind the wing was the fuselage proper, the sides consisting of spruce and plywood girders, interconnected by spruce and plywood frames. The fin was built integrally with the fuselage, and the tail unit was an all-wood cantilever structure.

The Bernard floats followed what had then become usual design, in so much that they had integral fuel tanks and were fabricated from duralumin and of single-step V-bottom configuration. They were, however, mounted to N-shape struts which were attached to a rectangular duralumin frame that formed the base of the wing centre-section. Wire bracing extended from floats to wings and between the floats. Lamblin radiators for engine cooling were mounted on the float struts of the HV.42.

The pilot, too, was accommodated in the centre-section of the multi-purpose wing, with the cockpit opening coming at the wing trailing-edge. Wing span was 30 ft 2 in (9·19 m) and length overall 28 ft 7 in (8·71 m).

It is clear the Bernard machines were not conspicuous for their clean lines. On the other hand, those constructed by Nieuport-Delage were very similar to the more advanced Macchis, with thin-section wire-braced monoplane wings set in a low-wing configuration, slender streamlined fuselage and neat and conventional tail unit.

They were, however, dominated by their enormous single-step floats which were longer than the fuselage, mounted on four slender struts and extensively wire-braced. Power plant was to consist of the same Hispano-Suiza engine chosen to power the Bernard HV.42.

But by the summer of 1929 little progress had been made with the power plants, although Bernard and Nieuport-Delage each had airframes awaiting their new engines. Efforts had been made to allow for team training, using a base on Lake Hourtin, near Bordeaux. Here a team of pilots of the French Naval air service trained to the best of their ability on hack machines, while Sadi Lecointe and Florentin Bonnet stood by to test the new machines as soon as they became available.

On 6 August 1929, Bonnet was killed when flying in one of the Nieuport 62 single-seat fighters which had been used for high-speed training. This, it seems, must have represented the last straw for France, for within days of the fatal accident they announced their withdrawal from the contest.

HRH The Prince of Wales photographed with the Italian team. Left to right: Lieutenant R. Cadringher, Lieutenant G. Monti, Captain A. Canaveri, Lieutenant-Colonel Mario Bernasconi, Warrant-Officer T. Dal Molin and Sergeant Major F. Agello

Giovanni Monti in the M.67 is towed to shore after an air test

German participation also failed to materialise. It had been reported that the Dornier company was to produce a seaplane contender, but it seems likely that their pre-occupation with Lufthansa long-range seaplane experiments, as well as their involvement in the Do X project, made it impossible to give any serious attention to a Schneider aircraft.

Italy, however, regarded the matter as one of prime importance, not only to her industry but to the prestige of the new regime. The defeat at Venice had been galling, especially as subsequent events had shown their M.52R to be an advanced and reliable machine. Nonetheless, they had been beaten at home by a British team, and it was pretty certain that if the Trophy was to be brought back to Italy a very determined effort would need to be made.

This was soon mounted by the energetic General Balbo who, taking note of Britain's broad-scale approach to the contest in 1927, decided also to involve a larger percentage of the Italian aviation industry.

Thus, Macchi was chosen without hesitation, and Fiat, Piaggio and Savoia-Marchetti were all asked to produce competitive designs. Fiat and Isotta-Fraschini were expected to develop new world-beating power plants.

Let us look first at the Macchi machine, again evolving from the genius of Castoldi and which, derived from the M.52, had the designation M.67. Its general appearance was similar to that of its predecessor but, like Mitchell, Castoldi had been compelled to scale up the design to cater for a heavier and more powerful engine. In the Italian's case, this was a new Isotta-Fraschini 18-cylinder liquid-cooled in-line engine of broad-arrow configuration, designed by Giustino Cattaneo. Developing approximately 1,400 hp, its choice had arisen for very much the same reason that the Rolls-Royce had supplanted the Lion in the new machine designed by Mitchell. Namely, that like the Lion, the Fiat AS.3 was considered to have reached its full development potential.

Principal external differences between the new M.67 and the M.52 of 1927 lay in elimination of sweepback of the wing, and provision of additional radiator surface to cater for oil cooling of the more powerful engine. The one other external distinguishing feature at the outset was the use of a three-blade propeller to make full utilisation of the additional power.

Construction of the monoplane wing set in low-wing configuration was conventional all-wood, except that skins consisted largely of metal surface radiators, the remaining area being covered with plywood. Wire bracing followed the same layout as for the M.52. The fuselage was a composite structure, consisting of metal forward of the cockpit to provide a rigid mounting for wing, engine and float struts. A wood semi-monocoque aft structure lead to what had become a feature of the Macchis, a cantilever cruciform tail unit. Oil coolers were mounted on the outer surface of each side of the fuselage.

Fuel for the power plant was carried in duralumin tanks in the floats, but the floats themselves were of wooden construction. On their upper surface, between the float struts, additional surface radiators were applied to provide more oil cooling capacity.

Wing span of the M.67 was 29ft 5in (8·97m), wing area 145·5sq.ft (13·52m^2) and maximum take-off weight 4,740lb (2,150kg), which was 1,400lb (635kg) more than the M.52.

The Fiat company, responsible for the earlier AS.2 and AS.3 engines which, though proving unreliable in the contests, had enabled Italy to set new world speed records, was also a builder of aircraft. Having acquired the assets of the old Ansaldo company they continued with that product line, which meant that their main experience was concerned with the design and construction of landplanes.

Their new machine to be one of Italy's contenders in 1929 was designated C.29, and bore a distinct resemblance to the Macchis: the only at-a-glance difference concerned the tail unit, the tailplane and elevators of which were almost in alignment with the upper surface of the fuselage.

Construction, however, differed very considerably, with each major assembly being a composite structure in an endeavour to exploit weight-saving to the full. The monoplane wire-braced wing, set in a low-wing configuration, had two duralumin spars, braced to each other by steel struts and making a rigid frame that was additionally braced diagonally by high-tensile steel wire. Ribs were of wood, and the wing skins were a combination of surface radiators and duralumin sheet.

Basic fuselage structure comprised four tubular steel longerons located by formers and lattice bracing, alloy stringers maintaining the fuselage contour which was covered by aluminium skin. Tail unit was an all-wood cantilever structure with duralumin skins.

Floats, similar to those of the Macchis, were of the single-step V-bottom type, constructed of wood, and carried on four tubular struts that were also wire-braced; each contained a fuel tank.

Wing span of the C.29 was 21ft 8½in (6·62m), length overall 24ft 7¼in (7·50m), height overall 9ft 0in (2·75m) and wing area 86·11sq.ft (8·0m^2). Maximum take-off weight was only 2,557lb (1,160kg), so that the aim of producing a lightweight structure had been achieved.

Power plant was, as might be expected, of Fiat design and construction, and comprised a new lightweight 12-cylinder in-line liquid-cooled engine of V-form, following the basic layout of the AS.2 and AS.3. With a bore and stroke of 5·43in (13·8cm) and 5·51in (14·0cm) respectively, it had a compression ratio of 8. Maximum power output was 1,000hp at 3,200rpm, and with a dry weight of only 728lb (330kg) the Fiat AS.5, as it was designated,

Opposite page: (*top*) The year 1929 saw the 'new look' in Italian aircraft, although it was only the Macchis that reached the starting line. Fiat's C.29 with 1,000hp AS.5 engine . . . (*centre*) the Piaggio P.7c in hardware form . . . (*bottom*) and a cutaway drawing showing the engine installation

C 29
129

P7-127

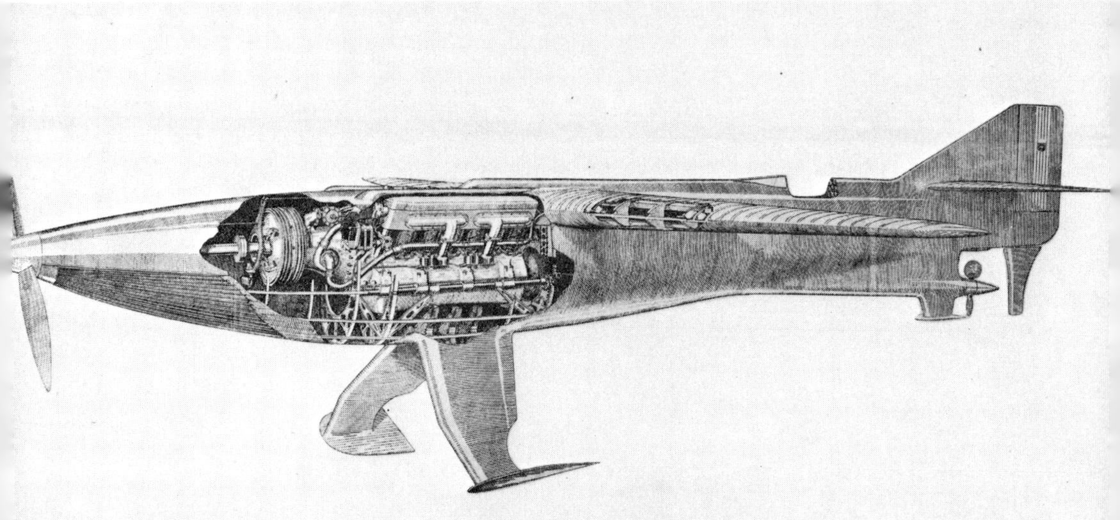

was for a number of years the lightest weight 1,000 hp engine in the world.

SIAI's Savoia-Marchetti S.65 was one of two quite revolutionary designs. It was one which attempted to resolve the problems associated with propeller torque, and at the same time to benefit from the availability of considerably more power without involvement with temperamental over-boosted engines.

It was a wire-braced low-wing monoplane without a conventional fuselage. Two narrow booms extended from the wing structure to carry the tail unit, and were braced at their aft end by two inverted Vee struts carried on rear extensions to what would otherwise have been fairly narrow and conventional floats. A central nacelle provided accommodation for two Isotta-Fraschini in-line liquid-cooled engines of 1,000 hp each, that in the forward position driving a two-blade metal tractor propeller, the aft engine driving a similar pusher propeller. Between the two engines sufficient space was allowed to accommodate the pilot's cockpit, and the engine/cockpit nacelle was mounted on four robust struts, strut-braced, and mounted on the floats. Fuel for the engines was contained in the floats.

It was a far-sighted design, for not only should the two moderately-powered engines promise a high degree of reliability, but the contra-rotating propellers were expected to eliminate all torque problems, permitting the use of much narrower floats of reduced frontal area and buoyancy.

However, most revolutionary of all the Italian designs was that produced by Ing Pegna of the Piaggio company, one which has been described as a hybrid resulting from the crossing of an aeroplane with a submarine.

Humorous although this comment was intended to be, it had a vestige of reality. Pegna had realised for some time what an immense improvement in the aerodynamic efficiency of the racing seaplane airframe could be realised if only it could be relieved of the enormous floats.

So he designed a fuselage and wing structure which was watertight, so that it could float in the water. From its in-line power plant a tail-shaft could be clutched-in to drive a conventional marine propeller mounted in the rear fuselage. Hydrofoil surfaces were provided fore and aft, and it was the intention that the marine propeller would give it sufficient speed to lift the entire structure on the hydrofoils, when the conventional tractor propeller would be clutched-in to allow the aircraft to become airborne. The hydrovanes and their supporting struts would have minimal frontal area, offering virtually no drag by comparison with floats and their massive supporting struts. Additionally, the slight incidence of the hydrovanes would add a small component of lift.

The cantilever wooden monoplane wing was set in a high-wing configuration and was of elliptical plan form. A three-spar structure with wooden ribs and plywood skins, it was specially constructed to make it completely waterproof. Surface cooling radiators were provided on both upper and lower surfaces. Ailerons occupied almost 75 per cent of the wing trailing-edges.

Last but not least, the Savoia S.65. This head-on view shows clearly how similar was the frontal area of floats and fuselage

Another non-starter in 1929 was the American Mercury racer

The fuselage was of oval cross-section, built up with bulkheads and longerons, skinned by a double layer of plywood sandwiching a water-proofed fabric. Buoyancy of the fuselage was enhanced by two watertight compartments, plus a number of aluminium boxes located in the rear fuselage. The tail unit was also of wood/plywood construction, the rudder post extending below the fuselage structure to carry a water rudder.

Power plant comprised an 850 hp Isotta-Fraschini 12-cylinder in-line liquid-cooled engine of V-form, driving through clutch and shaft mechanisms either a two-blade metal tractor propeller for conventional flight, or a two-blade variable-pitch metal water propeller. The complication of pitch-variation of the water propeller was chosen so that, in flight, it could be set to offer minimum drag. A specially-constructed mechanically-operated rubber gland was mounted on the conventional propeller shaft to ensure there was no ingress of water when the aircraft was in its near-submerged at-rest state on the surface.

Designated as the Piaggio Pc.7, its wing span was 28 ft 8½ in (8·75 m), length overall 29 ft 0 in (8·84 m), height overall 8 ft 0 in (2·44 m) and wing area 90·9 sq. ft (8·35 m^2). Maximum take-off weight and speed were estimated as 3,709 lb (1,682 kg) and 373 mph (600 km/h) respectively.

Not only had General Balbo done his utmost to procure the most advanced aircraft to compete in Britain, but he had also ensured that the Italian high-speed pilots were brought together at Desenzano in plenty of time to allow for adequate practice off the water of Lake Garda in the M.52s of the previous contest. They were most unlucky with the weather and it was not until August that they began to receive their new aircraft.

Commanded by Lieutenant-Colonel Mario Bernasconi, the team included Captains A. Canaveri and G. Motta, Lieutenants R. Cadringher and G. Monti, Warrant Officer T. Dal Molin, and Sergeant-Majors F. Agello, Gallone and Huber, and it did not take long for them to discover that two of the aircraft were non-starters.

It is hardly surprising that these were the two most revolutionary aircraft. Despite repeated trials with the Piaggio Pc.7, it proved impossible for the clutch of the marine propeller to provide a non-slip drive. Transition from water taxying to flight was never achieved, and the project was abandoned. The Savoia S.65 was plagued with power plant and airframe problems, and it was soon apparent that these would not be eliminated in time for the machine to have a chance of bettering the performance of the S.5 in the last contest.

The Fiat C.29, looking rather like the tried and proven Macchis, was more successful. Initial taxying trials had shown the floats needed adjustment, but when this had been done the first flight was most promising. During its second flight the Fiat machine caught fire but its pilot, Francesco Agello, managed to land safely and ground crews extinguished the flames before serious damage resulted.

Setbacks of this nature, in conjunction with bad weather, plagued the Italian pilots in the short time remaining before they and their aircraft were due to sail for England.

Fortunately, the C.29 had not been seriously damaged and was soon ready for further testing at the hands of Agello. On this occasion he could not get the seaplane to lift off the water at his first attempts. When he did eventually succeed in becoming airborne, pulling off in a steep climb, the aircraft was presumably in a stalled condition. Down went the nose, but before Agello could level out the Fiat met the water with such force that the floats were smartly wiped off, the aircraft plunging to the bottom of the deep lake. Happily, Agello escaped with nothing worse than a few bruises and scratches, but the C.29 was effectively eliminated from the contest. A second example had been built, but was not ready for testing before the time came for it to be crated for transit.

Three of the Macchi M.67s had been built, but at that time only one had been delivered to Lake Garda. It had already been flown by Captain Motta with promising results, and it was decided to press on with the tests to gain the maximum experience with this machine.

On 22 August, following another spell of bad weather, Guiseppe Motta was making a fast run over the lake at low level when the Macchi dived steeply, smashing into the water and killing the pilot. Thus, he was the second man to die during preparations for the 1929 contest.

As the two remaining M.67s were not yet ready for test, the Italians asked the Royal Aero Club for a postponement to allow them adequate time to field a properly representative team. Once again the British committee declined, citing their rigid interpretation of the contest rules, a decision upheld by the FAI. Britain then announced officially that, in the event of no competition being offered, their team would fly over the course to take the Trophy.

It was accordingly decided by the Italians that, despite their state of unpreparedness, they would do their utmost to contend on the appointed day, and every effort was made by the Macchi company to ensure that their two machines were got off to England without further delay. On arrival, they would have to make their initial flights.

It might have been prudent for the Royal Aero Club to have enquired the state of progress of the British team before their point blank refusal of the Italian request. They, too, were experiencing their share of problems, as was the sole American contender.

'Al' Williams was still suffering from the excess weight of the Mercury racer and, try as he might, he had found it impossible to lift the machine off the water with the power developed by the installed Packard engine. On only one occasion, on 18 August, did he succeed in putting a few inches of airspace between floats and water before the power of the overheated engine fell away and the Mercury returned to the surface.

In view of the near approach of the contest it was decided to ship the Mercury to England, taking with it the more powerful Packard engine which would be installed en route. It was announced that Williams, aircraft, new engine and Mr John Kean, chief engineer of the Naval Aircraft Factory, would sail aboard the SS *Leviathan* on 21 August, or on an alternative vessel three days later. Then, at the last minute, the US Navy withdrew its support and a bitterly disappointed 'Al' Williams was forced to withdraw from the contest.

The British team at Calshot had enthusiastically received their first S.6 (N.247) following its launch on 5 August. Orlebar was to make the first test and, having positioned himself for the take-off run, pushed the throttle wide. Immediate disillusionment came as the machine swung wildly to port, digging the float so deep in the water that the port wingtip seemed almost to be scraping the surface. No matter what he tried the results were the same; after about twenty minutes he gave up the struggle and taxied back to base for a consultation with Mitchell.

It was decided to make the next test with no fuel in the port float and only 50 Imperial gallons (227 litres) in the starboard float. This attempt ended more quickly than the first, for the starboard fuel pump failed and, without sustenance, the engine called it a day. But so that taxying tests could continue a small quantity of fuel was put in the port float, and in this condition Orlebar managed to get the S.6 on the step at about 40 mph (64 km/h).

Both Orlebar and D'Arcy Greig tried again, unsuccessfully, during the morning of 10 August, but it was not until later in the afternoon, when a breeze had begun to ripple the surface of Southampton Water, that Orlebar managed to get the S.6 into the air for the first time. It was only a brief flight for there were a number of snags apparent, including a tendency to drop the port wing, engine vibration, tail heaviness and engine tick-over too fast, so that the S.6 wanted to keep on flying when the engine was throttled right back. Orlebar had to cut the engine to put her down safely after only a few minutes of flight.

All of these problems were capable of resolution without too much difficulty. A slight rigging adjustment corrected the port-wing-low tendency, engine tick-over was adjusted and the vibration cured by mixture adjustment, and finally a bungee was added to the control column to off-load the tail heaviness.

During the following flights the S.6 began to show its potential, but it was soon discovered that as more power was applied the engine cooling system began to approach boiling point long before the full throttle position. This required the provision of more surface cooling, and Mitchell not only put additional coolers on the floats, but arranged also to put a degree of airflow through the wing to cool the inner face of the wing surface radiators. This was achieved by including tiny air scoops in the wing

Which ever way you look at it . . .

. . . the unfortunate Gloster VI was a clean looking aeroplane

leading-edges and vents in the trailing-edges, and the combined effect of this modification plus the new radiators on the floats proved sufficient to control the temperature within acceptable limits.

It was not until 21 August that the first Gloster VI (N.249) was rigged and ready for flight, but bad weather prevented Orlebar from making the first test until 25 August. Unlike the S.6, it became airborne quickly, but had reached a height of only about 20 ft (6 m) when the engine went dead. Orlebar made a successful landing and the machine was towed shorewards.

This was to be the continuing story of the Gloster VI aircraft prior to the 1929 contest, for trouble with the fuel system made the engine prone to cut out at any moment, especially in turns. Despite untiring efforts by the pilots of the High Speed Flight and by the Gloster and Napier engineers, the problem could not be isolated and, as a result, the beautiful Glosters were withdrawn from the contest. Britain was thus reduced to two defenders, the S.6s, so it was decided to field one of the S.5s from the previous event.

On 29 August the Italians arrived at Calshot, showing a little gamesmanship by bringing a total of six aircraft. These comprised two Macchi M.67s, the Macchi M.52R which still retained the world speed record, a Macchi M.52 for practice, as well as the second Fiat C.29 and the Savoia-Marchetti S.65 to give the British something to think about.

First to fly was the M.52, soon available to the Italians pilots for practice, but it was not until 4 September that Monti was able to fly the first of the M.67s. There was no attempt on his part to use full throttle and its capability was a worrying enigma for the British pilots. Both teams took advantage of good weather to fly as much as possible, but this amounted to very little individual time.

On 4 September Dal Molin had the misfortune to foul a floating hazard on take off in the M.52R, holing a float. Although he was able to land without difficulty, his machine took on a frightening-looking list and was towed hurriedly to the security of dry land.

The following day was also available for practice, and on 6 September when the teams had finalised their entries for the navigability test the weather was almost too perfect. Every pilot there would have liked to see some ripples on the glasslike water. However, the navigability tests proceeded without problems. Dal Molin's mount, the M.52R was serviceable again and he, together with Macchi M. 67 (No. 7), sporting a three-blade propeller and flown by Cadringher, and M.67 (No. 10) flown by Monti, all completed the test and were anchored for the water tightness test in a sheltered area north of Calshot Castle.

None of the British team had run into difficulty, and their two S.6s and

Opposite page: (*top*) All of the Supermarine trio completed the 1929 course. D'Arcy Greig's S.5 . . . (*centre*) R. L. R. Atcherley's S.6, although he was disqualified . . . (*bottom*) and the S.6 N247 with which Flying-Officer H. R. Waghorn notched up Britain's second consecutive win

N 219
5

N 248
8

N 247
2

single S.5 when anchored added to the colourful sight: the world's six fastest seaplanes riding calmly on the water, a peaceful overture to the excitement of the following day.

For the British team it was not to prove the peaceful prelude they could have wished. As the water tightness test reached mid-point, 'Batchy' Atcherley's S.6 (N.248) was seen to have developed a decided list. Since it could not be removed without disqualification, a sleeping Mitchell was almost dragged from his bed, where he was trying to offset the effects of working through the small hours. His opinion was that the S.6 would just about remain afloat for the requisite six hours, which it did, before being hurriedly beached for repair to the leaking float.

Final checks were given to the engines of the British machines to ready them for the morrow, a part of that routine being the fitting of re-conditioned sparking plugs. As a mechanic withdrew a plug from one cylinder of Waghorn's aircraft he noticed a fleck of white metal on the electrode.

Sufficiently experienced to know this must spell trouble, he showed it to Flying-Officer Moon. He, in turn, quickly called A. C. Lovesey of Rolls to give his opinion. It was decided that a serious mechanical failure had occurred within that cylinder and the two alternatives were an engine change or block change. The former was not allowed by the contest regulations, but it was permissible to change the block.

This demanded that a team of experienced mechanics should be available and Moon's men did not have the qualifications and, in any event, were already sleeping the sleep of exhausted men: how was the problem to be resolved? Fortunately, a team of Rolls-Royce fitters from Derby had been given leave from the works to see *their* engines perform in the race, and they were speedily rounded up from various hotels in Southampton and set the difficult task of a block change without suitable equipment.

Such was their spirit and skill that by the time Orlebar put in an early appearance on the following morning the job had been completed, the engine run up and passed as satisfactory.

The block which had been removed had a badly scored cylinder and a damaged piston with broken rings. Why? This was the factor worrying the Rolls engineers, and they could assume only that with engines ticking over a pool of fuel collected in the volute casing of the supercharger. When the throttle was opened for power a mass of neat petrol became drawn into one or more cylinders, destroying the film of lubrication and causing rings or piston to seize. The only possible solution as a temporary measure was to ensure that no engine had prolonged periods of slow running prior to the race.

The day of the race, 7 September, was as near perfect as anyone could have wished, setting a seal on the mounting excitement of the participants and spectators. The crowds were there in greater force than ever, and for once the Royal Aero Club had excelled themselves in making adequate arrangements for those who wished to enjoy the sights and sounds of the race, and be kept *au fait* with its progress.

Starting and finishing point was opposite Ryde pier, but the four-sided course differed considerably from that chosen in 1923. From Ryde pier to the first pylon off Seaview, Isle of Wight, was a distance of 2·86 nm (5·30 km), when a moderate turn put the competitors on an ENE heading for a leg of 4·50 nm (8·35 km) to a sharp turn around a destroyer-mounted pylon, identified as the Hayling turn, with a distance of 4·48 nm (8·29 km) to the next pylon off Southsea pier. A moderate port bank on to a heading almost due west led to the fourth, and most acute turn, at another destroyer-mounted pylon in mid-Solent off West Cowes, 8·86 nm (16·43 km) distant, leaving a final stretch of 6·28 nm (11·63 km) back to Ryde pier. The total circuit was 26·98 nm (50 km), which had to be lapped seven times.

First away was Waghorn, and using the take-off technique they had developed in practice he was soon off the water and heading for Seaview at a cracking pace, a faint trail of smoke serving to denote the line of his passage long after the S.6 had disappeared from sight.

He, in fact, had got off to a somewhat erratic flight path, confused by the mass of ships of all shapes and sizes that provided waterborne platforms for countless additional spectators, but which helped camouflage the turning points. This accounted for a rather disappointing first lap speed of 324 mph

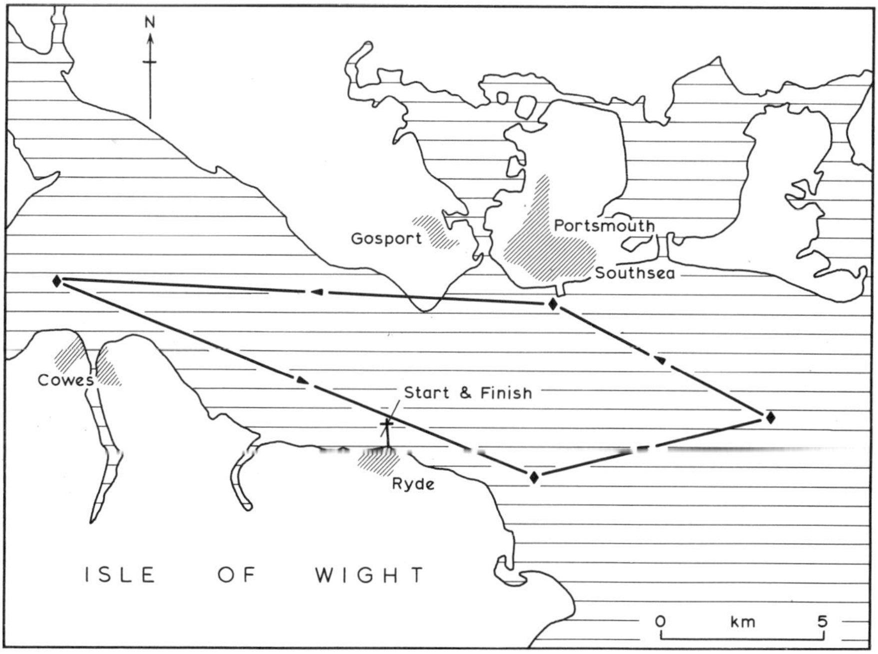

10. Schneider Trophy Contest Course: Cowes 1929

(521 km/h). The next was better, at 329 mph (529 km/h) and the third one of his fastest at 331 mph (533 km/h).

By then, however, Dal Molin was airborne in the M.52R, the Italians wisely leaving the M.67s to start as late as possible so that they could avoid pushing them unnecessarily if the British speeds were not eye-opening. Unfortunately they were.

By the standard set by Waghorn, Dal Molin's first lap of 286 mph (460 km/h) seemed something of an anticlimax, but it was clear that at any rate he and D'Arcy Greig were likely to provide an exciting race for the spectators. In fact, it was Greig who was next in the air, flying full out to record a first lap speed 2 mph (3·2 km/h) slower than that of Dal Molin.

Meanwhile, Waghorn was suffering similar agonies of mind as those which had troubled Webster at Venice. His 'Heath Robinson' lap counter showed six neatly punched holes. One lap to go, but as he passed the Seaview pylon his engine misfired. His heart skipped several beats, but though the engine roared back to life he was far from calm. Soon it was cutting and banging miserably, continuing all around the circuit and finally, having completed the last turn, it gave up completely with the finishing line almost in sight. A dejected and defeated Waghorn was down on the sea. He did not know then that, like Webster, he had attempted an extra lap and run out of fuel.

Cadringher was the second Italian in the air, but limited to using below maximum engine revolutions to prevent engine failure, and partially blinded and almost asphyxiated by exhaust fumes whipped into the cockpit, he could not better D'Arcy Greig's speed for the first lap. But whilst he could gulp a breath of reasonably pure air every now and then, his eyes could not recover as speedily from the effects of the fumes. It needed only minutes longer for tears to blur his vision to danger point. Wisely, he turned of the circuit and landed.

Next away was Atcherley, immediately suffering a differing vision problem which he related later: 'During my take-off my goggles became opaque with brine from the spray and I found I could no longer wipe them clear with my left glove. I knocked them up from my eyes but the slipstream took charge and snapped them from the strap behind my helmet. Although I carried a spare pair round my neck, I found I could not get these up to my eyes with one hand to spare.'

There was only one thing to do. Tuck down as far as possible in the cockpit and press on regardless. It didn't help one's vision, of course, and the Seaview turn was coming up fast. Let's look at it from Commander Alan Goodfellow's point of view:

'Batchy came near to killing me—nearer I think than any German ever did—when I was in charge of the Seaview turning point, which consisted of an old destroyer on which a pylon some thirty feet high (9 m) had been mounted. As the race was between British and Italian teams we had two observers of each nationality . . . In order that there should be no possibility of mistake I decided that I and one of the Italian observers should climb to the top of the pylon, leaving the other two on deck . . . Dick Atcherley duly took off in his Supermarine S.6 and headed in our direction. As he came rapidly nearer we realised that he was heading straight for the top of the pylon, including the two observers, and it appeared almost inevitable that the top of the pylon was going to be "bumped off" in more senses than one. At the very last moment he saw us and swerved sharply, passing not more than a wing span inside the pylon. The moment the incident was over the Italian observer turned to me and asked fiercely, "You disqualify?". I nodded my head sadly, whereupon he danced an excited jig on top of our somewhat perilous perch and shouted down to his fellow Italian observer on the deck, "Eliminato, Eliminato". He probably doesn't know to this day how near he came to getting my foot in his backside . . .'

Atcherley, of course, was unaware that he had been eliminated and continued to set up some cracking speeds, his best lap the fastest of the entire race at 332 mph (534 km/h). Orlebar had, of course, been advised of the disqualification before Atcherley completed his first lap, but decided to raise an objection on principle. When the true facts were known, he was just as quick to withdraw it.

One more pilot was to suffer rather more than bitter disappointment that day. This was the last of the Italians to take the air, Lieutenant Giovanni Monti, and their last real hope to wrest the Trophy back from Britain that year.

Charging off at fine speed, he appeared to be travelling very fast. It was something of a disappointment to the Italians to find that his lap time was only 301mph (484km/h), nowhere near enough to beat Waghorn but perhaps good enough for second or third place.

Even this minor success was to be denied, for Monti was already suffering from the fume problem that had defeated Cadringher. Worse was to befall, for almost immediately after completing his first lap a serious leak in the engine cooling system sprayed him with near-boiling water and steam. Despite the additional lack of visibility and the agony of his scalds, Monti managed to put down safely in the emergency landing lane beyond the Seaview turn.

It was all over. Britain had won with Waghorn's fine 328·63 mph (528·88 km/h), an achievement which was to win him the Air Force Cross. Dal Molin was second at 284·2 mph (457·38 km/h), and D'Arcy Grieg in third place at 282·11 mph (454·02 km/h).

Now Britain had two consecutive victories tucked beneath her belt. Only one more was needed to make the Trophy hers for all time, an attainment that seemed within reach. General Balbo had different ideas of course, commenting '. . . we have now finished playing our part as sportsmen. Tomorrow our work as competitors will begin.'

Clearly, they intended to do their utmost to break the British grasp on the coveted prize. But there was not a single Englishman present at the victory banquet at which Balbo spoke those words who did not believe that Britain would defend the contest in 1931: hopefully they would win.

The Royal Air Force's 'flying squad' had cleaned up the 1929 contest, bringing great credit to Britain's aviation industry. Scotland Yard's Flying Squad hadn't done so badly either, picking up a long-sought eight-man gang of international pickpockets working their way through the skyward-gazing crowds of enthralled spectators.

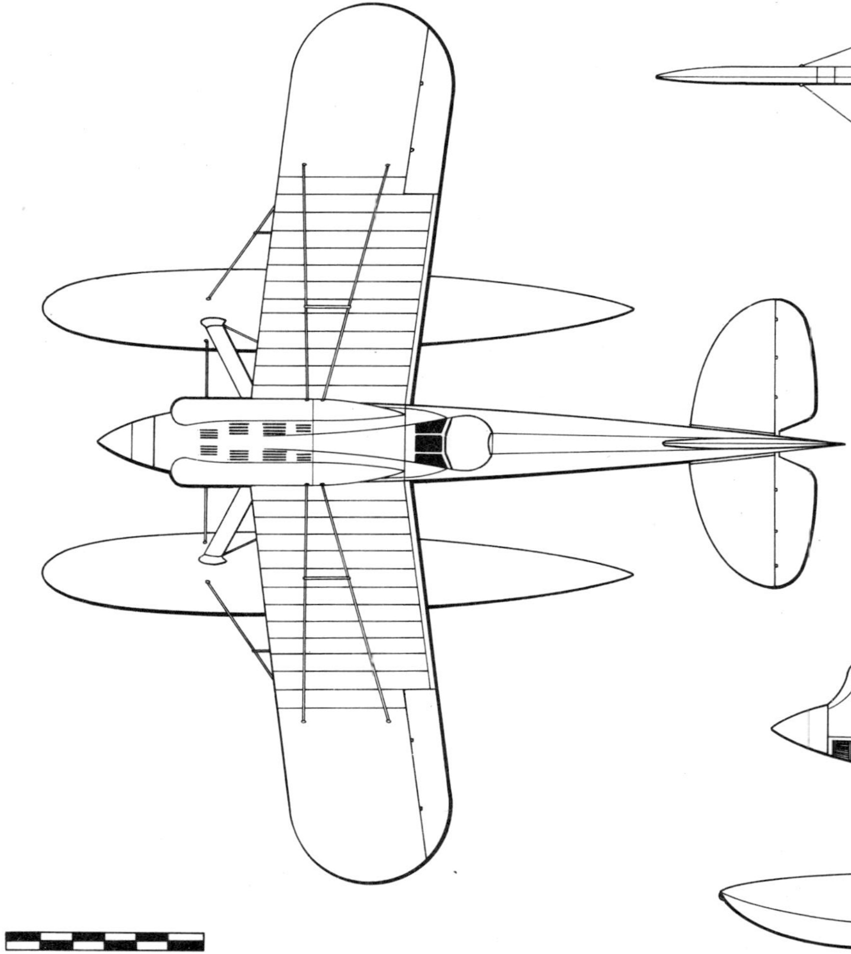

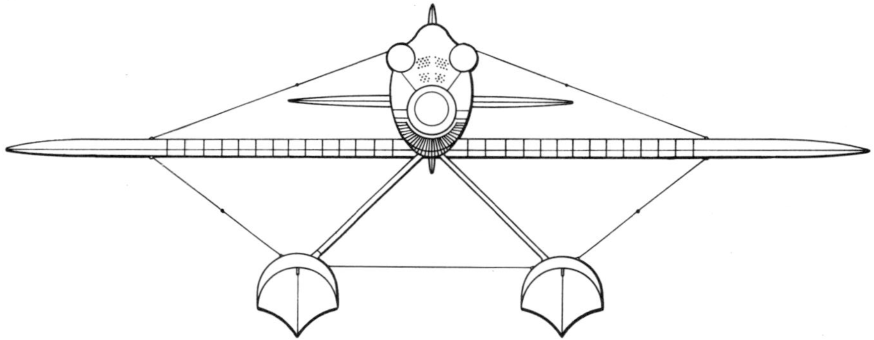

Macchi M.52R (1929)

Wing Span: 25 ft 9 in (7·85 m)
Length Overall: 23 ft $4\frac{3}{4}$ in (7·13 m)
Wing Area: 117 sq. ft (10·87 m^2)
Weight Empty: 2,580 lb (1,170 kg)
T-O Weight: 3,263 lb (1,480 kg)
Max Wing Loading: 27·89 lb/sq. ft
(136·17 kg/m^2)
Horsepower of Power Plant: 1,000 hp

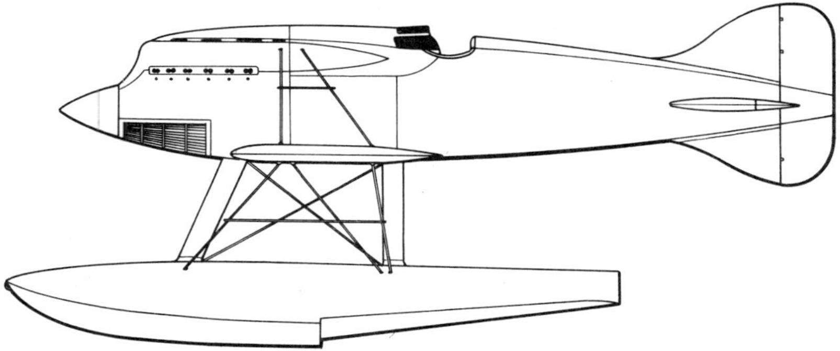

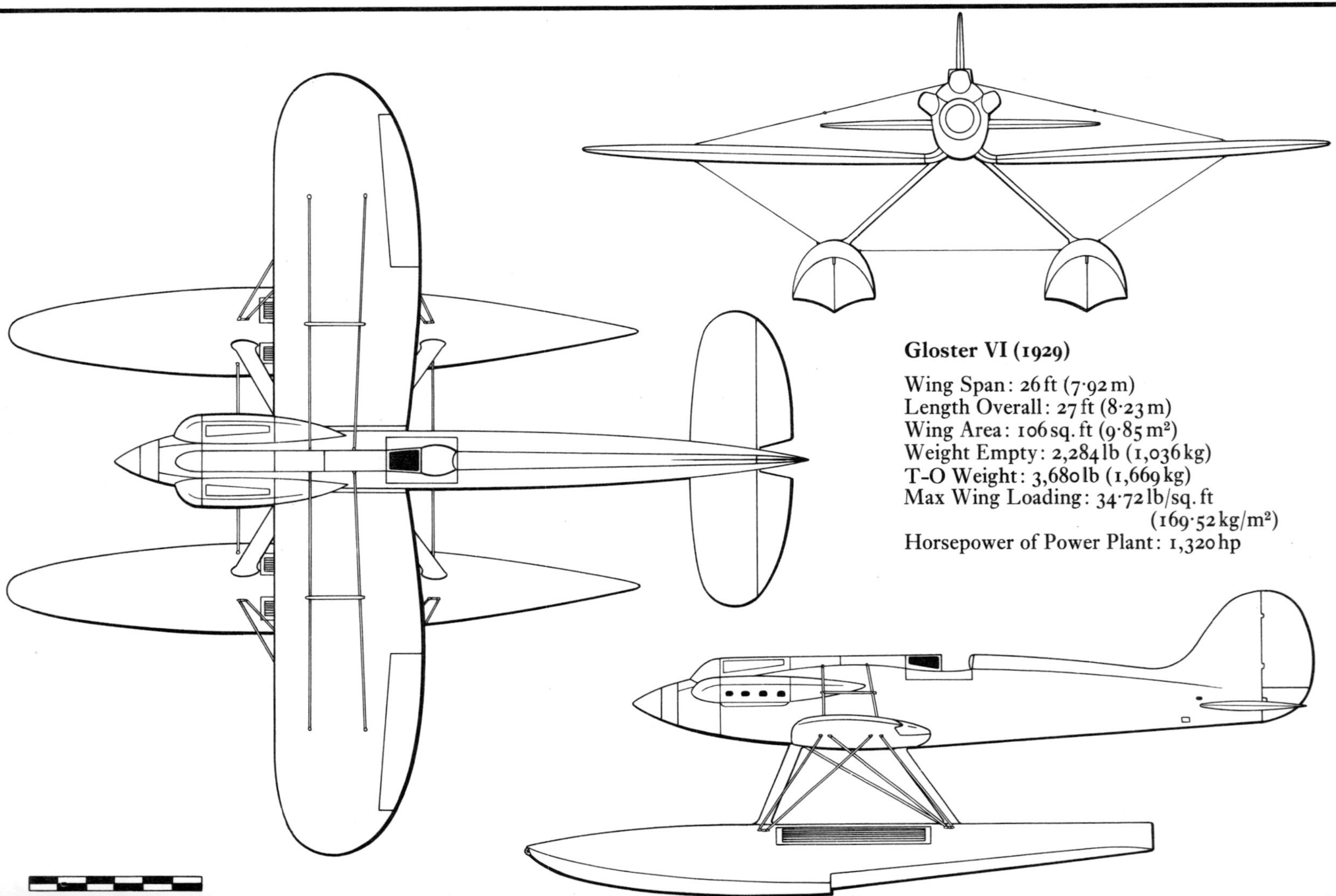

Gloster VI (1929)

Wing Span: 26 ft (7·92 m)
Length Overall: 27 ft (8·23 m)
Wing Area: 106 sq. ft (9·85 m²)
Weight Empty: 2,284 lb (1,036 kg)
T-O Weight: 3,680 lb (1,669 kg)
Max Wing Loading: 34·72 lb/sq. ft (169·52 kg/m²)
Horsepower of Power Plant: 1,320 hp

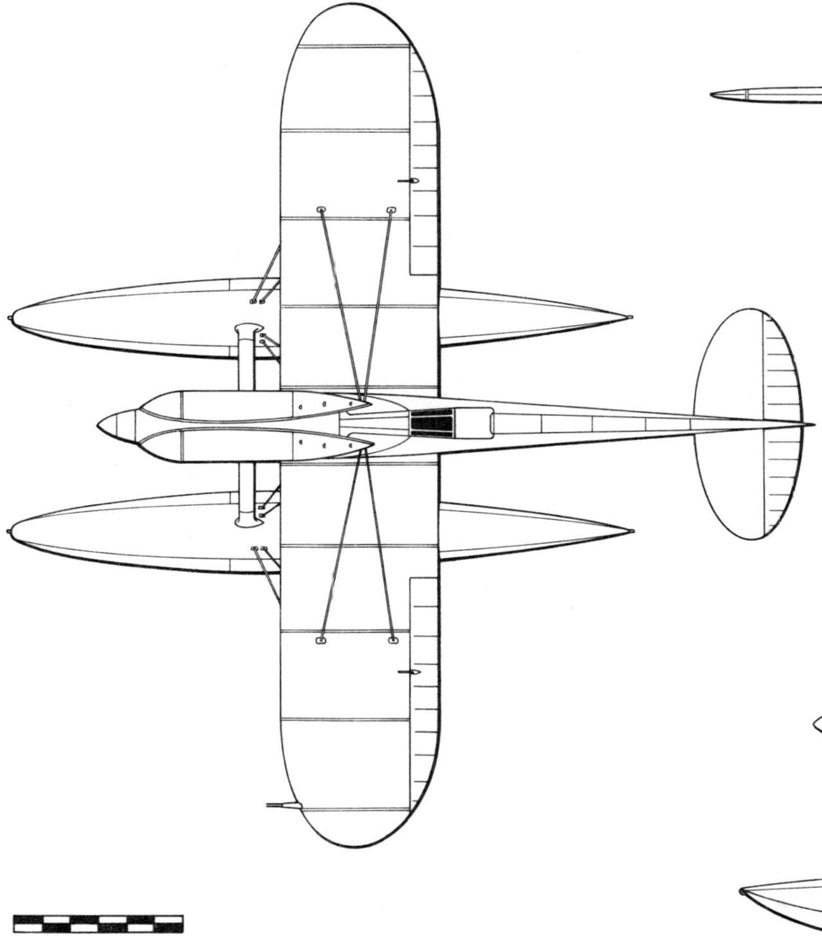

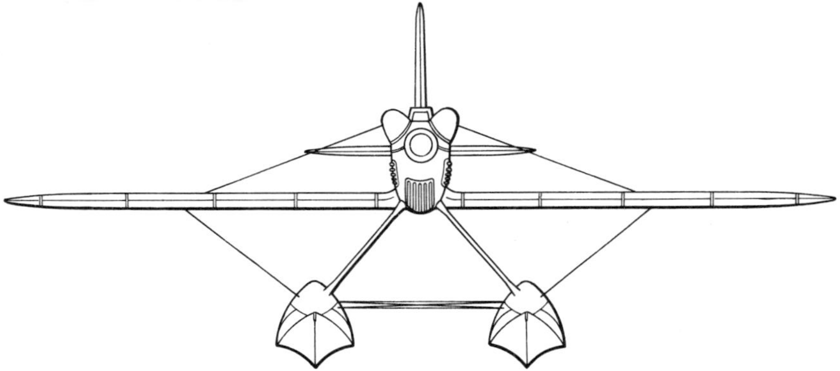

Supermarine S.6 (1929)

Wing Span: 30 ft (9·14 m)
Length Overall: 26 ft 10 in (8·18 m)
Wing Area: 145 sq. ft (13·47 m²)
Weight Empty: 4,471 lb (2,028 kg)
T-O Weight: 5,771 lb (2,618 kg)
Max Wing Loading: 39·80 lb/sq. ft (194·32 kg/m²)
Horsepower of Power Plant: 1,900 hp

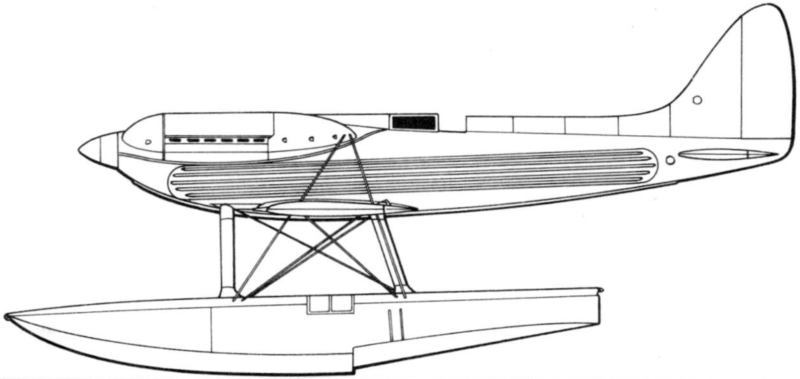

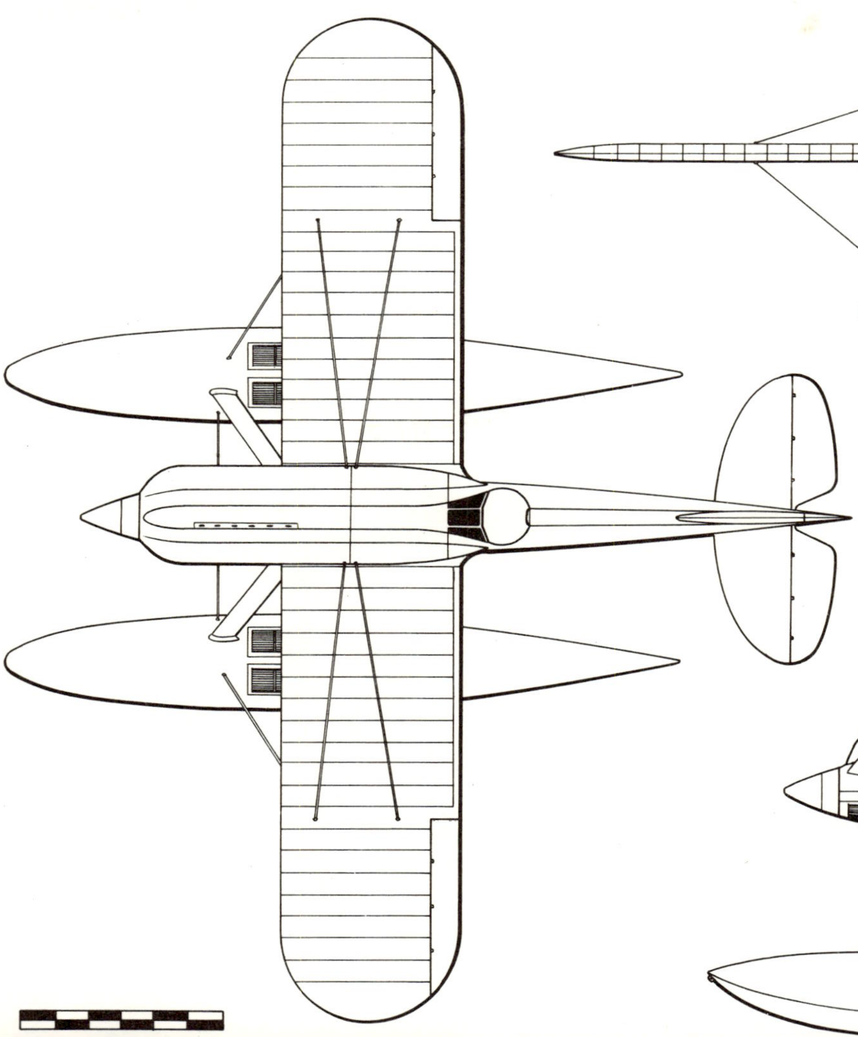

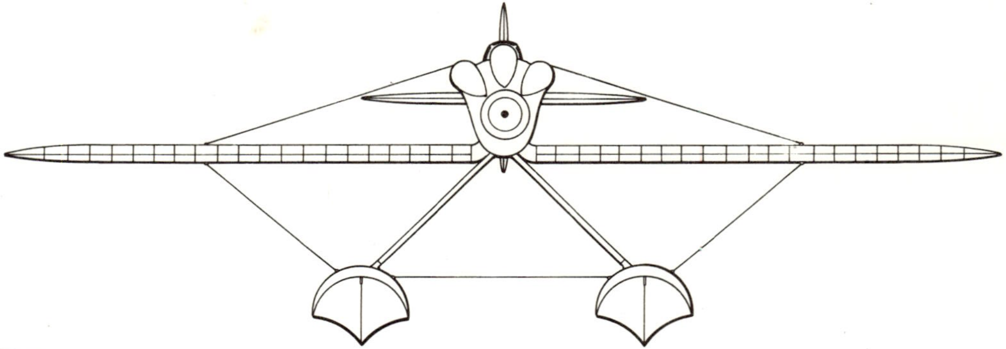

Macchi M.67 (1929)

Wing Span: 29 ft 5 in (8·97 m)
Length Overall: 23 ft $5\frac{1}{2}$ in (7·15 m)
Wing Area: 145·5 sq. ft (13·52 m²)
Weight Empty: 3,890 lb (1,765 kg)
T-O Weight: 4,740 lb (2,150 kg)
Max Wing Loading: 32·58 lb/sq. ft (159·07 kg/m²)
Horsepower of Power Plant: 1,800 hp

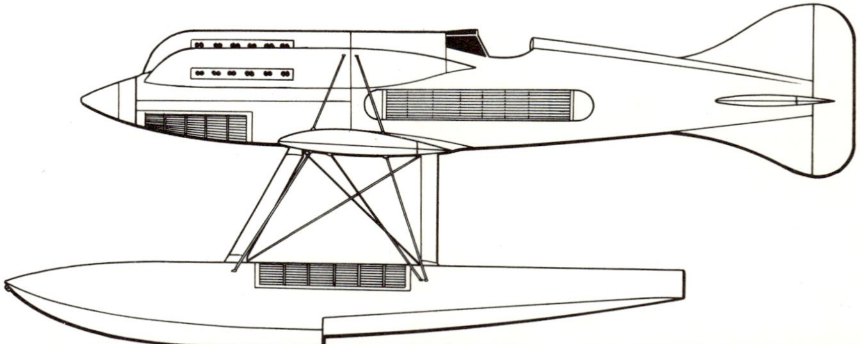

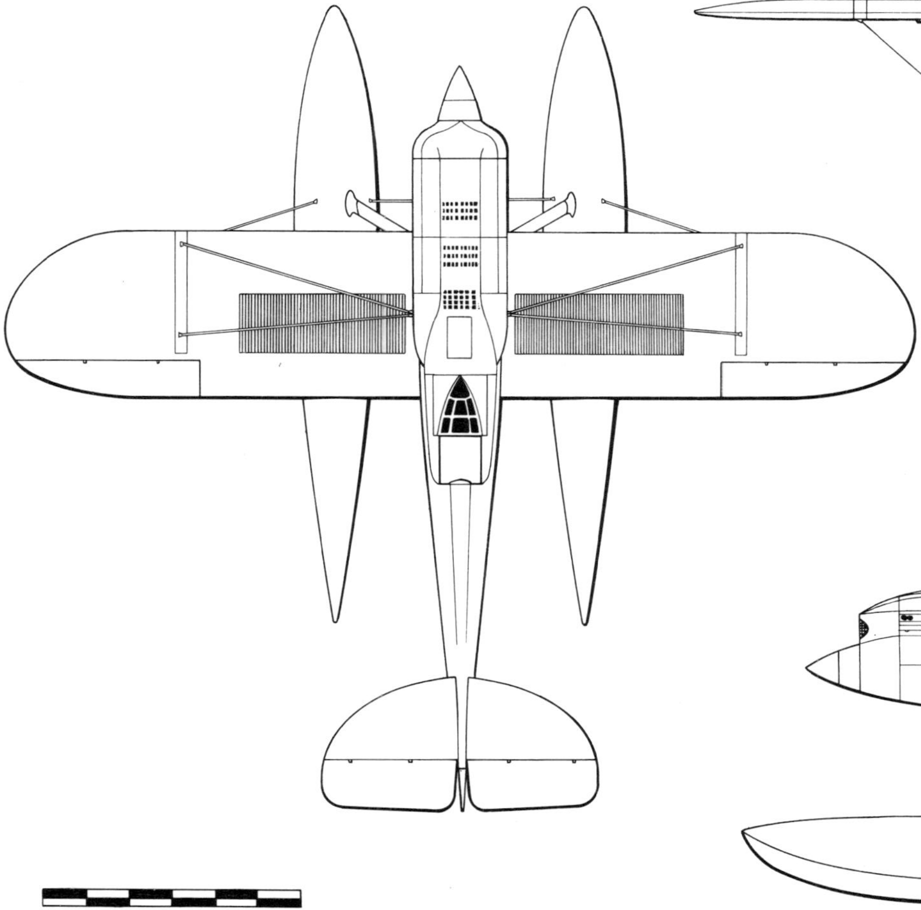

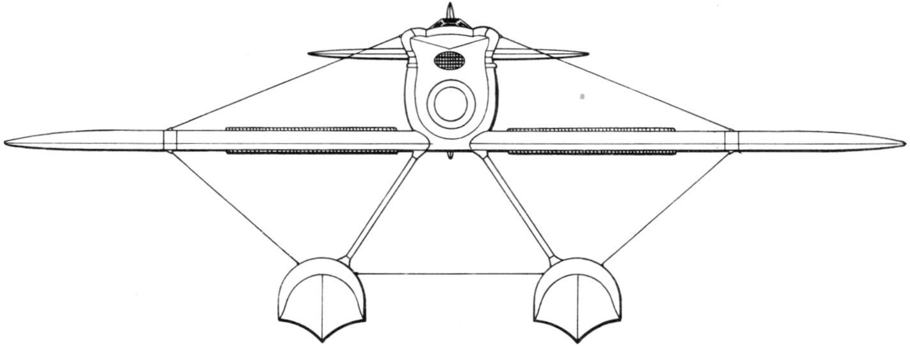

Fiat C.29 (1929)

Wing Span: 21 ft $8\frac{1}{2}$ in (6·62 m)
Length Overall: 24 ft $7\frac{1}{4}$ in (7·50 m)
Wing Area: 86·11 sq. ft (8·0 m²)
Weight Empty: 1,984 lb (900 kg)
T-O Weight: 2,557 lb (1,160 kg)
Max Wing Loading: 29·69 lb/sq. ft (144·96 kg/m²)
Horsepower of Power Plant: 1,000 hp

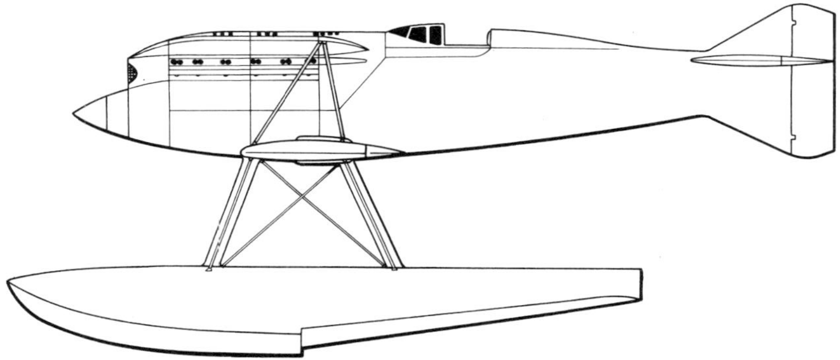

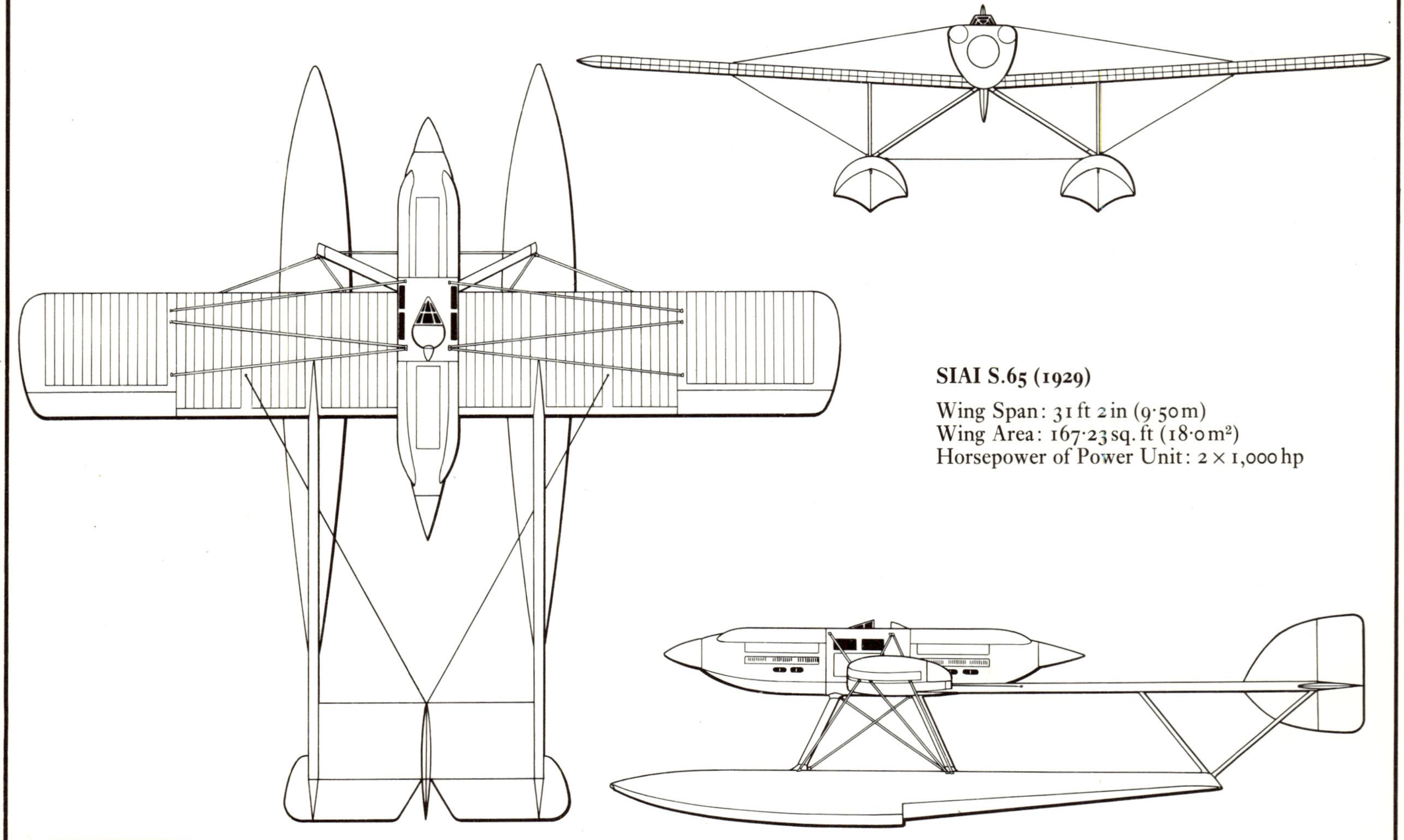

SIAI S.65 (1929)

Wing Span: 31 ft 2 in (9·50 m)
Wing Area: 167·23 sq. ft (18·0 m²)
Horsepower of Power Unit: 2 × 1,000 hp

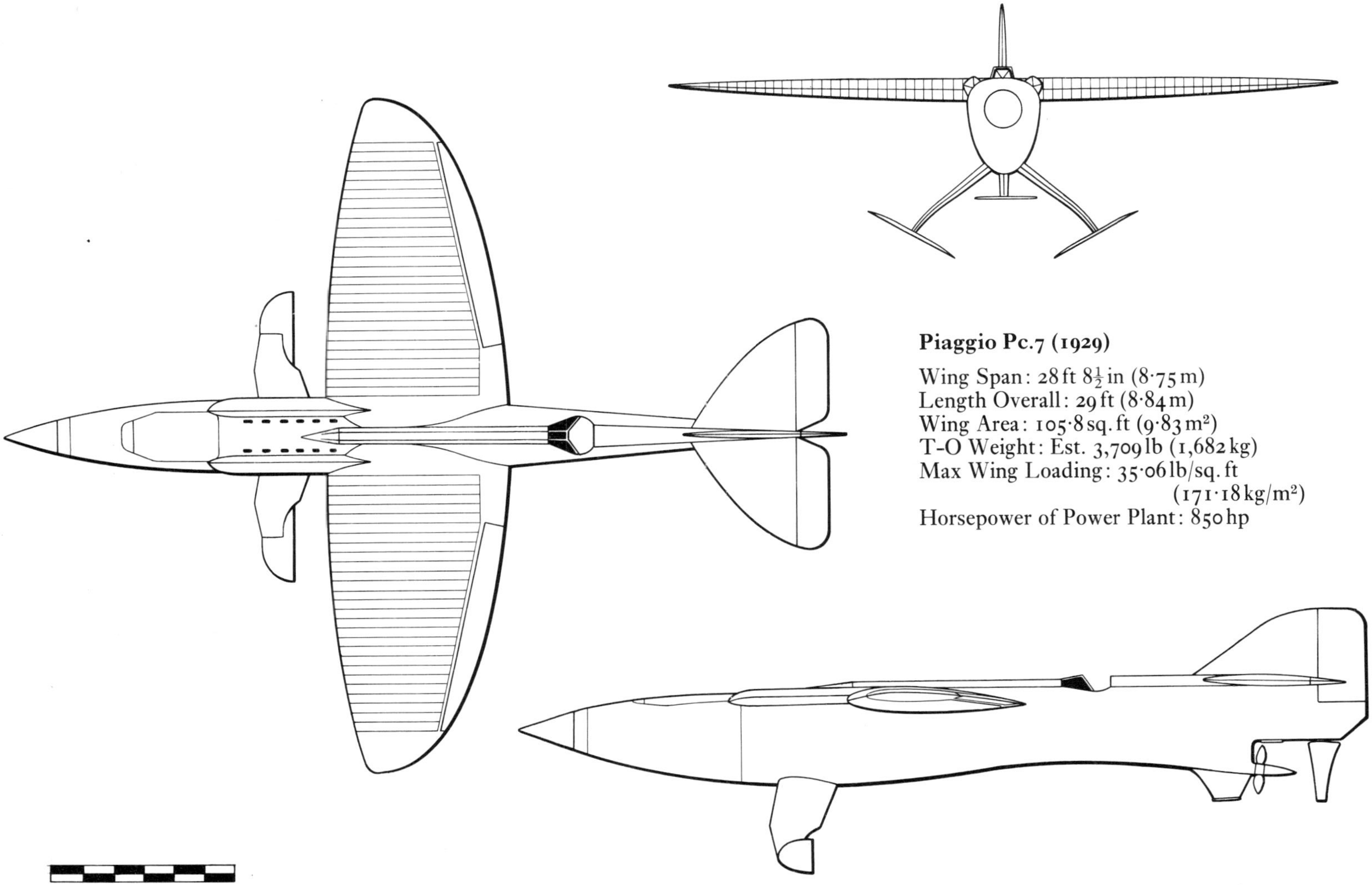

Piaggio Pc.7 (1929)

Wing Span: 28 ft 8½ in (8·75 m)
Length Overall: 29 ft (8·84 m)
Wing Area: 105·8 sq. ft (9·83 m²)
T-O Weight: Est. 3,709 lb (1,682 kg)
Max Wing Loading: 35·06 lb/sq. ft (171·18 kg/m²)
Horsepower of Power Plant: 850 hp

12

To be or not to be

1931

Present at the victory banquet following Britain's retention of the Trophy in 1929 was the country's Prime Minister, Mr Ramsay MacDonald. Having wined and dined well, and swayed by the general atmosphere of exuberance he had said, when called upon to make a speech: 'We are going to do our level best to win again.'

In fact, any other course was unthinkable, and the two victories resulting from Air Ministry involvement and the dedicated work of the High Speed Flight left little doubt that the Air Council would mount a worthy effort to ensure that Britain would win in 1931 and secure the Trophy.

When, in due course, it became known that neither the Government nor Air Council wanted anything further to do with the Schneider Trophy Contests, it came as a staggering shock to the aviation industry and British public alike.

C. G. Grey settled himself firmly in his editorial chair, ensured that his pen was well charged with ink and wrote a typically scathing comment:

'. . . there are at least four diametrically, or at any rate radically, opposed views about this announcement:

(a) 'And a very good thing too. Now we shall discover whether there are any real sportsmen in England who will spend some money for the honour of British sport.

(b) 'And a very good thing too. We waste too much time and money on these spectacular efforts. Let the Italians have the silly old Trophy and let's settle down to make saleable commercial aeroplanes.

(c) 'The Government's attitude is a disgrace to the nation. To let us be beaten by a lot of Latins is selling the birthright of the Anglo-Saxon race. Governments have been put out of action for less.

(d) 'A Government which will give £80,000 to subsidise a lot of squalling foreigners at Covent Garden and will refuse £80,000 to win the World's greatest advertisement for British aircraft is unworthy of the Nation.

'Personally I find myself in agreement with all four views, and several others as well. Which I suppose really means that I think it serves us all, I mean all of us concerned with Aviation, jolly well right for letting the Government having anything to do with it in the first place.'

And as if that were not enough, he reserved another spate of ink-stained wrath for the unfortunate Prime Minister:

'The curious and awkward position of Mr MacDonald is, in the face of his pronunciamento on board the SS *Orford* on the night of our last victory, quite naturally explained by the fact that on that occasion he was speaking on behalf of the British nation, whereas now in going back on that statement he is merely speaking on behalf of the British Government, which definitely does *not* represent the nation.'

The whole situation seemed extremely puzzling, especially as after the 1929 contest the members of the High Speed Flight had thrice raised the world speed record. First, on 10 September 1929, Flight-Lieutenant George Stainforth had made an attempt with the Gloster VI, the engine of which had been induced to behave itself in straight and level flight, although still something of a handful in turns. N.249 averaged a speed of 336·3 mph (541·22 km/h).

Then, a few hours later, Orlebar had another crack at the record with S.6 N.247, but the weather conditions had deteriorated a little and he had difficulty in aligning the seaplane for the runs over the measured course which, the same as that used by Stainforth, extended from Calshot Spit to Agwi Pier. Nevertheless, the record was raised significantly to 355·8 mph (572·604 km/h).

A final attempt, two days later, was again made by Orlebar and, on this occasion, he managed to add almost 2 mph (3·2 km/h) to record an average of 357·7 mph (575·66 km/h). Thus, Stainforth's and Orlebar's records in the Gloster VI and Supermarine S.6 respectively were submitted to the FAI for ratification.

It was in the aftermath of this success that the announcements had come which raised angry response from all those concerned with British aviation, those who were pro-aviation and an even larger body of persons concerned with national prestige.

The attitude of the Air Council was similar to that expressed at an earlier date by the US Army and Navy, namely that Royal Air Force participation in the contests had given much needed impetus to the development of high-speed aircraft, but that sufficient new data had been accumulated to make any future participation an unrealistic expenditure of public money.

The Government's attitude was even more to the point: they simply were not prepared to allocate the necessary money needed for participation in 1931, a figure which they estimated as being between £100,000 and £200,000. Furthermore, they pointed out that prior to 1927 Britain's contestants had been the entries of private individuals or those of private enterprise and that, in the economic conditions prevailing at the end of 1929, it would be wrong for the government to allocate funds for prestigious rather than practical needs.

The battle raged on throughout 1930. In mid-November Lieutenant-Commander Kenworthy rose in the House of Commons to ask the Under-Secretary of State for Air whether, before deciding that the Royal Air Force would not participate in 1931, he was assured that the Trophy would be defended by private companies or persons.

Mr Montague replied to the effect that the Government's decision to leave the question of entry to private enterprise was taken on grounds of principle and policy, not upon a calculation of the probability of private entries. He emphasised that until 1927 the responsibility for British participation was undertaken by private enterprise and that the Government considered that in the existing conditions created by two consecutive British successes it should be quite practicable for the former tradition to be resumed.

It was an unbelievable situation; many considered it intolerable, especially the Royal Aero Club who met on 19 January 1931 to discuss its every aspect. A subsequent statement concerning this meeting concluded: '. . . it was decided . . . to explore every avenue whereby the Trophy may be defended. The Club will leave no stone unturned to achieve this object, and feels sure that this is in general harmony with the wishes of the British public.'

One of the avenues was another approach to Parliament. On 27 January Ramsay MacDonald received a deputation which included Sir Philip Sassoon, Chairman of the Royal Aero Club. It was pointed out that participation would involve a sum not exceeding £100,000, and that the Royal Aero Club had already been promised financial support amounting to £22,000. The Prime Minister was non-commital, but promised to reconsider the matter.

Perhaps the Prime Minister had already been a little shaken by constant attacks from the British press. The *Daily Mail*, a stalwart supporter of aviation from its earliest days, carried large headlines on 23 January which shouted: 'If we let the Schneider Trophy go aeroplane trade will go too. Government blunder. Public astounded.'

It is interesting to conjecture whether the combined pressure of press, organisations like the Royal Aero Club and Society of British Aircraft Constructors, together with public opinion, would have forced the Government's hands, for the situation had progressed to a point where no holds were barred. The *Daily Mail*, for example, had discovered that the Under-Secretary of State for Air, Fred Montague, was a member of the Magician's Circle. 'The disappearance of the Schneider Trophy appears to be one of his most amazing feats', was their sarcastic comment.

Happily for the government, their face was saved by the public-spirited action of an eccentric, ebullient, generous-hearted and extremely patriotic woman. Christened Fanny Lucy Radmall, she was the daughter of a Camberwell box-maker, but by what could almost be described as a fairy tale of circumstance she had, at her third marriage, become the wife of Sir Robert Houston, wealthy owner of a shipping line. At his death in 1926, Lady Houston became the richest woman in Britain and, approached by a friend, Colonel the Lord Sempill, agreed to put up the necessary money to ensure that Britain would take part in the 1931 contest.

Her cheque for £100,000 was sent to the Secretary of the Royal Aero Club, who lost little time in thumping it down on Ramsay MacDonald's desk. The moment of decision had come: Britain would now be able to defend the Trophy.

In Italy, of course, there had been no similar doubts. It was 1931 or never so far as they were concerned, and if General Balbo's will-power had been the deciding factor the Trophy would not now rest in Britain.

Almost immediately the Italian contingent returned home, the preparations for 1931 began. The first matter to be resolved was whether anything could be salvaged from the widespread efforts made prior to the 1929 contest. Only two of the machines were worthy of consideration in view of the performance of the British machines in setting the post-contest world speed records. These were the tandem-engined Savoia S.65 and the Macchi M.67, but all too soon one of these was tragically eliminated from any further consideration.

On 18 January 1930, in an attempt to capture the world speed record back from Britain, Tomasso Dal Molin had been killed when the S.65 plunged into the waters of Lake Garda. In that bitter moment the Italians had lost not only a promising machine but also a highly skilled pilot.

This left only the M.67. Balbo was well aware of the past achievements of the Macchi/Fiat combination, and it needed little consideration for him to reach the conclusion that the nation's best chance lay in backing this team to win. It was up to Mario Castoldi and Tranquillo Zerbi to bring the Trophy home to Italy.

Castoldi had few doubts concerning the aerodynamic efficiency of the M.67. He had, however, been greatly impressed by the concept of the Savoia-Marchetti S.65, for it was clear to him that the elimination of propeller torque could offer a number of very significant advantages that would enhance the performance of a derivative of the M.67. He summarised these as follows:

- (i) Contra-rotating propellers would eliminate propeller torque
- (ii) Elimination of torque would (a) make take-off much easier and (b) allow a smaller float volume which if used to reduce frontal area would eliminate considerable drag
- (iii) The rear propeller would benefit from the fact that the forward propeller had already accelerated the airstream, allowing the former to increase still further the velocity of this mass airflow.
- (iv) Dividing high engine power output between two propellers would allow the use of smaller-diameter higher-efficiency propellers.

However, experience with the S.65 had shown that the pilot's position between the two engines was far from ideal; that it had proved impracticable to synchronise the propellers effectively; and that due to this lack of synchronisation and the considerable distance separating the propeller discs, the aerodynamic stability of the aircraft had been affected adversely, especially in manoeuvring flight. It was essential to bring the propellers more closely together.

This was, of course, a question for discussion between airframe and engine designers, their get-togethers producing the idea for a revolutionary power plant which in due course received the Fiat designation AS.6. It derived from the lightweight AS.5 which had been used to power the Fiat C.29, a reliable engine of considerable promise.

Dr Zerbi planned to mount two AS.5 engines in tandem on a common crankcase. Instead of regarding them as two engines, the company referred to it as a 24-cylinder in-line liquid-cooled unit of V-form. The two crankshafts were in alignment, but unconnected, and each engine drove a separate propeller via individual reduction gearing to co-axial shafts. These two shafts, one rotating inside the other, passed between the two cylinder banks of the forward engine, while the rear engine drove a centrifugal supercharger which was used to boost both engines.

With a bore of 5·12in (13·0cm) and stroke of 5·51in (14·0cm), the AS.6 had a total cylinder capacity of 51·1 litres, and compression ratio of 7. In its fully developed form, subsequent to the 1931 contest, it had a maximum crankshaft speed of 3,300rpm, propeller shaft speed of 1,980rpm, and a maximum take-off rating of 3,100hp. Dry weight of this remarkable engine was only 2,050lb (930kg), giving a power/weight ratio of just over 1·5hp per pound.

Castoldi was excited by the prospect of an engine with a theoretical power output of around 2,500–3,000hp and one which, because of the use of what was virtually two moderately powered units working together, promised a high degree of reliability. Furthermore, for the first time, he need fear no problems from propeller torque.

His resulting aircraft design was that of a beautifully clean low-wing monoplane, designated MC.72 (MC: Macchi-Castoldi), the resemblance to the parent M.67 plain for all to see. The two-spar wing, of all-metal construction, utilised a bi-convex symmetrical aerofoil section, and was wire-braced to fuselage and floats. Almost the entire upper and lower surfaces were used as surface coolers, twin skins housing a mass of flat-section copper tubes with inlet and outlet manifolds at the wing leading-edge and aft of the rear spar respectively. Ailerons were conventional, and similar to those of the M.67, but as loadings could well be considerably higher in a turn the control column was increased in length to keep the input forces as low as possible.

The fuselage was of composite construction, the forward portion comprising a high-strength truss tubular structure, within which the engine was mounted and to which the wings, float struts, and the aft wooden monocoque fuselage were attached. The forward section was cowled with light alloy, and the aft section which included the pilot's cockpit was of all-wood and skinned with plywood. The cantilever tail unit was also of all-wood construction, the ventral fin and rudder having reduced area by comparison with the M.67. Rudder control was differentially geared to allow of small movements in high-speed flight and large movements for low speed and taxying.

From the earlier comments on reduced float sizes, resulting from the elimination of propeller torque, one might have expected to see diminutive floats. In fact, they still looked enormous, but would of course have been considerably larger if the problem of propeller torque had not been eliminated, for the maximum take-off weight of this aircraft amounted to 6,409 lb (2,907 kg). All-metal floats with snap-head rivet construction were built for evaluation against the usual all-wood single-step V-bottom floats favoured by Castoldi. They were shown to reduce speed by 9·3 mph (15 km/h), so wooden floats carried on broad-chord steel-tube streamline struts were used instead. These each contained metal fuel tanks, which were pressurised by compressed air to raise the fuel to two small gravity feed tanks in the fuselage. Oil was contained in a tank in the fuselage nose.

The wing surface radiators for the engine liquid cooling system were supplemented by additional cooling surfaces on the wide-chord struts and by radiators on the rear upper surface of the floats. The forward upper surface of each float, as well as that between the float struts, carried surface coolers, in addition to those on each side of the fuselage, to serve the needs of the oil system.

The Fiat AS.6 power plant installed in the MC.72 for the 1931 contest was rated at 2,500 hp, and this drove two contra-rotating two-blade metal propellers, the pitch of which was ground-adjustable. Wing span of the MC.72 was 31 ft $1\frac{1}{2}$ in (9·50 m) and wing area 165·76 sq. ft (15·4 m^2).

From across the Atlantic there was no more than a promise of financial backing for a private venture, the irrepressible 'Al' Williams resigning his commission in the Navy so that he could devote full time to fund raising and constructional efforts. It was all to no avail and nothing materialised as hardware. Consequently, there was no contender from the United States.

In France the situation was rather different, for it will be recalled that they had not been ready in time to take part in the previous contest. The performance set up by the winning machine, and the subsequent world speed record set by the S.6, made it clear there was little point in merely making sure that the designs of two years earlier had now attained a requisite degree of reliability. Performance requirements had risen to a new plateau and would, presumably, climb still higher by the time the competitors lined up for the 1931 contest. Already the sights were being raised to the 400 mph (644 km/h) mark.

In addition to the Bernard and Nieuport-Delage companies, the Société Aéronautique Française, founded by M. Dewoitine, was also approached to design a racing seaplane to add strength to the French team. It was all rather chaotic, the circumstances aggravated by the Royal Aero Club which at a meeting of the FAI held in Paris in mid-January 1930 had proposed some changes in the regulations.

That which proved most controversial was that the 'good intent' deposit for would-be competitors should be raised to 200,000 francs (£1,600), it being argued that the cost of organising these events had risen so steeply that it was essential to have an assurance of the number of aircraft likely to be involved. It was considered such a deposit would ensure that only serious contenders would make application for entry.

The second proposal was that the navigability and water tightness tests in their existing form should be scrapped, to be replaced by a take-off and alighting test immediately prior to the speed contest. Thus, competing aircraft would take off, land, taxi on the surface and then take off again to complete the speed course. This would involve new problems for aircraft designers, as the float structure would need to be capable of accepting a landing at almost maximum take-off weight. The primary purpose behind the proposition was to enable the event to be completed in a single day, rather than impose the all too frequent problem of getting two separate days that provided acceptable flying conditions for such high-speed aircraft. It was suggested also that the closing date for entries should be 31 July 1930.

The FAI agreed on the first two proposals but left until a later meeting a decision as to whether the closing date for entries should be that suggested by the Royal Aero Club.

There was an immediate protest from both the French and Italian aero clubs, their main concern being the amount of deposit required. Thus, at a general meeting of the FAI held in June, it was agreed that the former deposit of £50 should apply to entries received before 31 July. Immediately, the French and Italian aero clubs took advantage of this and each made their entry of three aircraft to the Royal Aero Club. The British club declined to accept these, arguing that the decision reached by the FAI in January was final. Italian reaction was that a deposit of £1,600 per aircraft was ridiculous: if the Royal Aero Club were incapable of organising the 1931 contest without such a condition, then the Italian club would be quite prepared to stage the contest in Italy, the deposit being limited only to £50.

In an endeavour to resolve this impasse the FAI suggested a compromise, that entries prior to 31 July should be subject to a deposit of £50, those made between 1 August and 31 December a deposit of £1,600. The Royal

Aero Club maintained stubborn indifference, arguing that the original decision had been agreed upon in a constitutional manner and was therefore legal and binding.

The battle raged on, and at another FAI meeting held on 12 September the international body said that in the interests of sportsmanship final agreement must be reached. They ruled that members of the Royal Aero Club must attend a further meeting to be held on 30 November to agree upon and finalise the rules governing the 1931 contest. The wrangle ended without change: the final date for entry was fixed as 31 December 1930, the deposit £1,600, the venue to be once again in the Spithead/Solent area, and the contest to take place between 31 August and 19 September 1931.

From France came reports that the Lorraine and Renault companies were to develop new power plants for the contest. That of the former company was designated as the Radium, an inverted 12-cylinder in-line liquid-cooled V-form engine, designed by M. Barbarou. It was to be supercharged, the centrifugal blower turning at 28,000 rpm, and was expected to develop 2,200 hp at 4,000 rpm. The inverted configuration had been chosen so that its installation in the airframe would allow improved forward visibility for the pilot during taxying and the critical take-off and landing phases of flight.

The engine being developed by Renault was also a 12-cylinder in-line liquid-cooled engine, but of conventional V-form, supercharged and

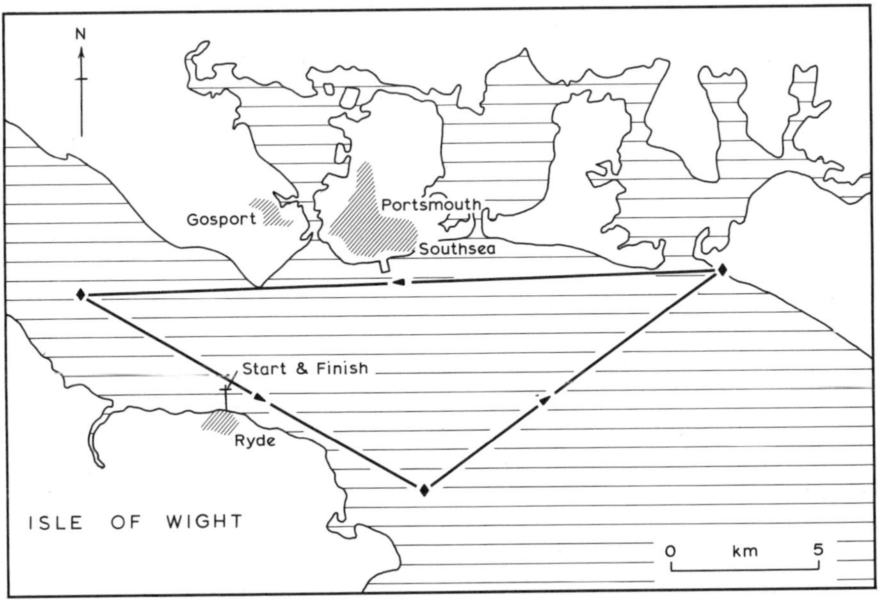

11. Schneider Trophy Contest Course: Cowes 1931

geared, and reported to be in the 1,500–2,000hp class, with a dry weight of 1,540lb (698kg).

Meanwhile, a team of French pilots began their training at Lake Berre, near Marseilles, under the command of Captain Amanrich. They had adopted the concept, originated by the British High Speed Flight, of bringing together a team of service pilots skilled in high-speed flight, but having no experience of waterborne operations. For their early training an FBA flying-boat was available, with Nieuport 62 landplane fighters for high-speed practice, and it was not until some months after their formation that one of the 1929 Bernard aircraft, re-designated HV.41, became available for use as a high-speed seaplane trainer. They were to receive also a Bernard HV.120, basically the same as the HV.42, but with wing surface radiators replacing the Lamblin type and minor changes in dimensions.

The Nieuport-Delage machine which had failed to materialise in time for the 1929 contest emerged eventually under the designation ND.450, and had received its initial flight tests on Lake Hourtin in the hands of Sadi Lecointe. As these tests had shown the desirability of certain modifications, the aircraft was flown back to Paris on 24 July by Fernand Lasne. In alighting on the Seine it crashed, the pilot escaping without serious injury, but the ND.450 was decidedly the worse for wear.

The spirits of the French team were at low ebb, and reduced to nought when on 30 July Lieutenant Bougault, flying the Bernard HV.120, crashed at Berre and was killed. The cause of the accident has never been determined satisfactorily, but there had been considerable difficulty in selecting a suitable propeller to give a reasonable compromise between take-off and high-speed performance. On a number of occasions propellers had been damaged by water during take-off, and it was assumed that this had been the contributary cause of Bougault's death, the propeller breaking up in flight and either incapacitating the pilot by injury or by causing vital damage to the aircraft. Technical investigation of the wreckage had shown that a sparking plug was missing from the engine, and the conclusion of the investigators was that this had penetrated the windshield and caused the pilot to lose control. Either of the suggested causes may have been responsible, and was as near as anyone could come to an explanation for the accident.

This was, however, just about the final blow so far as France was concerned. Although desultory efforts continued for a short period after the fatal accident, time was running out fast.

Italy, too, was not finding the going easy. Fiat's new AS.6 engine was proving something of a handful, and as early as 29 April 1931 General Balbo had indicated that all was not well when he stated that he could not 'affirm with certainty that we shall take part this year'.

A couple of months later the first MC.72 had arrived at Desenzano where, once again, the Italian team were training. It was demonstrated at once that the contra-rotating propellers had eliminated the torque problem: for the first time take-off was as easy and predictable as that of a landplane. The trouble was that the engine could not be brought to anywhere near full power without spluttering and backfiring, some of the backfires being frighteningly violent. Despite this, the MC.72 had shown a hint of its potential as a racing aircraft by recording speeds of up to 375 mph (604 km/h).

As testing continued, the engine was found to be running far too hot, and this coupled with the irregular running gave every indication of carburation problems associated with weak mixture conditions. On 2 August the courageous Monti, who had been scalded in the M.67 at Cowes and had since been promoted to Captain, was testing the MC.72. During a particularly bad spell of irregular running he made a low level sweep over the maintenance area so that engineers on the ground could better hear for themselves the distressing behaviour of the engine. Within seconds the aircraft was reduced to splintered wreckage as it smashed into the unrelenting waters of Lake Garda and Giovanni Monti was dead.

With both the French and Italian teams deep in difficulties, it was not surprising that their respective aero clubs should approach the Royal Aero Club for a postponement. The requests were made on 3 September, only nine days before the appointed day for the race, both representatives pointing out their particular problems. Both, no doubt, reminded the Royal Aero Club of the precedent created by the Americans in 1924, when it had not been possible for Britain, France or Italy to get their contenders to Baltimore in time to compete. Then, the American decision to postpone the contest for twelve months had caused the Royal Aero Club to express their great appreciation of such sporting action.

Now, faced with a similar situation, the Royal Aero Club refused to even consider a postponement, once again shielding themselves behind a strict interpretation of the rules. The same course could have been adopted by the United States in 1924. No question of regulations had been raised by them or the British at that time, so one cannot help but question which nation had the better appreciation of sportsmanship.

And to make sure there should be no subsequent confusion, on the following day the Royal Aero Club announced officially that, in the event of no opposition being presented, the British team would fly over the course to take the Trophy. One could, presumably, argue in their defence that this was a final attempt to force one or other of the teams to put up some opposition. Whether or not this was the case it brought no response: the Air Ministry confirmed on 5 September that there would be no foreign competition.

As a postscript to Italy's efforts, it must be recorded that two days before the race the Italians lost the second of the three Macchi MC.72s that had been built. Flown by Lieutenant Stanislao Bellini, it was making a high-speed low-level pass over Lake Garda when it crashed into rising ground on the far side. Subsequent investigations proved that an intake explosion had set fire to the gravity fuel tank behind the engine, enveloping Bellini in a broad tongue of flame. It was to mark the end of development of the MC.72 for some time.

Britain's efforts to win the Trophy for the third and final time have been ignored so far as, in view of the fact that there was no foreign participation in the contest, it seems better to relate it as an unbroken story.

The no-go situation that had been brought about by combined government and Air Council determination not to defend the Trophy in 1931 had reduced very considerably the period of time that might have been available to produce a completely new aircraft for the purpose.

In fact it was not until the last day of January 1931 that things began to move, which meant there was little more than seven months available in which to develop the two aircraft and engines that would represent the hard core of the British team, supplemented by the S.6s which had done such noble work in 1929.

Inevitably, more power was needed. Within the time scale mentioned above, the design and development of a new engine was impossible. Fortunately, the Rolls-Royce engineers were satisfied that the 'R' engine could be made to yield more power. To do so it would require that both crankshaft and centrifugal blower should run faster, that the air intake should be capable of admitting more air, and reciprocating components would need to be strengthened to withstand the extra stresses of higher engine speed and power.

Stated in so many words the task seems simple enough: the realisation of these 'simple' alterations almost brought the team of engineers to despair.

To begin with, the changed rules of the contest imposed new problems, for after an initial take-off and subsequent alighting, the engine must be capable of reliable tick-over and of a second full-power take-off before beginning the speed course. Because of this extra requirement before the speed course, it meant that higher power was needed to cope with the task of getting additional loads of fuel and oil into the air as well. Desirably, therefore, fuel and oil consumption should be reduced and power increased to give the aircraft in which it was installed the best possible chance of success.

Tests to determine the best approach began with the engines of 1929 vintage. Increased crankshaft revolutions, coupled with modification of supercharger diffuser vanes, increased air intake volume and higher supercharger speeds were most promising as regards the ultimate achievement of the desired power. But the increased rotational speed of the engine produced a staggering increase in oil consumption; at the outset totalling some 50 Imperial gallons (227 litres) an hour. This was completely unacceptable for two reasons: the sheer problem of oil storage capacity in the tank at the base of the fin, and the resulting changes in trim that would result as this large quantity of oil was consumed.

The pistons of the original 'R' engines had three compression rings and one oil scraper ring, and a first approach involved the use of more rigid compression rings. This had no material affect on oil consumption, and resulted only in serious scoring of the cylinder barrels. The final solution was to lay in the use of two oil scraper rings, modification of the crankcase breathers, an improved oil scavenging system and utilisation of a greater capacity sump. The combined effects of these measures brought oil consumption down to an acceptable figure of around 13 Imperial gallons (59 litres) an hour at maximum rpm.

Improvement in fuel consumption was achieved by careful study of inlet valve opening and exhaust valve closure, together with another closely related factor, namely the optimum point at which to initiate ignition of the mixture in the cylinder. Desirably, the mixture should be as weak as reasonably possible, but weak mixture conditions inevitably bring higher operating temperatures. While it might prove possible to dissipate this extra heat by careful attention to the entire cooling system, its immediate effect was to cause pre-ignition of the mixture in the cylinder due to the heads of the exhaust valves becoming red hot.

Experiments in America had shown that sodium-cooled valves might offer a solution, and this new prospect was explored. Such a valve has hollow stems, partially filled with metallic sodium. This liquid metal is shaken up and down as the valves open and close, heat being transferred from the head of the valve and up the stem, into an area where liquid-cooled valve guides can effectively dissipate much of this heat.

The new valves were immensely successful, the temperature of the valve head remaining below a point where it would cause pre-ignition, even with mixtures significantly weaker than those used in the 1929 engines. In the final analysis, the extra power developed by the 1931 engines was achieved with a lower specific fuel consumption.

When bench testing of the new engine began a spate of mechanical failures occurred. Most serious were main bearing and crankshaft failures, and it was not until a balanced crankshaft was adopted that this problem was eliminated. It is worth recording that the load on the centre main bearing at full power was in the order of nine tons. Other bearings, supercharger gears, valve springs, and the valves themselves, were all subject to mechanical failure under full power conditions until, one by one, methods were found to enable them to withstand the new stresses imposed.

It can be imagined that the roar of one of these engines in full cry on its test bed was more than ear shattering. It is not perhaps appreciated that simultaneously three other Kestrel engines were kept running at full throttle: one to blow a cooling stream of air over the crankcase; one to keep the test house free of exhaust gases; and the third giving a simulated 380 mph (612 km/h) airflow over the test engine air intake to allow of carburation adjustments under conditions similar to those that would be experienced in flight. It is not surprising that a large proportion of the residents of Derby were fully aware when a test run was under way.

The measure of progress is given by the fact that in April 1931 an engine could be run at full throttle for about twenty minutes before failure. Another three months of painstaking work was needed to increase this to beyond the half-hour mark. It was not until 3 August that an engine approached the required one-hour endurance, achieving a run of 58 minutes and developing 2,360 hp. On 12 August an engine completed the full one-hour endurance test, producing 2,350 hp at 3,200 rpm without failure. The maximum power produced by one of these engines during this development period was 2,783 hp.

What of the airframe to receive this remarkable engine?

The task of defending the Trophy had once again fallen to Supermarine and R. J. Mitchell. They, like Rolls-Royce, had little enough time in which to carry out their job, and it was clear from the outset that it was impossible to design and build a completely new aircraft.

The only course available was to modify the design of the S.6 to accept the more powerful engine promised by Rolls-Royce. Thus evolved the S.6B, its basic dimensions the same as those of the S.6 of 1929, except that overall length increased by 2ft 0in (0·61m) due to the use of longer floats. Tailplane area was also reduced from 15·8 sq. ft (1·47 m^2) to 15·0 sq. ft (1·39 m^2).

Well aware that more engine power meant also more heat to be got rid of, the significance of Mitchell's comment to A. J. Rowledge, mentioned in the previous chapter, can be better understood. In fact, it was necessary to provide, as nearly as possible, for the dissipation of some 40,000 BTUs per minute. To this end the larger floats proved invaluable, all of the top surface extending down to the chines being occupied by surface radiators. Air vents in the cooling system were faced forward into the airstream so that increased air pressure would help to control the boiling point, but so efficient was the design of the cooling system that even when boiling point was attained the loss was confined to steam, rather than water. However, it was a condition that could be tolerated, even though it proved impossible to use full throttle without causing boiling if the air temperature exceeded 17°C (62·6°F). It was quite normal for the water temperature to be in the region of 88–90°C (190–194°F) at take-off, steadily rising as the flight progressed, so that the pilots of the S.6Bs had to throttle back to maintain a water temperature not exceeding 95°C (203°F). Thus arose what many would consider a curious situation for a racing aircraft: it was not flown at full throttle, but to a water temperature, this being the governing factor of maximum airspeed.

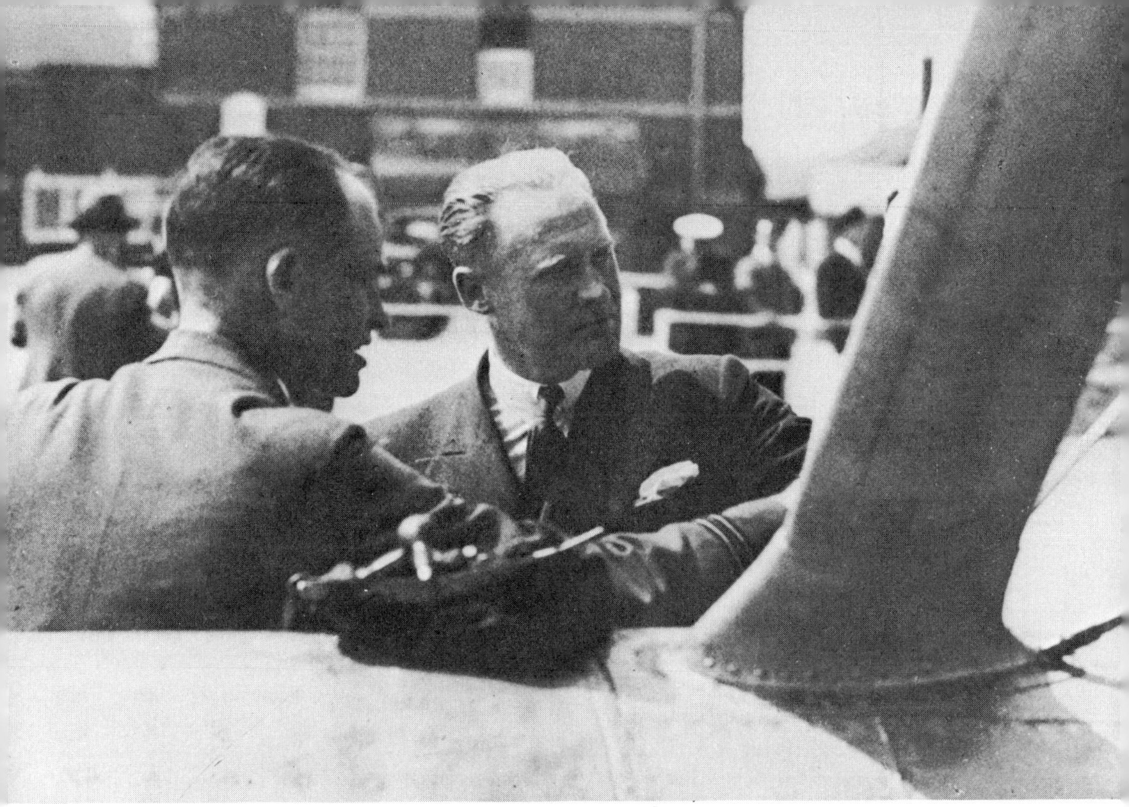

The architect of victory. R. J. Mitchell talking 'shop' with Flight-Lieutenant F. W. Long

The all-important ground crews busily at work

Temperature control of the engine's cooling system was not the only problem to be resolved for, of course, the lubricating oil was hotter also. An additional area of surface cooling was provided by taking the oil from the tank back to the engine via a fuselage 'keel', and small vanes were placed in the oilways within the fin to ensure that the maximum volume of oil was brought into contact with the cooler outer surface skin. A change was made also in the oil circuit, hot engine oil passing down both fuselage coolers to the top of the fin, returning from the collecting tank at its base via the under-fuselage 'keel'. So effective was this new system that a temperature drop of between 30 and 40°C (86–104°F) was obtained between engine outlet and inlet oil.

The two S.6s of 1929 were modified to have the new floats as designed for the S.6B, and were also to have the new engines as soon as they became available. In this modified form they were re-designated S.6As.

After the 1929 contest the High Speed Flight had returned to Felixstowe to continue with experimental work, but a number of changes in personnel were soon to follow. Atcherley, Grieg, Waghorn and the engineer officer, Moon, were all sent to pastures new. Orlebar and Stainforth remained, soon to be joined by Flight-Lieutenant F. W. Long. Stainforth was next to go, being replaced by Flight-Lieutenant J. N. Boothman, and another addition was Flight-Lieutenant E. J. L. Hope.

When the decision was made to participate in the 1931 contest, further postings were made to strengthen the team, including the welcome return of George Stainforth, plus Flying-Officer L. S. Snaith and Lieutenant R. L. Brinton from the Fleet Air Arm, while Flight-Lieutenant W. F. Dry became the new engineer officer.

Available as 'hack' machines for the early training of the newcomers were an Armstrong Whitworth Atlas (J9998), as well as a trio of Fairey types: Firefly, Fleetwing and Flycatcher. Once promoted to the 'hotter' machines, they found available a Gloster IVA, two Supermarine S.5s, as well as the two Gloster VIs, but the latter were not expected to be capable of any sustained effort.

The Flight had hardly got under way before Brinton was posted away again, but the remainder of the team got down to work as and when weather would permit, pending the move back to Calshot during May. The same old combined disadvantages of open sea and east wind were less worrying to the old hands than in the previous year. At least they were not plagued by the constant problem of floating debris and the wash of large vessels that made life at Calshot far less rosy than it might otherwise have been.

But Calshot was the real thing, and as soon as the High Speed Flight arrived there in mid-May they all began at once to feel a surge of excitement, with the first of the modified S.6As due any day. In the meantime there were the two S.5s, two Gloster VIs and the Gloster IVA with which the team could practice. The Gloster VIs had become far more reliable as a result of modification to their air intakes at Felixstowe, this involving a new forward-facing type. Even this had caused a completely new kind of trouble at the outset, when a fairly large proportion of a wave had been sucked in by the supercharger, damaging the fan blades. A changed position of the intake, although still forward-facing, overcame this problem and the VIs became valuable training machines.

It was not until 20 May that the first of the modified S.6As (N.247) arrived, and Orlebar could hardly wait to get his hands on the controls. He didn't even manage a taxying test, for a combined leaking float and leaking fuel tank was supplying the engine with a sea water/fuel mixture that was not conducive to smooth running. Almost two weeks were to elapse before the fuel system was completely cleared of contamination, the float changed and the weather co-operative.

On 2 June Orlebar was at the controls again, and as the engine responded in full measure to the throttle he found that N.247 taxied well, was quickly up on the step, and then into the air in an unbelievably short time. The only snag was that he experienced a fair amount of vibration at full throttle, but as he eased back after take off it just as quickly disappeared. Perhaps a propeller blade was marginally out of track. He cruised around for a period at about 280 mph (450 km/h) and all seemed well, so he decided to give the S.6A its head to see how the new floats had affected maximum speed.

Air-Vice Marshal Long described to the author how: '. . . he was doing a low-level run over Calshot, and we were all watching, when we suddenly saw the tail start to oscillate violently. He throttled right back and landed straight ahead, far out in the Solent. This turned out to be rudder flutter, so violent that it had sheared all the rivets in the last bay of the fuselage.'

To Orlebar it had seemed that a crash was inevitable, for the S.6A was at a height of only about 300 ft (91 m) when the flutter began, and travelling at close upon 350 mph (563 km/h). He did well to maintain control, fighting to hold the aircraft steady until the speed dropped to just below 200 mph (322 km/h) when, just as suddenly, the vibration stopped, allowing a greatly relieved pilot to make a hurried landing.

N.247 was sent back to the works for repair; horn balances were applied to the rudder, the ailerons being similarly treated as a safety precaution. N.248 was given the same modifications, as well as the two new S.6Bs. In addition, the last bay of the fuselage was strengthened by the application of doubler plates.

N.248 was the first to become available for flight training, and was also the first to have the new uprated engine. Orlebar was responsible for the air test on 26 June, frustrated after only a few minutes of flight by the engine spluttering and producing so little power that he was forced to land. The fuel filters were found to be choked. When cleaned all was well again—for a short time. Again the filters were cleaned out, only to be followed by another forced landing for the same cause.

The critics. Left to right: Flight-Lieutenant F. W. Long, Squadron-Leader A. H. Orlebar and Flight-Lieutenant Dry (Engineer Officer)

The backer. Squadron-Leader Orlebar introduces Lady Houston to Flight-Lieutenant F. W. Long: behind him stands Flight-Lieutenant J. N. Boothman, soon to settle ownership of the Trophy

It was found that this cycle of trouble was due to the exotic fuel attacking a compound used in the fuel system joints, and it was not until all the surplus jointing material had been dissolved that the trouble was eliminated.

Consequently, it was 3 July before Flight-Lieutenant Long was able to make what could be called a completely successful flight in N.248. Later the same day a second flight was made by Flight-Lieutenant Hope, but he had been airborne for only a few minutes when a section of the engine cowling began to blow loose and he decided it was wise to make an immediate landing before it became detached. Unfortunately, a liner coming to anchor off the mouth of the Hamble had been using full engine revolutions to manoeuvre, creating a nasty swell. As the seaplane touched down the floats hit the swell, throwing the machine some 20 ft (6 m) into the air. Before Hope could collect her with a burst of throttle, the port wing dipped and N.248 cartwheeled but did not sink. The water-logged and despondent pilot clung to the floats until picked up, and although apparently uninjured, it was found subsequently that he had received a damaged ear drum as a result of the accident, eliminating him from further active participation in the contest.

Having served as a life raft for Hope, N.248 considered she had done quite enough and went to the bottom. It was not until three days later that a combination of diver and salvage vessel brought her back to the surface for return to Supermarines for extensive repairs.

By 8 July N.247 was back again at Calshot and was soon at work. Experience showed that under certain conditions of wind and water the machine was difficult to handle at take-off, a vicious swing developing as the engine was opened up and which almost immediately led to porpoising. Eventually a technique to overcome this was evolved, the aircraft being headed at least 45° out of wind, so that the swing brought the nose back into the wind, by which time the speed had increased sufficiently for the rudder to become effective.

With this difficulty resolved practice went ahead, and by the time that Boothman and Snaith had both gained some experience with N.247 the long awaited moment arrived with receipt of the first S.6B (S.1595) on 21 July.

Knowing how to cope with the swing on N.247, Orlebar did not anticipate any real difficulty with the take-off. He was to discover that no matter how he tried he could not correct the swing on the S.6B, which gyrated in frustrating circles until the engine was throttled back. Three further days of test ended in failure, culminating with a new headache when S.1595 fouled a barge, holing the surface radiator. A wing change was essential and, in the meantime, a collective mass of brains concentrated on the swing problem. N.247 was fundamentally the same as the new S.6B, differing primarily in weight and propeller installation.

Since, for test purposes, nothing could be done about the weight, it was

The machines. S.6B serial S1595 . . .

. . . and the reserve, S1596

decided to make some tests by fitting the smaller-diameter propeller of the S.6B to N.247. Immediately it proved impossible to get the S.6A into the air. They had hit upon the right solution, and when S.1595 was ready for test again on 29 July, complete with a larger diameter propeller, she got off the water with little difficulty.

Nonetheless, considerable time was spent in arriving at the most suitable propeller, a diameter of 9 ft 1½ in (2·78 m) proving the final selection. How valuable a variable-pitch propeller would have been, with a fine pitch setting for use at take-off to allow the engine to produce its full power. As it was, when the engine was run to full power on the ground in a 'chocked' condition, the maximum crankshaft revolutions that could be developed with the installed propeller were about 1,850, thus only some 56 per cent of maximum power was available at the critical moment of take-off.

While all this worrisome period had been in progress, Lieutenant Jerry Brinton had been posted back from the Fleet Air Arm to replace Flying-Officer Hope. He was greeted enthusiastically, for during his short stay at Felixstowe he had proved to be popular and was also a capable pilot. It did not take long for him to become re-acquainted with the training seaplanes, and it was considered that he was ready to try his hand with the S.6A.

Experience had shown that to prevent the floats from porpoising at the moment of lifting on the step, the control column must be pulled right back, and as flying speed was gained it still had to be held there, despite an uneasy feeling that the aircraft was hanging in the air, suspended by the propeller alone. But provided the column was held there the speed would gradually build up, when control reaction became quite normal. Unfortunately, this holding of the aircraft in a near-stalled position immediately after lift-off was completely foreign to the average pilot.

This had been carefully explained to Brinton, but there was always a little apprehension as a pilot made his first take-off in the S.6A. Those who watched saw him make a short run to get the feel of the swing and the inclination to porpoise on the step. Then he positioned himself for take-off, and there was nothing wrong with his run at all until, having gained a height of about 10 ft (3 m) the tail came up and the aircraft smacked back on the water. Clearly, he had instinctively eased the stick forward on becoming airborne.

N.247 bounced smartly back into the air at an even steeper angle of attack. With engine at full throttle in an attempt to gain airspeed, the seaplane hit the water again, bouncing almost 30 ft (9 m) into the air this time before plunging nose down to the bottom. The violence of this dive was too much for the human body and Jerry Brinton's neck was broken: the fourth man to die before the 1931 contest.

This tragic accident came as a severe blow to everyone at Calshot, but its impact was alleviated to some extent by the really hard work put in to ensure that each member of the team should be capable of his best.

There was so much to do and, with a very indifferent period of weather, so little time in which to do it. The first flight of the second S.6B (S.1596) was made on 12 August and proved quite uneventful until after about twelve minutes of flight the engine decided to call it a day. The same old problem: clogged filters. With pre-knowledge of the cause it did not take so long to rectify the problem this time, and soon it was possible for the pilots to practice with both S.6Bs to discover their capabilities and limitations.

It was difficult, of course, to arrive at the best means of making the fastest turn. Should it be steeply banked and tight, or more gentle with a climb in and dive out? It was a question resolved by fitting accelerometers and *g* recorders, this proving that a turn that produced 4–4½ *g* was the best, and one which could be tolerated by the pilot without any loss of vision due to the excess force of gravity restricting severely the supply of blood to the brain. The resulting temporary loss of vision was known as 'blacking-out' if all vision went, or 'greying-out' with only partial loss of vision.

Atcherley described his own experience of 'blacking-out' in an early test flight in a Supermarine S.5 prior to the 1929 contest: 'I went "out" halfway round a turn at Calshot Castle, and flew completely unconscious at about 500 feet (152 m) halfway back to Cowes before regaining my senses. Even then there was a very frightening lapse of seconds when one realised one *was* flying and had been "out", but still could not see or move one's hands . . .

'In my lapse of unconsciousness, I dreamt that I was sitting in the housemaster's garden at Oundle in a deck chair . . . I could see the flowers —and hear the bees—the noise of which got angrier and angrier, until I started to wonder where I had heard that noise before. Then I realised that it was the Napier engine in the S.5, and gradually came the frightening realisation that I was going like a bomb and might expect to hit the water any second . . . I was a very frightened officer!'

Both machines proved somewhat unstable on the floats, as well as during turns in the air, and Mitchell decided that this was due to the CG being too far aft, primarily due to the extra weight of oil in the tank at the base of the fin. This tended to conflict with the view of the pilots who complained of the aircraft having a feeling of nose heaviness.

Nonetheless, Mitchell's remedy was to reduce the quantity of oil in the tank by 4 Imperial gallons (18 litres), having discovered by experimentation that this left an adequate reserve for the duration needed to complete the 188·9 nm (350 km) course. In addition, he had about 25 lb (11 kg) of lead affixed in the nose of each float. His suggestion of a bungee on the control column to allow elevator trim adjustment was met by an outcry of complaint from the pilots so, instead, he added a 9 in × 1 in (22·8 cm × 2·5 cm) strip of duralumin to the trailing-edge of each elevator to provide ground-adjustable trim tabs.

The modifications greatly improved the handling characteristics of the aircraft, leaving only a few 'bugs' to be eliminated. One of these concerned the by-pass system that returned excess fuel from the gravity header tank to the floats. The tendency was for this fuel to migrate back to just one float tank, instead of being divided between the two, with a consequent upset to the aircraft's lateral trim. This was resolved eventually by the fitment of restrictors in the by-pass lines to balance the flow.

Then, on 6 September, S.6A N.248 was returned to the flight, having been restored to flying condition after Hope's crash. It behaved perfectly, so the three aircraft for the contest were just about as ready as they could possibly be.

As events had decreed that the contest would be a fly-over, it was necessary to settle the most suitable tactics since it was not intended that the three aircraft should race in competition. It was decided that S.1595 should be flown around the course first at a reasonable speed: if it failed for any reason then N.248 could be relied upon to follow and complete the course. If this was so, then S.1596 would be flown all-out over the 3-km speed course in Southampton Water to try and set a new world speed record.

But of the four pilots available, who should fly the three machines? George Stainforth elected to attempt the world speed record, so the three remaining were allocated to the three mounts in order of service seniority. Thus Boothman was to fly S.1595, Long N.248, and Snaith S.1596 if neither Boothman nor Long completed the Schneider speed course. If Boothman was successful, neither Long nor Snaith would have a chance to show their paces, but none complained of the arrangements.

With their aircraft as perfect as loving maintenance could ensure, all but the most vital instruments blanked off, lap counters fitted—comprising copper tabs that could be bent down—tubes installed to give a blast of fresh air for the pilots, and cleaned and polished to perfection, all stood by on the eve of the contest.

The course chosen for 1931 differed from that of 1929, once again being triangular in form. As before, the starting and finishing line was at Ryde pier, the first leg of 4·48 nm (8·3 km) to a pylon on a destroyer anchored off St Helen's Point. There, a turn on to a NE heading led to the second pylon, erected on the shore at West Wittering, 7·29 nm (13·5 km) distant. An acute turn on to the longest leg, 12·01 nm (22·1 km) led back along the south coast, past Southsea and Gosport, to the third pylon, again mounted on a destroyer, this being anchored in mid-Solent off East Cowes, and giving a final short stretch of 3·29 nm (6·1 km) back to the line at Ryde pier.

Public enthusiasm was considerable but, of course, nowhere near as great as it would have been had the French and Italians been contending ownership of the Trophy. One thing almost completely reliable, so far as Britain was concerned, was the weather: true to form, on the appointed day of the race, it subjected the area to wind and rain, causing postponement until the following day, Sunday 13 September.

Although Britain had won the Schneider Trophy, the Macchi M.72 was subsequently to prove a superb machine

On 23 October 1934, Francesco Agello and the M.72 set a world speed record, for seaplanes of 440·68 mph (709·204 km/h).

Was the date to be ominous? Happily, the weather relented, enabling spectators to turn up in their thousands. But the team were very conscious of the fact that the eyes of the world were upon them. Failure to complete the course on that day—in an event where they faced no competition—would be an utter fiasco.

The team gathered around a somewhat nervy John Boothman as, at two minutes past 1.0 p.m., S.1595 was got into the water, followed almost instantly by the sound of the starting gun.

Boothman took off without difficulty, landing again almost immediately as required by the new rule. This also demanded that he should remain on the water for a period of not less than two minutes, and he made sure the engine should not stall during his spell of inactivity by giving it short bursts of throttle. Then away again, with another clean take-off, and speeding towards the St Helen's turn.

There were no problems, everything going as planned as he flew with the engine throttled back slightly to maintain a steady water temperature, and each of his seven laps were consistent within 4 mph (6·4 km/h) of each other, to record a final average speed of 340·08 mph (547·31 km/h). The Trophy had been won: one bright achievement in a Britain troubled by economic and political problems, and beset by rising unemployment.

Later in the afternoon S.1596 was readied for George Stainforth to have an attempt on the world speed record. In this attempt he would not be compelled to restrict throttle opening, for even if the water in the cooling system reached boiling point, there was time for it to fall comfortably below that temperature as he throttled back, turned and re-aligned the aircraft for the ensuing run over the measured course.

This, too, proved uneventful, and his four runs established a new world speed record of 379·05 mph (610·02 km/h).

Supermarine, Rolls-Royce and the High Speed Flight had made it: thanks to the generosity of Lady Houston!

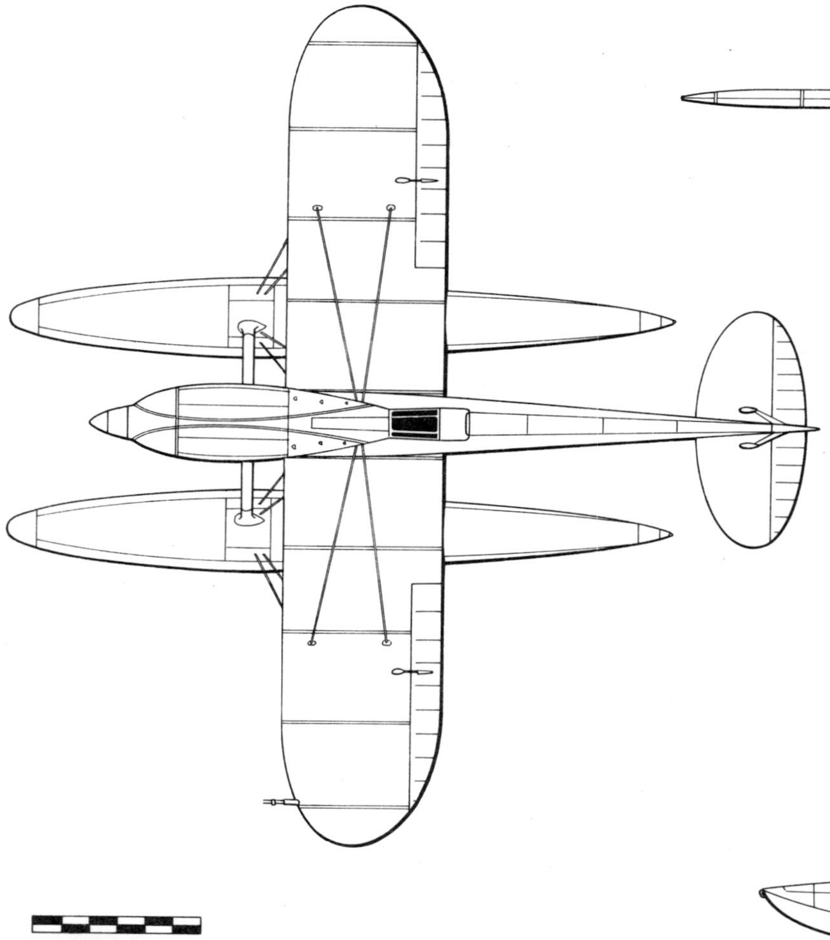

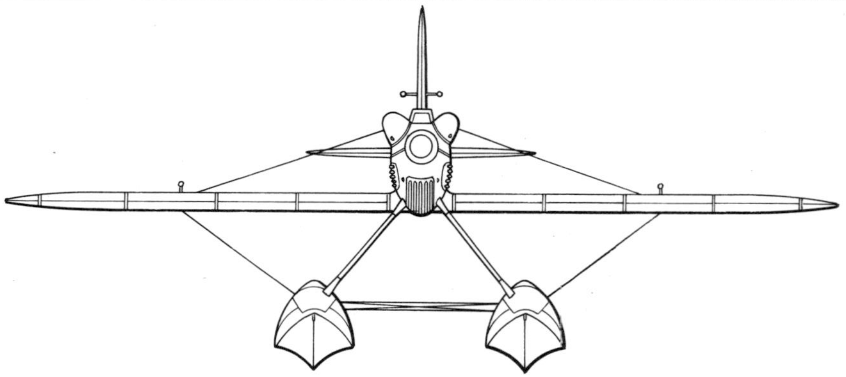

Supermarine S.6B (1931)

Wing Span: 30 ft (9·14 m)
Length Overall: 28 ft 10 in (8·79 m)
Wing Area: 145 sq. ft (13·47 m^2)
Weight Empty: 4,590 lb (2,082 kg)
T-O Weight: 6,086 lb (2,761 kg)
Max Wing Loading: 41·97 lb/sq. ft (204·91 kg/m^2)
Horsepower of Power Plant: 2,650 hp

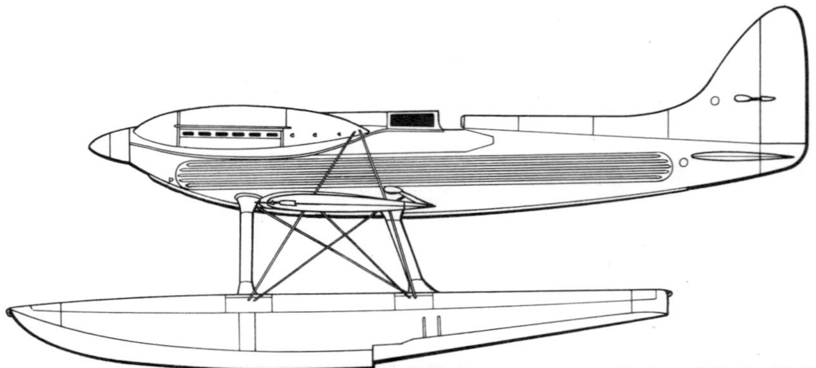

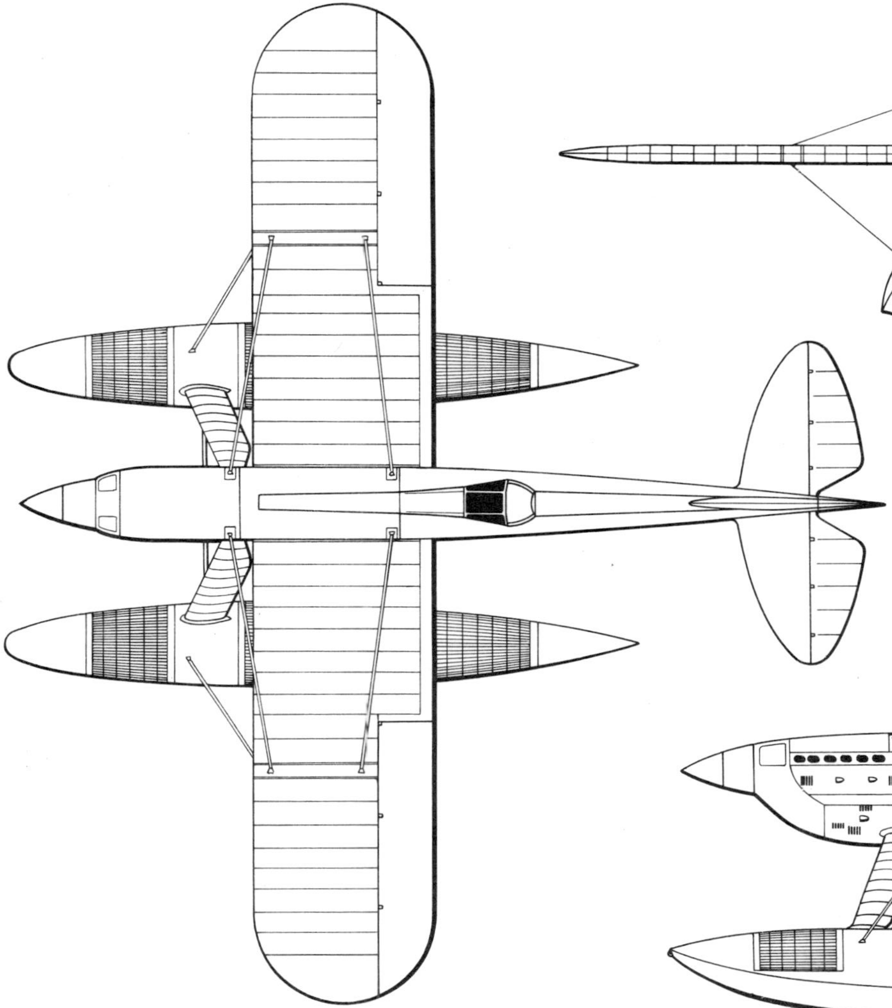

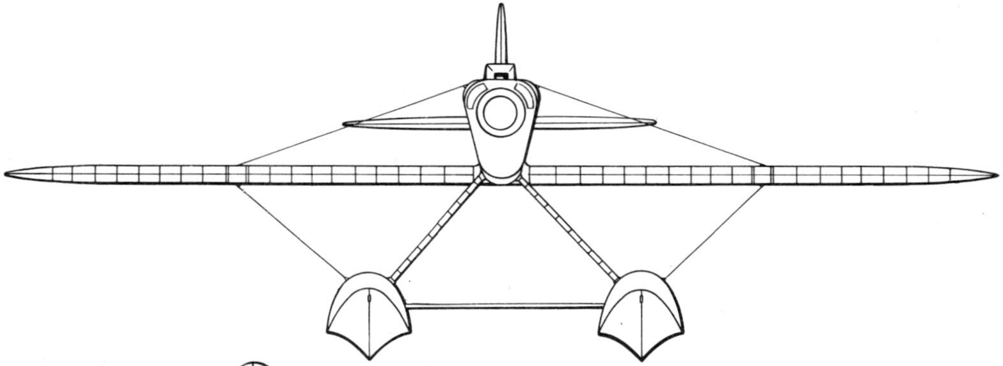

Macchi M.72 (1931)

Wing Span: 31 ft $1\frac{1}{2}$ in (9·49 m)
Length Overall: 27 ft $6\frac{3}{4}$ in (8·40 m)
Wing Area: 165·76 sq. ft (15·4 m²)
Weight Empty: 5,512 lb (2,500 kg)
T-O Weight: 6,409 lb (2,907 kg)
Max Wing Loading: 38·66 lb/sq. ft (188·75 kg/m²)
Horsepower of Power Plant: 2,500 hp

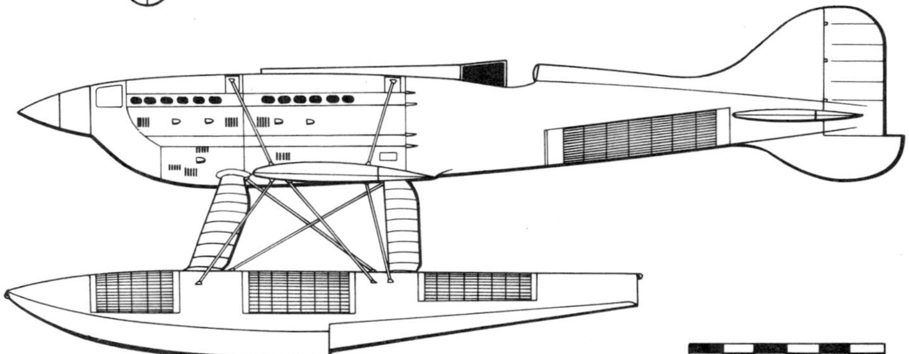

13

Cart follows the horse

How does one begin to summarise this exciting period of aviation history? The Trophy belonged to Great Britain. Had it been worth all the endeavour? C. G. Grey had characteristic comment to make in *The Aeroplane*:

'There is a story about a man who bought a horse from a Yorkshire horse-coper, a species which is known to be one of the keenest of its kind. When he had bought the horse and paid for it, he said to the dealer: "Now I have bought the horse, tell me what's the matter with him?" The dealer replied: "There's nowt much the matter wi' 'im. 'E 'as nowt but two faults." "Good, tell me what they are," said the buyer. "Well," said the dealer, "the first fault is that if thee lets 'im loose in a field, 'e takes a 'ell of a lot of catchin'." "Then, what's his second fault?" "Well," said the dealer, "when thee 'ast catched 'im 'e's no dam use."

'Somehow the Schneider Trophy is like that. It has taken an awful lot of catching. And now we've got it its no real use.'

But, of course, CGG was among the first to appreciate precisely what the 'catching' had done for British aviation in terms of the development of aircraft and engines capable of new standards of performance. If the government of the time had chosen to jump upon this new technological band waggon, then we would have had the most powerful air force in the world when the moment came for confrontation with the Third Reich.

There was, however, more to come. Another attempt was made to raise the world speed record beyond the 400 mph (644 km/h) mark for the first time, and Rolls-Royce had prepared a special engine for the task, referred to usually as the 'sprint' engine. Increased boost pressure and the use of a special fuel 'cocktail' comprising 30 per cent benzole, 60 per cent methanol and 10 per cent acetone, and including one part per thousand of tetraethyl lead, enabled the 'sprint' to develop 2,530 hp. Installed in S.6B S.1595 and flown by George Stainforth once again, the record was duly established on 29 September 1931, at an average speed of 408·8 mph (657·90 km/h). Responsible for concocting the strange fuel mixtures used by these high-powered engines was F. Rodwell Banks (later Air Commodore), of the Ethyl Export Corporation. Much of the credit for the astounding power output of the 'R' and 'sprint' engines is due to him.

Rolls-Royce had learnt a great deal in developing this engine which, via the Goshawk, led to the P.V.12 (P.V.: private venture) which was to earn its place in aviation history as the Merlin. For example, from experience they had gained with the test engines they had wrecked in trying to gain the maximum power output from the 'R', it became possible to arrive at a life expectation for highly stressed components. Unless it proved possible to develop those components to withstand even greater stress, it was found much cheaper to remove and replace them at regular intervals, rather than smash up a valuable engine.

But despite the wealth of knowledge that had been gained, it required another four years of hard work before the first Merlin I passed its bench test in December 1935.

By then R. J. Mitchell and Sydney Camm of the Hawker Aircraft company, had begun the design of the Spitfire and Hurricane respectively. In fact, Mitchell started the design of a high-speed monoplane fighter in 1932, and Air Vice-Marshal F. W. Long recalled how he and John Boothman had been shown the wooden mock-up of this aircraft during that year, asked by Mitchell to give their comments on the cockpit layout.

This evolved as the Supermarine Type 224, called unofficially the Spitfire, and which was powered by the Rolls-Royce Goshawk engine. Developed from the Kestrel, and using new techniques learned from the 'R' engine, the Goshawk had an evaporative cooling system. It was a system that was neither popular nor particularly successful, and only a limited number of Goshawk engines were built.

Only a single example of the Type 224 was built for testing by the Royal Air Force, but it was a direct ancestor of the prototype Spitfire K5054, first flown by Captain J. ('Mutt') Summers on 5 March 1936. This was to become developed into a brilliantly successful fighter aircraft. Sadly, R. J. Mitchell did not live to see this success, dying of tuberculosis on 11 June 1937 at the young age of 42.

Because it tells something of the man, rather than his achievements, a comment by 'Batchy' Atcherley is superior to most of Mitchell's obituaries:

'. . . He was a man with an alert and inquisitive mind, and in spite of his very considerable attainments in the world of aircraft design he was always ready to crack a joke or take on [in conversation] anyone on his own wavelength. He was always keen to listen to pilot's opinions and never pressed his own views against theirs . . . He set his sights deliberately high, for he had little use for "second-bests". Yet he was the most unpompous man I ever met.'

In the final analysis, should Britain have won the Trophy at all? In so doing had she displayed an unsportsmanlike attitude? From an American point of view, quite definitely yes. When faced with a 1931 kind of situation at Baltimore, in 1924, the Americans had postponed the contest for twelve months to allow the contenders to prepare.

From the Italian point of view it could not be quite so definitely yes. For example, they in 1922 had advanced the date of the contest without prior consultation with anyone, an action quite outside the scope of the regulations. But, as events were to prove, they felt they had been deprived of the opportunity of participating in a contest in which an outstanding combination of aircraft and engine should have ensured that, in that confrontation at any rate, the Trophy would have been taken home to stand in the Aéro-Club d'Italia for at least two years—perhaps much longer.

From the British point of view, there was really no alternative to proceeding with the contest in 1931. The money with which to defend the Trophy had been donated by Lady Houston: it could not be expected that any private individual would put up a similar sum again. The preparations had been made and with the request for postponement coming only nine days before the day of the contest it was impossible to put back the clock.

After the contest, Italy continued with development of the Macchi MC.72, or it would perhaps be more accurate to say with the engine to power it. Rodwell Banks was invited by General Crocco to visit the Fiat works, and once there he was soon able to resolve their problems. Bench testing of the AS.6 had always proved satisfactory, but when the engine was installed in the aircraft the mixture was invariably excessively weak. The nett result was violent backfiring, and with an induction system that was almost 7 ft (2·13 m) long, this could prove both explosive and destructive.

Banks showed the Fiat engineers how Rolls-Royce had simulated ram air conditions across the engine intake, allowing accurate setting of the carburation system under the equivalent of flight conditions. This, together with his specialised knowledge of exotic fuel mixtures enabled Fiats to develop the AS.6 to provide a reliable power output of 3,100 hp at 3,300 rpm, the reduction gearing bringing the contra-rotating propeller shaft speed down to 1,980 rpm.

On 10 April 1933, flying the Macchi MC.72 at Lake Garda, Francesco Agello set a new world speed record of 423·82 mph (682·07 km/h). Eighteen months later Agello and the MC.72 established another world speed record of 440·68 mph (709·20 km/h), a record to remain unbeaten until mid-1939. Then Germany raised the figure twice, first by the Heinkel He 112 and finally with the Messerschmitt Me 109, but both of these aircraft were landplanes. Italy's world speed record for seaplanes remained unbeaten until 1961.

History has some strange quirks. Despite the proven capability of the Italian aircraft industry to build high-speed aircraft powered by in-line liquid-cooled engines, the Italian Air Ministry ruled in 1933 that the industry was to concentrate on the development of radial air-cooled power plants for use in military aircraft. It was to Germany they had to turn in 1940 when they needed urgently high-powered in-line engines.

The Rolls-Royce Merlin, on the other hand, went from strength to strength, powering a legion of different and world-beating aircraft, and it is necessary to mention only the British Avro Lancaster, de Havilland Mosquito, Hawker Hurricane, Supermarine Spitfire and the American P-51 Mustang, which did so much to help bring Allied victory in the European theatre of operations in the second World War.

It had all begun so simply and differently—the wish of Jacques Schneider to advance long-range maritime aviation. In this respect his aim was not realised directly, but the aviation industry of the world and free people everywhere must forever owe much to the little man who dared to dream. What advanced dreams too, of intercontinental aviation at a time when even a cross-Channel flight was a great adventure.

This is one thing that we 'caught' and kept when we gained the Schneider Trophy: a permanent memorial to a man of courage and vision.

Appendix: Schneider Trophy results

FIRST CONTEST: 16 April 1913, at Monaco. 28 laps each of 10 km : 280 km : 173·98 miles : 151·09 nm

Race number	Aircraft	Engine	Pilot	Representing	Remarks
—	Borel Monaco	160 hp Gnome	Géorges Chemet	France	Eliminated in trials
—	Breguet	110/115 hp Salmson/ Canton-Unné	Henri Brégi	France	Eliminated in trials
—	Breguet	200 hp Salmson/ Canton-Unné	René Moineau	France	Eliminated in trials
19	Deperdussin	160 hp Gnome	Maurice Prévost	France	1st 45·75 mph (73·63 km/h)
2	Morane-Saulnier	80 hp Gnome	Roland Garros	France	2nd 30·42 mph (48·96 km/h)
6	Nieuport	100 hp Gnome	Dr Gabriel Espanet	France	Retired lap 8
5	Nieuport	160 hp Gnome	Charles Weymann	USA	Retired lap 25

SECOND CONTEST: 20 April 1914, at Monaco. 28 laps each of 10 km : 280 km : 173·98 miles : 151·09 nm

Race number	Aircraft	Engine	Pilot	Representing	Remarks
—	Aviatik Arrow	150 hp Benz	Victor Stoeffler	Germany	Crashed during trials
—	Deperdussin	160 hp? Gnome	M. Janoir	France	Third team reserve
—	Deperdussin	160 hp Gnome	M. Parmelin	Switzerland	Reserve
—	Deperdussin	160 hp? Gnome	Maurice Prevost	France	Retired with engine failure
—	Deperdussin	160 hp Gnome	William Thaw	USA	Withdrew after seeing Pixton's times
7	F.B.A. flying-boat	100 hp Gnome Mono	Ernest Burri	Switzerland	2nd 51·00 mph (82·08 km/h)
—	Morane-Saulnier	80 hp Gnome	Lord Carbery	Britain	Crashed during trials. Completed 2 laps in Deperdussin borrowed from Janoir
—	Morane-Saulnier	160 hp Gnome	Raymond Garros	France	Withdrew, broken propeller
5	Nieuport	160 hp Gnome	Dr Gabriel Espanet	France	Retired 16th lap
6	Nieuport	160 hp Gnome	Pierre Levasseur	France	Retired 17th lap. Made second attempt in borrowed Nieuport, retired after 9 laps
1	Nieuport	160 hp Le Rhone	Charles Weymann	USA	Withdrew after seeing Pixton's times
3	Sopwith Schneider	100 hp Gnome Mono	C. Howard Pixton	Britain	1st 86·78 mph (139·66 km/h)

THIRD CONTEST: 10 September 1919, at Bournemouth. 10 laps each of 29 nautical miles : 230·30 miles : 370·63 km

Race number	Aircraft	Engine	Pilot	Representing	Remarks
—	Avro 539A	240 hp Siddeley Puma	Captain H. A. Hamersley	Britain	Team reserve
1	Fairey IIIA	450 hp Napier Lion	Lieutenant-Colonel Vincent Nicholl	Britain	Retired 1st lap
2	Nieuport 29-C-1	300 hp Hispano Suiza	Lieutenant Jean Casale	France	Did not start
7	Savoia S.13	250 hp Isotta-Fraschini	Sergeant Guido Janello	Italy	Completed 11 laps, subsequently ruled to be incorrect laps
3	Sopwith Schneider	450 hp Cosmos Jupiter	Harry Hawker	Britain	Retired 1st lap
6	SPAD-Herbémont	340 hp Hispano-Suiza	Sadi Lecointe	France	Did not start
5	Supermarine Sea Lion	450 hp Napier Lion	Basil D. Hobbs	Britain	Retired 1st lap

FOURTH CONTEST: 21 September 1920, at Venice   10 laps each of 37·117 km : 230·63 miles : 200·28 nm

Race number	Aircraft	Engine	Pilot	Representing	Remarks
—	Nieuport-Macchi M.12	550 hp Ansaldo	Giovanni de Briganti	Italy	Withdrawn
—	Nieuport-Macchi M.19	680 hp Fiat A14	Arturo Zanetti	Italy	Withdrawn
7	Savoia S.12	550 hp Ansaldo	Lieutenant Luigi Bologna	Italy	Fly-over: 107·22 mph (172·55 km/h)
—	Savoia S.19	550 hp Ansaldo	Guido Janello	Italy	Withdrawn

FIFTH CONTEST: 7 August 1921 at Venice. 16 laps each of 24·6 km : 393·6 km : 244·57 miles : 212·39 nm

Race number	Aircraft	Engine	Pilot	Representing	Remarks
1	Macchi M.7	250 hp Isotta-Fraschini	Giovanni de Briganti	Italy	1st 117·90 mph (189·74 km/h)
14	Macchi M.7	250 hp Isotta-Fraschini	Piero Corgnolino	Italy	Retired on last lap
4	Macchi M.19	680 hp Fiat A14	Arturo Zanetti	Italy	Retired
5	Nieuport-Delage	300 hp Hispano-Suiza	Sadi Lecointe	France	Damaged during trials

SIXTH CONTEST: 12 August 1922, at Naples. 13 laps each of 28·5 km : 370·5 km : 230·22 miles : 199·93 nm

Race number	Aircraft	Engine	Pilot	Representing	Remarks
—	C.A.M.S.36	300 hp Hispano-Suiza	V. Roman	France	Withdrawn before trials
—	C.A.M.S.36	300 hp Hispano-Suiza	Captain Teste	France	Withdrawn before trials
10	Macchi M.7	260 hp Isotta-Fraschini	Piero Corgnolino	Italy	4th 123·7 mph (199·07 km/h)
9	Macchi M.17	260 hp Isotta-Fraschini	Arturo Zanetti	Italy	3rd 139·75 mph (224·9 km/h)
8	Savoia S.51	300 hp Hispano-Suiza	Alessandro Passaleva	Italy	2nd 143·20 mph (230·46 km/h)
14	Supermarine Sea Lion II	450 hp Napier Lion	Henri Biard	Britain	1st 145·7 mph (234·48 km/h)

SEVENTH CONTEST: 28 September 1923, at Cowes. 5 laps each of 37·2 nm : 186 nm : 214·18 miles : 344·69 km

Race number	Aircraft	Engine	Pilot	Representing	Remarks
6	Blackburn Pellet	450 hp Napier Lion	R. W. Kenworthy	Britain	Crashed during trials
10	C.A.M.S.36*bis*	360 hp Hispano-Suiza	Lieutenant Pelletier d'Oisy	France	Damaged in collision, withdrawn
9	C.A.M.S.38	360 hp Hispano-Suiza	Lieutenant de Vaisseau Hurel	France	Retired during 2nd lap
3	Curtiss CR-3	465 hp Curtiss D-12	Lieutenant Rutledge Irvine	USA	2nd 173·46 mph (279·16 km/h)
4	Curtiss CR-3	465 hp Curtiss D-12	Lieutenant David Rittenhouse	USA	1st 177·38 mph (285·46 km/h)
11	Latham L.1	2 × 400 hp Lorraine-Dietrich	J. Duhamel	France	Engine failure, withdrawn
5	Naval Aircraft Factory TR-3A	265 hp Wright	Lieutenant Frank Wead	USA	Withdrawn
7	Supermarine Sea Lion III	550 hp Napier Lion	Henri Biard	Britain	3rd 157·17 mph (252·94 km/h)
—	Wright NW-2	700 hp Wright T-3	Lieutenant A. W. Gorton	USA	Crashed before trials

EIGHTH CONTEST: 26 October 1925, at Baltimore. 7 laps each of 50 km : 217·48 miles : 188·86 nm

Race number	Aircraft	Engine	Pilot	Representing	Remarks
2	Curtiss R3C-2	600 hp Curtiss V-1400	Lieutenant G. T. Cuddihy	USA	Retired during last lap
3	Curtiss R3C-2	600 hp Curtiss V-1400	Lieutenant J. H. Doolittle	USA	1st 232·57 mph (374·28 km/h)
1	Curtiss R3C-2	600 hp Curtiss V-1400	Lieutenant R. A. Ofstie	USA	Retired during 6th lap
5	Gloster III	700 hp Napier Lion	Hubert Broad	Britain	2nd 199·17 mph (320·53 km/h)
4*	Gloster III	700 hp Napier Lion	H. J. L. Hinkler	Britain	Crashed during trials
7	Macchi M.33	435 hp Curtiss D-12	Giovanni de Briganti	Italy	3rd 168·44 mph (271·08 km/h)
8	Macchi M.33	435 hp Curtiss D-12	Riccardo Morselli	Italy	Withdrawn
4	Supermarine S.4	700 hp Napier Lion	Henri Biard	Britain	Crashed during trials

*Bert Hinkler's Gloster III was given the race number 4 after Biard's crash.

NINTH CONTEST: 13 November 1926, at Hampton Roads. 7 laps of 50 km each : 217·48 miles : 188·86 nm

Race number	Aircraft	Engine	Pilot	Representing	Remarks
2	Curtiss F6C-1 Hawk	440 hp Curtiss D-12	Lieutenant W. G. Tomlinson	USA	4th 136·95 mph (220·39 km/h)
6	Curtiss R3C-2	600 hp Curtiss V-1400	Lieutenant F. C. Schilt	USA	2nd 231·36 mph (372·34 km/h)
2*	Curtiss R3C-3	700 hp Packard 1A-V-1500	Lieutenant W. G. Tomlinson	USA	Crashed during trials
4	Curtiss R3C-4	708 hp Curtiss V-1550	Lieutenant G. T. Cuddihy	USA	Retired during last lap
1	Macchi M.39	882 hp Fiat AS.2	Lieutenant Adriano Bacula	Italy	3rd 218·01 mph (350·85 km/h)
5	Macchi M.39	882 hp Fiat AS.2	Major Mario de Bernardi	Italy	1st 246·50 mph (396·70 km/h)
3	Macchi M.39	882 hp Fiat AS.2	Captain Arturo Ferrarin	Italy	Retired during 4th lap

*Race number 2 and Lieutenant Tomlinson were transferred to the Curtiss F6C-1 Hawk after the crash of the Curtiss R3C-3.

TENTH CONTEST: 26 September 1927, at Venice. 7 laps each of 50 km : 217·48 miles : 188·86 nm

Race number	Aircraft	Engine	Pilot	Representing	Remarks
1	Gloster IVB	875 hp geared Napier Lion VIIB	Flight-Lieutenant S. M. Kinkead	Britain	Retired during 6th lap
2	Macchi M.52	1000 hp Fiat AS.3	Major Mario de Bernardi	Italy	Retired during 2nd lap
5	Macchi M.52	882 hp Fiat AS.2	Captain Federico Guazetti	Italy	Retired during 6th lap
7	Macchi M.52	1000 hp Fiat AS.3	Captain Arturo Ferrarin	Italy	Retired during 1st lap
—	Short/Bristow Crusader	650 hp Bristol Mercury	Flight-Officer H. M. Schofield	Britain	Crashed before trials
4	Supermarine S.5	900 hp Napier Lion VIIA	Flight-Lieutenant S. N. Webster	Britain	1st 281·66 mph (453·28 km/h)
6	Supermarine S.5	875 hp geared Napier Lion VIIB	Flight-Lieutenant O. E. Worsley	Britain	2nd 273·01 mph (439·36 km/h)

ELEVENTH CONTEST: 7 September 1929, at Calshot. 7 laps each of 50 km : 217·48 miles : 188·86 nm

Race number	Aircraft	Engine	Pilot	Representing	Remarks
4	Macchi M.52R	1000 hp Fiat AS.3	Warrant-Officer T. Dal Molin	Italy	2nd 284·20 mph (457·37 km/h)
7	Macchi M.67	1400 hp Isotta-Fraschini	Lieutenant Remo Cadringher	Italy	Retired during 2nd lap
10	Macchi M.67	1400 hp Isotta-Fraschini	Lieutenant Giovanni Monti	Italy	Retired during 2nd lap
5	Supermarine S.5	875 hp geared Napier Lion VIIB	Flight-Lieutenant D'Arcy A. Greig	Britain	3rd 282·11 mph (454·01 km/h)
8	Supermarine S.6	1900 hp Rolls-Royce 'R'	Flight-Officer R. L. R. Atcherley	Britain	Disqualified for cutting a pylon
2	Supermarine S.6	1900 hp Rolls-Royce 'R'	Flight-Officer H. R. Waghorn	Britain	1st 328·63 mph (528·87 km/h)

FINAL CONTEST: 13 September 1931, at Calshot. 7 laps each of 50 km : 217·48 miles : 188·86 nm

Race number	Aircraft	Engine	Pilot	Representing	Remarks
1	Supermarine S.6B	2350 hp Rolls-Royce 'R'	Flight-Lieutenant J. N. Boothman	Britain	Fly-over: 340·08 mph (547·305 km/h)
—	Supermarine S.6B	2350 hp Rolls-Royce 'R'	Flight-Lieutenant F. W. Long	Britain	1st reserve
—	Supermarine S.6A	1900 hp Rolls-Royce 'R'	Flight-Officer L. S. Snaith	Britain	2nd reserve

Index

C

G

W

Z

Guido Fuga • Lele Vianello

Marco Polo

TESTIMONIES OF AN EXTRAORDINARY JOURNEY

Translation David Graham

lineadacqua

Seconda edizione

lineadacqua Edizioni Eventi srl
San Marco 3717/d
30124 Venezia

Tel/fax 0415224030
info@lineadacqua.it
www.lineadacquaedizioni.it

Project Manager Federcio Acerboni e Luca Zentilini
Coordinamento editoriale Franca Brancovich e Silvia Troni

VES QUE VINC · VEN QUE VOY · VIENI CHE VADO · 你来我往

BANCO SAN MARCO
GRUPPO BANCO POPOLARE DI VERONA E NOVARA

VENETIA STVDIVM

PMV
Società del Patrimonio per la Mobilità Veneziana

Contents

'travellers ne'er lie,
though fools at home comdemn'em.'

William Shakespeare The tempest

It is less than 70 years since Byzantium was sacked by armed pilgrims. They were led cynically but shrewdly by old Doge Enrico Dandolo who, ignoring the aim of liberating the Holy Sepulchre, concentrated on a strategic, more lucrative prize. So I arrived in Venice from the valleys of

Bergamo at a time of plenty. The sack of the Eastern Empire had filled the state coffers, and sacred relics, marbles and magnificent sculptures had been brought as spoils of war to embellish the city. The magnificent horses above the entrance to St Mark's basilica are the most triumphant symbol of this. I liked the atmosphere in this strange place, compared to the narrow-mindedness where I'm from, without any walls around you but protected by a magnificent lagoon. Here you came into contact with the world and, if you had the will and the ideas, you could do profitable business. This is how in about ten years I found myself running a small company importing

precious stones, which made me wealthy and allowed me to buy into the Venetian nobility. This aspect seemed more modern and realistic to me, too: not aristocrats of imperial or papal origin, but intelligent men who had made it on their own, who had taken risks and built up solid fortunes. They are the repositories of the state's power, and here there is one rule in force: you're Venetian first, then Christian. This idyllic picture has now been broken by the taking of Constantinople in 1261 by Michael Paleologus, supported by the Greeks and, worse still, the Genoese, historic rivals in the economic expansionism of the Serenissima. So what had been a Venetian mercantile stronghold is now occupied by Genoa, forcing the Venetian Republic to look for new trade routes. This was why my Polo friends, jewel traders who had had a warehouse in Constantinople, left that city, which no longer offered them security, for Sougdeia on the northern shores of the Black Sea. Here they came into contact with the Tartar world, which led to them embarking on an extremely long journey toward the remote lands of Gog and Magog.

Anno Domini 1271. It's just past Easter and we can finally weigh anchor. This brisk northerly wind will push the 'muda' down the Dalmatian coasts and beyond the Greek ones to our destination: the port of Lajazzo. A 'muda' (for non-Venetians) consists of 30 or more galleys and ships fitted out for trading. There are also some navy galleys that will act as escort to protect us from attacks by the pirates that infest these waters and by

enemies of our Republic. My name is Andrea Zen and I am the captain of a big galley equipped with oars and sails. As well as the sailors, the oarsmen and the goods, there are numerous merchants on board and some soldiers on their way to relieve others in distant eastern posts where the flag of St Mark flies. We have also taken on board a large number of pilgrims on their way to the Holy Land, but three of the passengers deserve a special mention: Matteo and Nicolò Polo and the 17 year-old son of the latter, Marco. I already know the young man, having seen him numerous times on the quays at Zattere and Rialto, stopping sailors and merchants just back, me included, to ask for news about his father and uncle, who had left years before for Tartary. I remember him listening with fascination to the stories of those people returning from remote places. His father and uncle had made a long journey lasting a good eight years, going as far as Bukhara and even further, reaching Cathay, the immense land of the Great Khan. It's said in Venice that they came back rich from this trip and with an embassy from the great King of the Mongols to the Pope. Now they are on board this ship to go back to those far-off lands, as they had promised the Great Khan. Just a moment! I hear a trumpet blast! It's time to weigh anchor, slip the moorings and man the oars!

I bear the name of Erasmus Ohller of Mainz, a notable by profession. I am heading to the Holy Land to fulfil a vow. I had decided to travel as far as Bari by land, but was advised not to as the roads are not very safe. I have already been robbed – by bandits when crossing the Alps – and had to pay a large sum of money to get away. Then I heard that sea voyages to the holy places are a proper organised business in Venice. The pilgrim just has to pay and is assured of the Republic's protection for the whole trip. On the ship I got to know young Polo; I studied Latin and can make myself understood. Here on board the food leaves a lot to be desired and the water is foul-smelling. During the first days of sailing I suffered from sea-sickness to the point of feeling much debilitated, and the boy did all he could to assist me. He is a genuinely kind person and is thirsty for knowledge. He wanted to know about the customs and ways of the people in my parts. He is travelling with his father and uncle to lands where the Latin people have never been seen. God bless him. When I am in Jerusalem I will pray for him.

My name is Theobald Visconti, or rather I should say Gregory X, as this is the name I have chosen now that I have been elected Pope. On 1 September in this year of our Lord, the provost Cardinals gathered in Viterbo decided to elect me after the Holy See had been vacant for more than three years. Before setting off for Brindisi and going to Rome, I have to put things in order here in the east. One of the many things is to send an answer to the great sovereign of the Mongols, Kublai Khan. To do so I have had the Polo brothers recalled from Lajazzo. They are getting ready to return to those far-off lands as my ambassadors with a holy relic: an ampoule of the oil that burned in the sepulchre of our Lord Jesus Christ. This is to meet a request made to me personally by the Khan, as his wife, a Nestorian Christian, considers this oil a powerful talisman. Along with other gifts and my special blessing, I will send them some letters with proposals for peace and an alliance between Tartars and Latins against our common enemy: Muslim expansion. Unfortunately I cannot grant his request of a hundred wise men to spread the Christian message in that immense empire; I am sure that I wouldn't find even a tenth of that number in these parts and it would take some years to put them together even searching all over the Latin world. But two Dominican envoys will leave with the Venetian brothers: Brother Nicolò da Vicenza and Brother Guglielmo da Tripoli, great authorities on theology and Muslim doctrine. I have invested them with unlimited powers; they may ordain priests and consecrate bishops. God bless this long and difficult journey.

GENOA
VENICE
ROME
CURZOLA
CONSTANTINOPLE
SOUGDEIA
TRABZON
LAJAZZO
TABRIZ
ACRE
BAGHDAD
JERUSALEM
YEZD
MASHAD
HERAD
KERMAN
HORMUZ
AFRICA
ARABIA
ARABIAN SEA
THE INDIAN OCEAN

their trust in my experience. This is not a good time. There is a war on and we have to make a big detour north, going through Lesser and Greater Armenia and beyond; hoping not to run into any bands of Mamelukes, the fierce, ruthless horsemen of Turkish-Circassian origin who charge around plundering these regions. Not long ago they burned the city of Sys and killed hundreds of people. We will try to avoid them. Yesterday two Venetian merchants arrived with a fine looking young man, who I think is the son of one of them. They asked me if they could join us – they want to reach the port of Hormuz. They also seemed to have an interest in gemstone trading so I gave them the name of a trader in Kerman, a relative of my wife. They chose three good horses and some mules for the journey. I had recommended camels, but they said that the horse is faster if they need to flee. Sensible answer. Now I have to check the water-bags...

It seems as if today will never end. The dust gets in everywhere and I am forced to inhale it, despite the turban that leaves only my now reddened eyes uncovered. I advised the young man by the name of Marco riding beside me to cover himself in the same way. He and his father and uncle are heading for far-off Hormuz. For many years I have been trading fabrics and carpets woven in these areas, which many say are among the most beautiful in the world. Through my work I have had dealings with Latin people and have learnt to understand their language, so to break the monotony we started to talk. We talk about everything. He is eager for knowledge and asks me about the customs and traditions of my people. In the evening when we are tired and gather round the fire, I see this young man listening enraptured to the tales of the old, widely-travelled caravan guides who have been to distant places. I can't express his amazement when, some days ago, the caravan went across a vast plain and Mount Ararat rose up before us in all its majestic isolation. As the book of books says, it is the mountain where the Ark made by the patriarch Noah rested after 150 days when the waters of the flood finally abated. It now remains buried among its perennial snow. The mountain is sacred and no man can reach its peak alive. Malevolent spirits lurk there and anyone daring to go beyond the furthest borderline is taken by these demons and thrown into a deep abyss. The land here is called Georgia. The King, like his subjects, is Christian, but subject to the Tartars, a proud and ferocious people from the distant steppes of the east.

Their princes, known as khans, govern these provinces, with rich pasturelands for their numerous livestock. Our caravan has made the most of them, too, to rest the animals. We are camping in this valley and I have decided to show the young Latin the surrounding area, which is really beautiful with its inaccessible mountains and narrow passes that even stopped the great Alexander. He built a fortress there called the 'Gate of Iron' to keep out the barbarians from the east. There are numerous castles and villages around here that I know well, having, as I said, traded the silk and gold cloth called 'muslin' in this area. The local people are very industrious and friendly and have invited us to a falcon hunt, a common practice here. They use beautiful birds that are as swift as an arrow. Last night I saw young Marco get a real fright when soaring flames suddenly leapt from the plain and lit up the sky like daytime. My camp neighbours, also frightened, said they were the blades of the sword of the Archangel Gabriel, but that's not true. There is an oil here that gushes up from underground and is used for fire and light. It is also used to tan the hides of animals. People come from far away to get it, but there are also some heathens who worship this fire. In three days the caravan will reach Tabriz, 'the city that cures fever', as it is called, and where all the caravans from the most remote parts converge. Here I will be able to sell my carpets and, God willing, do some good business. I have already said goodbye to my young travelling companion as the caravan is carrying on to Hormuz.

I've been riding these lands for weeks, but this is my job: to be on the lookout and inform my superiors of all that happens in this border area. That means days and days of complete solitude in these endless lands. This morning I caught three rabbits, so will finally be able to eat some fresh meat. In the last few days I have fed only on the blood of my horse, drinking it directly from a vein I opened up in its neck with my knife. In this way we Mongols can last for more than ten days without cooking food. Our diet is usually varied and unrestricted. I have eaten horse, wolf, fox, cat, rat and lice. In my village, last winter, I ate the placenta of my father's mare after it had foaled. It had been days since I'd seen another human being, but this afternoon a cloud of dust suddenly appeared on the horizon. I hid among the grass and waited. After a while I began to make out the shape of a group of merchants with their pack animals. It's my job to find out where they're going, so I mounted my horse and galloped in their direction, taking my bow out of the quiver – you never know. But these people seemed to wait calmly for my arrival, which seemed unusual. After all, I'm a Mongol warrior and we're famous for being a bloodthirsty people. I was extremely surprised when the one that seemed to be their leader greeted me in my own language, showing me the

big golden tablet with the seal of my heavenly Lord. It is called a 'paiza' and is a safeguard for all territory under the sovereignty of the Great Khan, guaranteeing protection, respect, hospitality and assistance to he who carries it, on pain of death. I dismounted and prostrated myself face down on the ground. The same man then firmly ordered me to get up, asking me for information on the road they have to take and whether it is safe. I explained to them that the 'pax mongola' rules throughout the empire and a naked virgin with a golden plate on her head could cross it unharmed. They laughed and seemed reassured. They are courteous people and offered me some food. I shared my rabbits with them.

My name is Battista di Chiavari and I have been living in the city of Tabriz for years. Only the Lord knows whether or not I will ever see Genoa again. We Genoese have extended our trading area to these regions by bringing our ships from the Black Sea to the Caspian, sailing up the Don, then pushing on overland for many leagues beyond the River Volga. An extraordinary venture but a very profitable one for our traders. Along with the goods, the last caravan from Lajazzo brought with it three Venetians, also merchants. I went to meet them immediately. Our cities are at war with each other every now and then, but political grudges and disputes mean nothing in these remote parts. You do business and that's all.

What's more, they bring fresh news. They told me that Christianity finally has a new Pope, praise the Lord. Their name is Polo and I remember having dealings with one of their relatives in far-off Sougdeia some years ago. I invited them to my home and after dinner we talked about goods and prices, but I also had to satisfy the curiosity of the youngest one, who fired

questions at me about the city of Baghdad, which he considers legendary, but unfortunately won't be able to see. During their travels, the caravan guides had amused themselves by describing it as a fabulous city with a thousand minarets, where the domes of the palaces are covered with gold; inhabited by cruel caliphs and powerful, malevolent wizards, cheated by cunning thieves who make off with beautiful, sensual women on flying carpets... The naive boy believed all these tales and I had to let him down. Baghdad is certainly a fine city where good business can be done, but it is not like he was told. I contented him by telling a couple of stories: the first about Caliph Al-Musta'Sim and his greed, and how he paid for that venal sin. This took place around 1250, when Baghdad was invaded by a horde of Tartar warriors under the command of Prince Hulagu. After they had overwhelmed the army and taken the Caliph prisoner, the Mongols entered the now undefended city and massacred more than 70,000 people. The slaughter stopped only after 40 days. When Hulagu found out about the Caliph's immeasurable wealth, he asked why he hadn't used those enormous deposits of gold and precious stones to pay an army of mercenaries to defend the city and its people. When he found out that it was only because of his greed, he had him locked up in a tower with all his treasure, forcing him to survive on that. It is said that he died a week later. The second is more recent, and is remembered as 'The Miracle of the Mountain'. It tells of the Caliph of Baghdad, who had a great hatred for all Christians. One day, having read a passage from the Gospel of St Mathew, where it says that a Christian equal to a mustard seed would be able to move a mountain, he threatened to kill the entire Christian community if it could not carry out such a thing within ten days. Imagine the frenzied search for a holy person able to perform this miracle and thereby save thousands of innocent people from certain death! The time passed relentlessly and the search gave no results. All hope seemed lost, when the Angel of the Lord appeared to the Bishop, pointing out a shoemaker as the appointed person. He was an honest, decent man at the point of having

an eye taken out for having given in to temptation, avidly admiring the legs of a beautiful client of his. But he refused the entreaties of the people, until convinced by their constant pleading. He was taken to a plain at the foot of the mountain and placed in front of a cross. The old man started to pray and the mountain began to crumble and change. The Caliph and his dignitaries were so struck by the event that they converted. When the Sultan died they found a cross around his neck. This last tale must have made an impression on young Marco, as he didn't utter another word, remaining quiet and thoughtful all evening. Perhaps because it is such a nice story. Tomorrow they resume their travels and I am sorry. I gave them a box of salted sturgeon's roe...

We have finally arrived in Saveh. It is a beautiful evening. The doors of the harem will stay closed till dawn, the fires have been lit and the animals given their ration of hay. Now we can sit around the fire. Sometimes there is someone in the caravan who can play some instrument; it's nice then to be able to lie back after so much walking and listen to some music or a song about pretty girls awaiting our return. Today I was paid to accompany a young Venetian beyond the hill to the east where the Three Wise Men are buried in a big mausoleum. More than a thousand years ago they made a long journey to pay tribute to a great prophet, whose birth had been announced by mysterious signs in the firmament. Their travels had been guided by a star that led them to the cave where the baby lay. Each of the three offered a symbolic gift: gold to find out whether he was an earthly king, incense to find out whether he was divine and myrrh to find out whether he was eternal. The boy's mother reciprocated with a simple wooden box. The Wise Men, whose names were Caspar, Melchior and Balthasar, left again, full of curiosity about the contents of the box. After a long journey to these environs, they decided to open it and found only a small stone. Disappointed and not understanding the meaning of the gift, they threw it into a well. A thick, black oil immediately began to gush forth and a flash of lightning ignited it. After this portent, the three regretted having doubted the baby prophet. To atone for their error they built a temple where fire is considered sacred and is still today guarded and worshipped. When they died they were buried together in a beautiful tomb. It is said that their bodies remain intact and they seem to be sleeping. No one has ever been able to explain the meaning of that gift.

BLACK SEA
TRABZON
ERZURUM
LAJAZZO
CYPRUS
ACRE
JERUSALEM
BAGHDAD
AFRICA

CASPIAN SEA
MASHAD
BRIZ
ALAMUTH
KORASHAN
SAVA
YAZD
KERMAN
HORMUZ
PERSIAN
GULF

My name is Hasan and I live in Kerman with my wife, who was born here. Our parents betrothed us when we were still children to strengthen their business ties. I've got a small jewellery shop in the old part of the city. I moved here from Badakshan where my parents deal in stones from that region: balas' and spinels as beautiful as rubies, and the finest lapis lazuli in the world: stones of an extremely intense blue of unmatched purity. Perhaps you know that it is the preferred stone of our people, a cosmic image of the starry night. We hang it round the necks of our children and animals to ward off the evil eye. Not far from Kerman there is a mountain where turquoise is also mined, with the bluest through to the greenest shadings – another magnificent stone that protects against negative influences. The best come from the mountains of Nishapur, the city north of here where Omar Khayyam, my favourite poet, was born. The local craftsmen, serious, industrious people, are renowned for their skill at making damask swords, armour and all the gear for armed riders. A lot of the people in my tribe have blond hair. It is said in our parts that we are descendants of the peoples

who followed the great conqueror Ishkander. It was in the year 670 of the Hejira that I first met the three Venetian merchants, who came through the door of my little shop in Kerman. I said the first time because, after about 20 years, they came back after a long stay with the Great Khan. They came to see me and traded some lapis lazuli and turquoise for some sapphires and amethysts brought from India.

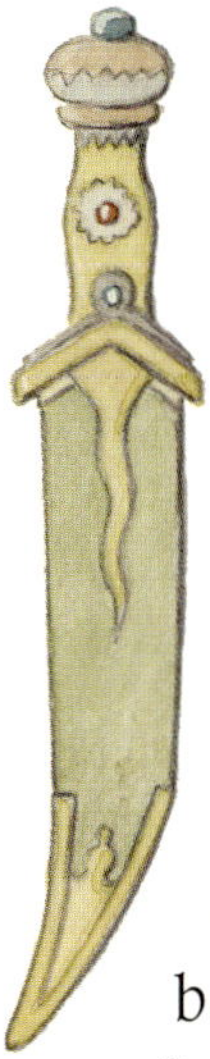

The one that had then just been an inquisitive boy, called Marco, had turned into a confident man with a fine beard and a good knowledge of the Persian language. He told me about their city suspended in the water and incredible stories of their epic journey; they showed me some tablets of gold that are a safeguard for the entire Mongol empire to prove the truth of their meeting with the Great Khan. Now I will tell you some of the things I learnt about their travels in our regions. They had already passed through here on their way to Hormuz in search of a ship to the east, when they ran into a band of the notorious Karaunas in the Rudbar region. They are half-breed bandits, of Tartar fathers and Indian mothers, led by a nephew of the Great Khan, a certain Nigudar, who has gathered an army of 10,000 men. They come down from a land to the north of India in search of goods and animals to plunder. They cast diabolical spells that alter the course of the day, turning day into night. In the midst of an ambush, in total

darkness, the three Venetians found refuge in a nearby castle, but a large number of their travelling companions were taken as slaves and some killed. Young Marco, still shocked by that terrible encounter, asked me about the Old Man of the Mountain and the Assassins, and I told him what I knew. It is a story that began about 200 years ago with Hasan- i Sabbah and his conversion to the Ishmaelite faith. A sect of the chosen had gathered around the Master and had built and occupied a series of virtually impregnable castles and fortresses in the Elburz mountain region below the Caspian Sea. The most famous was that of Alamuth, clinging to the almost inaccessible rocks. It concealed a fantastic version of Paradise in its secret gardens, where young girls sang to the tune of the oud amid perfumes and magnificent incense, while others danced and played the reed pipes between brooks and springs of milk, honey and wine. Here they raised young men from the age of 10 to 20, making them think they were in a paradise on Earth of the most seductive bliss. Then, when it was

necessary to crush some enemies, they were made to drink potions of opium and hashish (giving rise to the term 'assassins'). They were then taken outside and, when they awoke, were confounded by stark reality before the Master. He offered them the chance to go back to their golden refuge as soon as they had carried out the required deed. Trained in the perfidious art of ambushed killing, these young fanatics, scornful of death, left on their mission with the dream of going back to their secret paradise. The Assassins had earned the respect and dread of various kings, who feared those highly devoted killers and paid taxes to the Old Man to ensure their protection. It was not until the arrival of the Tartars from the east, not long ago, that an end was finally put to this fanatical faction. Hulaguh sought to completely wipe out the sect and seized the castles until the last fortress capitulated out of hunger after a three year siege. With the few survivors killed and Khwurshah, the last Great Master, captured, the story of the Old Man of the Mountain came to an end. Marco seemed satisfied with the story I had told him, and listened to and joined in the discussion on

what the adults told me about their visit to Hormuz, which had made them decide not to carry on by sea. Citizens of a sea power, they had found a big port with every kind of person and product, from the most precious spices to the finest fabrics, all in a seething human mass amid gigantic elephants shipped from India and other exotic animals. But the thing that had made them change their mind was the poor state of the ships. These were still built to ancient methods using wood lashed together with coconut fibre, had a single mast and seemed fairly unstable. They were then shocked by the region itself, with its torrid heat and fearful stories of funeral rites. So they decided to come back to our city and continue by land. Having left Kerman after our last meeting, I heard later, they headed north across a desert area where the only water is brackish, green and undrinkable, so they had to wait until they reached the caravanserai at the Gobiam oasis (Kubanan), ten days' walk away, for new supplies. After a long desert crossing they reached a province where

they saw the 'Solitary Tree', an enormous tree with a tall, thick trunk that towers over a vast, otherwise treeless plain. They continued after a long journey to Shibarghan, a city renowned for its sweet melons, and then to Balkh, the

ancient capital of Bactria, where the mythical Ishkander married Rossane... our distant forebears... who knows? The city, with its rivers and fertile lands, is now in decline after the massacre perpetrated by the Mongols who spared neither cat nor dog, but it remains an important trading centre because of its favoured position where the peoples of several different regions come together. They passed through Kunduz and reached the city of Talikhan, known for its salt mountain, which they say could suffice until the end of the world. They then travelled through areas where the people practise banditry and are even more dangerous because they are always drunk on wine, but without any nasty meetings. And so they came to Ishkashim, divided by a great river.

They then crossed the border of Badakshan, governed by a descendant of the Ishkander lineage, and found themselves in the region of my people, as I mentioned before. They stayed there for about a year and met my relatives who sold them lapis lazuli. They were struck by the big baggy pants worn by our women, which made them laugh. Their prolonged stay was partly due to a long illness that struck young Marco, who was cured when taken to the highest part of the mountains, famous for the salubrity of the air that drives all evils away. Making the most of their long stay, they visited some of the outlying regions, inhabited by dark-skinned people all adorned with earrings, pearls and precious stones. Seven days' travel took them to Kashmir, where the people live to the Buddhist rule. They are dark and thin and have an extraordinary knowledge of the magic arts. They said that the shamans there know how to weave very powerful spells, they can make the idols speak and know how to alter the course of time and other frightening, unimaginable sorcery. The country is temperate and the people eat rice and meat. They also practise fasting in keeping with their religion, which is observed in many monasteries. But going back to our region, apart from

the mines of precious stones and silver, lush pastures with big flocks of magnificent wild sheep, springs of purest water and lofty mountains, the most beautiful horses in the world are bred here. They are thought to be of royal descent, from the same stock as Bucephalus, Ishkander's mythical horse. The people, devoted to the Prophet, are proud, and the mcn are expert hunters: they are accomplished ar-chers and also use the magnificent falcons of the area. In short, you will have realised that I love my country, but the three Venetians also liked it well enough during their long stay. Strange that they didn't find a wife, like Ishkander did.

It was a windy morning, it must have been more or less 1273 according to the Gregorian calendar. I had just argued with my wife and was going back up to the bazaar for a piece of cloth to give her to make amends when I met these three honourable foreigners. They introduced themselves as Venetians, citizens of a rich, far-off land in the west. They said they were heading for the capital of Tartary to take important messages to our Prince. It turned out they had a letter from the head of the Roman Church and so I told them about our people, Nestorian Christians. I don't know how we came to be converted, but many of us here follow this rule and we also have several churches. They explained that, as far as the Prince of the Roman Church is concerned, we are heretics, but I don't understand the matter very well. It seems that there is no agreement on the figure of the mother of Christ, who for us gave birth to a man chosen by God, while for the others she gave birth to God; the thing leaves me a bit puzzled. Even though the Great Khan is sympathetic to our religion, possibly because his wife is Nestorian, here we are despised for our open ways, the practice of usury and our fondness for drinking. After we had exchanged these thoughts on our religion, they told me about their journey from Badakhshan to here in Kashgar. It had taken them more than two months' walking. In the Wakhan region they had come across the

extraordinary wild sheep with their enormous spiral-shaped horns. The local people there use them as furnishings and heap them up to mark the roads when the country is covered in snow. They had gone up to Pamir, the place that touches the sky, where the air is so rarefied that you get dizzy and even the colour of fire is different. There are no houses, but the pastures are lush and the animals fatten up in ten days. They then went down to the Bolor region amongst hunters dressed in skins; evil, unfriendly people. This road, I learnt later, had been taken by the two older merchants about ten years earlier. They had also passed through Kashgar, but evidently I did not meet them that time. They had taken a more northerly route and had also been to Samarkand, the big trading centre, so I told them a story that happened there and that I love: the miracle of the Nestorian church dedicated to St John the Baptist. Not all that long ago, the Lord of Samarkand, Ciagatai, brother of the Great Khan, became a Nestorian Christian and the jubilant community wanted to celebrate by building a new church. During construction work, they laid a fine stone belonging to the Muslim community as a base for the big central column supporting the structure.

This aroused discontent in the Saracen community, and when poor Ciagatai died some time later they wanted the return of that stone so tactlessly taken. The most influential members of the Nestorian community tried to re-purchase it, or to come to some kind of agreement so as not to have to remove the base of the column supporting the sacred temple, but they received a blunt refusal from the Muslim people, who were, furthermore, considerably more numerous. In order to appease them, the new Lord of Samarkand ordered the stone to be returned to its rightful owners, and the Christian community was plunged into deep sorrow, not knowing what to do. On the morning the big monolith was to be removed, the people who came to watch were astonished to see the big column suspended like an enormous stalactite four hands' breadth above the disputed stone. The miracle was greeted with joy by the faithful, but left the Muslims disconcerted. They recognised in that divine sign a grander answer to the mere squabbles that divided the two communities, so the stone remained in place.

I met these three Venetians, at least that's how they identified themselves, in the bazaar at Lop. They were looking for a guide to undertake a crossing of the insidious sands of the Gobi. Someone suggested they look for Yolltyi: that's my name and I'm a guide for the deserts of this region. They had come from Kashgar, having crossed the province of Khotan in eight days and taken another ten to go through the cities of Pem and Charchan, which are famous for

jasper and chalcedony, things I understood interested the travellers. We'll leave out the stories of their travels and come to the crossing of the desert regions that was to take them to Suchow. I advised against using horses and suggested using our magnificent camels for this section of the journey: extraordinary animals that are the best suited to facing the impervious desert. Here the problem isn't marauders, but water, food and the buran, the wind that is at times frightening, raising clouds of sand and stony dust, and making progress hellish. You need provisions for about 30 days, which is how long the shortest route takes, so I gathered together seven camels, three sheep, a dozen chickens, a fine rooster and two Tibetan mastiffs. It is a good idea to tie bells around the animals' necks to make them easier to find, because even a little wind is enough to frighten and disperse them. The journey proceeded without any unpleasant surprises and during the long night camps I got to know the travellers better. The two older men had already passed through our regions many years ago and seemed less surprised, but the younger one, Marco, was curious about every new thing and was not content with what he saw, he liked to hear stories. So I told him about the spirits that inhabit these arid regions.

If you don't keep close to the caravan, they appear in the likeness and with the voices of your companions and ask you to follow them, getting you irrevocably lost in the desolate wastelands where there are no points of reference. You can hear them call you with the sound of drums or visions of armies, that ominously force you to leave the road and so mark your end. I told him about the strange origin of the first King of the Uiguri, who was not born from a woman like us humble mortals,

but from a tree fungus. I told him about the amazing stone wool made with a mineral taken from the quarries of Chingitalas, with which they make fire resistant fabrics; indeed, if they get dirty, all you have to do is put them in the flames and they come out clean. Marco didn't believe me, but his relatives confirmed my story and told how, on their first trip, they had taken a similar cloth to the head of the western church, a gift from the Great Khan, to wrap around the shroud of the Christians' prophet. In accordance with my plans, we left the arid lands of the Gobi after about a month and came to Suchow, the end of my mission. But, despite saying our farewells, I continued to see them; or rather, I saw them again on my return with other travellers a few months later. I later learnt that they stayed for about a year, making excursions to the outlying regions where they saw the gigantic golden Buddhas.

Yochi is my name and I am not happy. I've got a beautiful wife who loves me and a small holding that allows me to live decently in a small town in the province of Komul. I live in a very peaceful, happy community that likes its festivals, when we entertain ourselves playing music and dancing; basically, everything would be

fine if it weren't for an old tradition my people are proud of. Here the guest is sacred in the real sense of the word. If someone knocks at your door, you have to pack your bags, leaving your house and your women, wife and daughters at the stranger's disposal. They cheerfully do their utmost to entertain the guest until he decides to leave your home and continue his journey. This is how, one day, three travellers from a far-off place that I've never heard of before ended up in my house, having asked for information from my daughter, who was in the garden next to the road. Invited to come into our house, they stayed for several days and so I had to leave my things and take refuge with a relative. The

young one called Marco was delighted with the welcome he was given by my pretty daughter. He didn't seem to believe what was happening to him, but the others also showed a kind of amazement at the situation. The embarrassing thing is that, a while ago, the Lord of the Tartars, Mangu Khan, asked our community to stop this ancient practice, which earns us the derision of our neighbours. After a certain time the people grew melancholy and saw ominous signs in their miserable crops, so sent a delegation to the Prince to obtain the right to go back to the old ways again, and so to offer our house and our beautiful women to every passing guest. Now everyone here is happy and content, but whenever I hear someone knock on the door I feel my stomach tighten and I suffer like a beaten dog.

CASPIAN SEA
SAMARKAND
BADAKSHA
MASHAD
HERAT
SHIBARGAN
BALKH
KORASHAN
KERMAN
DE
GULF OF HORMUZ
GUJARAT
CAMBAY
INDIA
ARABIAN SEA

KASGHAR
AMIR
KHOTAN
PEM
CHARCHAN
LOP
SUCHOW
KOMUL
THE GOBI DESERT
TIBET
BAY OF BENGAL

Many moons have now passed since the arrival here in Campigiù of these three westerners, who are waiting to be received by our Lord, King of all the Mongols. To tell the truth, the Great Khan has been informed of their presence in this province and he immediately sent a large escort, with orders to make their stay as comfortable as possible. But they will have to wait. No one can pass this border without a top level 'paiza'. The ones they have are not very influential. What's more, the young man has no credentials and the officials in these parts are very suspicious. These are difficult times. Our Lord Kublai is at the moment involved in serious political affairs, primarily the submission of the peoples of southern China. They do not want to be governed by us, who they consider barbarians. The whites will have to wait. During this long stay I have watched the young foreigner wander around the city streets with avid interest; today he finally decided to approach me. I am the leader of the military forces in

this area so have free access to all the territories and have decided to take him to see the big camp several days' trek away, beyond those hills where the sun rises. He was very excited at the idea and wanted to leave the same day. His father and uncle will stay here, presumably to do business. After crossing a short stretch of desert we entered Karakorum, 'the black city', with its endless fortifications. While we were riding I told Marco about the exploits of the courageous Yusugei Temugin, Lord of 'all those who live in felt tents', better known as Ghenghis Khan. He was the first Emperor of the Mongol people, the one who managed to unite a wild, primitive people and, by imposing order and discipline, lead them to world domination. It is said that when the new Chinese Emperor Chi'n demanded public submission from him, Ghenghis Khan looked sternly to the south and, after spitting on the ground, ordered the advance, setting off a war that lasted a good 23 years, until the ultimate defeat and flight of the arrogant Chi'n from

Beijing, the capital of the empire. Intrigued by this story, Marco wanted to know about the great battle fought by Ghenghis Khan against the Christian Priest King known in his parts as Prester John. Well, this King, who we call Unkahn, had tried to make us Mongols submit to his tyranny, taxing us and our animals, and separating us from each other in distant, desolate lands. It was the great Ghenghis who reunited us and freed us from the slavery imposed by this arrogant King. The Mongol people thus began to return from the most remote areas and place themselves under his orders. Finding himself at the head of so many courageous soldiers, Ghenghis Khan decided to leave those wild lands. With this enormous, determined army, he began subjugating towns and entire cities, taking over more and more new land. Once he had taken a region, he personally selected a governor for it, who ruled with such exemplary methods that the inhabitants had nothing to fear. As head of this increasingly powerful multitude of followers, he decided to send envoys to Unkhan charged with asking for his daughter as his wife. But the powerful sovereign

scornfully replied that he would never marry his daughter to a slave, threatening death to the envoys and to their master himself. Infuriated by this response, Ghenghis Khan assembled a powerful army and declared war. The two armies met on a vast plain. But before the clash, the Great Khan called his wizards and astrologers to learn the outcome of the imminent battle. They split a cane into two equal parts and wrote the names of the contenders on each. They then put them on the ground and began to study their ancient books of magic formulas. After a little while, the canes began to fight like snakes and the piece with the name of Ghenghis Khan ended up on top. Such was the enthusiasm for this sorcery that the Mongol army crushed the enemy like fury. Prester John was killed in the battle and Ghenghis Khan married his daughter. Six years after this epic event, fate decreed that the Lord of all the Mongols should be struck by an arrow during the siege of Ming-Heia fortress and subsequently die from the wound. All the Mongol people lamented the 'Prince of the Ocean', but in their own way: the coffin crossed the steppe escorted by a thousand horsemen cloaked in black, who had the horrendous task of killing every living being that crossed their path. He was buried on Mount Altai and, in keeping with Mongol custom, the tomb was trampled on by a thousand horses and no trace of it remains. Ah, there are the fires of the camp. I will send this inquisitive young man to a clan chief to act as his escort. I have to go back to Campigiù.

The sun was about to go to sleep behind the hills when the dogs started barking loudly and the children stopped playing and started looking at the small black dots on the horizon raising a big cloud of dust. It wasn't long before I recognised the standard of the leader of the Campigiù military forces. A tanned young man was at his side, dressed like us, but his features and the shape of his eyes betrayed his origins. He was one of those people from the lands of the setting sun. Without getting off his horse, the leader handed this young foreigner over to me, charging me with showing him our customs and ways. I am a reserved and quiet type, so was fairly uncomfortable. But this young man, called Marco, put me at ease. He is a friendly person and speaks our language, having been stopped in this part of the border for more than a year with his father and uncle, waiting to be received by our Lord of all the lands, Kublai. Our people place great importance on hospitality. The guest is sacred, but he shouldn't expect anything special; we are people of few words. Before admitting him to my yurt, whose entrance must always face south, I explained that anyone who enters has to leave their whip

and stick outside. Once inside, he has to sit on the left side, reserved for men. We have very ancient formalities that must be respected. After getting him to put on the *khadag*, the ritual scarf, I made him comfortable. When we were seated I noticed him looking inquisitively at the rope hanging from the ceiling. I explained that it is for grabbing to ensure that the wind, which blows very strong here, doesn't carry everything away. Our house of wood and felt has no roots and is made to be taken down and moved by yak, not the wind. My father and brothers are already seated. After the ritual offerings to our spirits, and sips of milk, biscuits and cheese, we will move on to the bowls of kumis, our liquor made from fermented milk.

We will soon end up talking about the weather and the recent harsh winter. Tomorrow I'll take him to see our herds of horses that are fast and strong and can run for an incredibly long time. The horse is the essential, indispensable part of the life of we Mongols. Our children know how to ride before they can walk, and ride with a confidence that is astounding to an outsider. In our calendar the year of the horse is considered a lucky year. The Prince of the Ocean, the great Ghenghis Khan, was born under this sign. I am watching our young guest and can see his eyes closing.
Perhaps he's tired, or it may be all the kumis my brother amuses himself by constantly pouring him.
Better let him sleep.

I am moving uncomfortably among the curtains and stuccoes of the summer pavilion of my Lord Kublai, King of Kings, Chief of Chiefs, Absolute Lord of all Mongols and Sovereign of China, 'Ruler of All' as his name says. Everything is ready, tomorrow is the twenty-eighth day of the August moon and the Great Khan will leave this palace of curtains to celebrate the ancient magic rite of the summer solstice. The ritual is as always organised by the shaman sorcerers. Kublai will sprinkle the milk of white mares on the ground and sky to protect all the things that belong to him. After the ceremony we will leave for the new capital, Ta-Tu. I have for many years had the onerous task of organising everything to perfection and it is not easy, believe me, to move the thousands of people that make up my Lord's retinue. His five wives will leave first, with their respective escorts, then the hundreds of concubines, then he with his utterly loyal Kasitan, his personal guard counting 12,000 warriors. And then all the others: princes of royal blood, vassals, great dignitaries, shamans, astrologers, the military classes, warriors, jesters and jugglers. Then there are the 5000 elephants and the same number of camels. Today my Lord wanted a last hunt to be organised before his departure. I had the big, open-roofed, tiger-skin lined cabin prepared and it will be transported on the backs of four elephants from where, stretched out on a bed of cushions, he will amuse himself watching his gyrfalcons hunting in the sky. He doesn't lie around out of laziness, but because of the gout from which he suffers terribly. Those know-all Chinese doctors attribute it to too much meat, but we are Mongols and have always eaten meat. It is our main food, and they can keep their bowls of rice and all the other things cooked in steam. Kublai was drunk again yesterday during the banquet, which worries me. I wouldn't want him to end up like Uncle Ogodei or his brother Hulagu, dead in the grip of a delirium. I am the only one who can prevent him overdoing it. He is fond of me and has kept me at his side since I was small, after my father died in battle saving his life. I have for some time also had the task of teaching court manners to the three foreigners from the distant west, especially the young one who moves around the rooms with a certain self-assurance, because he knows he is liked by the Great Khan. He is a careful, polite young man, but his presence in the court seems to displease the strict black Lama. I will try to ensure they don't meet. Since they are all away hunting, I have taken off my boots and am walking barefoot on the grass from the distant steppe that my Lord has had laid around the palace so as not to forget, as I mentioned, that he is a Mongol, child of the grass and the wind. It's a lovely, pleasant feeling. We adore the infinite spaces where our horses gallop free, but unfortunately we are losing these values. The luxury and way of life of the people of Cathay are having a negative influence on us. One of these days I will take heart and ask my Lord for permission to leave. I'll go back to the land of my forebears and talk to the wind.

I have been observing these three foreigners for some days now, and they move freely through the rooms of my Lord Kublai Khan's summer pavilion. I had read in the fire of their arrival in these lands. The Great Khan treats them cordially, especially the young one, who he seems to have taken a liking to. When they arrived, a couple of moons ago, they gave our Lord a gift from their high priest. It is a talisman of great powers, from the sepulchre of their god who they say is all-powerful. But how can a god who allows himself to be killed and, rather than eliminate his enemies, pardons them, be powerful? But the mother of our Khan follows this religion and that is why there are numerous converts throughout the empire. In any case, religious tolerance is a prerogative of all the Khans, begun under the great Ghenghis. Kublai, on the other hand, recalling his nomad origins, wants numerous shamans from the steppes with him in their clothing of rags and coloured

ribbons. They know how to alter the course of time and to evoke malignant spirits to the sound of the big drum or by reading the shoulder blades of sacrificed animals. But it is us, the lamas belonging to the Sakyapa sect, who are the most powerful and most feared. During the banquet I saw the three westerners astonished, then terrified, when my brothers made the cups of wine in the centre of the room move to the hands of our Lord without anyone touching them. All this power means that the great Khan is very respectful of us and, between you and me, also fears us. As far as the three clumsy foreigners go, I had thought of getting rid of them in some way, but I read in the fire that they will return home... I can't do anything about it.

My friends in Cambuluc (Khanbalig) call me 'wooden arse' because of my skill at jumping from one horse to another on the long rides I have to do at the service of the Great Khan, carrying the most urgent messages to all the regions under his rule. I had stopped in one of the 10,000 buildings set up for postal couriers every 25 miles along the roads of the kingdom. We stop at these for a change of horses and, if there is no hurry, to rest and refresh ourselves. That was how I met a clever foreigner called Marco Polo who was on his way from Cambaluc to the south of the country on a long mission in the service of the Khan. He had mastered our language and, over a light meal we shared, he asked me about the postal system linking the various parts of the country to the military and administrative centres and the royal palace. I explained that the pony express service is used for messages that have special priority, unlike the normal despatches that are sent by runners, who pass them on to other runners at the special buildings set up for them every five miles.

The sound of the bells they carry on their belts alerts the next runner to get ready; in this way ten days' distance can be covered in 24 hours. At night, the pony express has to proceed less rapidly so as not to hinder the runners, who carry lamps to light their way and signal their presence. Every changeover of couriers is noted in special registers by a kind of notary. He had found his lodgings very comfortable and was impressed by the stable of more than 300 horses. The strange thing is that we met again about five months later in one of these service buildings near T'ai-yuan-fu, a wine and silk production centre. This is more or less the story he told me then of the long trip that had taken him as far as Burma. After two days in a westerly direction he had passed the castle of the Golden King, a powerful person who did not want to submit to Prester John, but who was captured by him thanks to some traitorous servants and made to watch over the livestock for a couple of years as punishment. After this long humiliation and having made an act of submission, he was released by Prester John with great honours and fine gifts.

About 20 miles further south he had passed the big Huang-ho river, which my people call the 'black river', and reached the rich, noble city of Hsi-an-fu governed by Mangalai, son of the Great Khan. He had ridden across beautiful plains for three days and then gone into an area of mountains and valleys for 20 days, where the forests are full of game, bears, wolves and tigers, to the joy of the hunters. There are also lots of small musk deer. These secrete small balls from their abdominal glands to mark out their territory, which are the source of musk, the substance used for the prized perfume. He had then come to Cheng-tu-fu in the province of Sichuan, an ancient city divided by a big river that is so wide it seems more like a sea. He crossed it on a fine, stone bridge with columns supporting a richly decorated roof and wooden shops lining its sides, where various products are sold and handcrafts made. Big ships come up from the sea bringing goods and the numerous merchants bustling around the city. A few days' travel to the west is the region of Tibet, still marked by the devastation of Mongke Khan's war of conquest. The people, dressed in rags, didn't make a very good impression on him; indeed, he said that

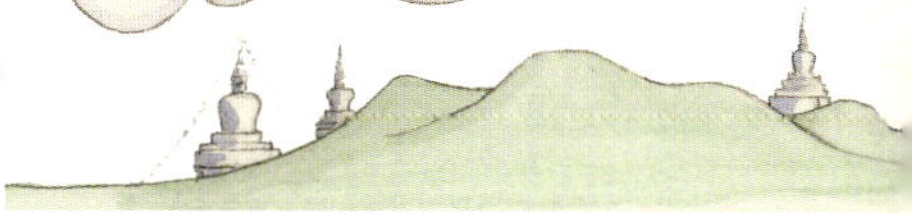

they were the greatest swindlers and thieves in the whole world. The predominant smell there is musk, but the thing that most struck him was the importance of magic in that society, with very powerful sorcerers and astrologers. They value coral above all else, using it for barter and hanging it around their necks as a good luck charm. He told me about the giant bamboo they burned at night in the camps to keep the wild beasts of the region at bay. The explosions these made in the fire were so loud and frightening that the horses had to be blindfolded, their ears muffled and their hooves tied with iron stocks to prevent them escaping in the dark. He also told me about the custom the mothers have of offering their daughters of marriageable age to passing merchants.

After they have lain with the girl they give her a small jewel to show their enjoyment, and the more jewels a girl displays, the more desirable she is seen as for marrying. Once they are married, they stay faithful to their husbands and woe betide anyone touching them! I think it's because he's young, but these licentious aspects of our customs seemed to particularly intrigue the traveller; indeed, when talking about the nearby region of Kaindu, the first thing he mentioned was a proposal for sex made by the women of the place, who are particularly free with the visitors. He spoke to me of the beautiful turquoise that is mined from a big mountain and the deals paid for in salt, in blocks carrying the seal of the Great Khan; this is also bartered for gold, which is less valued, so many merchants go there to exploit the profitable trade. They drink wine made from wheat and rice seasoned with lots of spices of which the country is very rich, from ginger to cinnamon. A very pleasant drink, according to Marco. After ten days' travelling he had found himself in Karajang, a big province containing seven kingdoms, governed by one of Kublai's sons. The people use cowrie shells taken from the sea in India as money, which they make into necklaces to adorn themselves. The worst thing in that region is the presence of big crocodiles and poisonous snakes, but even more frightening was the custom, forbidden by Kublai, of keeping guests in the house if they are of a particularly pleasant appearance in order to keep the positive spirit they emanate in their home. After another five days he had come to a place where the men have dazzling smiles, as they coat all their teeth in gold.

Their arms and legs are tattooed and they don't follow any particular religion, but worship the oldest in the family because they say they are all descended from him. He was struck by the story of the epic battle that had been fought a few years earlier by the Khan's expeditionary force against the powerful army of the King of Mien and Bengal. The Tartar forces led by General Nasir-ed-din numbered 12,000 well-trained horsemen, facing an army of 40,000 men, both infantry and horsemen, supported by 2000 war elephants with turrets housing archers. The impact of the enormous armed elephants on the Tartar cavalry at first knocked them off balance and the commanders had difficulty controlling the ensuing panic. They were forced to retreat into the forest and dismount, tying their horses to trees so they wouldn't flee. The archers then launched a shower of arrows at the elephants, which ran among the trees, smashing the wooden turrets they had on their backs. Making the most of the change of situation, the now reassembled cavalry unleashed an attack of such force that they overwhelmed the enormous Burmese army and were finally victorious, exacting a very high price from the proud King Narasimhapati. After this legendary battle, the Great Khan also wanted elephant garrisons for his army. He had eventually come to the border of India in the kingdom of Mien, where he saw pagodas of gold and silver, and visited a place where the inhabitants tattoo their whole bodies with birds, lions, dragons and other fantastic designs. In the nearby province of Amu, the men and women wear precious gold and silver bracelets on their arms and ankles, and have beautiful horses. He never tired of

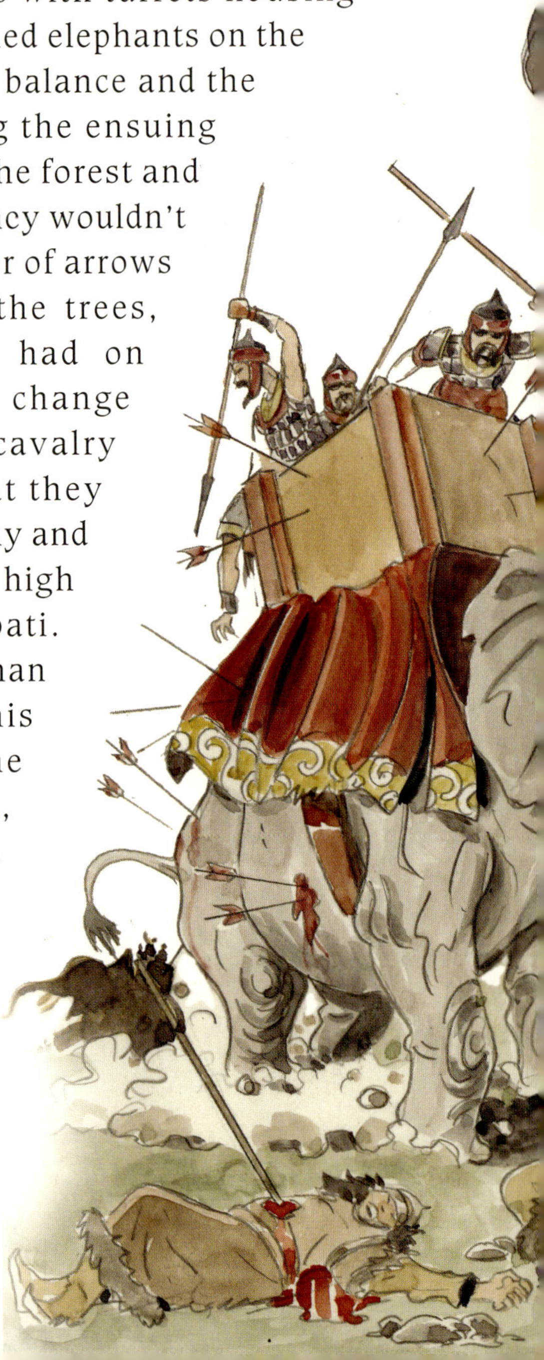

recounting the marvels he had seen and heard, jogging his memory with the written notes he kept for his final report to Kublai; and he talked and talked and talked. I can understand why our Prince was so taken by him and assigned him this mission.

PEM
CHARCHAN
THE GOBI DESERT
SUCHOW
KOMU
LOP
TIBET
SI-NGAN-
SICHUAN
CHENG-TU-FU
KAINDU
KARAJANG
PAGAN

CAMBALU
(BEIJING)
HO-KIEN-FU
AI-YUAN-FU
CATHAY
PIJU
HO-CHUNG-FU
CHENG-CHOW
SUCHOU
KINSAI
MANGI
FU-CHOW
ZAITON
SEA OF
CHINA

I belong to a small community of European residents living in these remote lands. Some arrived as prisoners during the Mongol invasion that reached Poland and Hungary, and some were moved by a spirit of adventure, like myself, tired of the humdrum of Cologne. I am an engineer and my name is Yosemain. I crossed half the world and faced thousands of adversities to get to these parts, where I found a rich and developed society that welcomed me warmly. I have also met a colleague from here, a Nestorian Christian by the name of Alauting, and we sometimes work together. They build magnificent stone bridges and excavate big canals here, so there is plenty to do. I socialised with the three Polos immediately, as is often the case when you live a long way from your own people and have the chance to meet others of your culture who are easier to get on with. At a certain point they got involved in a special

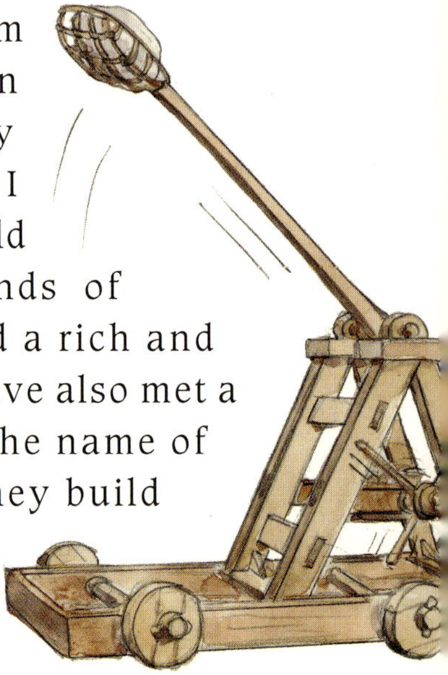

project for the Great Khan. My three new friends, who are in close contact with the powerful Lord and his advisors, had recommended building three war machines that they thought could have resolved an impasse in a siege that had been worrying Kublai and for which no end was in sight. All the rest of China had submitted to the new Mongol power, but the city of Siang-yang-fu had resisted for five years. It seemed inaccessible to the Khan's forces, being connected to the mainland on one side and protected on the others by a deep lake that also provided it with food. This was how my colleague and I came to design and build three mangonels, as were once used in the west, capable of catapulting 300 pound stones over a long distance. The new war machines were sent by ship and, once positioned, began targeting the houses in the besieged city with heavy rocks. The disruption caused panic among the inhabitants, compelling the city to surrender. The Lord of the Eternal Heaven was extremely happy, adding to the prestige of my three Venetian friends, who were already in his good books. Excellent prospects opened up for myself and my partner, too, working with the powerful Mongol army. I will always be grateful to fate for bringing me into contact with the Polos, who really are special people.

I don't know exactly where to start; whether to tell of my city Hangchow (or Kinsai as we prefer to call it, perhaps because it means 'paradise city') or my work at one of the big public baths, where I met a very inquisitive foreigner called Marco. Merchants come here from remote parts of the world and frequent our baths, but this visitor, apart from having a nice smell, had something special: not by chance, I learnt, he had been appointed by Kublai Khan in person to visit the regions of the empire and make reports on the situation in the various provinces. He appreciated our liking for cleanliness and thought the baths were grand and comfortable, nothing like the small and slightly squalid ones, he said, in his city, called 'stue'. He was proud of his homeland, which he praised as being very special, but here he was impressed by the immense size of things.

There are thousands of stone bridges, enormous squares for the markets, paved roads, rivers and canals forming a dense communication network, and a fine lake where you can laze around in comfortable boats in merry company or with the charming local girls. He was fascinated by this very refined society with its lively intellectual and business life, which had only recently submitted to the Lord of the Tartars. He admired all the things here that to me seem completely normal, probably because I grew up here. He had been impressed on his travels by the modesty and virtue of the girls in Codifù, but here, in the arms of the young courtesans, he had found an artfulness that made him feel he was floating on air. Indeed, it is said that when the foreign merchants go back to their own countries and are asked about where they have been, they say are back from paradise: Kinsai. He liked being washed with cold water, refusing the special rooms for foreigners who want hot water. He liked the tonic effect it had on his body and he always wanted to hear and tell stories. There are 3000 of these baths in our city, but Marco, a nice, affectionate person, always came back here during his stay and asked to be assisted by Chiang Ch'ing, which is my name. After a visit to a shadow theatre, he also invited me to go out on the lake with him and, stretched out comfortably on the boat, observing the splendour of the palaces and temples, said to me that something like this could perhaps be organised in his city and may have a future. He had many doubts about the magic he had seen on his interminable journey, but told me that in Codifù he had had a chance to discover the effectiveness of a practice used to find lost or stolen things. With the help of an old temple priestess, he had found a lost ring that had been given to him by a merchant in Kerman.

The beat of life is strong in Zaiton. Merchants come from all over to do business in our city, which is rich in sought-after goods. Ships from the Indies laden with precious goods come through our port. There are people from upper India who come to our master tattooists to get their limbs decorated. Enormous quantities of pepper and spices are sold here and our government takes large sums by charging tariffs on all transactions. It's easy to find me on the quays of the port, where I do small deals with foreigners and direct them to hostelries or some particular market. I have learnt to distinguish them at a glance, which country they come from and what I can offer them. I was struck by this person who, although he has the features of people from the far-off west, was dressed in Tartar costume, spoke the language and moved confidently through the seething crowds at the port. They say he's Venetian. I don't know what that means, but I quickly realised that he didn't like me. I tried to direct him to some lodgings and offer him my services to find some girls or some special goods.

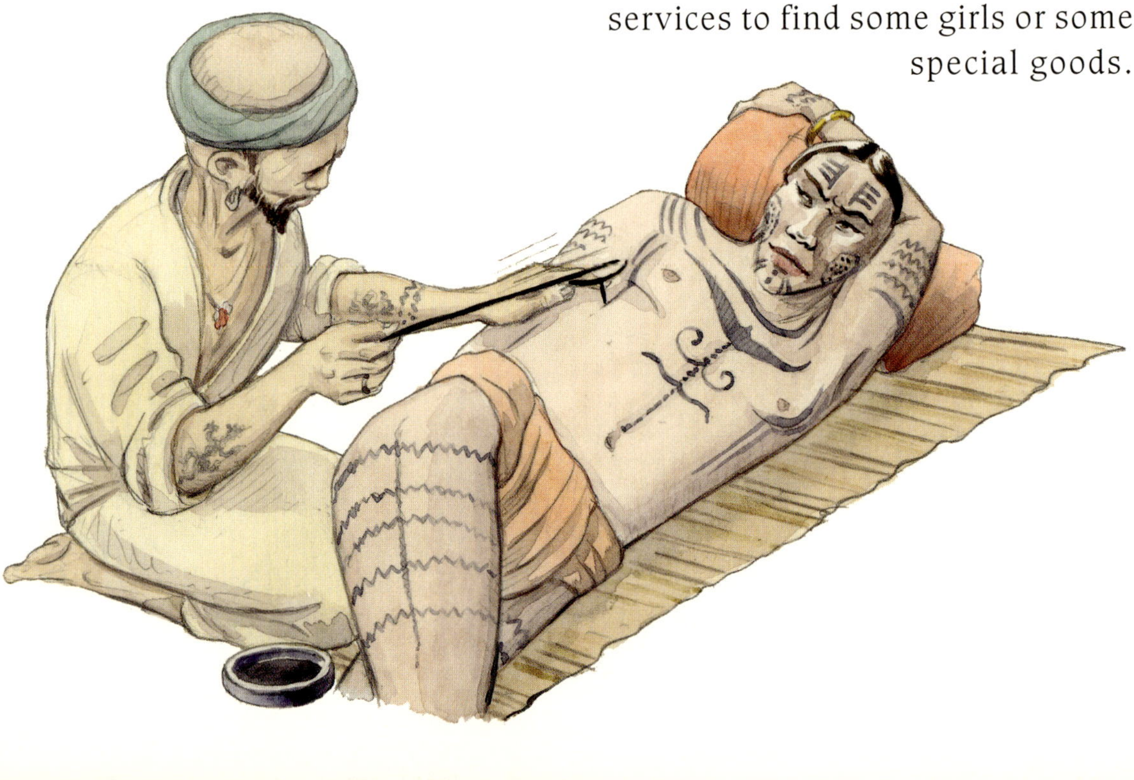

樞府窯

I suggested our beautiful porcelain, but he knew more than I do above where and how it is made. He had already visited the city of Tinju, the production centre for these magnificent supplies, and didn't want to know about my good offices. I followed him for a while trying to figure out what would interest him, but although he looked at everything with great curiosity, he didn't show any sign of dipping into his pockets. I realised that it was better to let the prey go; it's not worth insisting, it's just a waste of time, and Zaiton is a big port full of more amenable people. I saw him again a long time after with a big entourage of dignitaries and soldiers embarking with a considerable escort fleet to accompany, so they said, a Tartar Princess betrothed to a Persian Prince; so a friend of the Mongol Lord, not of us Chinese.

The sadness that can be read in the face of my Lord Kublai is great. Today, after much hesitation, he has finally decided to let the three Latins leave for their home in the far-off west. To tell the truth, he didn't want to even consider letting them go, but reasons of state prevailed. They will accompany the future bride of Arghun, the Ilkhan of Persia, the second most politically important person among the Mongols to Kublai, by sea. The Princess, dignitaries and a large escort left some time ago travelling overland, but after a good eight months they had to turn back. A new internecine war between Mongols had made the journey unsafe, and they thought the voyage by sea would be less risky. It seems that these delegates considered the three westerners experts in navigation, having returned from a long mission to India made almost entirely by sea. So they worked hard to convince the Great Khan and he finally accepted. He will provide a fleet of 14 Chinese built ships. All this was done very reluctantly: my Lord is now very old and

alone, the courtesans around him are no longer sincere and, furthermore, he has a great affection for the three Latins, especially the younger one, Marco, for whom he has always had a liking since his arrival a good 17 years ago. Now he has become a mature, trustworthy man and I think the Great Khan has the same feelings for him as a father for his son. After having given in to the insistent appeals of Arghun's representatives, he wanted to see the three Latins for the last time, giving them golden tablets of privileges and guarantees, and some letters for the Pope and the Catholic sovereigns of the west. The atmosphere in the palace hall is glum. During these formalities my Lord's eyes were glazed and misty. I see him consign the last letter with eyes lowered and then go off, disappearing behind the red curtains. For my part, for the umpteenth time I put off making my request to go back to the steppes of my forebears.

We thank the gods that finally, after five months' halt, they allow us to weigh anchor and leave this treacherous coast fraught with dangers. Our departure from the port of Zaiton was very different, accompanied by the blessings of our Lord Kublai Khan. I can still hear the music and sound of cymbals that celebrated our departure as we sailed away. Now there are only arrows, spears and the frightening howls of the fierce natives accompanying our exit from this cove. If I think of the pride with which I accepted the absolute command of this fleet, now halved, which numbered a good 14 ships of heavy tonnage... Four have been burned and the crews massacred by the people of this

place, who are merciless and eat human flesh. Luckily for us the three Latins accompanying Princess Cocachin, future bride of Arghun of Persia, the reason for this sea voyage, had a defensive fort built along the coast in which we managed to protect her and her numerous retinue of maidservants and dignitaries. My sailors in the meantime died defending the ships from the continuous attacks by these wild people in light, rapid canoes. Now the shrieks are far behind and the arrows fall harmlessly into the wake of our ship. Gods willing we are safe! I look dejectedly at our remaining ships: there are only five. We had to abandon two because more than half the crew had been killed and it was impossible to sail them; the others were lost in the frightening storms we ran into before reaching this diabolical place called Sumatra. These ships, built by Chinese shipbuilders, are examples of very advanced engineering. They have a single deck, beneath which there are about 60 cabins that are the width of the hull; each one is a small, comfortable, independent cabin. They have four or five masts, the first and last of which can be raised or lowered at will. The sails are fitted with battens that make them manoeuvrable in any wind and allow them to be reefed if necessary. But the most amazing feature is the sealed bulkhead compartments along the whole length of the hull, meaning that the ship can float even if it is holed after running into rocks. And yet these whales of the sea sank before my eyes, when the spirits were against us. Now we are sailing westward again; the journey is still long and many other unknowns await us.

I have been an ant, but also an eagle, and who knows how many other forms my spirit has taken in its terrestrial peregrinations. Now I am a simple monk who wants to free himself from the wheel of incarnations and attain much-coveted enlightenment. 'Birth is pain, old-age is pain, sickness is pain, death is pain; union with what you do not love is pain, separation from what you love is pain. Pain is not achieving what you desire.' It is necessary to remove avidity by cancelling desires, easy to say, but it requires meditation, meditation and more meditation, and one life is not always enough. The material bonds that plunge us into the painful ocean of the cycle of existence are strong. This inquisitive stranger, who I met some time ago during his stay here in Ceylon with a delegation of Tartar lords, loved to hear about these things. The diplomatic role played by a man from the furthest west as part of the Khan's court seemed strange to me, but then I had understood his special qualities by talking to him. They had come to negotiate the translation to Tartary of the sacred relics of the Buddha held in our temple. Kublai wanted two teeth and a miraculous porphyry bowl, which when filled for one person could satisfy five. According to the Saracens these were relics linked to the figure of Adam; indeed, on the island there is a mountain known as Adam's Peak. The question is not important to us monks, we have other concerns if we want to attain enlightenment. There had been another diplomatic mission from the powerful Mongol Lord to obtain the biggest

ruby in the world from the King of Ceylon, a fabulous stone without impurities that is part of our sovereign's treasure. The request was, however, refused. We have the most beautiful rubies in the world here: exquisite sapphires, amethysts and topazes. To some Muslims this is the earthly Paradise and Adam's Peak is the footprint of that wise man, the father of all men. The Hindus think it belongs to Shiva, while we Buddhists link it to Buddha. In any case, it causes a constant pilgrimage of worshippers from the three religions. The inquisitive person was called Marco Polo and I saw him disembarking once again from a Chinese ship heading for Hormuz.

He introduced his father and uncle who had accompanied him on a journey that had kept them far from home by now for more than 20 years. He was enchanted by the story of Siddhartha Gautama, the Indian Prince who became Buddha, revealing to us the way of self-discipline and deliverance. He seemed deeply moved by the precepts of our rule and, who knows, perhaps we have found another devotee.

I belong to the Brahmin caste, my name is Ramaswamy and I've got a small fleet of boats for harvesting pearls, the most precious produce of our sea. Merchants from east and west come here to Malabar to bargain for these jewels coveted by all the princes of the world. I met Marco by chance as he was wandering around the moorings of the boats preparing to leave for the rich pickings. He asked me if he could come on board and accompany the craft in its work. I offered him a wad of betel leaves to chew and put him in the boat with the Sadhu sorcerer, who has to keep the ferocious fish away from the fishing area with his spells, which only work during the day. The men dive into an area that is not very deep and gather the oysters on the bottom with their precious content. He was enthusiastic about the experience and then introduced his relatives accompanying him who were interested in buying some pearls. The variety of birds, including the multi-coloured parrots, the enormous bats, monkeys, black panthers and dangerous snakes: everything fascinated him, but most

of all he was interested in the stories and customs of our peoples. He wanted information on the tomb of a saint of his religion who had died and was buried in a small town in the area: St Thomas, whose sacred remains lie in a church in Malabar. The holy man, collected in prayer, had been mistakenly shot with an arrow by a hunter aiming at a peacock. Marco told me that he had been in our country as a messenger from the Tartar Lord not long ago, but had not visited this area.

He was surprised that the people go around naked, covered only by a cloth. Even the King himself does not wear clothes but covers his limbs with all kinds of jewellery. He asked me lots of questions on our religion and was particularly intrigued by our funeral rites, wherein the wife of the deceased is often thrown onto the pyre burning the body of her dead husband, and by the worship of cows and the rules followed by the yogis, ascetics who go around naked smeared with ash and would not kill even an ant. He stayed a few days, time to stop and get provisions, then continued his return journey sailing along the coast in the direction of Gujarat, a route full of perils due to the presence of pirates.

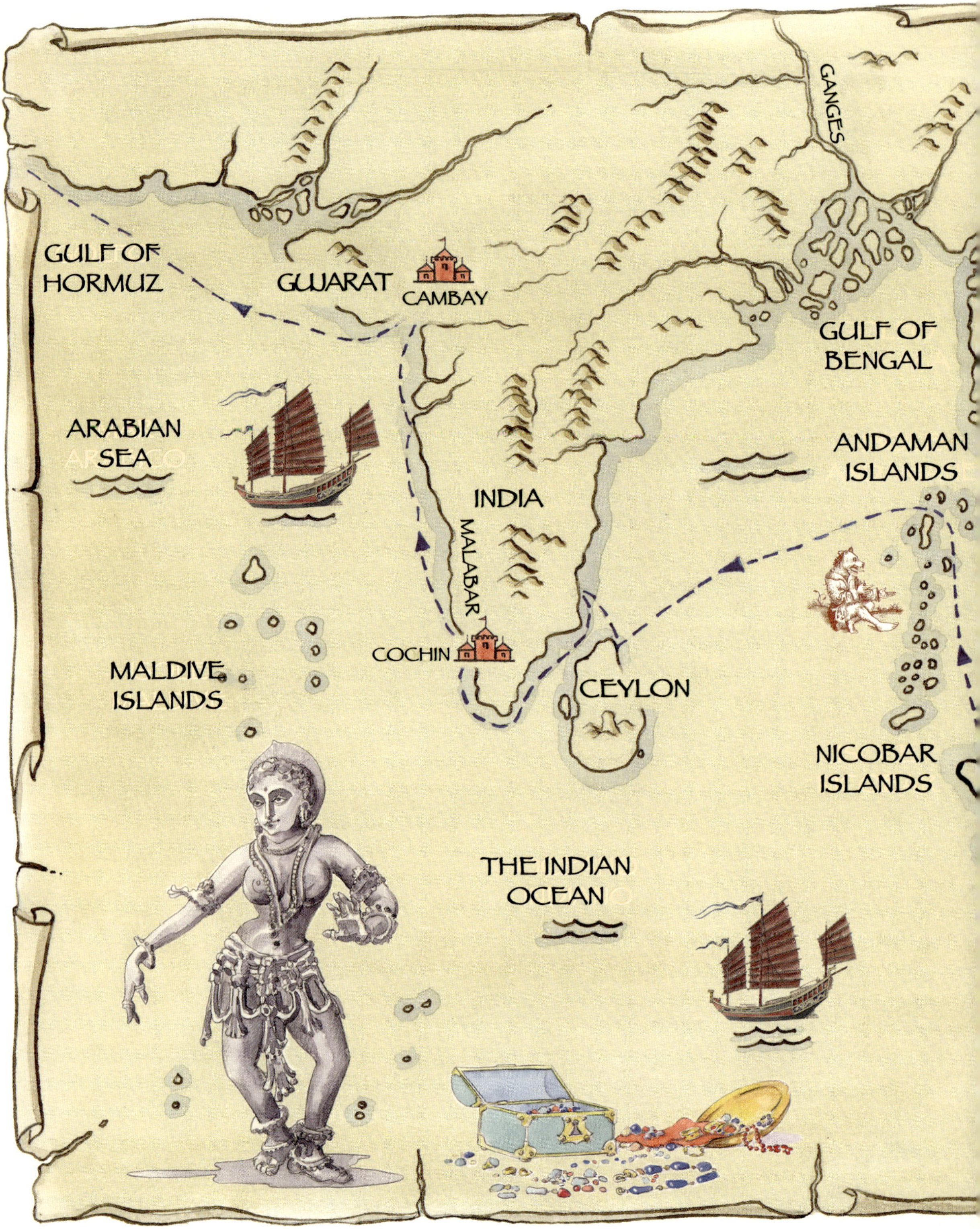
GULF OF HORMUZ
GUJARAT
CAMBAY
GANGES
GULF OF BENGAL
ARABIAN SEA
ANDAMAN ISLANDS
INDIA
MALABAR
COCHIN
MALDIVE ISLANDS
CEYLON
NICOBAR ISLANDS
THE INDIAN OCEAN

CATHAY
FU-CHOW
MANGI
ZAITON
AGAN
SEA
OF CHINA
BORNEO
SUMATRA

Who knows why I always have to stay up on this yard scanning the horizon in search of some ship to loot! It must be because of my lack of enthusiasm in the raids. We don't make any distinction: regardless of what ensign the ships hoist, they are all booty to us. Sometimes we manage to get good spoils, but there are lots of us, more than 100 boats, and in the end the sharing out doesn't come to much. We keep not only the cargo, but also the women and children, who we sell for a good price to the merchants in the interior. We release the men, though, so they can go back to trading and accumulate more riches, which we will then be able to steal again. We may seem ruthless, but I have to say that the people who do this in the islands further south are much crueller. If the person captured there can't pay a ransom, they kill him and, after inviting their friends and relatives, eat him with much celebration. Our life is not that easy. The merchant ships have recently been escorted by smaller boats whose crews are armed to the teeth, determined not to be plundered. At times it is impossible to board them, but every now and then we end up getting one and then we are happy and celebrate for several days when we get back to land. But look, down there, where the sun rises! I see sails! They're Chinese ships. It looks like a small fleet. The one in the middle is flying a blue flag, so there must be some dignitary or very important person on board. Now I have to light the fire to signal the fleet to the other boats further off. They will certainly be well armed, but they are heavy ships, we'll try to lure one into the shallows... now, excuse me, but I have to go.

I thought it was one of the numerous passing merchant ships that travel according to the monsoons, the winds that govern sailing in our seas. My name is Maulani. I am an official of the port of Khambhat and keep a record of all the vessels that tie up at our quays. But the visitor's ship, a big Chinese junk, wasn't anchored here in the port because it is too shallow and, to avoid the same disaster that had struck others accompanying it, took refuge on the other side of the gulf of Gandhar. Marco Polo was the name of the traveller and he recounted – in Persian, my native language – a fascinating story of a journey lasting 20 years. He was accompanying a Tartar Princess with her entourage. They had survived shipwreck and attacks by pirates that had sorely tried his mettle. He was visiting the city and was enchanted by its cosmopolitan atmosphere, which reminded him of his home, where they prefer to look to the sea than the mainland. Commerce unites our inhabitants closer than blood; here the finest houses belong to foreign merchants. Gujarat has plenty of goods to offer, from indigo to cotton, pepper and ginger, not to mention our work with leather. This is dyed in beautiful colours and used to make blankets sewn with gold and silver threads, a product highly sought after by Arab princes. The most important crafts in our region are sewing and

embroidering, carried out with great skill and in fantastic patterns unmatched anywhere in the world. Our guest was intrigued by the Arab almanac I showed him with the chart describing the movement of the winds in the Indian Ocean. I showed him how the circulation of traffic in our seas is one way, governed by the movement of the monsoons. From October to March those of the north-east blow, moving shipping from

China to the African ports, while from April to September the south-west monsoons move it in the other direction. The sailors much prefer sailing in the Indian seas with the north-east monsoon. The skies are clear and the starry nights are like an open book for taking bearings, and the waters are more or less calm, apart from the rare hurricane, which is not the case in the rainy season brought by the south-west monsoons. It is unthinkable to attempt voyages against the wind, resulting in dead periods that keep whole communities of merchants and sailors in our ports, where they are forced to wait for the weather to change, sometimes for several months, which strengthens relationships and stimulates new deals. This was the period when the ships were moving from the Far East and heading on to the ports of Hormuz, Aden and the African coast. Marco Polo was following this same direction, then continuing westward, dreaming of his much-loved Venice.

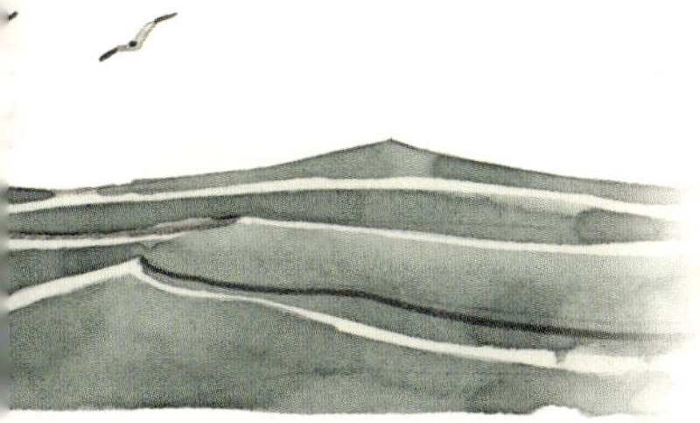

Bismillah! I exclaimed, when, to my great distress, I saw only one junk from the expected fleet enter the port of Hormuz. We had been advised by the Great Khan's highly efficient postal system of the arrival of 14 ships carrying three ambassadors named Oulaurai, Pusciai and Coia with Princess Cocachin. As luck would have it the dignitaries were all safe and sound. They were accompanied by three Venetians who were highly commended by Kublai Khan and had taken advantage of the mission to put themselves on the road home to Venice. They had already passed these shores about 20 years earlier. They had been thinking of sailing to Cathay then, but had not been impressed with our ships and had preferred to travel overland. Now perhaps they will have appreciated the sense of the construction techniques we use, making smaller, more flexible vessels with lashed planking that are more easily able to withstand the dangers of our seas, not like those enormous, rigid Chinese junks. I was here, by then for a couple of months,

with the delegation that was to have welcomed and accompanied the noble passenger to the court of the Prince of Persia. Unfortunately our King Arghun has in the meantime died and the young bride is now to marry his son Ghazan. The weather had got very debilitating, with a burning sun, so we hurried to leave Hormuz to continue, as arranged, toward the camp of the young Prince north of the region of the Dry Tree. The Venetians had already travelled these roads and, when going through Kerman, wanted to visit a jewel merchant they had met previously. They were happy not to meet with the same nasty surprises of 20 years ago, however. They told me about the two Male and Female islands in the Arabian Sea, where the two sexes live separated, and of Socotra, a whale hunting centre and flourishing, commercial, pirate emporium. During the journey bringing us closer to our destination, I noticed a certain sadness in the face of the young Tartar Princess. She seemed to have taken a liking to that strange family of foreign merchants and to be unhappy at their forthcoming separation. I repeatedly caught her confiding in them and at times heard her sobbing.

My name is Ebegai and I was assigned by my noble Lord to look after the young Princess Cocachin on the tormented journey toward her new life as consort to the Prince of the Khanate of Persia. I have lived with this responsibility for more than two years; luckily Marco was there to help in the more difficult moments. Now we have finally arrived at our destination and everything should be easier. I can't describe the thousands of dark eyes that greeted us here at the camp; a good lot of handsome lads – perhaps even I might end up getting married among these folk. I grew up in a yurt: my parents were nomads. But everything changed when some government representatives came to our tribe on a mission to select attractive girls for our Celestial Lord. Weighed, measured and sniffed, I passed all the selections and found myself among the Great Khan's favourites. I lived in the royal apartments in his grandiose palace and, dressed in precious clothes, felt as if I had gone into a dream. But the Prince knew and understood my restless spirit and when he found himself needing to choose a trusted lady to accompany the betrothed to Persia, he called me and offered me this mission. He lost a devoted girl, who would certainly have eventually been married to one of his barons, but knowing the secret part of my heart he knew that I would have happily accepted. Before letting me go he told me a story by the Persian poet, Rumi, about a merchant who kept a parrot in a beautiful cage. Before leaving for India, the merchant asked his beloved bird to tell him if it had anything to say to its cousins in that country. The parrot said only: 'Tell them that I am closed up in a cage'. When he arrived in India, the merchant went up to some parrots and delivered his message, at which one of the birds fell to the ground dead. On his return home he grudgingly told his much-loved parrot what had happened, and it in turn fell to the ground stone dead. The dismayed merchant opened the cage and took out the poor parrot, which, taking flight, told him that his Indian brother had revealed death as a way to be free.

It was early afternoon when I heard someone knocking at my door. I thought it was the boy from my shop near the walls of old Byzantium, who usually comes to let me know how things are going. I was instead surprised to see some familiar faces. It was my three cousins, by now given up for lost, and they were standing right in front of me dressed in eastern clothes. They were accompanied by a faithful servant they called Pietro. I am Mabilia Polo and, like others in my family, chose to live far from my homeland in pursuit of my business. I live with my cats near the racecourse in this amazing city, a wonderful place. I have to say that their long absence hadn't done them any harm. On the contrary, Marco, who was just a boy when he left and who I had never met before, seemed to me a fine 40-year old of elegant manner. They were pleased to feel some of the atmosphere

of home and I did my best to spoil them as much as I could for the few days they stayed. They had been planning at first to go to Sougdeia, but had then opted for Constantinople and were now counting on embarking for Venice on the first available ship. They had arrived from Trabzon, which they had reached with an escort of 400 horsemen provided by the Prince of Persia, but that hadn't saved them from being embezzled by the authorities in that city, who had lightened them of some of their possessions. They wanted to know everything about the general political situation and so, sitting down to a nice plate of 'sarde in saor', I brought them up to date on the constant rivalry between

the Serenissima and Genoa. The last Byzantine Emperor, Andronicus II, disheartened by the sad end of his excommunicated father, had decided to renounce his vow of loyalty to the Pope and restore the autonomy of the Orthodox church, partly because here it is said, better the Sultan's turban than the Cardinal's hat. His father's skilful diplomatic acrobatics had ensured 20 years' peace and he had also managed to make a dual treaty with Genoa and Venice. But the heir's choices on matters of security were very worrying. In order to save money he had dismissed the foreign mercenaries who ensured defences and dismantled the navy, entrusting the Genoese with the patrol of the seas. So the triremes lie abandoned in a state of disrepair and thousands of dismissed sailors have been taken on by the Turkish navy. The last vestige of Christian rule in Jerusalem had definitively gone with the fall of Acre in 1291. In short, the situation for the Venetian merchants, who had gradually returned to the city, was marked by uncertainty, while war with their rival Genoa was always on the point of breaking out.

The city still bore signs of the devastation wreaked on it by the Serenissima itself in the first years of the century, but it must be said that it is located in such a beautiful position that you still find yourself enchanted by certain views over the Golden Horn. No name was ever more appropriate. At sunset the sea is all a golden blaze. They asked me about the Pope and were surprised to hear of the death of Gregory X, whom they had met prior to their departure. In a single year the Roman church had actually seen four Popes succeed one another, one of whom was killed in his study when the ceiling collapsed. Now, after the abdication of Celestino V a few months after his election, Boniface VIII has been elected Pope. I told them about the last Doge, Pietro Gradenigo, who was elected at the age of 38 and found himself having to face these restless times. I suggested they go and visit the tomb of Doge Enrico Dandolo in the church of Santa Sofia, and their Tartar servant to go to the church of Our Lady of the Mongols, built by Princess Maria Paleologus, who was married to Abagu, the Grand Khan of the Tartars.

Anno Domini 1295. If there is one element that is completely extraneous to we Mongols it is water. Imagine how much I suffered on the long voyage that has brought me here to the lands of the setting sun. I should add that after all I went through from the port of Zaiton to Hormuz, my stomach can now put up with anything and at night I no longer dream of the demons of the abyss. I have now been at the service of Marco Polo for seven years, and I owe the name Pietro to him, from when I converted to Christianity. The voyage by sea was

calm, but the ship was small and uncomfortable compared to the junk on the first part of the journey. After we left the port of Constantinople we stopped in Negroponte, then I recall the island of Curzola because my master's family has a house there. Our arrival in their much praised Venice moved the Polos deeply. The city with its bell towers seemed a pink mirage hidden behind a forest of ship and boat masts. It is a strange place that rises out of the waters, criss-crossed with canals

where a seething human mass moves about on crafts of various shape. I was struck by my beloved horses. In the labyrinth of narrow streets they have a disoriented air, probably yearning to return to the countryside as soon as possible. The people looked at us with curiosity because of our clothing, and when we reached the home of the good Marco, even his family didn't seem to recognise their masters. It was as if they had seen some ghosts from the past, or beggars from who knows where. The general belief, I learnt later, was that the travellers, of whom no news had ever been heard, were long dead on the roads of the east. Once they had had a chance to wash and change into the same kind of clothes as the locals, the people seemed to reconcile themselves to their appearance. But the moment that really left their relatives and friends gaping was when they ordered me to bring their long, quilted, dust-covered coats and cut through the linings with a knife, revealing a real treasure of rubies, emeralds, diamonds, pearls, chalcedonies, turquoise, lapis lazuli and other precious stones hidden inside. Those who at first were greeted with suspicion became the heroes of the moment. Though it must be said that the stories of their travels revealed an astonishment in the faces of the onlookers that betrayed total disbelief.

I found myself on the deck in combat gear, scanning the horizon. The sky was still dark and the morning star shone brightly. I was worried, but the foolishness of youthful pride sustained me in what was to be my first battle. A companion offered me some Cypriot wine in a terracotta flask, from which I took a small sip to warm my heart and breathed deeply. It was dawn of 8 September 1298 when the two fleets met. In the Adriatic Sea, 95 galleys of the Serenissima led by Andrea Dandolo, Capitano da Mar, faced 85 ships of the Superba, under the command of Admiral Lamba Doria. The Genoese fleet, positioned nearer the coasts of the island of Curzola, was able to use the wind blowing off the land and broke the ranks of the Venetian galleys that had attacked. A skilful manoeuvre by Doria forced 15 of the galleys being kept aside into the point where the main commotion had been created. So the battle took a bad turn for us and, despite everyone fighting courageously, it was a terrible defeat; a real massacre. Only 11 ships managed to return home, the others being either sunk or captured, plundered and burned. I saw scenes I will never be able to forget; my sleep will never be the same again. It was on this dramatic occasion that I met Marco Polo, who had embarked on the same galley. My name is Giovanni da Fiume and I am a young crossbow-man in the service of the Serenissima. I had exchanged only a few words with Polo before the disastrous battle, but he didn't seem to me to be a real soldier. I often saw him during the voyage in the evenings consulting by candlelight some writings he kept close beside him in a bag, and it was only on the sad trip toward the Genoese prison that I got closer to this strange person. There were more than 7000 prisoners of every class, and I was still shocked by the action of our admiral who, not accepting the humiliation of defeat, committed suicide by beating his head against the main mast of the ship carrying us away. This mature man, who could have been my father, helped me accept the vagaries of chance. He told me an incredible story of a journey to the

limits of the known world, overcoming difficulties and unbelievable dangers. So I realised how, with those experiences behind him, he could be calmer than others. We were then divided during our imprisonment, which luckily ended in August the following year as a result of a new peace treaty between our cities.

'...Of course all that I recounted to Rustichello is not even half of what I saw and what happened to me...'

Marco Polo

Bibliography

Jurgis Baltrusaitis, *Il medioevo fantastico*, Adelphi, Milano 1973.
Franco Brunello, *Marco Polo e le merci dell'Oriente*, Neri Pozza, Vicenza 1986.
Edward Burman, *Gli assassini. La setta segreta dei sacri killers dell'islam*, Firenze 1988.
Italo Calvino, *Le città invisibili*, Einaudi, Torino.
D. Chaudhuri, *The Other Side of Marco Polo's Journey in India*, Calcutta 1926.
Roy C. Craven, *Indian Art*, Thames and Hudson, London 1976.
Alain Demurger, *Vita e morte dell'ordine dei Templari*, Garzanti, Milano.
Ross E. Dunn, *Gli straordinari viaggi di Ibn Battuta*, Garzanti, Milano 2005.
Jacques Gernet, *La vita quotidiana in Cina ai tempi di Marco Polo*, Fabbri Ed.
Richard Humble, *Marco Polo*, Dall'Oglio Editore, Milano 1982.
Sergej Kozin (a cura di), *Storia segreta dei mongoli*, TEA 2000.
Giancarlo Ligabue, *Il pane e la chiglia*, Erizzo Editore.
Giancarlo Ligabue e Grigore Arbore Popesco, *I cavalieri delle steppe*, Electa.
Marco Polo, *Il Milione*, Biblioteca Universale Rizzoli, Milano 2000.
Marco Polo, *Il Milione*, I Meridiani, A. Mondadori, Milano 1982.
Stefano Malatesta, *Il cammello battriano*, Neri Pozza, Vicenza 1997.
Kenneth Nebenzahl, *Mapping the Silk Road and Beyond*, Phaidon, London 2004.
John Julius Norwich, *Bisanzio*, Oscar Mondadori, Milano 2000.
G. Pauthier, *China*, Giuseppe Antonelli Editore, Venezia 1841.
Guglielmo di Rubruc, *Viaggio nell'impero dei mongoli*, Marietti 2002.
Robert Silverberg, *La leggenda del Prete Gianni*, Piemme, Casale Monferrato 1998.
S.R. Tornbul, *I mongoli*, Osprey .P.L.T.D.
V. Tretjakov, *Le voyage secret de Marco Polo dans le Thibet*, Odessa 1904.
Alvise Zorzi, *Vita di Marco Polo*, Rusconi.
Le vie della seta e Venezia, Leonardo De Luca Editori, Roma 1990.
Marco Polo e la via della seta, Universale Electa/Gallimard 1992.
Mongolia nelle steppe di Genghis Khan, Erizzo Editore.

C
A
T
A
I
O
Guidago
nanto
ainan
tolser
cori